Rudy Park

Rudy Park

The People Must Be Wired

by Darrin Bell & Theron Heir

**Andrews McMeel
Publishing**

Kansas City

03 04 05 06 07 BBG 10 9 8 7 6 5 4 3 2 1

ISBN: 0-7407-3807-0

Library of Congress Control Number: 2003106587

Rudy Park can be viewed on the Internet at:

www.comics.com/comics/rudypark

———— **ATTENTION: SCHOOLS AND BUSINESSES** ————

Andrews McMeel books are available at quantity discounts with bulk purchase for educational, business, or sales promotional use. For information, please write to: Special Sales Department, Andrews McMeel Publishing, 4520 Main Street, Kansas City, Missouri 64111.

To my grandpa Marty, a Rude Park, Colorado, tough guy turned wise and a generous patriarch.
With respect and love.

—T.H.

To Mom and Steven, who taught me everything that matters, and to Laura, who teaches me something new every day.

—D.B.

Introduction

Interview with Rudy Park.

Interviewer: Rudy, congratulations on the publication of your first book.

Rudy Park: Thank you.

Int.: So, what are you feeling on this momentous occasion?

R.P.: Horrible shame.

Int.: Shame? But . . .

R.P.: Listen. This is 2003, and we're putting out a book! Why not an ebook or an interactive TV show? Paper is so twentieth century. Be reasonable. Are we done? I'm getting a call on my digital camera/phone.

Int.: Why don't we move on. Tell us about the origins of the strip. How did *Rudy Park* get started?

R.P.: History bores me. If it's not the cutting edge, it's not relevant. There is absolutely nothing that will get me to talk about the past.

Int.: I'll give you a peek at the next Mac operating system.

R.P.: Let us begin with Ancient Rome. . . .

Int.: How about 1996? In Oakland.

R.P.: Theron Heir was a reporter at the *Oakland Tribune*, a local paper. He had an idea for a comic strip but was an abominable artist. Darrin was a student at UC Berkeley, where he drew editorial cartoons on the side for the *Los Angeles Times* and other newspapers. One day, he faxed a cartoon to the *Tribune*. Theron was standing at the fax machine when the cartoon came over. Theron saw the art, loved its style, and gave Darrin a call. The two started talking and discovered they had similar visions and humor, though they did differ considerably on my girth.

Int.: Pardon?

R.P.: When Darrin first conceptualized me, he imagined a fat guy who sat around all day at his computer. True story. When Theron saw the first images, he didn't know what to say. But he didn't want to be critical because this was a team effort. Eventually, though, thinner heads prevailed.

Int.: But they agreed on substance?

R.P.: Oh, yeah. They both thought there was big humor in the dot-com frenzy and the insatiable demand for technology. When they heard venture capitalists funded a business that sought to digitize gasoline, then send it over the Internet so you could fuel your SUV from your home computer, they laughed. They're cruel people who probably need medication.

Int.: You could see why they thought there was a niche, no? After all, it was an era when you could write a business plan on an Arby's napkin and get millions in financing and the cover of *Time* magazine. If you put a ".com" at the end of your company, it's value skyrocketed. Nine-year-olds were planning their retirements. And . . . what are you doing?

R.P.: Weeping.

Int.: Weeping?

R.P.: For a beautiful time gone by. It was an incredible era. Young people were onboard. We were part of a movement. We had a sense of purpose. We believed in something—something bigger than ourselves.

Int.: Which was?

R.P.: Smaller phones.

Int.: So you believed in something smaller than yourselves.

R.P.: Your kind saddens me.

Int.: You make the late '90s sound like the '60s.

R.P.: Exactly, but with better personal organizers. But then things got weird. The daily strip was launched nationally in newspapers on September 3, 2001. It was a pivotal week in American history. Just before that, the economy began its nosedive. I had just gotten laid off from my dot-com and had to take a job working the counter at House of Java Internet café. But, looking back, I count my blessings. A week later, the terrorists attacked. Trust me, this is not exactly the stuff of comic strips. I wouldn't have blamed Darrin and Theron one bit if they had packed it up and gone back to doodling editorial cartoons and writing newspaper stories about the Oakland Port Authority.

Int.: What did they decide to do?

R.P.: Our humble Internet café turned a little more chaotic, and our cast changed with the times. Sadie Cohen, one of the café regulars, wound up breaking bread with Dick Cheney. I found myself as point man on Operation Trojan Latte with Colin Powell. And Randy Taylor, another café regular, took a job undressing people.

Int.: He works in fashion?

R.P.: Airport security.

Int.: What's the most important thing you've learned so far?

R.P.: Life is more than technology; people are what's important. For instance, next time I probably shouldn't end a long-term relationship via text messaging.

Int.: Well, I can tell by the shrill beeping coming from your pants that our time is up. Any final thoughts?

R.P.: The world is changing again, and I'm ready to be on the forefront. If the revolution is televised, I plan to watch on a big-screen HDTV.

Int.: Thank you, Rudy, for taking the time to be with us today and for setting your cell phone on "vibrate" . . . for the first two-thirds of the interview.

R.P.: My pleasure. It's been my lifelong dream to be interviewed by Larry King.

Int.: I'm not Larry King.

R.P.: AWWW! I want this tape. (Scuffle ensues.)

(Fade to black.)

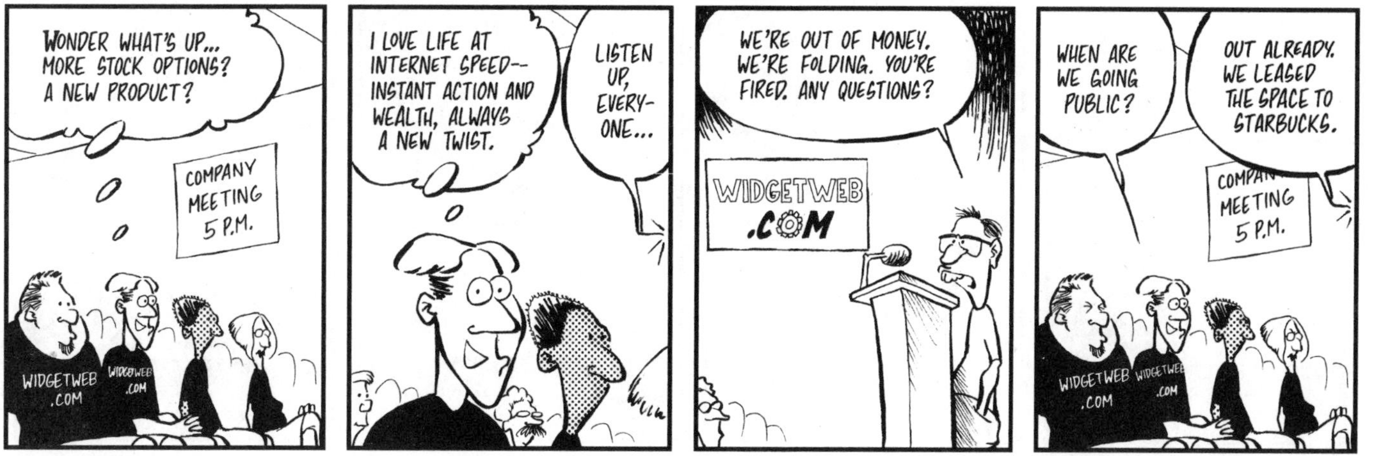
WONDER WHAT'S UP... MORE STOCK OPTIONS? A NEW PRODUCT?
COMPANY MEETING 5 P.M.
WIDGETWEB .COM
WIDGETWEB .COM
I LOVE LIFE AT INTERNET SPEED-- INSTANT ACTION AND WEALTH, ALWAYS A NEW TWIST.
LISTEN UP, EVERY- ONE...
WE'RE OUT OF MONEY. WE'RE FOLDING. YOU'RE FIRED. ANY QUESTIONS?
WIDGETWEB .COM
WHEN ARE WE GOING PUBLIC?
OUT ALREADY. WE LEASED THE SPACE TO STARBUCKS.
MEETING 5 P.M.
WIDGETWEB .COM
WIDGETWEB .COM

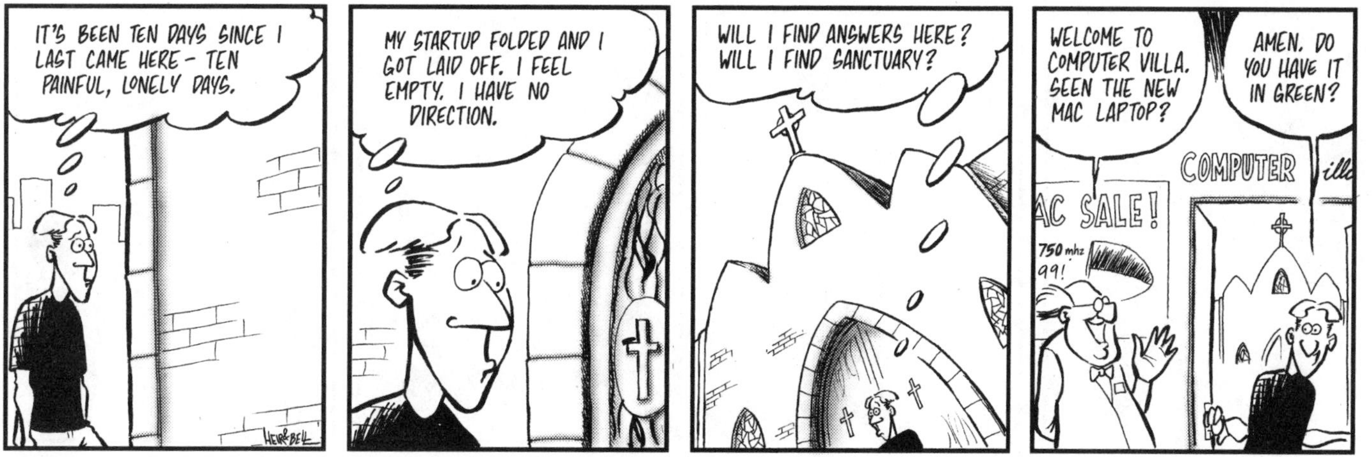
IT'S BEEN TEN DAYS SINCE I LAST CAME HERE - TEN PAINFUL, LONELY DAYS.
HEIR & BELL
MY STARTUP FOLDED AND I GOT LAID OFF. I FEEL EMPTY. I HAVE NO DIRECTION.
WILL I FIND ANSWERS HERE? WILL I FIND SANCTUARY?
WELCOME TO COMPUTER VILLA. SEEN THE NEW MAC LAPTOP?
AMEN. DO YOU HAVE IT IN GREEN?
COMPUTER
AC SALE!
750 mhz
99!

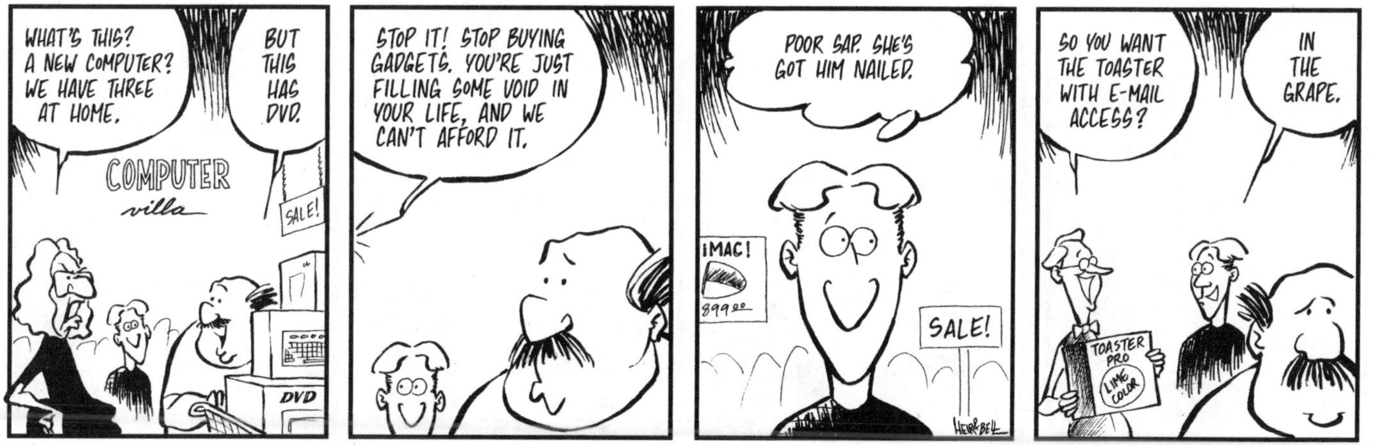
WHAT'S THIS? A NEW COMPUTER? WE HAVE THREE AT HOME.
BUT THIS HAS DVD.
COMPUTER villa
SALE!
DVD
STOP IT! STOP BUYING GADGETS. YOU'RE JUST FILLING SOME VOID IN YOUR LIFE, AND WE CAN'T AFFORD IT.
POOR SAP. SHE'S GOT HIM NAILED.
iMAC!
SALE!
HEIR & BELL
SO YOU WANT THE TOASTER WITH E-MAIL ACCESS?
IN THE GRAPE.
TOASTER PRO
LIME COLOR

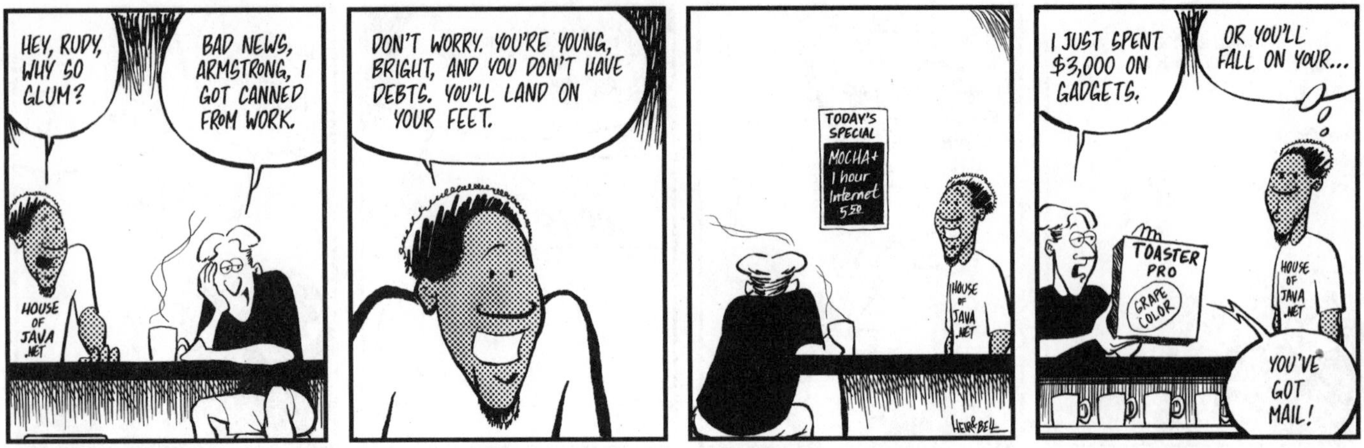
HEY, RUDY, WHY SO GLUM?
BAD NEWS, ARMSTRONG, I GOT CANNED FROM WORK.
DON'T WORRY. YOU'RE YOUNG, BRIGHT, AND YOU DON'T HAVE DEBTS. YOU'LL LAND ON YOUR FEET.
TODAY'S SPECIAL
MOCHA + 1 hour Internet 5.50
HOUSE OF JAVA .NET
I JUST SPENT $3,000 ON GADGETS.
OR YOU'LL FALL ON YOUR...
TOASTER PRO
GRAPE COLOR
YOU'VE GOT MAIL!
HEIR & BELL

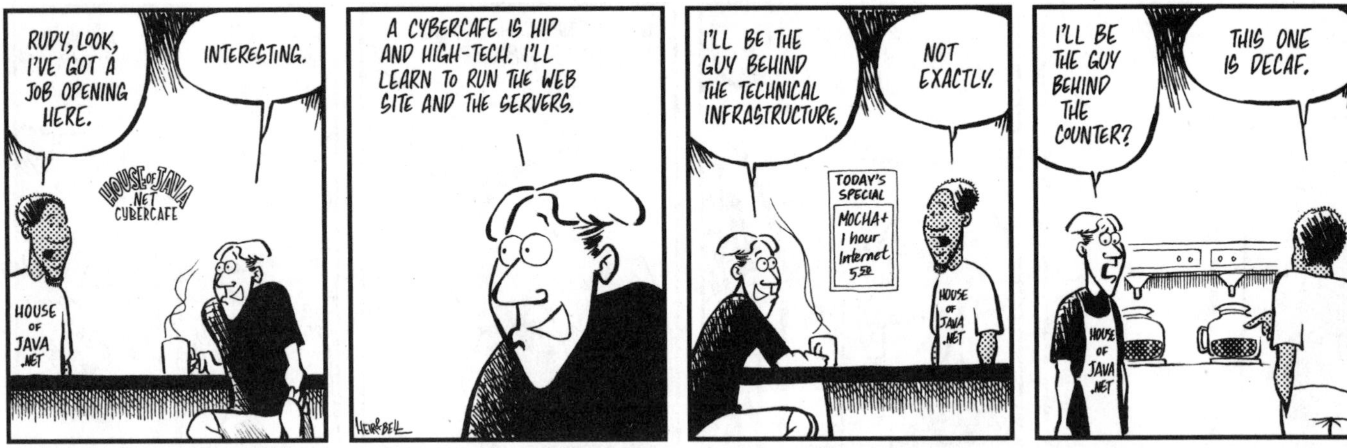
RUDY, LOOK, I'VE GOT A JOB OPENING HERE.
INTERESTING.
HOUSE OF JAVA .NET CYBERCAFE
A CYBERCAFE IS HIP AND HIGH-TECH. I'LL LEARN TO RUN THE WEB SITE AND THE SERVERS.
I'LL BE THE GUY BEHIND THE TECHNICAL INFRASTRUCTURE.
NOT EXACTLY.
TODAY'S SPECIAL
MOCHA + 1 hour Internet 5.50
I'LL BE THE GUY BEHIND THE COUNTER?
THIS ONE IS DECAF.
HEIR & BELL

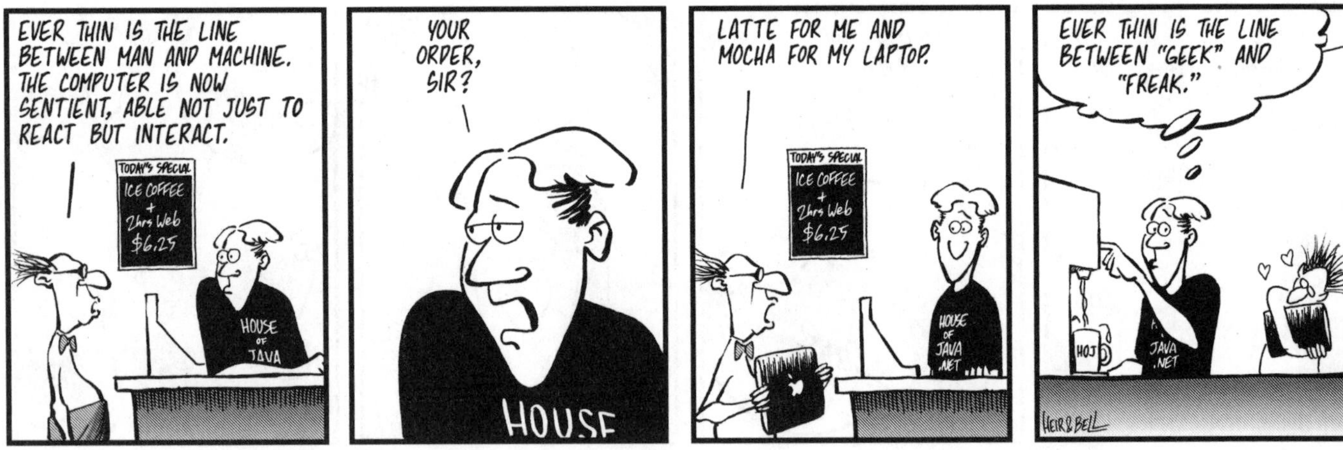
EVER THIN IS THE LINE BETWEEN MAN AND MACHINE. THE COMPUTER IS NOW SENTIENT, ABLE NOT JUST TO REACT BUT INTERACT.
TODAY'S SPECIAL
ICE COFFEE + 2hrs Web $6.25
YOUR ORDER, SIR?
LATTE FOR ME AND MOCHA FOR MY LAPTOP.
EVER THIN IS THE LINE BETWEEN "GEEK" AND "FREAK."
HOJ
HEIR & BELL

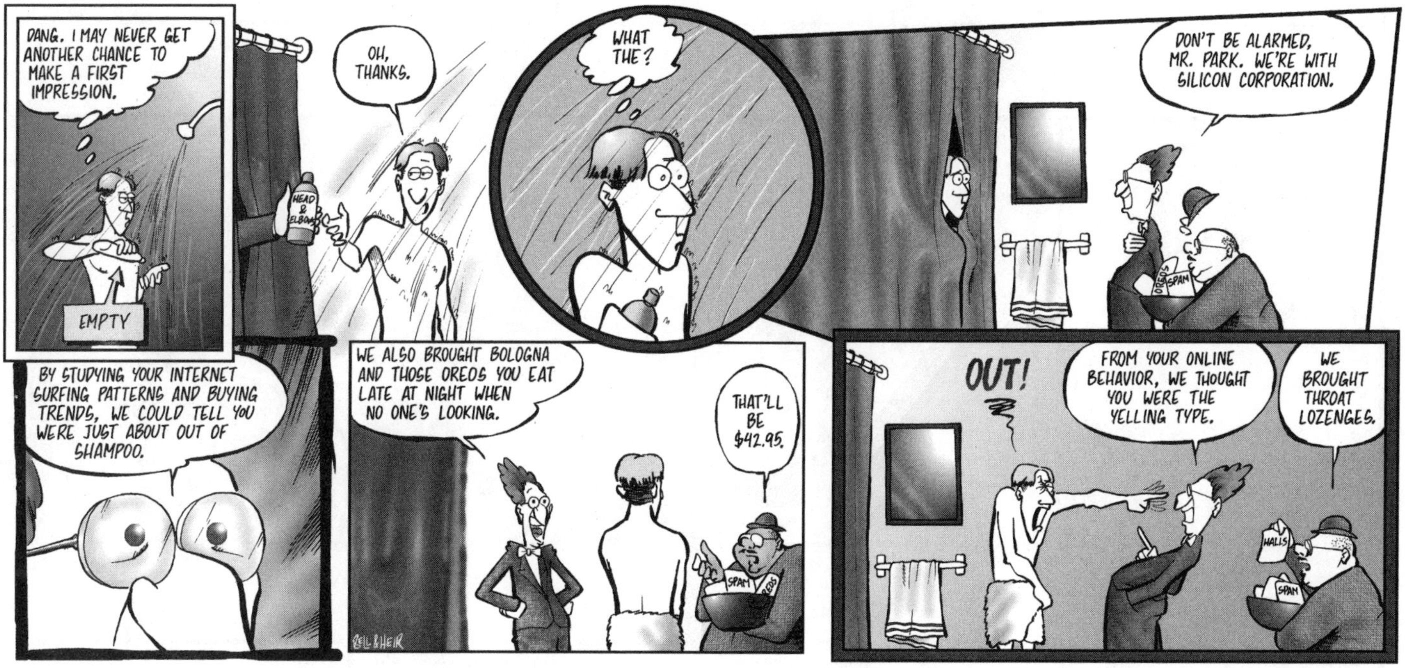
DANG. I MAY NEVER GET ANOTHER CHANCE TO MAKE A FIRST IMPRESSION.
EMPTY
HEAD & ELBOWS
OH, THANKS.
WHAT THE?
DON'T BE ALARMED, MR. PARK. WE'RE WITH SILICON CORPORATION.
OREOS
SPAM
BY STUDYING YOUR INTERNET SURFING PATTERNS AND BUYING TRENDS, WE COULD TELL YOU WERE JUST ABOUT OUT OF SHAMPOO.
WE ALSO BROUGHT BOLOGNA AND THOSE OREOS YOU EAT LATE AT NIGHT WHEN NO ONE'S LOOKING.
THAT'LL BE $42.95.
SPAM
OREOS
OUT!
FROM YOUR ONLINE BEHAVIOR, WE THOUGHT YOU WERE THE YELLING TYPE.
WE BROUGHT THROAT LOZENGES.
HALLS
SPAM

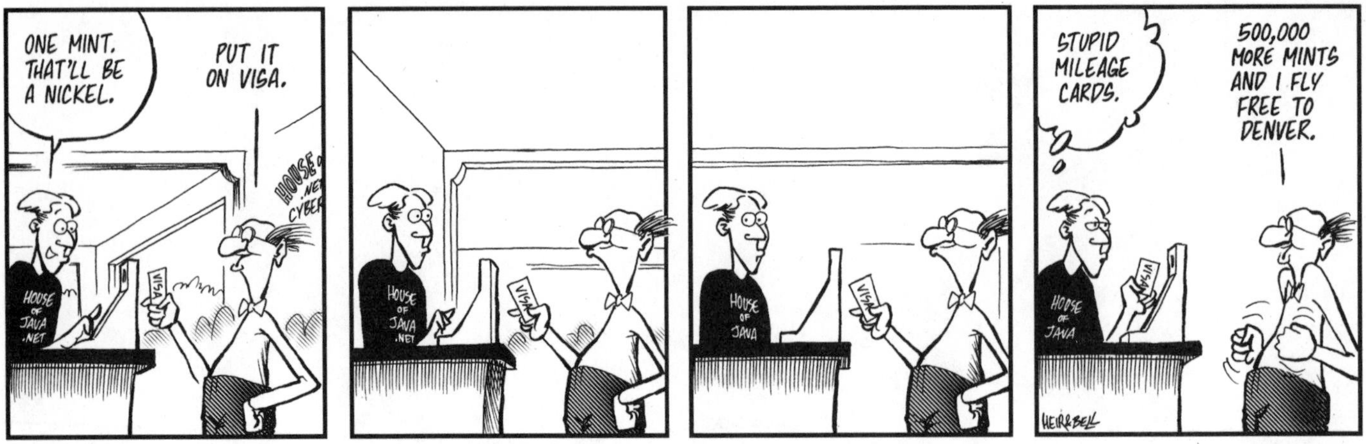
ONE MINT. THAT'LL BE A NICKEL.
PUT IT ON VISA.
STUPID MILEAGE CARDS.
500,000 MORE MINTS AND I FLY FREE TO DENVER.
HEIR & BELL

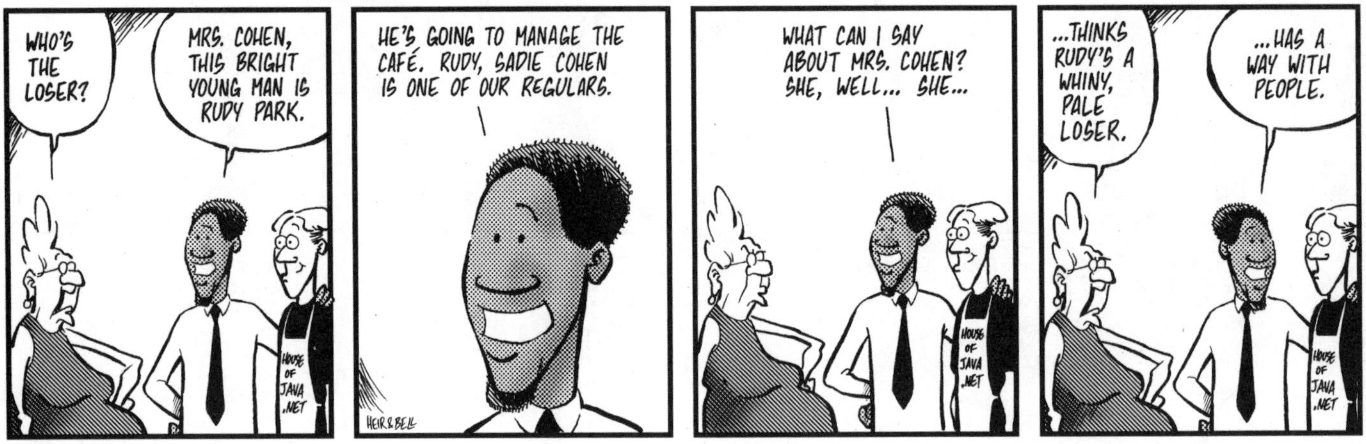
WHO'S THE LOSER?
MRS. COHEN, THIS BRIGHT YOUNG MAN IS RUDY PARK.
HE'S GOING TO MANAGE THE CAFÉ. RUDY, SADIE COHEN IS ONE OF OUR REGULARS.
WHAT CAN I SAY ABOUT MRS. COHEN? SHE, WELL... SHE...
...THINKS RUDY'S A WHINY, PALE LOSER.
...HAS A WAY WITH PEOPLE.
HEIR & BELL

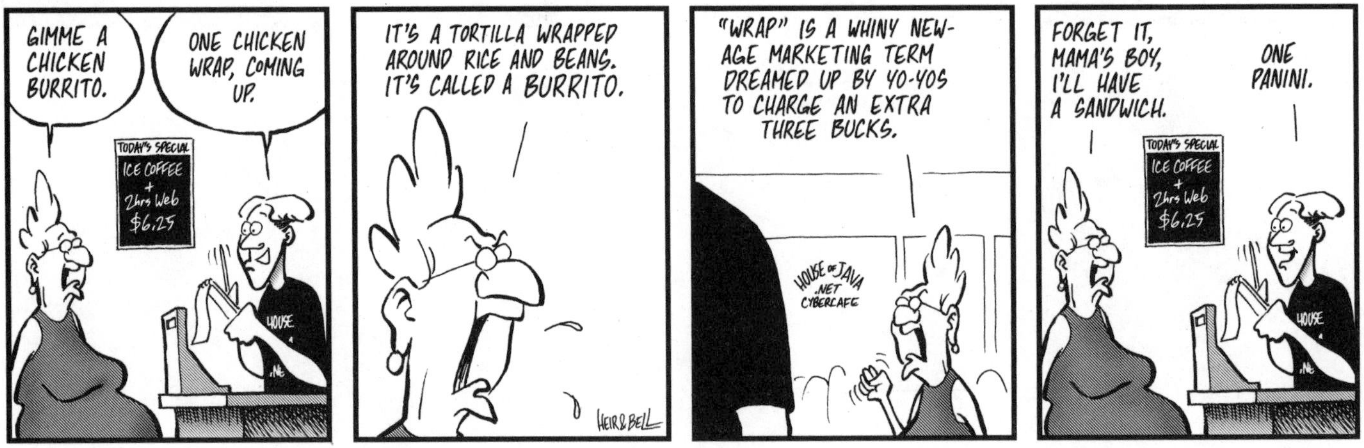
GIMME A CHICKEN BURRITO.
ONE CHICKEN WRAP, COMING UP.
TODAY'S SPECIAL
ICE COFFEE + 2hrs Web $6.25
IT'S A TORTILLA WRAPPED AROUND RICE AND BEANS. IT'S CALLED A BURRITO.
"WRAP" IS A WHINY NEW-AGE MARKETING TERM DREAMED UP BY YO-YOS TO CHARGE AN EXTRA THREE BUCKS.
HOUSE OF JAVA .NET CYBERCAFE
FORGET IT, MAMA'S BOY, I'LL HAVE A SANDWICH.
ONE PANINI.
HEIR & BELL

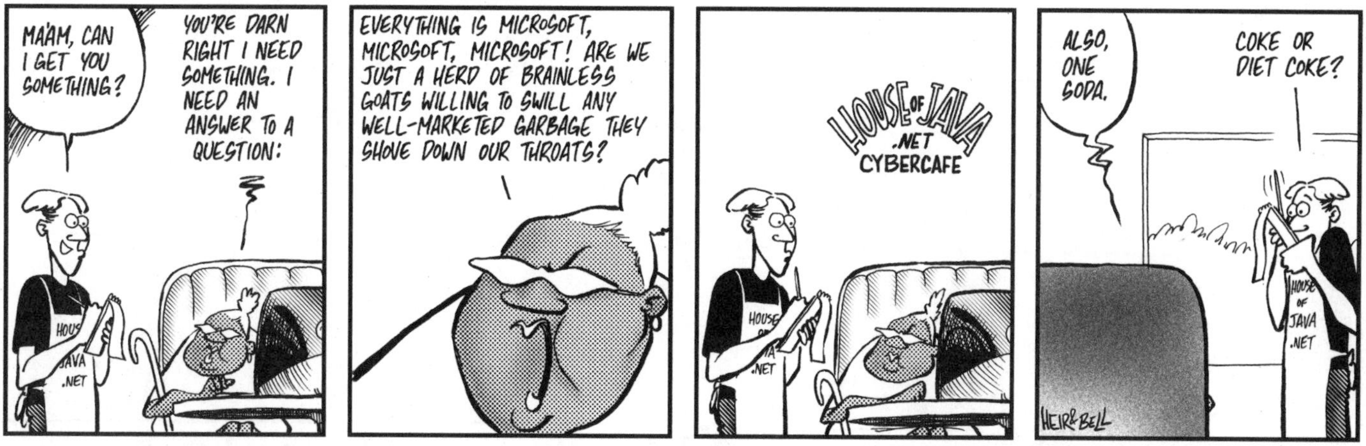
MA'AM, CAN I GET YOU SOMETHING?
YOU'RE DARN RIGHT I NEED SOMETHING. I NEED AN ANSWER TO A QUESTION:
EVERYTHING IS MICROSOFT, MICROSOFT, MICROSOFT! ARE WE JUST A HERD OF BRAINLESS GOATS WILLING TO SWILL ANY WELL-MARKETED GARBAGE THEY SHOVE DOWN OUR THROATS?
HOUSE OF JAVA .NET CYBERCAFE
ALSO, ONE SODA.
COKE OR DIET COKE?
HOUSE OF JAVA .NET
HEIR&BELL

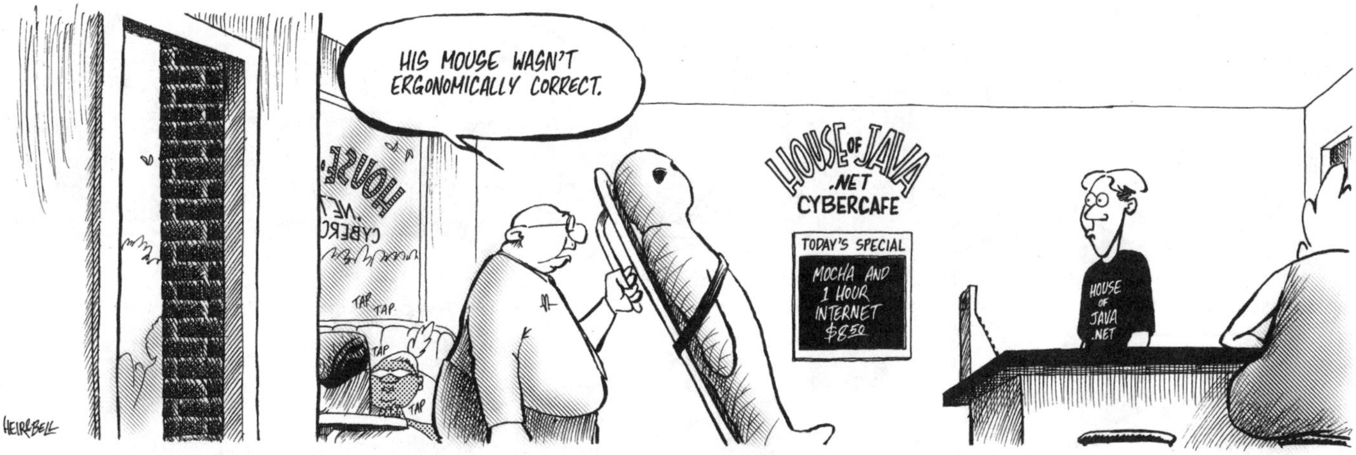
HIS MOUSE WASN'T ERGONOMICALLY CORRECT.
HOUSE OF JAVA .NET CYBERCAFE
TODAY'S SPECIAL
MOCHA AND 1 HOUR INTERNET $8.50
HOUSE OF JAVA .NET
TAP TAP TAP TAP
HEIR&BELL

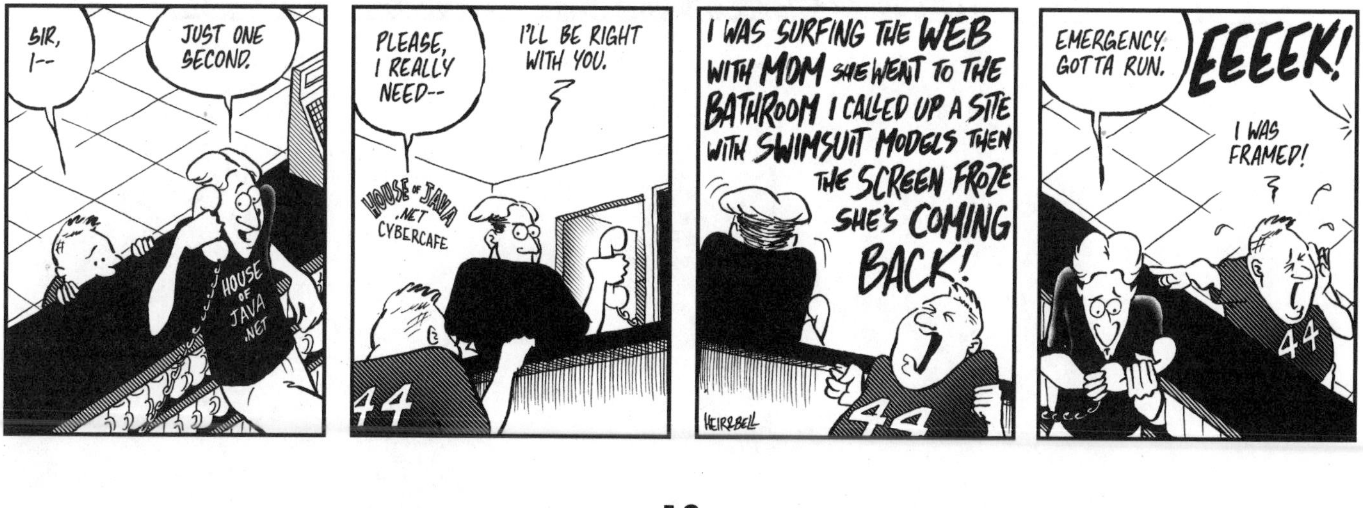
SIR, I--
JUST ONE SECOND.
PLEASE, I REALLY NEED--
I'LL BE RIGHT WITH YOU.
HOUSE OF JAVA .NET CYBERCAFE
I WAS SURFING THE WEB WITH MOM SHE WENT TO THE BATHROOM I CALLED UP A SITE WITH SWIMSUIT MODELS THEN THE SCREEN FROZE SHE'S COMING BACK!
EMERGENCY. GOTTA RUN.
EEEEK!
I WAS FRAMED!
HEIR&BELL

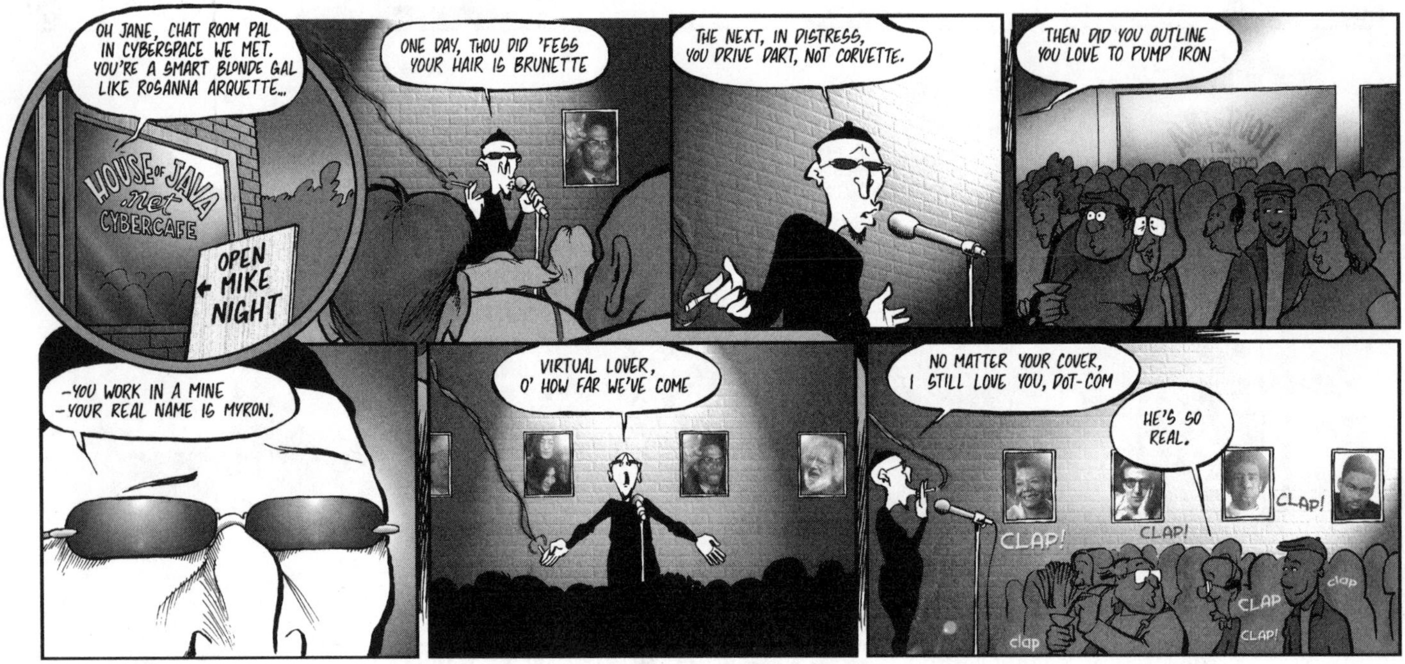
OH JANE, CHAT ROOM PAL IN CYBERSPACE WE MET. YOU'RE A SMART BLONDE GAL LIKE ROSANNA ARQUETTE...
HOUSE OF JAVA .net CYBERCAFE
OPEN MIKE NIGHT
ONE DAY, THOU DID 'FESS YOUR HAIR IS BRUNETTE
THE NEXT, IN DISTRESS, YOU DRIVE DART, NOT CORVETTE.
THEN DID YOU OUTLINE YOU LOVE TO PUMP IRON
-YOU WORK IN A MINE
-YOUR REAL NAME IS MYRON.
VIRTUAL LOVER, O' HOW FAR WE'VE COME
NO MATTER YOUR COVER, I STILL LOVE YOU, DOT-COM
HE'S SO REAL.
CLAP!
CLAP!
CLAP!
clap
CLAP
clap
CLAP!
clap

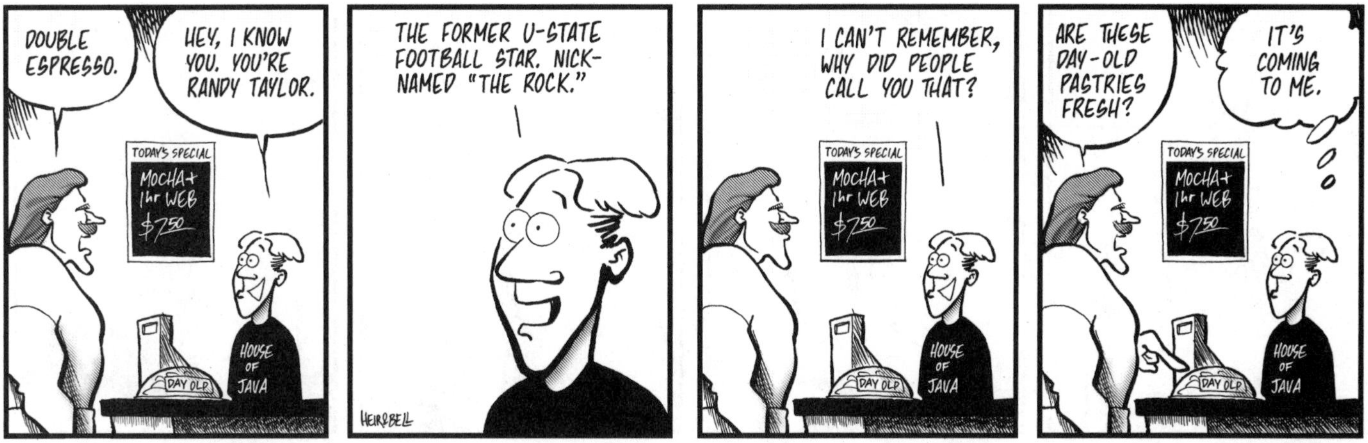
DOUBLE ESPRESSO.
HEY, I KNOW YOU. YOU'RE RANDY TAYLOR.
TODAY'S SPECIAL
MOCHA+ 1hr WEB $7.50
DAY OLD
HOUSE OF JAVA
THE FORMER U-STATE FOOTBALL STAR. NICK-NAMED "THE ROCK."
HEIR&BELL
I CAN'T REMEMBER, WHY DID PEOPLE CALL YOU THAT?
ARE THESE DAY-OLD PASTRIES FRESH?
IT'S COMING TO ME.

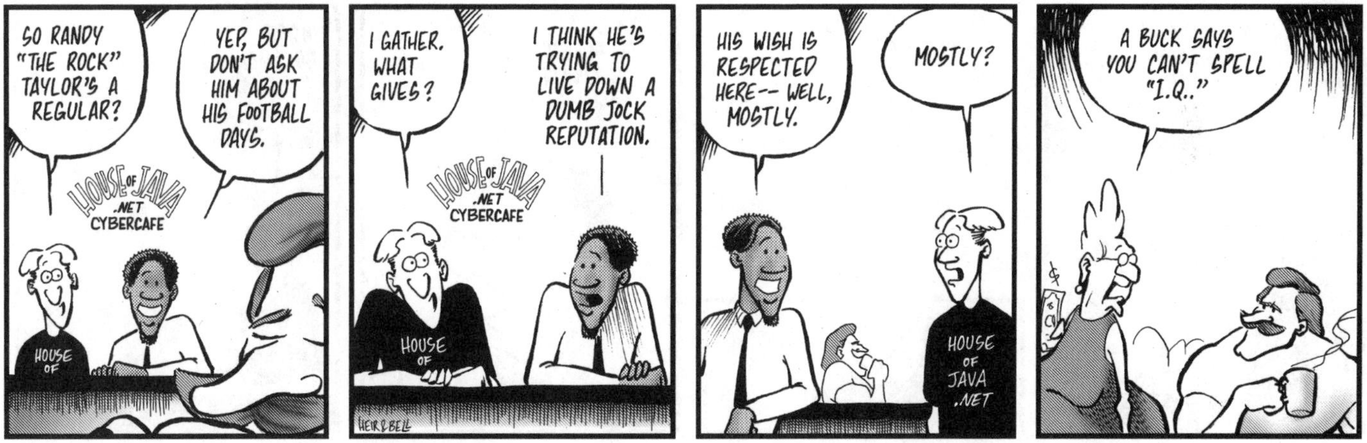
SO RANDY "THE ROCK" TAYLOR'S A REGULAR?
YEP, BUT DON'T ASK HIM ABOUT HIS FOOTBALL DAYS.
HOUSE OF JAVA .NET CYBERCAFE
I GATHER. WHAT GIVES?
I THINK HE'S TRYING TO LIVE DOWN A DUMB JOCK REPUTATION.
HEIR&BELL
HIS WISH IS RESPECTED HERE-- WELL, MOSTLY.
MOSTLY?
HOUSE OF JAVA .NET
A BUCK SAYS YOU CAN'T SPELL "I.Q.."

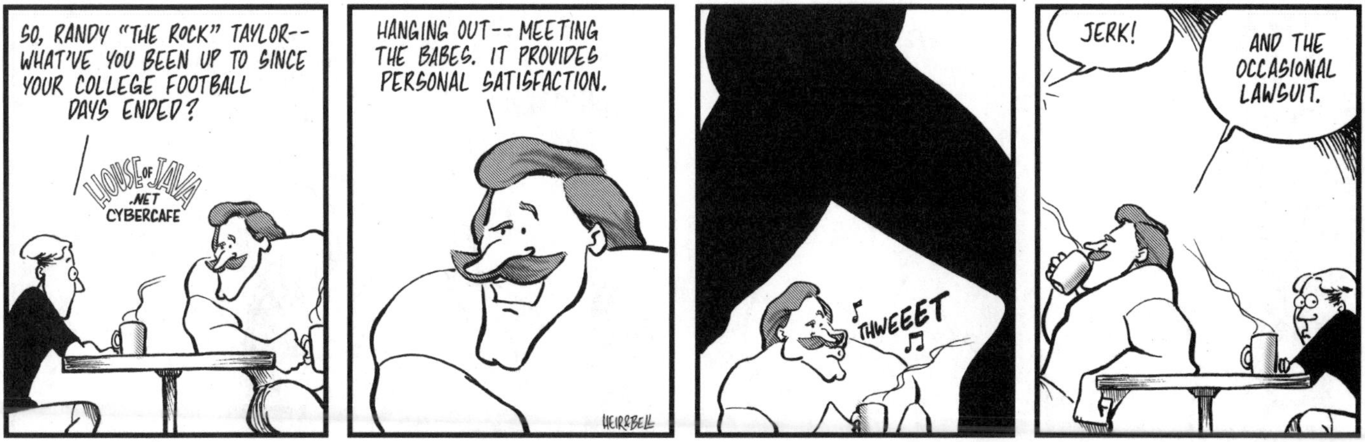
SO, RANDY "THE ROCK" TAYLOR-- WHAT'VE YOU BEEN UP TO SINCE YOUR COLLEGE FOOTBALL DAYS ENDED?
HOUSE OF JAVA .NET CYBERCAFE
HANGING OUT-- MEETING THE BABES. IT PROVIDES PERSONAL SATISFACTION.
HEIR&BELL
THWEEET
JERK!
AND THE OCCASIONAL LAWSUIT.

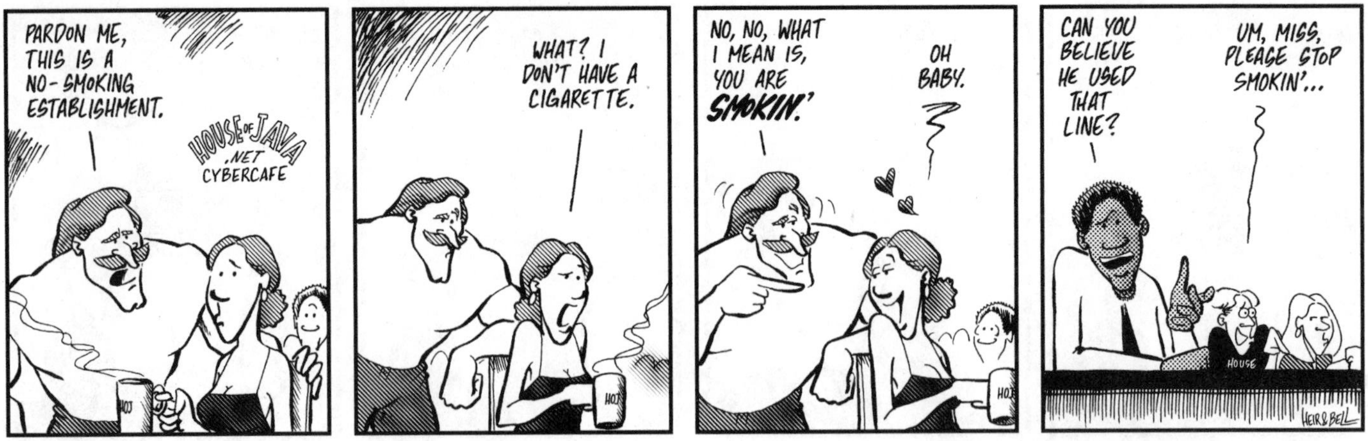
PARDON ME, THIS IS A NO-SMOKING ESTABLISHMENT.
HOUSE OF JAVA .NET CYBERCAFE
HOJ
WHAT? I DON'T HAVE A CIGARETTE.
HOJ
NO, NO, WHAT I MEAN IS, YOU ARE *SMOKIN'.*
OH BABY.
HOJ
CAN YOU BELIEVE HE USED THAT LINE?
UM, MISS, PLEASE STOP SMOKIN'...
HOUSE
HEIR & BELL

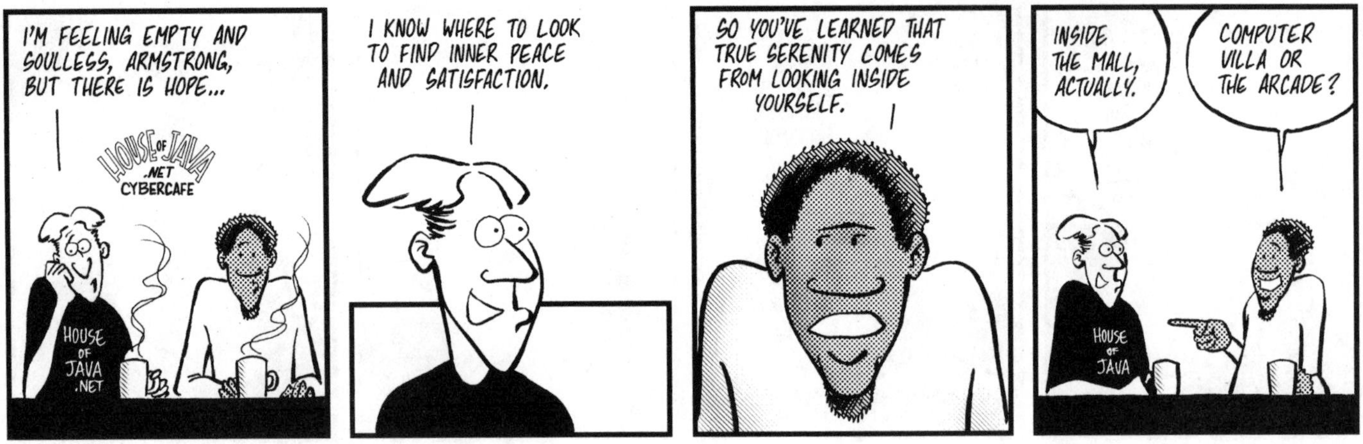
I'M FEELING EMPTY AND SOULLESS, ARMSTRONG, BUT THERE IS HOPE...
HOUSE OF JAVA .NET CYBERCAFE
HOUSE OF JAVA .NET
I KNOW WHERE TO LOOK TO FIND INNER PEACE AND SATISFACTION.
SO YOU'VE LEARNED THAT TRUE SERENITY COMES FROM LOOKING INSIDE YOURSELF.
INSIDE THE MALL, ACTUALLY.
COMPUTER VILLA OR THE ARCADE?
HOUSE OF JAVA

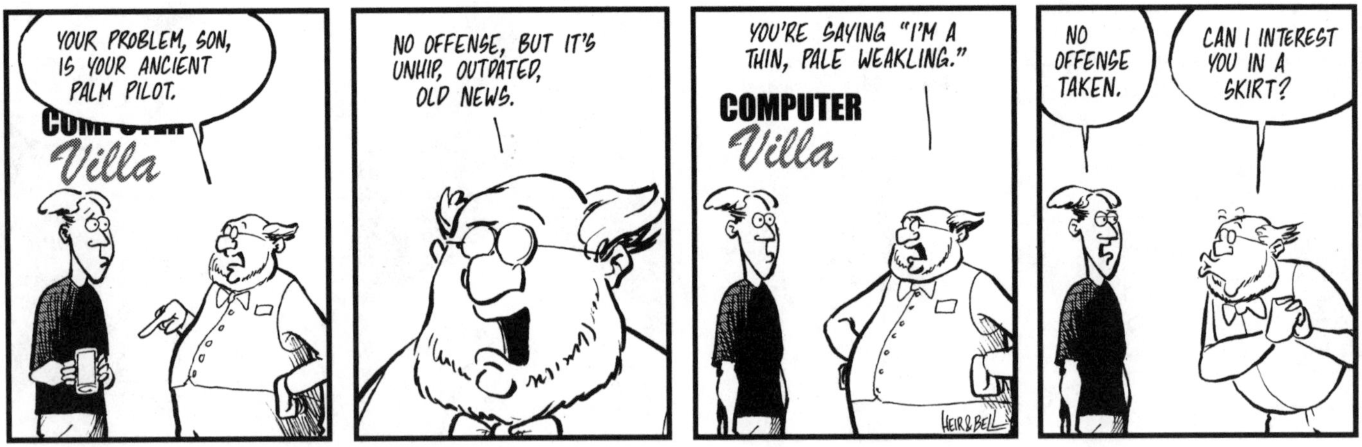
YOUR PROBLEM, SON, IS YOUR ANCIENT PALM PILOT.
Villa
NO OFFENSE, BUT IT'S UNHIP, OUTDATED, OLD NEWS.
YOU'RE SAYING "I'M A THIN, PALE WEAKLING."
COMPUTER Villa
HEIR & BELL
NO OFFENSE TAKEN.
CAN I INTEREST YOU IN A SKIRT?

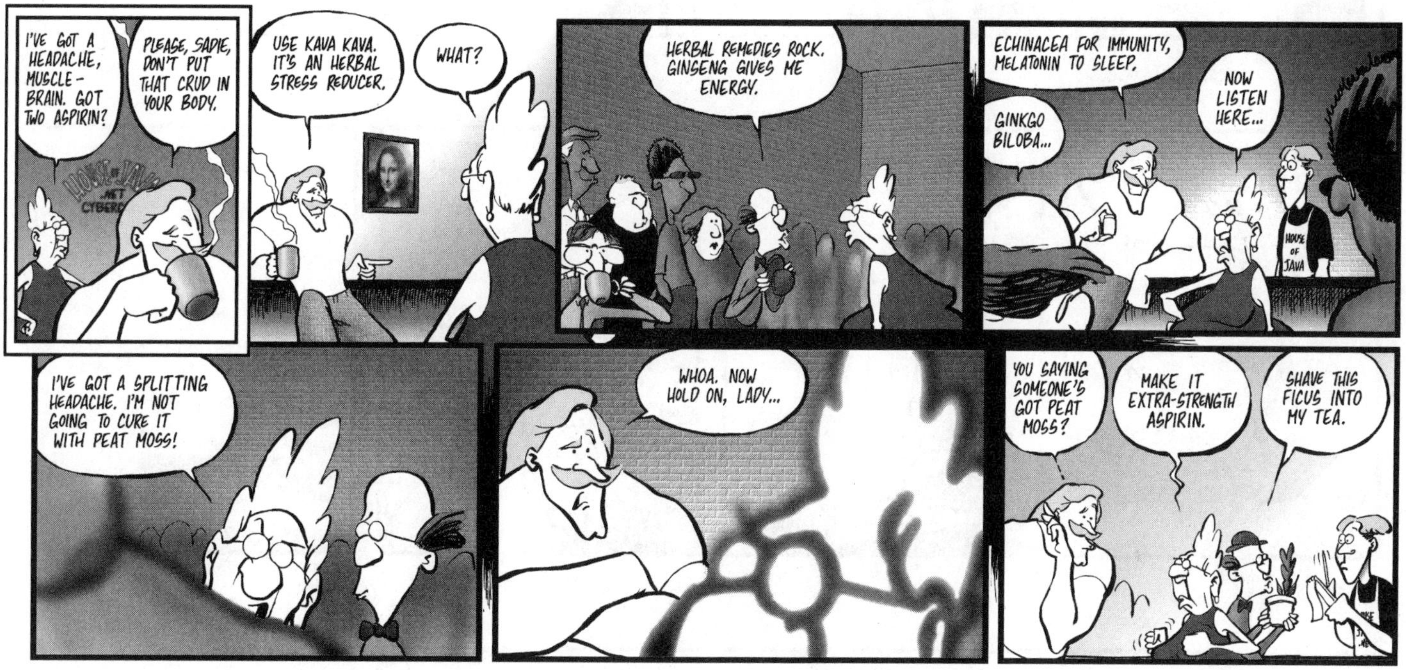

I'VE GOT A HEADACHE, MUSCLE-BRAIN. GOT TWO ASPIRIN?
PLEASE, SADIE, DON'T PUT THAT CRUD IN YOUR BODY.
USE KAVA KAVA. IT'S AN HERBAL STRESS REDUCER.
WHAT?
HERBAL REMEDIES ROCK. GINSENG GIVES ME ENERGY.
ECHINACEA FOR IMMUNITY, MELATONIN TO SLEEP.
GINKGO BILOBA...
NOW LISTEN HERE...
HOUSE OF JAVA
I'VE GOT A SPLITTING HEADACHE. I'M NOT GOING TO CURE IT WITH PEAT MOSS!
WHOA. NOW HOLD ON, LADY...
YOU SAYING SOMEONE'S GOT PEAT MOSS?
MAKE IT EXTRA-STRENGTH ASPIRIN.
SHAVE THIS FICUS INTO MY TEA.

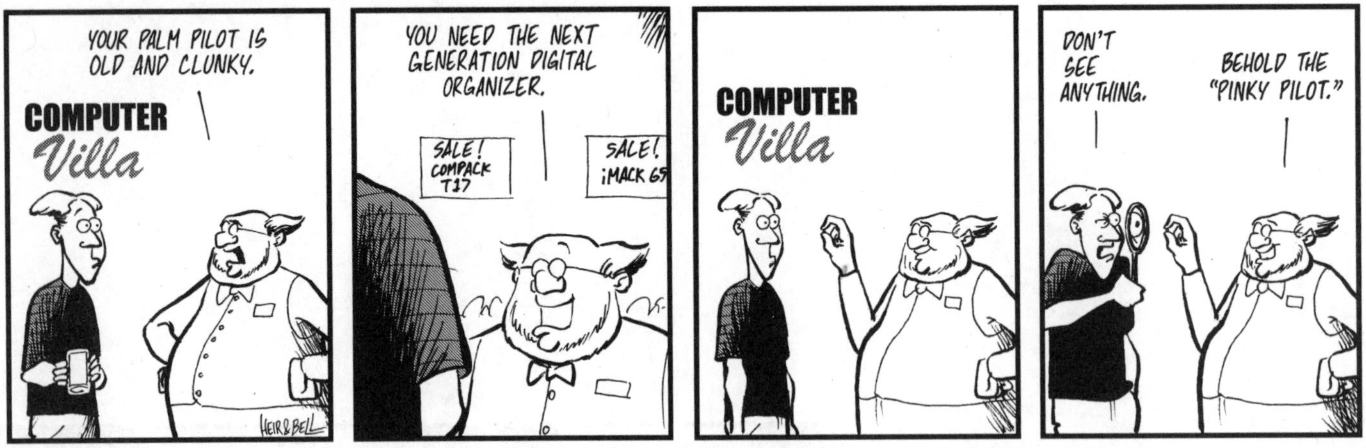
YOUR PALM PILOT IS OLD AND CLUNKY.
COMPUTER Villa
HEIR&BELL
YOU NEED THE NEXT GENERATION DIGITAL ORGANIZER.
SALE! COMPACK T17
SALE! iMACK 65
COMPUTER Villa
DON'T SEE ANYTHING.
BEHOLD THE "PINKY PILOT."

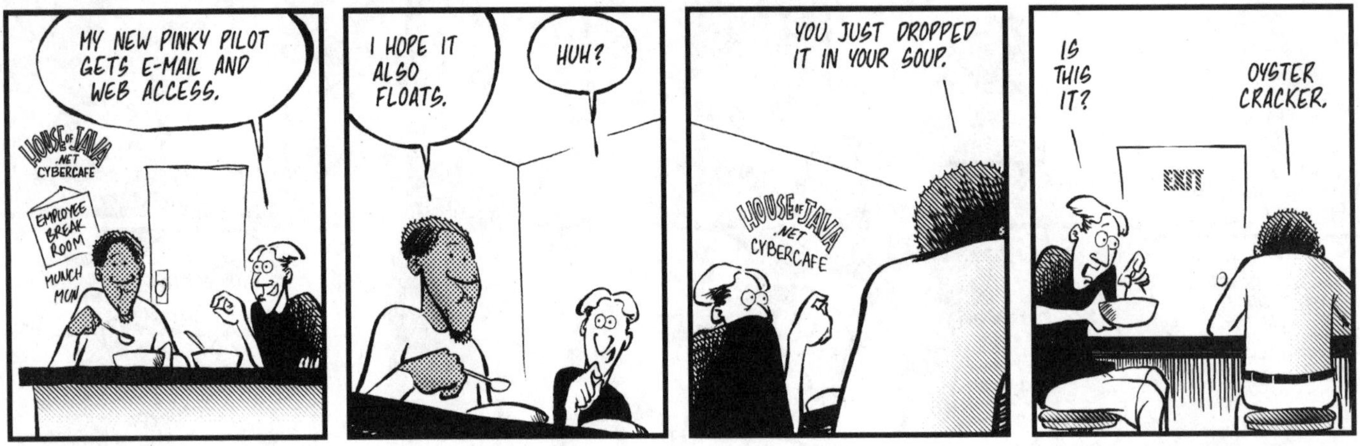
MY NEW PINKY PILOT GETS E-MAIL AND WEB ACCESS.
HOUSE OF JAVA .NET CYBERCAFE
EMPLOYEE BREAK ROOM
MUNCH MON
I HOPE IT ALSO FLOATS.
HUH?
YOU JUST DROPPED IT IN YOUR SOUP.
HOUSE OF JAVA .NET CYBERCAFE
IS THIS IT?
OYSTER CRACKER.
EXIT

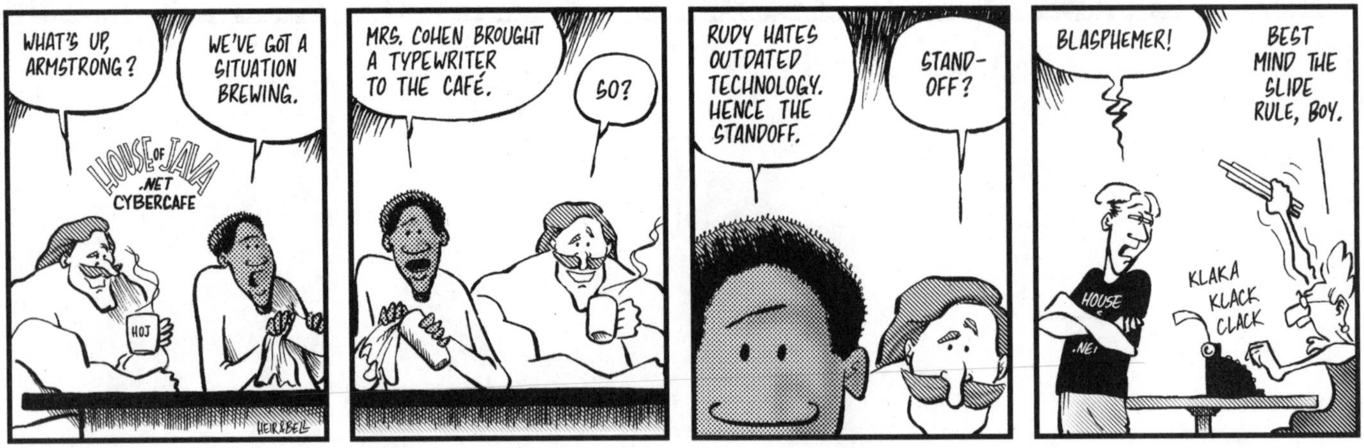
WHAT'S UP, ARMSTRONG?
WE'VE GOT A SITUATION BREWING.
HOUSE OF JAVA .NET CYBERCAFE
HOJ
HEIR&BELL
MRS. COHEN BROUGHT A TYPEWRITER TO THE CAFÉ.
SO?
RUDY HATES OUTDATED TECHNOLOGY. HENCE THE STANDOFF.
STAND-OFF?
BLASPHEMER!
BEST MIND THE SLIDE RULE, BOY.
HOUSE .NET
KLAKA KLACK CLACK

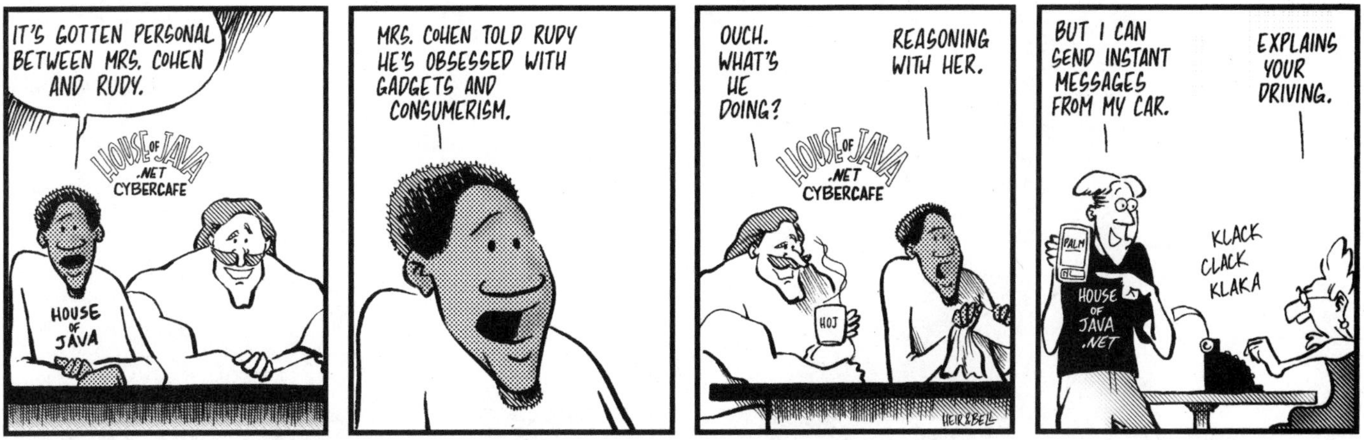
IT'S GOTTEN PERSONAL BETWEEN MRS. COHEN AND RUDY.
HOUSE OF JAVA .NET CYBERCAFE
HOUSE OF JAVA
MRS. COHEN TOLD RUDY HE'S OBSESSED WITH GADGETS AND CONSUMERISM.
OUCH. WHAT'S HE DOING?
REASONING WITH HER.
HOUSE OF JAVA .NET CYBERCAFE
HOJ
HEIR&BELL
BUT I CAN SEND INSTANT MESSAGES FROM MY CAR.
EXPLAINING YOUR DRIVING.
PALM
HOUSE OF JAVA .NET
KLACK CLACK KLAKA

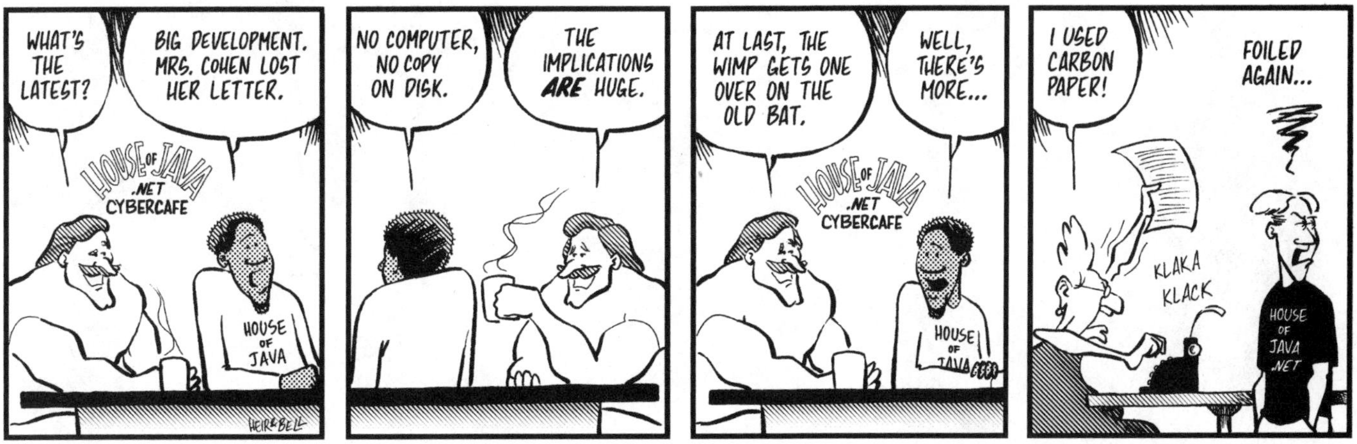
WHAT'S THE LATEST?
BIG DEVELOPMENT. MRS. COHEN LOST HER LETTER.
HOUSE OF JAVA .NET CYBERCAFE
HOUSE OF JAVA
HEIR&BELL
NO COMPUTER, NO COPY ON DISK.
THE IMPLICATIONS ARE HUGE.
AT LAST, THE WIMP GETS ONE OVER ON THE OLD BAT.
WELL, THERE'S MORE...
HOUSE OF JAVA .NET CYBERCAFE
HOUSE OF JAVA
I USED CARBON PAPER!
FOILED AGAIN...
KLAKA KLACK
HOUSE OF JAVA .NET

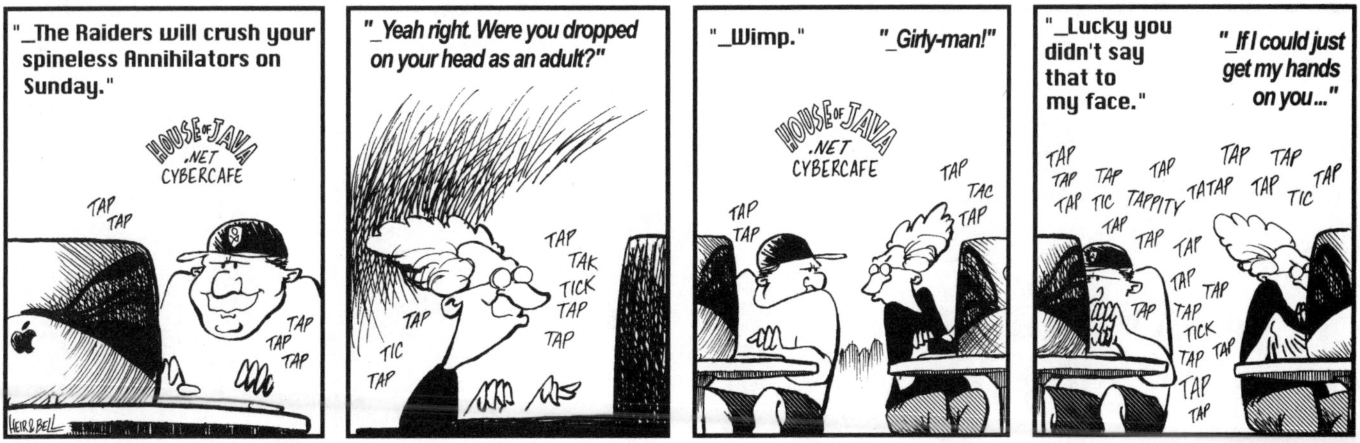
"_The Raiders will crush your spineless Annihilators on Sunday."
HOUSE OF JAVA .NET CYBERCAFE
TAP TAP
TAP TAP TAP
HEIR&BELL
"_Yeah right. Were you dropped on your head as an adult?"
TAP TAK TICK TAP TAP
TAP TIC TAP
"_Wimp."
"_Girly-man!"
HOUSE OF JAVA .NET CYBERCAFE
TAP TAP
TAP TAC TAP
"_Lucky you didn't say that to my face."
"_If I could just get my hands on you..."
TAP TAP TAP TAP TIC TAP TAPPITY TATAP TAP TAP TAP TAP TIC TAP
TAP TAP TAP TAP TAP TAP TAP TICK TAP TAP TAP TAP

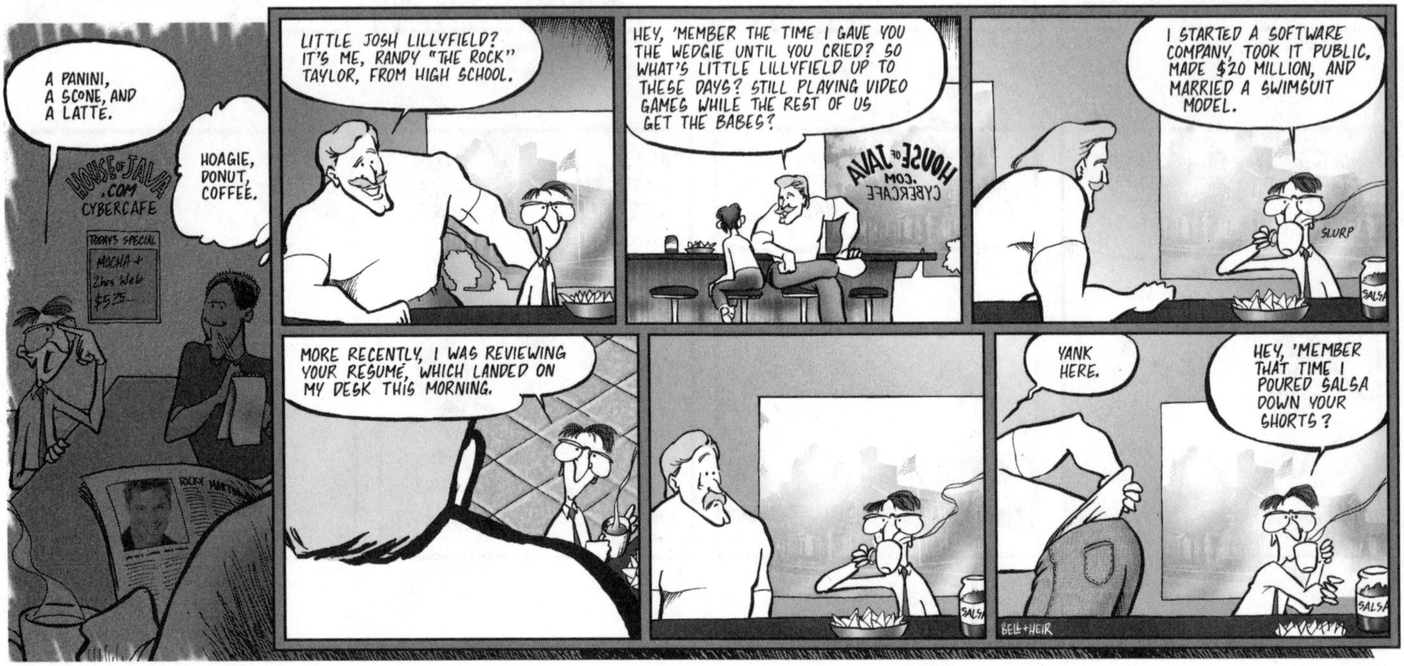
A PANINI, A SCONE, AND A LATTÉ.
HOAGIE, DONUT, COFFEE.
HOUSE OF JAVA .COM CYBERCAFE
TODAY'S SPECIAL MOCHA + 2hrs Web $5.75
LITTLE JOSH LILLYFIELD? IT'S ME, RANDY "THE ROCK" TAYLOR, FROM HIGH SCHOOL.
HEY, 'MEMBER THE TIME I GAVE YOU THE WEDGIE UNTIL YOU CRIED? SO WHAT'S LITTLE LILLYFIELD UP TO THESE DAYS? STILL PLAYING VIDEO GAMES WHILE THE REST OF US GET THE BABES?
I STARTED A SOFTWARE COMPANY, TOOK IT PUBLIC, MADE $20 MILLION, AND MARRIED A SWIMSUIT MODEL.
SLURP
SALSA
MORE RECENTLY, I WAS REVIEWING YOUR RESUME, WHICH LANDED ON MY DESK THIS MORNING.
YANK HERE.
HEY, 'MEMBER THAT TIME I POURED SALSA DOWN YOUR SHORTS?
BELL+HEIR

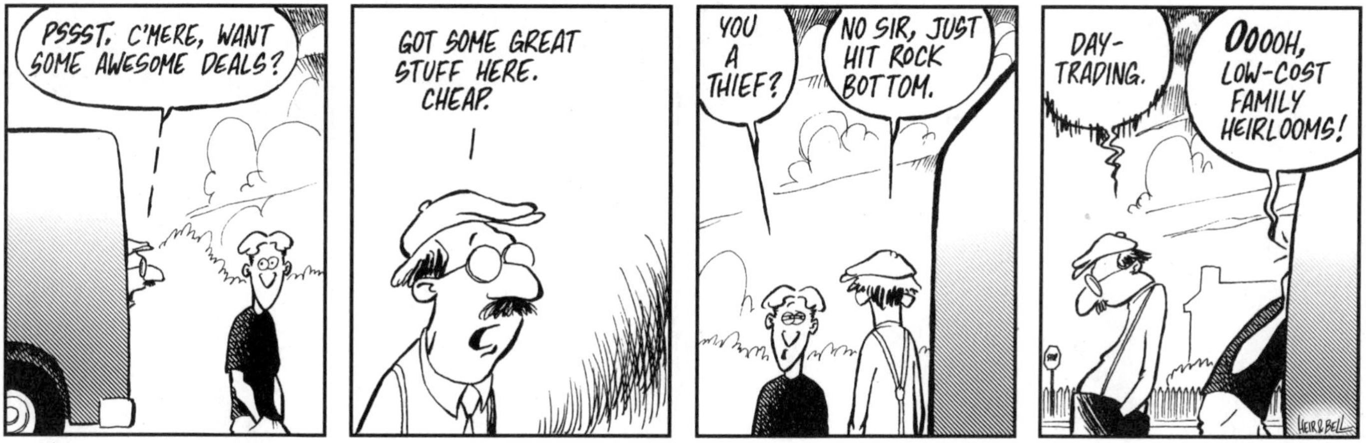
PSSST. C'MERE, WANT SOME AWESOME DEALS?
GOT SOME GREAT STUFF HERE. CHEAP.
YOU A THIEF?
NO SIR, JUST HIT ROCK BOTTOM.
DAY-TRADING.
OOOOH, LOW-COST FAMILY HEIRLOOMS!

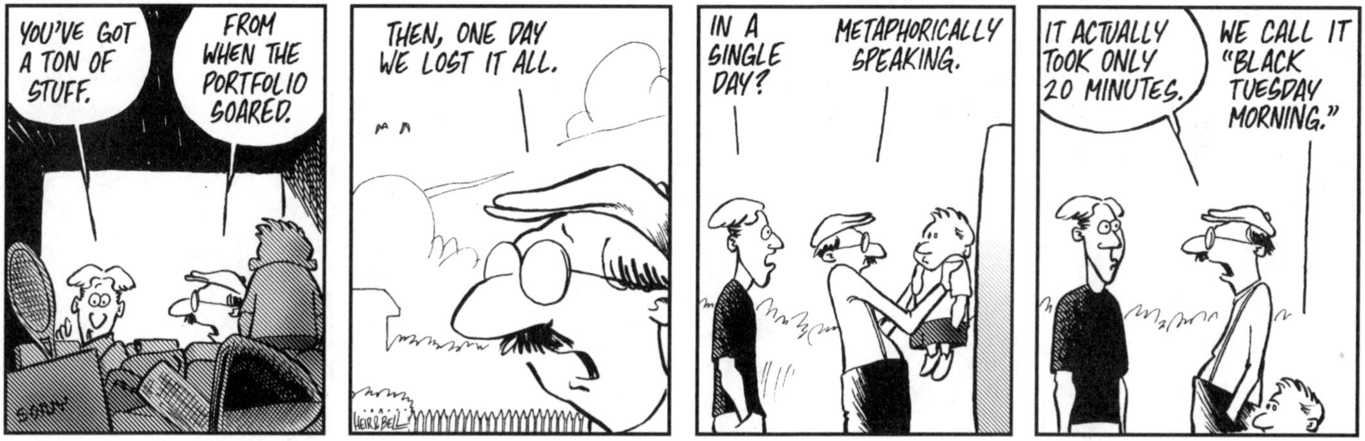
YOU'VE GOT A TON OF STUFF.
FROM WHEN THE PORTFOLIO SOARED.
THEN, ONE DAY WE LOST IT ALL.
IN A SINGLE DAY?
METAPHORICALLY SPEAKING.
IT ACTUALLY TOOK ONLY 20 MINUTES.
WE CALL IT "BLACK TUESDAY MORNING."

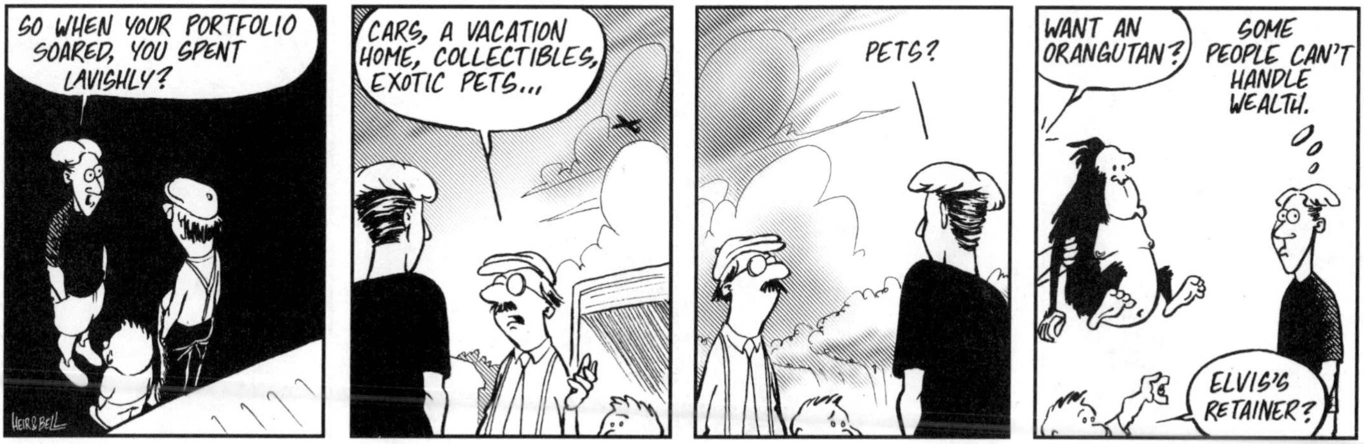
SO WHEN YOUR PORTFOLIO SOARED, YOU SPENT LAVISHLY?
CARS, A VACATION HOME, COLLECTIBLES, EXOTIC PETS...
PETS?
WANT AN ORANGUTAN?
SOME PEOPLE CAN'T HANDLE WEALTH.
ELVIS'S RETAINER?

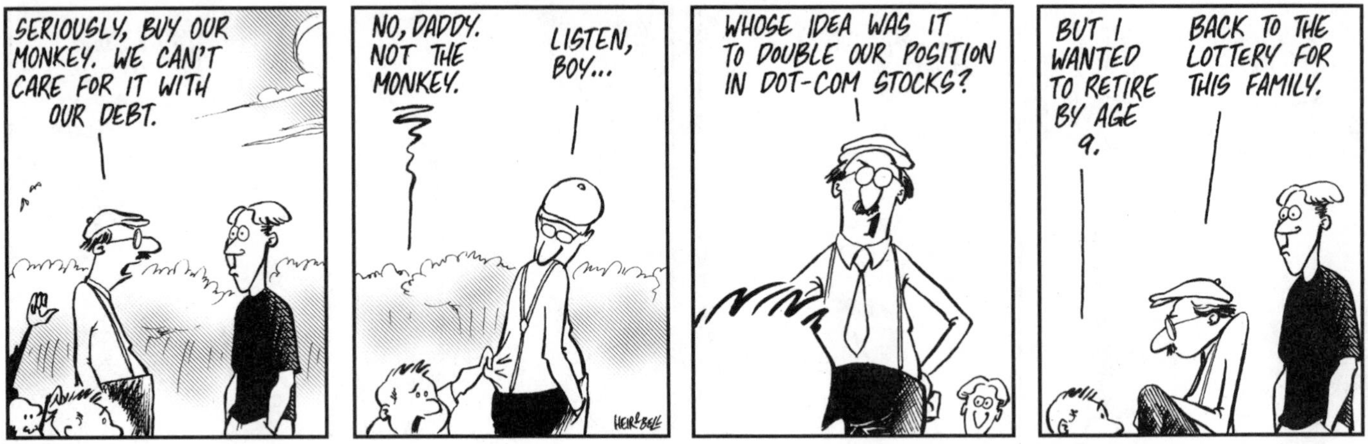
SERIOUSLY, BUY OUR MONKEY. WE CAN'T CARE FOR IT WITH OUR DEBT.
NO, DADDY. NOT THE MONKEY.
LISTEN, BOY...
WHOSE IDEA WAS IT TO DOUBLE OUR POSITION IN DOT-COM STOCKS?
BUT I WANTED TO RETIRE BY AGE 9.
BACK TO THE LOTTERY FOR THIS FAMILY.

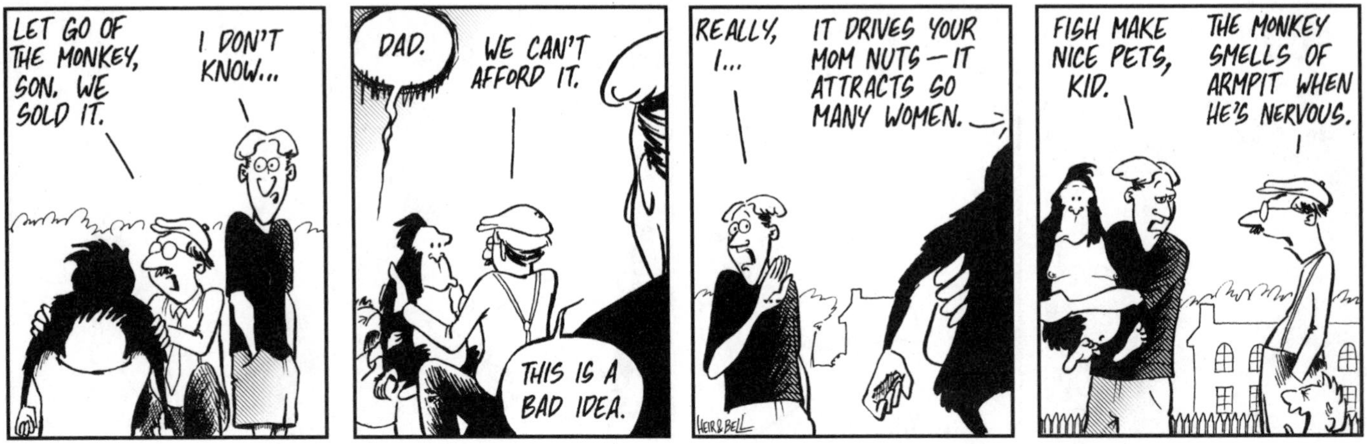
LET GO OF THE MONKEY, SON. WE SOLD IT.
I DON'T KNOW...
DAD.
WE CAN'T AFFORD IT.
THIS IS A BAD IDEA.
REALLY, I...
IT DRIVES YOUR MOM NUTS—IT ATTRACTS SO MANY WOMEN.
FISH MAKE NICE PETS, KID.
THE MONKEY SMELLS OF ARMPIT WHEN HE'S NERVOUS.

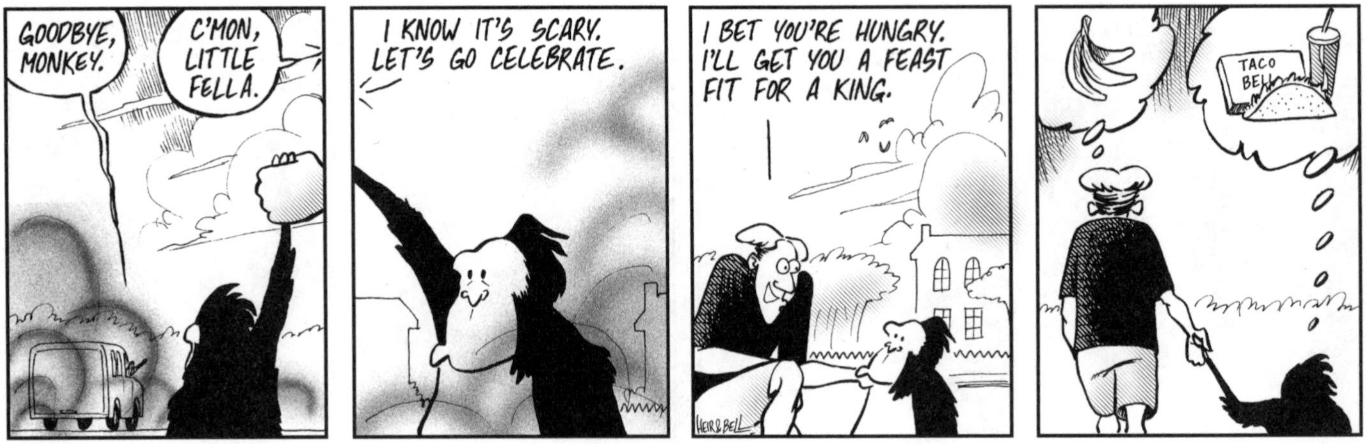
GOODBYE, MONKEY.
C'MON, LITTLE FELLA.
I KNOW IT'S SCARY. LET'S GO CELEBRATE.
I BET YOU'RE HUNGRY. I'LL GET YOU A FEAST FIT FOR A KING.
TACO BELL

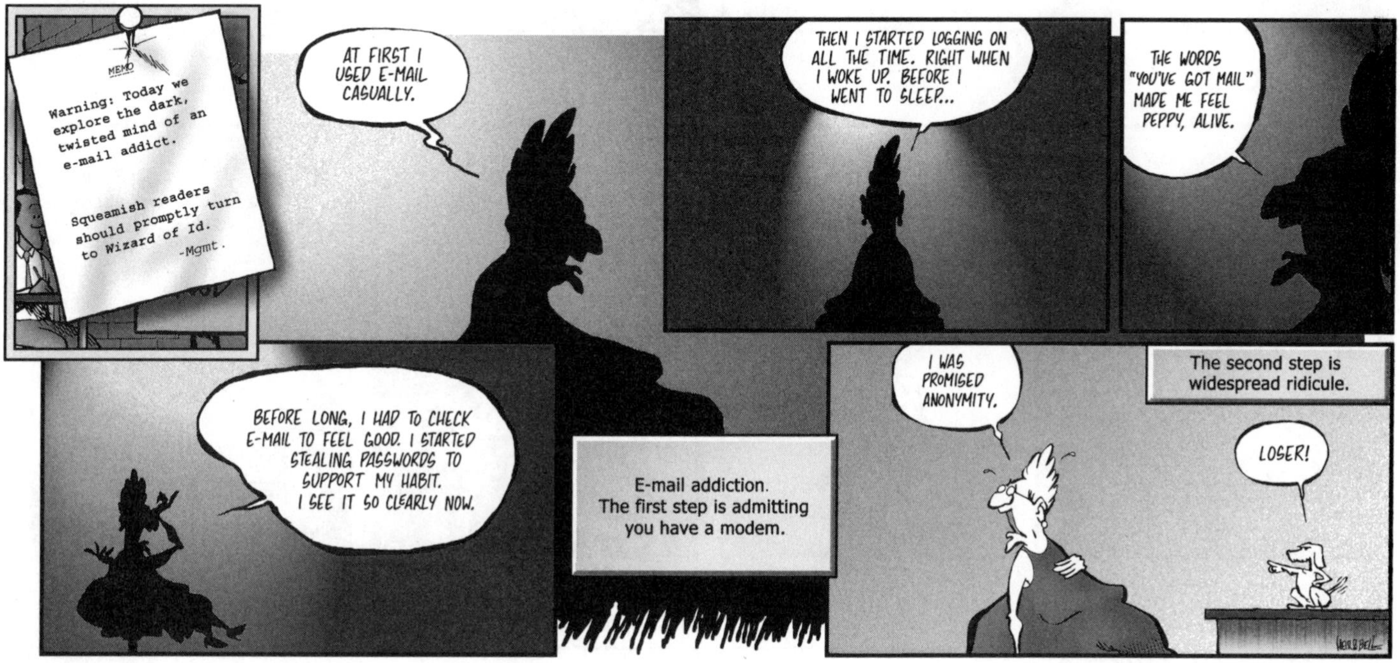
MEMO
Warning: Today we explore the dark, twisted mind of an e-mail addict.
Squeamish readers should promptly turn to Wizard of Id.
-Mgmt.
AT FIRST I USED E-MAIL CASUALLY.
THEN I STARTED LOGGING ON ALL THE TIME. RIGHT WHEN I WOKE UP. BEFORE I WENT TO SLEEP...
THE WORDS "YOU'VE GOT MAIL" MADE ME FEEL PEPPY, ALIVE.
BEFORE LONG, I HAD TO CHECK E-MAIL TO FEEL GOOD. I STARTED STEALING PASSWORDS TO SUPPORT MY HABIT. I SEE IT SO CLEARLY NOW.
E-mail addiction. The first step is admitting you have a modem.
I WAS PROMISED ANONYMITY.
The second step is widespread ridicule.
LOSER!

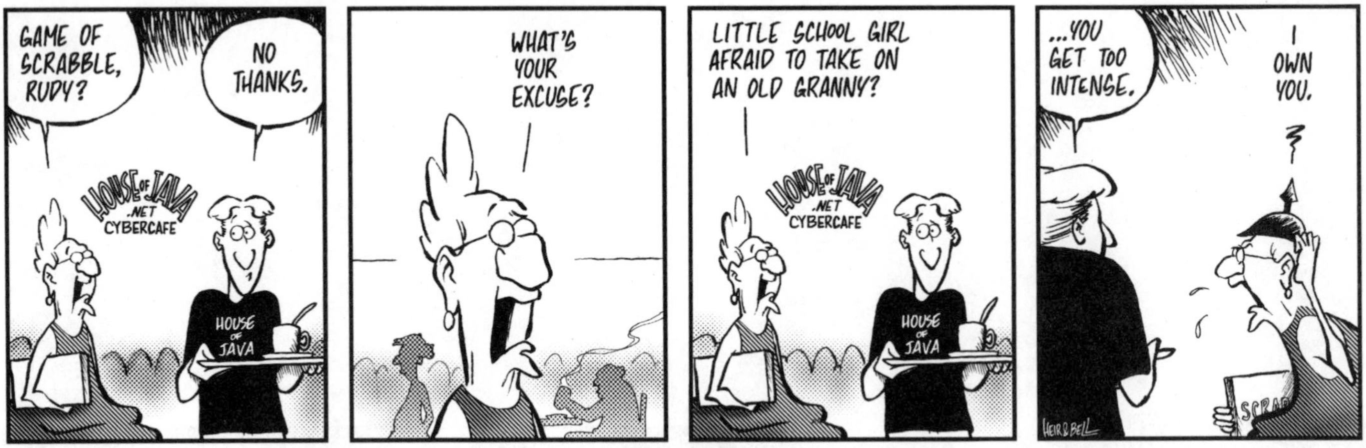
GAME OF SCRABBLE, RUDY?
NO THANKS.
WHAT'S YOUR EXCUSE?
LITTLE SCHOOL GIRL AFRAID TO TAKE ON AN OLD GRANNY?
...YOU GET TOO INTENSE.
I OWN YOU.

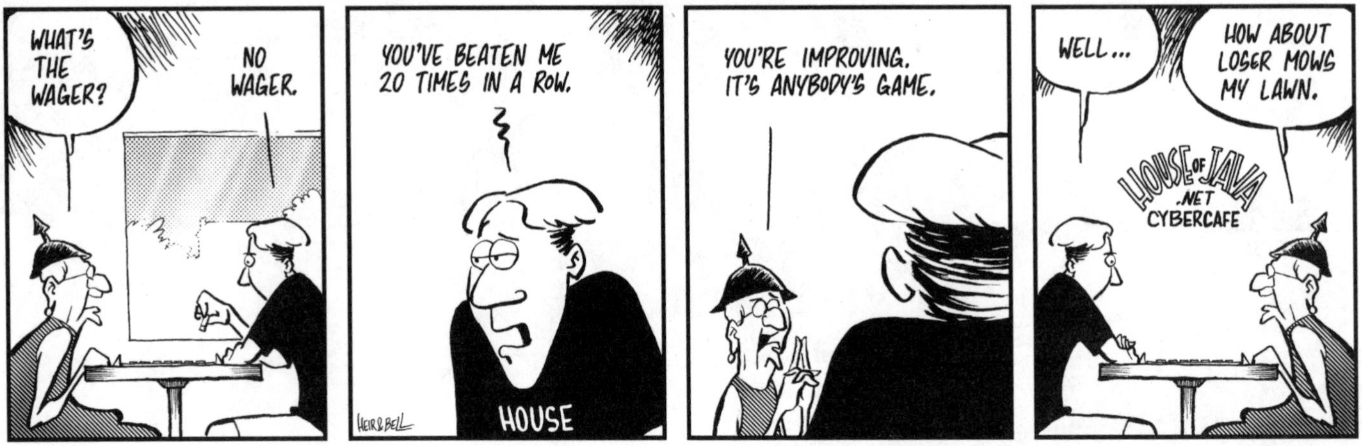
WHAT'S THE WAGER?
NO WAGER.
YOU'VE BEATEN ME 20 TIMES IN A ROW.
YOU'RE IMPROVING. IT'S ANYBODY'S GAME.
WELL...
HOW ABOUT LOSER MOWS MY LAWN.

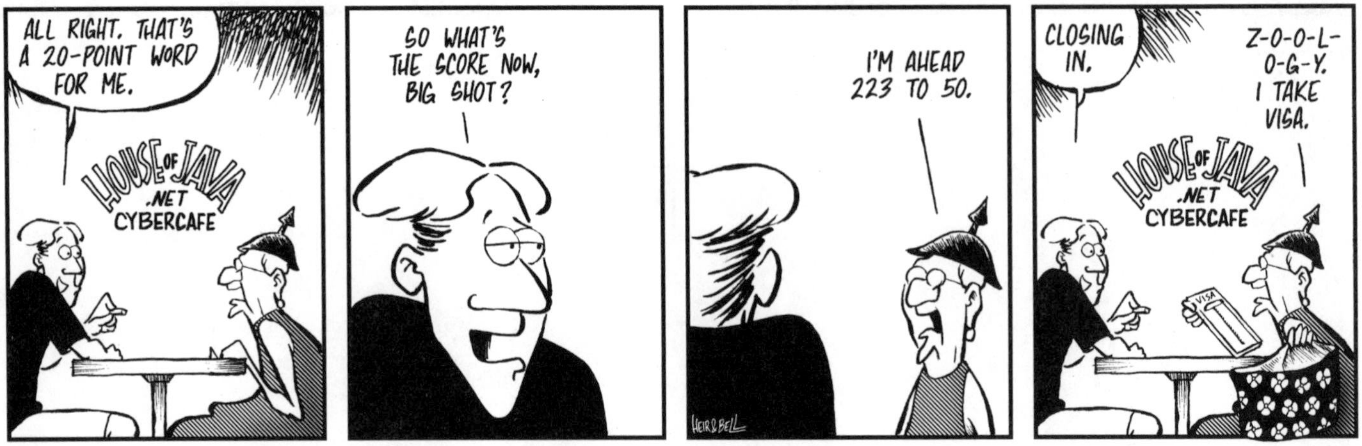
ALL RIGHT. THAT'S A 20-POINT WORD FOR ME.
SO WHAT'S THE SCORE NOW, BIG SHOT?
I'M AHEAD 223 TO 50.
CLOSING IN.
Z-O-O-L-O-G-Y. I TAKE VISA.

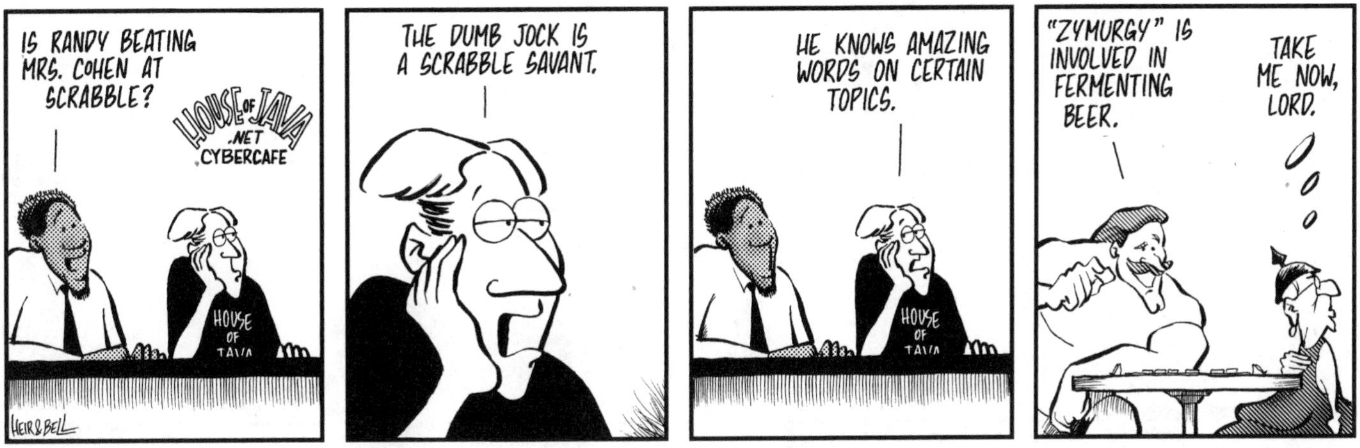
IS RANDY BEATING MRS. COHEN AT SCRABBLE?
HOUSE OF JAVA .NET CYBERCAFE
HOUSE OF JAVA
HEIR & BELL
THE DUMB JOCK IS A SCRABBLE SAVANT.
HE KNOWS AMAZING WORDS ON CERTAIN TOPICS.
HOUSE OF JAVA
"ZYMURGY" IS INVOLVED IN FERMENTING BEER.
TAKE ME NOW, LORD.

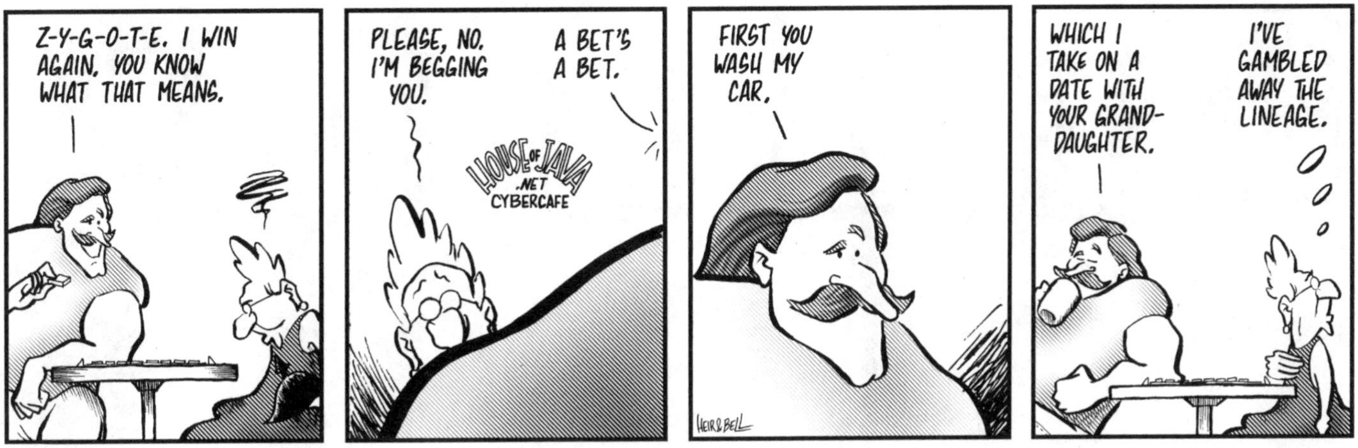
Z-Y-G-O-T-E. I WIN AGAIN. YOU KNOW WHAT THAT MEANS.
PLEASE, NO. I'M BEGGING YOU.
A BET'S A BET.
HOUSE OF JAVA .NET CYBERCAFE
FIRST YOU WASH MY CAR.
HEIR & BELL
WHICH I TAKE ON A DATE WITH YOUR GRAND-DAUGHTER.
I'VE GAMBLED AWAY THE LINEAGE.

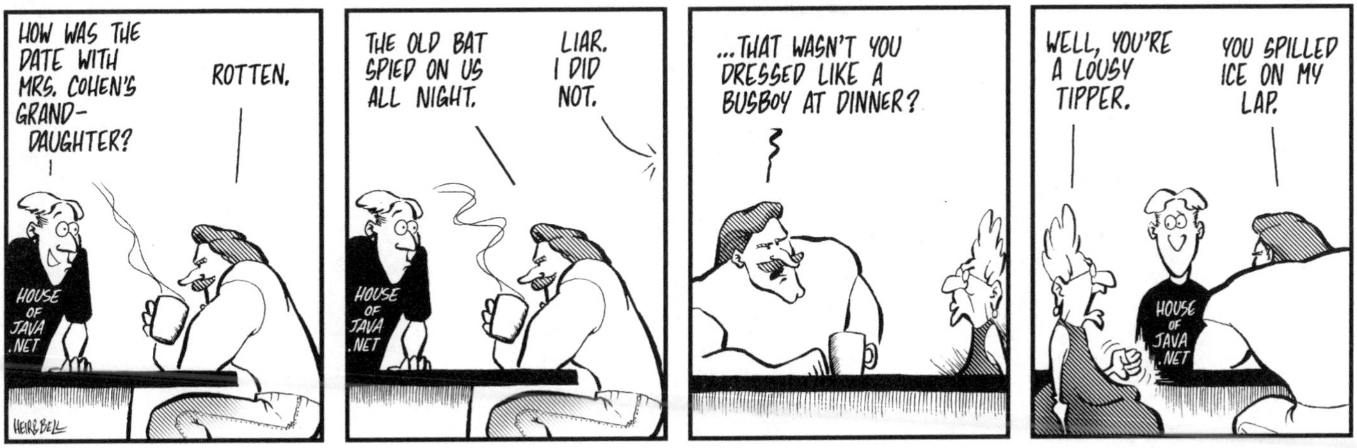
HOW WAS THE DATE WITH MRS. COHEN'S GRAND-DAUGHTER?
ROTTEN.
HOUSE OF JAVA .NET
HEIR & BELL
THE OLD BAT SPIED ON US ALL NIGHT.
LIAR. I DID NOT.
HOUSE OF JAVA .NET
...THAT WASN'T YOU DRESSED LIKE A BUSBOY AT DINNER?
WELL, YOU'RE A LOUSY TIPPER.
YOU SPILLED ICE ON MY LAP.
HOUSE OF JAVA .NET

IN RESPONSE TO A GROWING NUMBER OF ADS MAKING UNSUBSTANTIATED CLAIMS, THE **HONESTY IN ADVERTISING COALITION** OFFERS THE FOLLOWING REALITY CHECK.
H.A.C.
YOU LIKELY WILL NOT IMPROVE YOUR SLEEPING PATTERNS OR MOODS.
SNORT-THK
ZzzZZzzz
YOU WILL NOT LEARN FRENCH OR DEVELOP TIGHT BUNS.
YOU WON'T MAKE A KILLING IN REAL ESTATE OR PRECIOUS METALS. YOU WILL CONTINUE TO HAVE SEVERE CRAMPS.
YOU WILL REMAIN BALD, FAT, UNMOTIVATED, UNABLE TO TRAIN YOUR PET TO DANCE POLKA, AND DEEPLY ROMANTICALLY INADEQUATE.
H.A.C.
HONESTY. IT'S OUR ONLY HOPE.
H.A.C.
DANG.
SIDE EFFECTS FROM HONESTY INCLUDE DEPRESSION AND SEVERE CRAMPS.
PET POLKA!

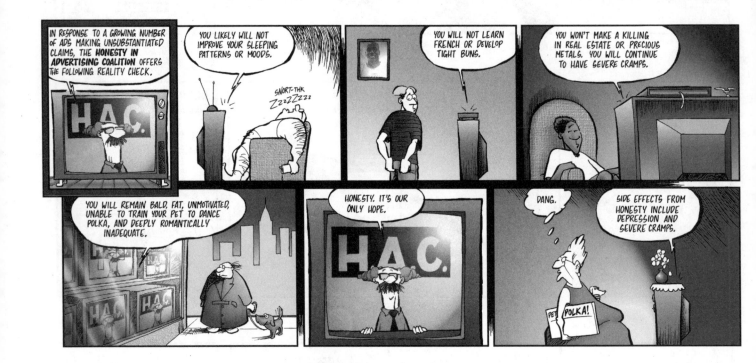

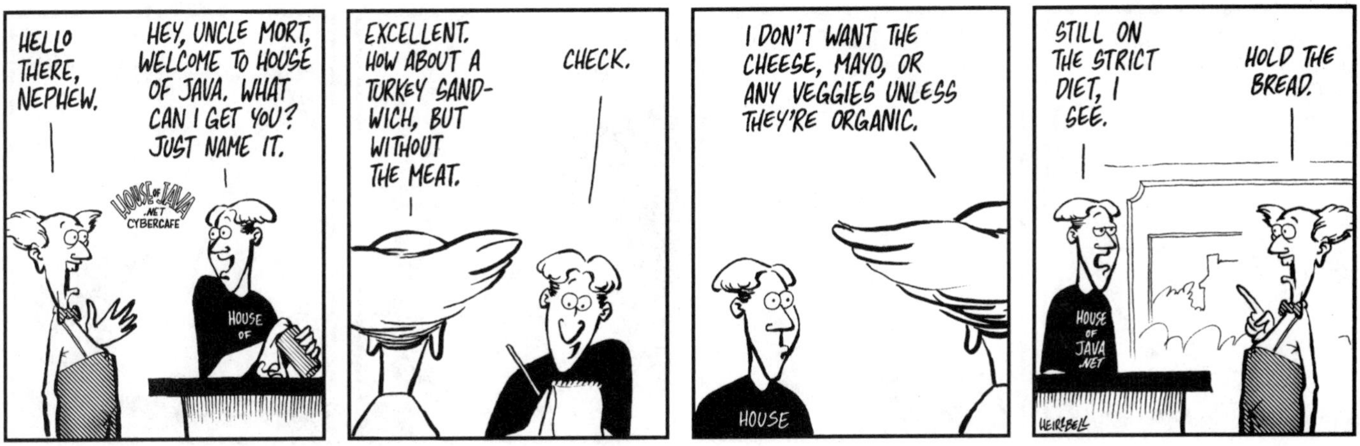
HELLO THERE, NEPHEW.
HEY, UNCLE MORT, WELCOME TO HOUSE OF JAVA. WHAT CAN I GET YOU? JUST NAME IT.
HOUSE OF JAVA .NET CYBERCAFE
HOUSE OF
EXCELLENT. HOW ABOUT A TURKEY SANDWICH, BUT WITHOUT THE MEAT.
CHECK.
I DON'T WANT THE CHEESE, MAYO, OR ANY VEGGIES UNLESS THEY'RE ORGANIC.
HOUSE
STILL ON THE STRICT DIET, I SEE.
HOLD THE BREAD.
HOUSE OF JAVA .NET
HEIR&BELL

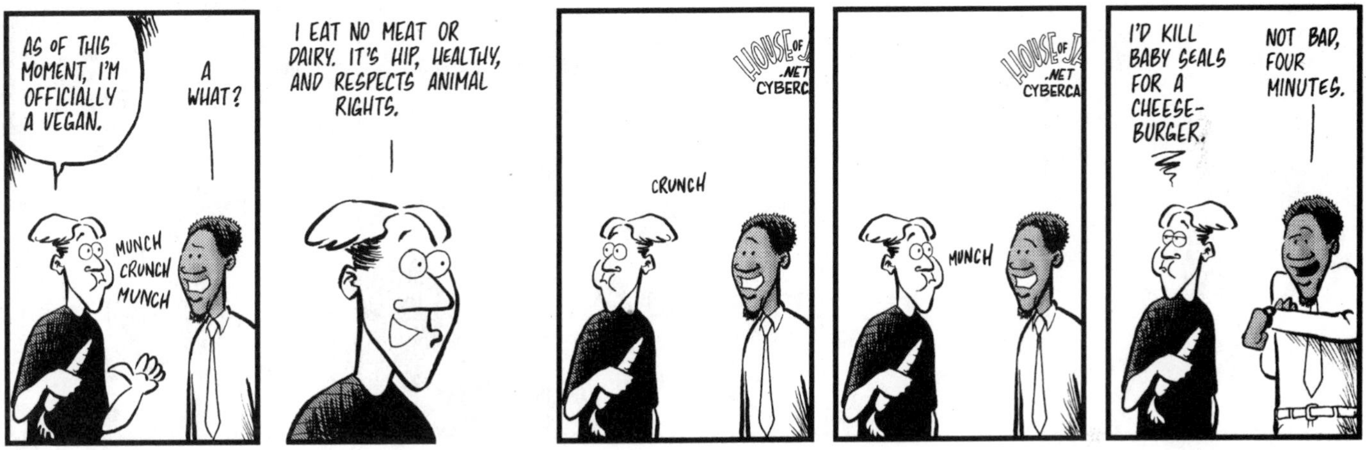
AS OF THIS MOMENT, I'M OFFICIALLY A VEGAN.
A WHAT?
MUNCH CRUNCH MUNCH
I EAT NO MEAT OR DAIRY. IT'S HIP, HEALTHY, AND RESPECTS ANIMAL RIGHTS.
CRUNCH
MUNCH
I'D KILL BABY SEALS FOR A CHEESEBURGER.
NOT BAD, FOUR MINUTES.

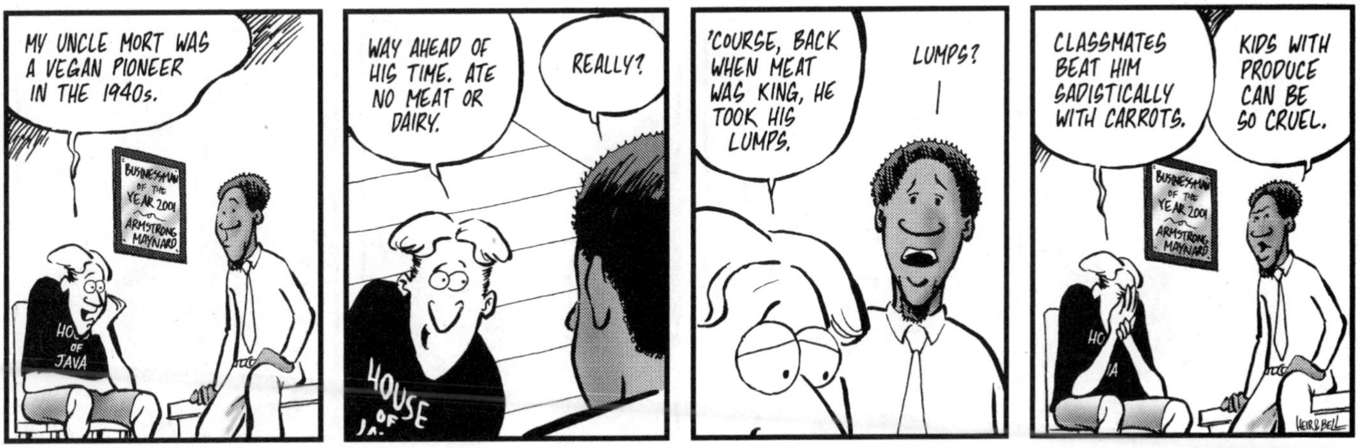
MY UNCLE MORT WAS A VEGAN PIONEER IN THE 1940s.
BUSINESSMAN OF THE YEAR 2001 ARMSTRONG MAYNARD
HOUSE OF JAVA
WAY AHEAD OF HIS TIME. ATE NO MEAT OR DAIRY.
REALLY?
'COURSE, BACK WHEN MEAT WAS KING, HE TOOK HIS LUMPS.
LUMPS?
CLASSMATES BEAT HIM SADISTICALLY WITH CARROTS.
KIDS WITH PRODUCE CAN BE SO CRUEL.
HEIR&BELL

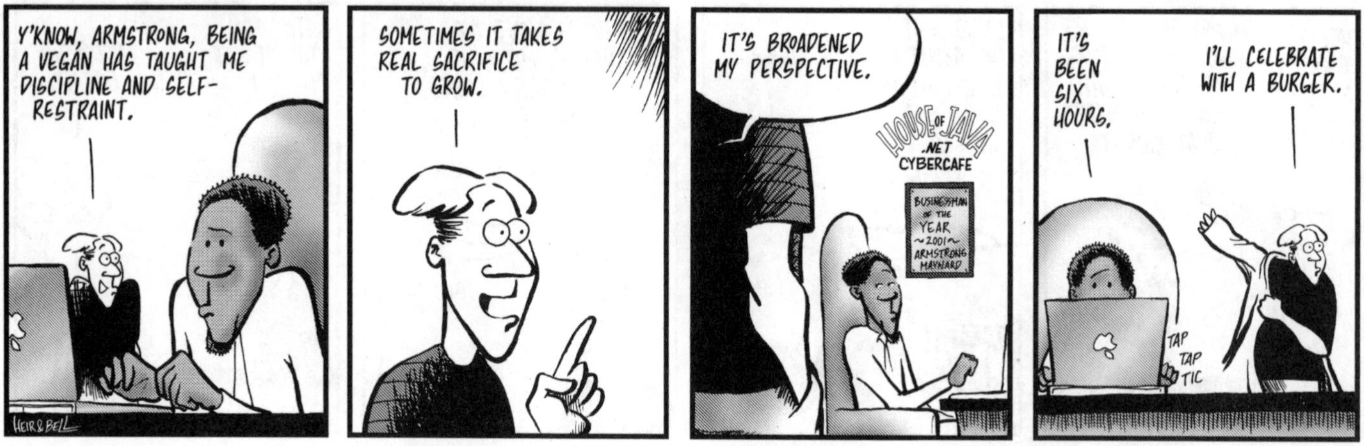

Y'KNOW, ARMSTRONG, BEING A VEGAN HAS TAUGHT ME DISCIPLINE AND SELF-RESTRAINT.
SOMETIMES IT TAKES REAL SACRIFICE TO GROW.
IT'S BROADENED MY PERSPECTIVE.
HOUSE OF JAVA .NET CYBERCAFE
BUSINESSMAN OF THE YEAR ~2001~ ARMSTRONG MAYNARD
IT'S BEEN SIX HOURS.
I'LL CELEBRATE WITH A BURGER.
TAP TAP TIC

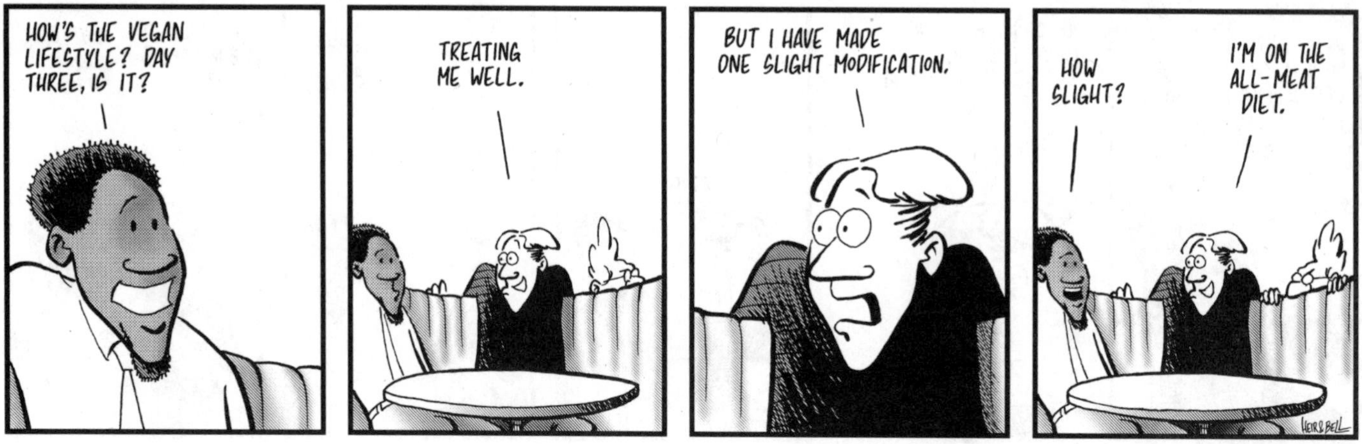

HOW'S THE VEGAN LIFESTYLE? DAY THREE, IS IT?
TREATING ME WELL.
BUT I HAVE MADE ONE SLIGHT MODIFICATION.
HOW SLIGHT?
I'M ON THE ALL-MEAT DIET.

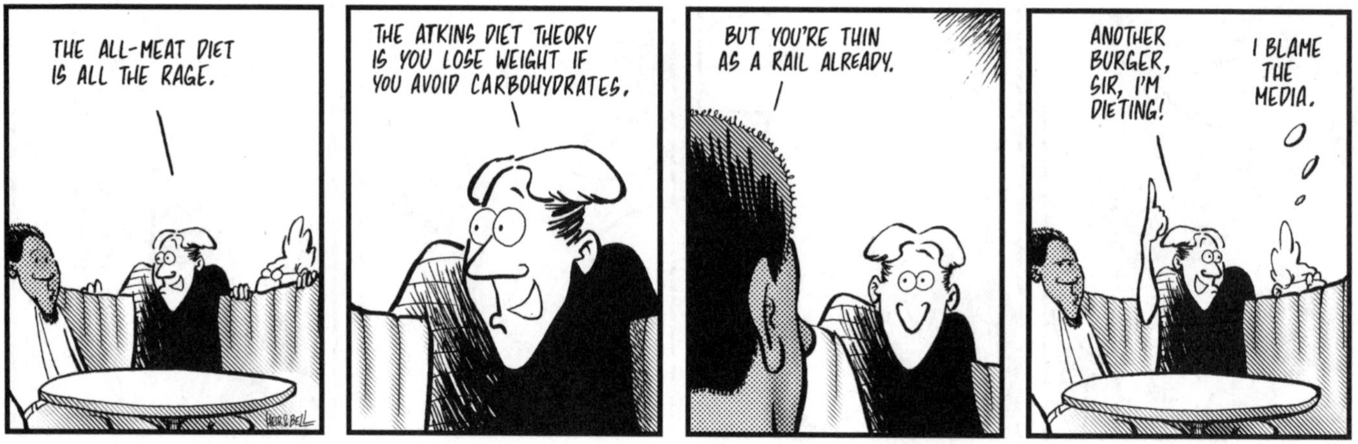

THE ALL-MEAT DIET IS ALL THE RAGE.
THE ATKINS DIET THEORY IS YOU LOSE WEIGHT IF YOU AVOID CARBOHYDRATES.
BUT YOU'RE THIN AS A RAIL ALREADY.
ANOTHER BURGER, SIR, I'M DIETING!
I BLAME THE MEDIA.

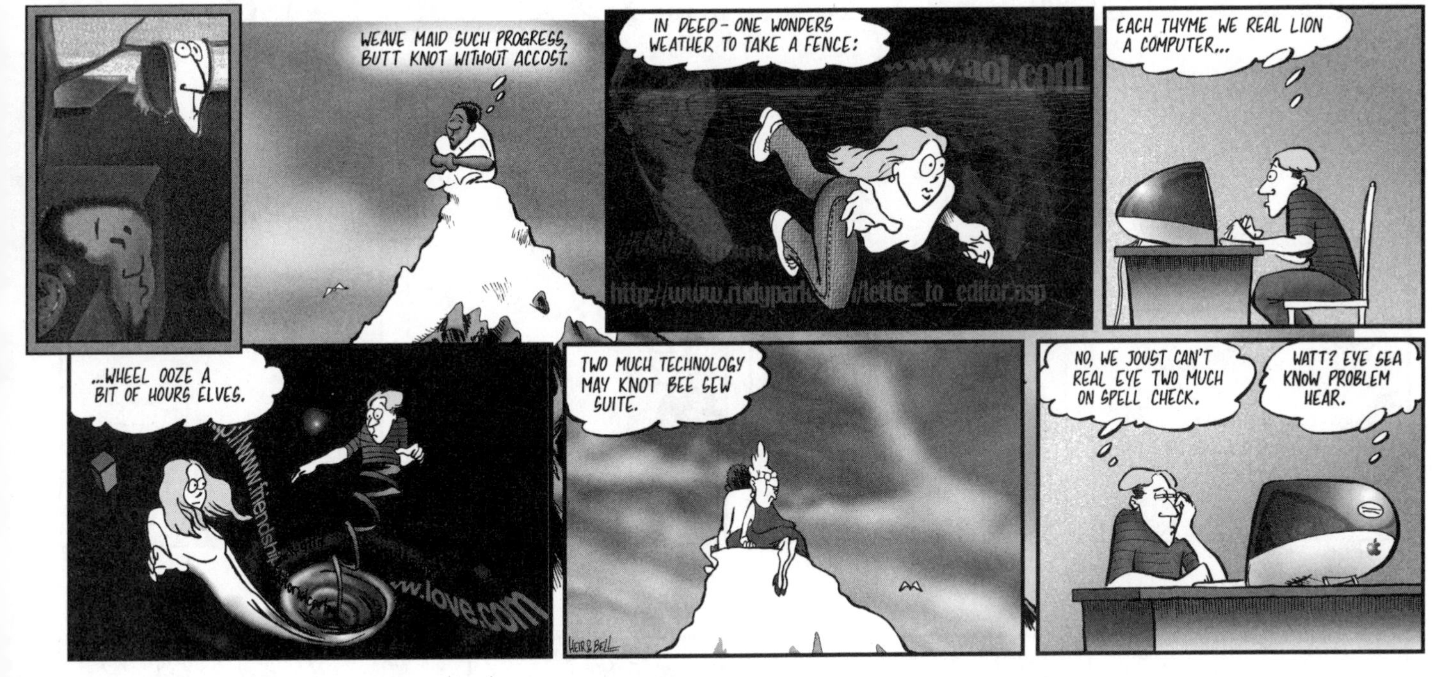
WEAVE MAID SUCH PROGRESS, BUTT KNOT WITHOUT ACCOST.
IN DEED - ONE WONDERS WEATHER TO TAKE A FENCE:
EACH THYME WE REAL LION A COMPUTER...
...WHEEL OOZE A BIT OF HOURS ELVES.
TWO MUCH TECHNOLOGY MAY KNOT BEE SEW SUITE.
NO, WE JOUST CAN'T REAL EYE TWO MUCH ON SPELL CHECK.
WATT? EYE SEA KNOW PROBLEM HEAR.

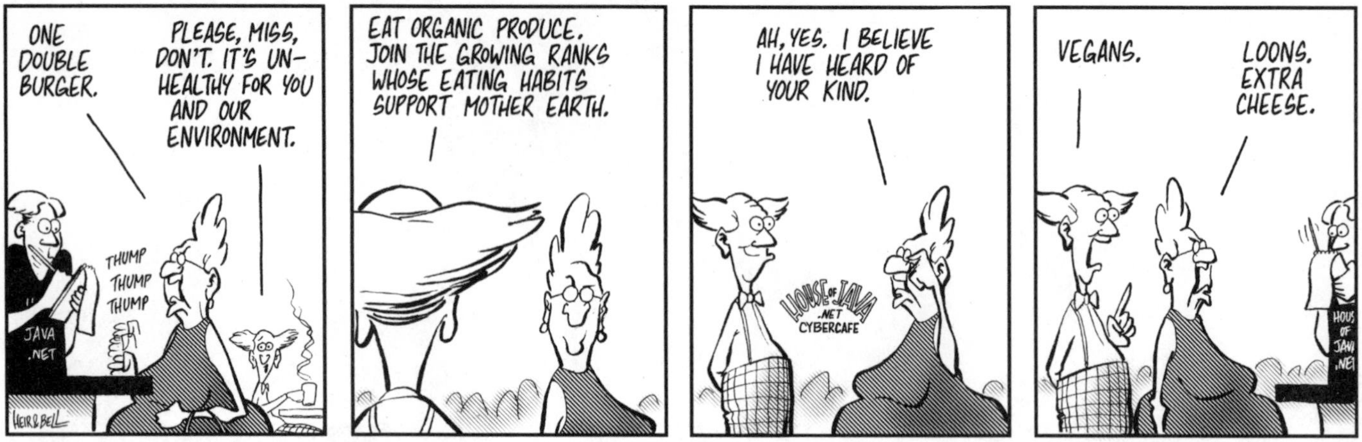
ONE DOUBLE BURGER.
PLEASE, MISS, DON'T. IT'S UN-HEALTHY FOR YOU AND OUR ENVIRONMENT.
THUMP THUMP THUMP
JAVA .NET
EAT ORGANIC PRODUCE. JOIN THE GROWING RANKS WHOSE EATING HABITS SUPPORT MOTHER EARTH.
AH, YES. I BELIEVE I HAVE HEARD OF YOUR KIND.
HOUSE OF JAVA .NET CYBERCAFE
VEGANS.
LOONS. EXTRA CHEESE.

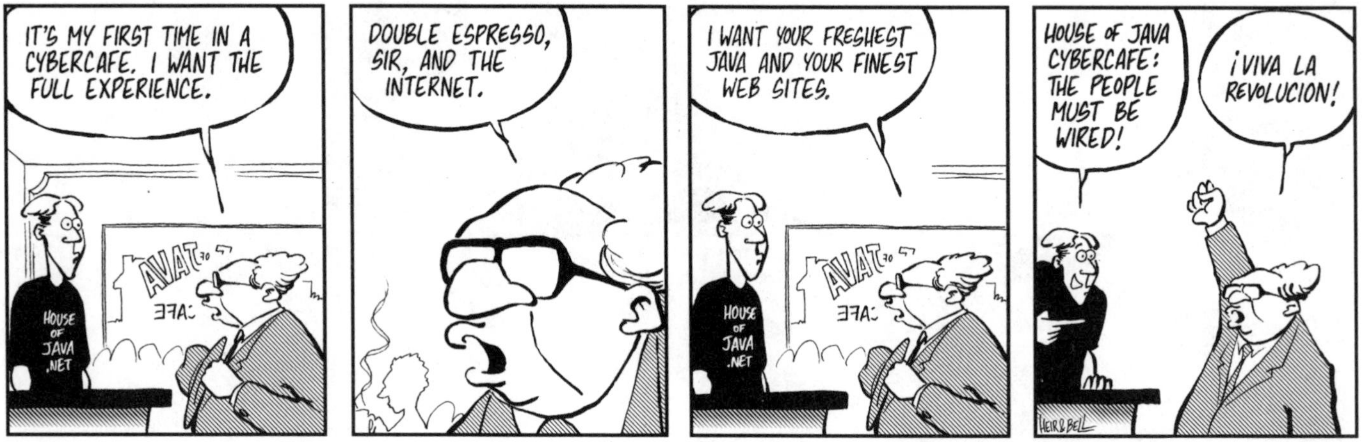
IT'S MY FIRST TIME IN A CYBERCAFE. I WANT THE FULL EXPERIENCE.
HOUSE OF JAVA .NET
DOUBLE ESPRESSO, SIR, AND THE INTERNET.
I WANT YOUR FRESHEST JAVA AND YOUR FINEST WEB SITES.
HOUSE OF JAVA .NET
HOUSE OF JAVA CYBERCAFE: THE PEOPLE MUST BE WIRED!
¡VIVA LA REVOLUCION!

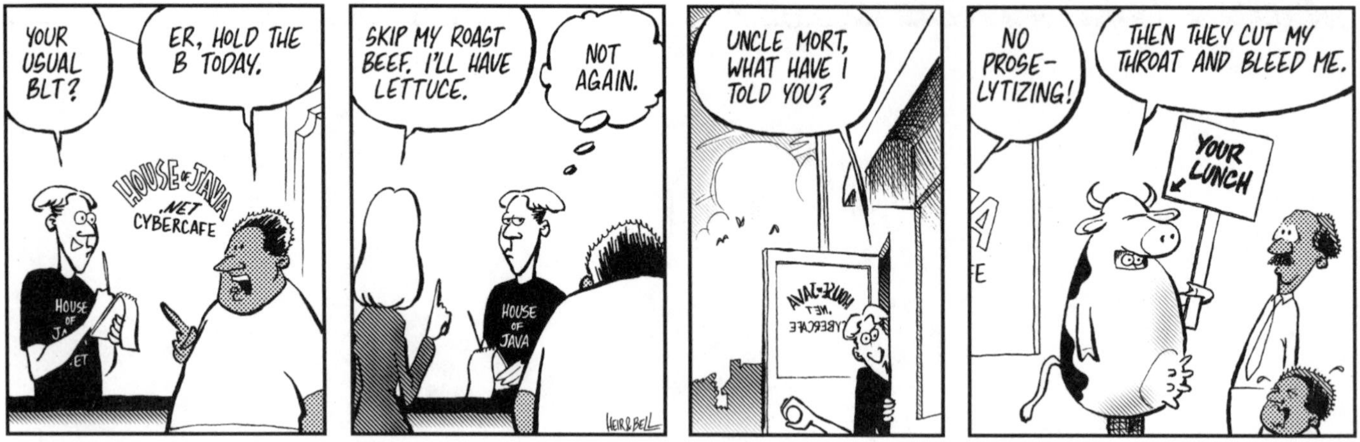
YOUR USUAL BLT?
ER, HOLD THE B TODAY.
HOUSE OF JAVA .NET CYBERCAFE
SKIP MY ROAST BEEF. I'LL HAVE LETTUCE.
NOT AGAIN.
HOUSE OF JAVA
UNCLE MORT, WHAT HAVE I TOLD YOU?
NO PROSE-LYTIZING!
THEN THEY CUT MY THROAT AND BLEED ME.
YOUR LUNCH

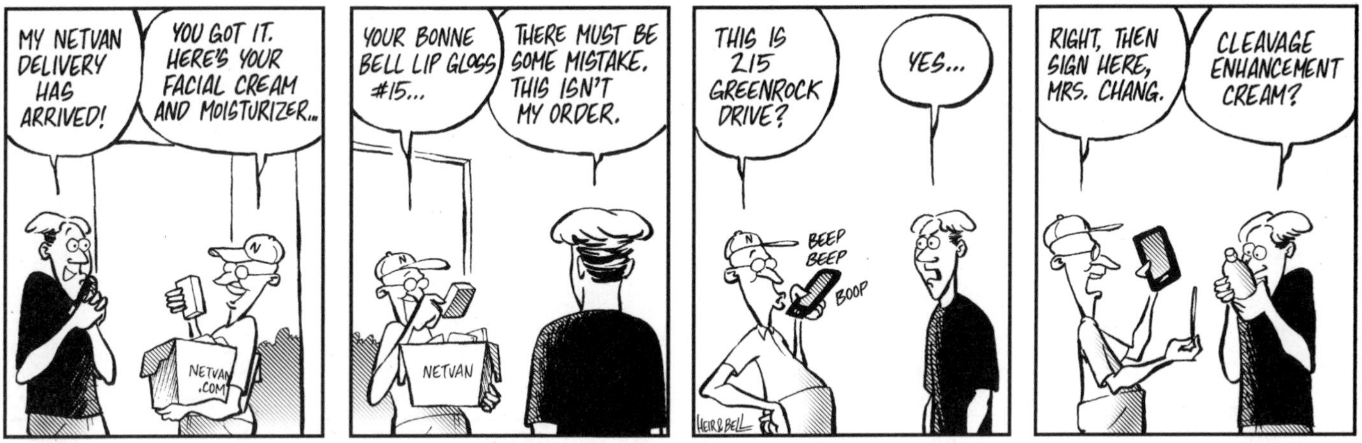
MY NETVAN DELIVERY HAS ARRIVED!
YOU GOT IT. HERE'S YOUR FACIAL CREAM AND MOISTURIZER...
NETVAN .COM
YOUR BONNE BELL LIP GLOSS #15...
THERE MUST BE SOME MISTAKE. THIS ISN'T MY ORDER.
NETVAN
THIS IS 215 GREENROCK DRIVE?
YES...
BEEP BEEP
BOOP
RIGHT, THEN SIGN HERE, MRS. CHANG.
CLEAVAGE ENHANCEMENT CREAM?

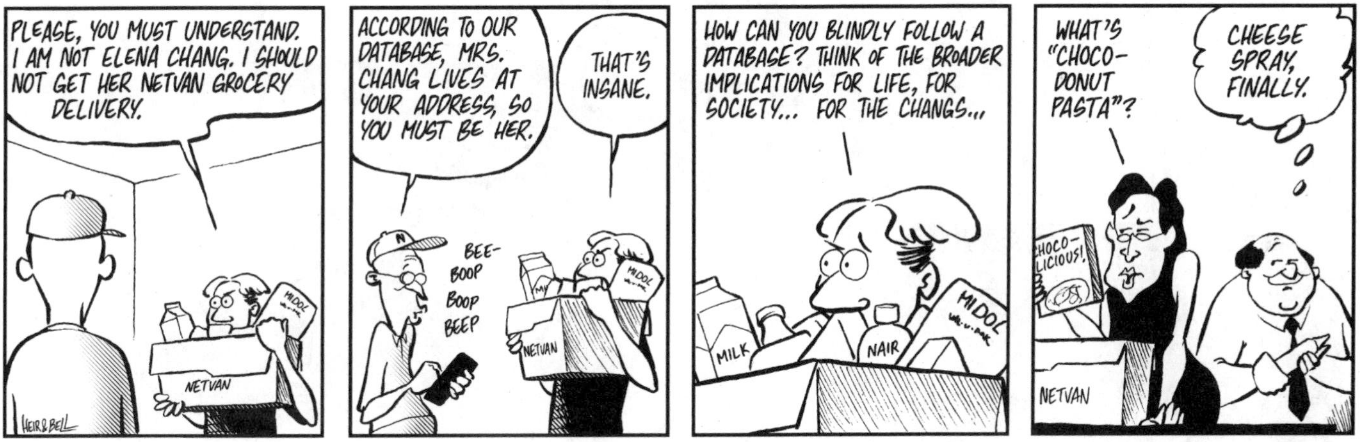
PLEASE, YOU MUST UNDERSTAND. I AM NOT ELENA CHANG. I SHOULD NOT GET HER NETVAN GROCERY DELIVERY.
NETVAN
ACCORDING TO OUR DATABASE, MRS. CHANG LIVES AT YOUR ADDRESS, SO YOU MUST BE HER.
THAT'S INSANE.
BEE-BOOP
BOOP BEEP
NETVAN
HOW CAN YOU BLINDLY FOLLOW A DATABASE? THINK OF THE BROADER IMPLICATIONS FOR LIFE, FOR SOCIETY... FOR THE CHANGS...
MILK
NAIR
MIDOL
WHAT'S "CHOCO-DONUT PASTA"?
CHEESE SPRAY, FINALLY.
CHOCOLICIOUS!
NETVAN

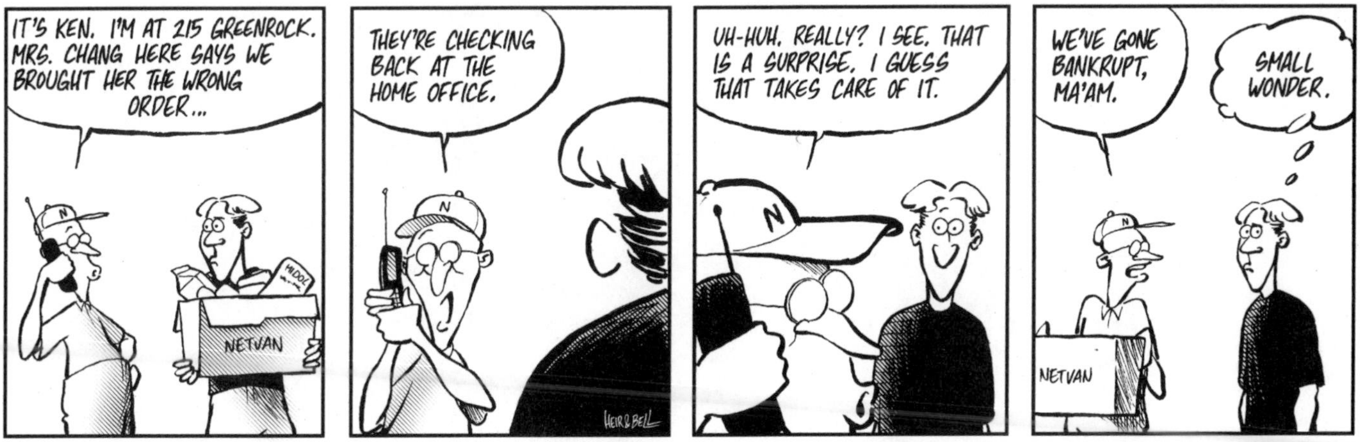
IT'S KEN. I'M AT 215 GREENROCK. MRS. CHANG HERE SAYS WE BROUGHT HER THE WRONG ORDER...
NETVAN
THEY'RE CHECKING BACK AT THE HOME OFFICE.
UH-HUH. REALLY? I SEE. THAT IS A SURPRISE. I GUESS THAT TAKES CARE OF IT.
WE'VE GONE BANKRUPT, MA'AM.
SMALL WONDER.
NETVAN

AT LAST, WE MAKE CONTACT WITH EARTH.
I HOPE THEY TAKE VISA.
GREETINGS, EARTHLING BROTHERS, WE COME IN PEACE!
DIAL "9"
Hello, and thank you for calling Earth. You've reached our automated answering service.
...For technical support, press "one."
To dial by name, press "two." To speak with a live operator, press "three."
...Sorry, no operator is available at this time. Please try your call again.
LET'S BLAST 'EM.
...Para instrucciones en español, oprima el numero "cuatro."
DIAL "9"

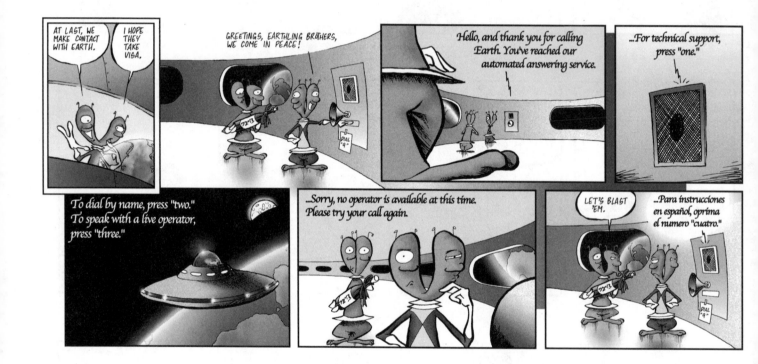

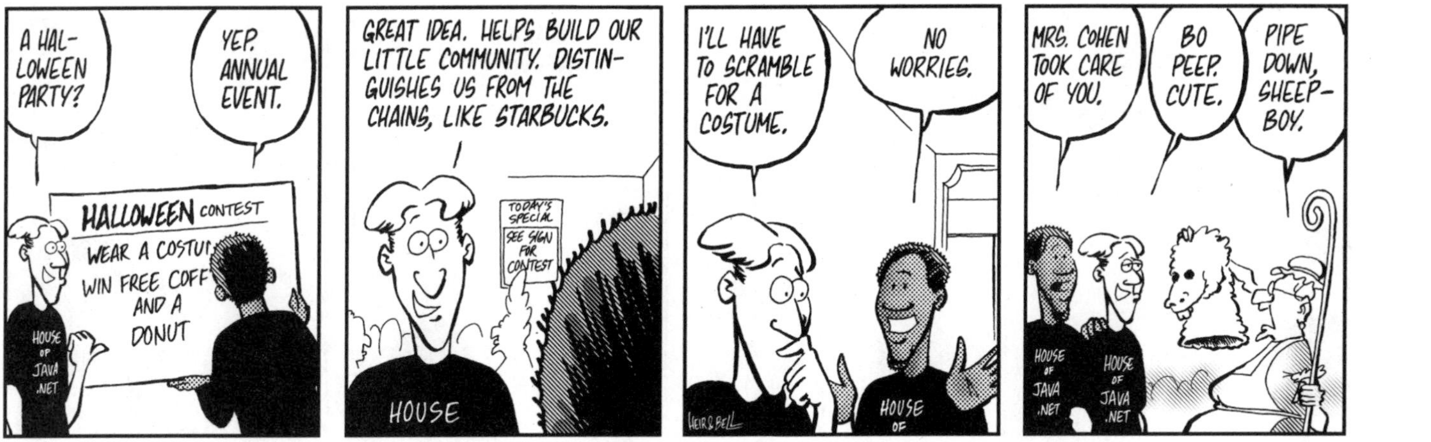
A HAL-LOWEEN PARTY?
YEP. ANNUAL EVENT.
HALLOWEEN CONTEST
WEAR A COSTUM
WIN FREE COFF
AND A DONUT
HOUSE OF JAVA .NET
GREAT IDEA. HELPS BUILD OUR LITTLE COMMUNITY. DISTIN-GUISHES US FROM THE CHAINS, LIKE STARBUCKS.
TODAY'S SPECIAL
SEE SIGN FOR CONTEST
HOUSE
I'LL HAVE TO SCRAMBLE FOR A COSTUME.
NO WORRIES.
HOUSE OF
HEIR & BELL
MRS. COHEN TOOK CARE OF YOU.
BO PEEP. CUTE.
PIPE DOWN, SHEEP-BOY.
HOUSE OF JAVA .NET
HOUSE OF JAVA .NET

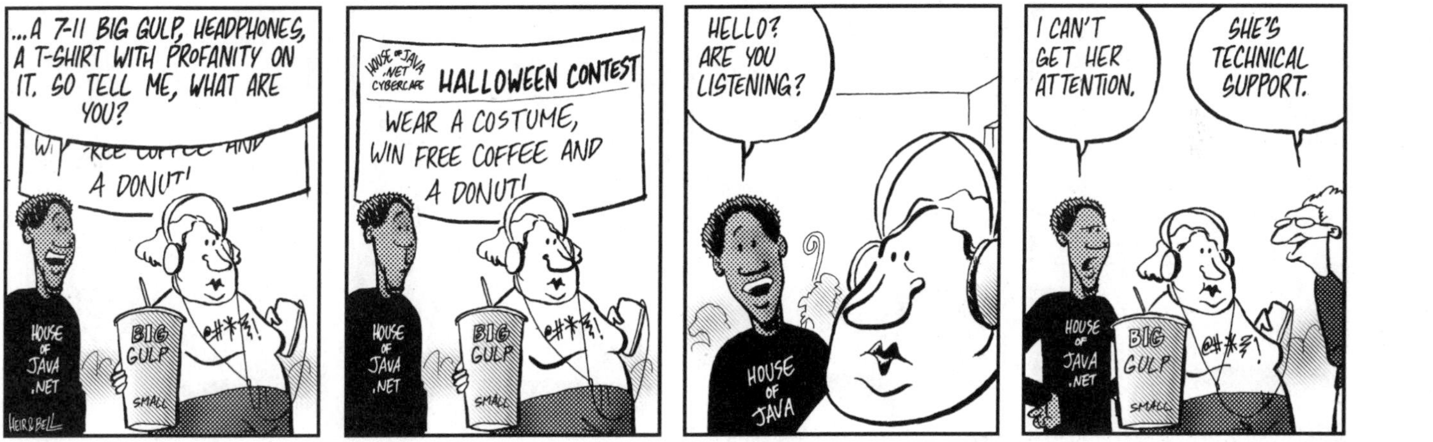
...A 7-11 BIG GULP, HEADPHONES, A T-SHIRT WITH PROFANITY ON IT. SO TELL ME, WHAT ARE YOU?
A DONUT!
HOUSE OF JAVA .NET
BIG GULP
SMALL
@#*%!
HEIR & BELL
HOUSE OF JAVA .NET CYBERCAFE
HALLOWEEN CONTEST
WEAR A COSTUME, WIN FREE COFFEE AND A DONUT!
HOUSE OF JAVA .NET
BIG GULP
SMALL
HELLO? ARE YOU LISTENING?
HOUSE OF JAVA
I CAN'T GET HER ATTENTION.
SHE'S TECHNICAL SUPPORT.
HOUSE OF JAVA .NET
BIG GULP
SMALL

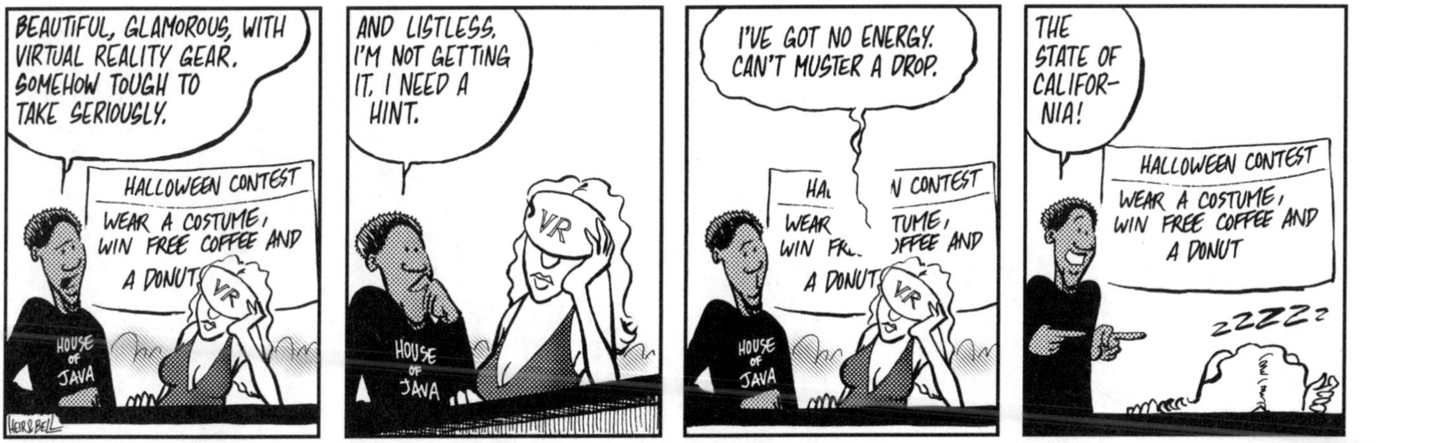
BEAUTIFUL, GLAMOROUS, WITH VIRTUAL REALITY GEAR. SOMEHOW TOUGH TO TAKE SERIOUSLY.
HALLOWEEN CONTEST
WEAR A COSTUME, WIN FREE COFFEE AND A DONUT
VR
HOUSE OF JAVA
HEIR & BELL
AND LISTLESS. I'M NOT GETTING IT. I NEED A HINT.
VR
HOUSE OF JAVA
I'VE GOT NO ENERGY. CAN'T MUSTER A DROP.
HOUSE OF JAVA
THE STATE OF CALIFOR-NIA!
HALLOWEEN CONTEST
WEAR A COSTUME, WIN FREE COFFEE AND A DONUT
ZZZZZ

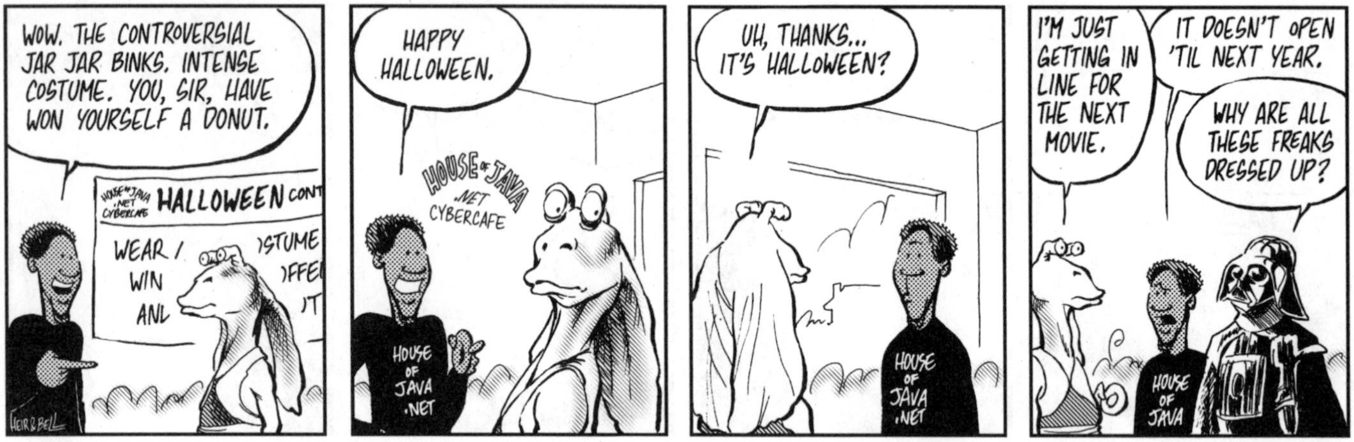
WOW. THE CONTROVERSIAL JAR JAR BINKS. INTENSE COSTUME. YOU, SIR, HAVE WON YOURSELF A DONUT.
HOUSE of JAVA .NET CYBERCAFE HALLOWEEN CONT
WEAR
WIN
HEIR & BELL
HAPPY HALLOWEEN.
HOUSE of JAVA .NET CYBERCAFE
HOUSE OF JAVA .NET
UH, THANKS... IT'S HALLOWEEN?
HOUSE OF JAVA .NET
I'M JUST GETTING IN LINE FOR THE NEXT MOVIE.
IT DOESN'T OPEN 'TIL NEXT YEAR.
WHY ARE ALL THESE FREAKS DRESSED UP?
HOUSE OF JAVA

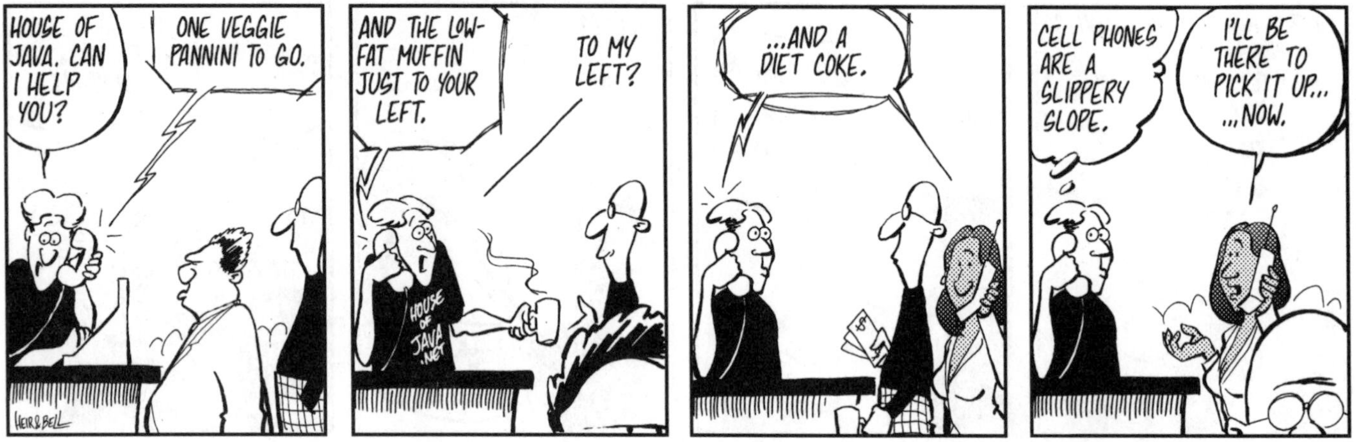
HOUSE OF JAVA. CAN I HELP YOU?
ONE VEGGIE PANNINI TO GO.
HEIR & BELL
AND THE LOW-FAT MUFFIN JUST TO YOUR LEFT.
TO MY LEFT?
HOUSE OF JAVA .NET
...AND A DIET COKE.
CELL PHONES ARE A SLIPPERY SLOPE.
I'LL BE THERE TO PICK IT UP... ...NOW.

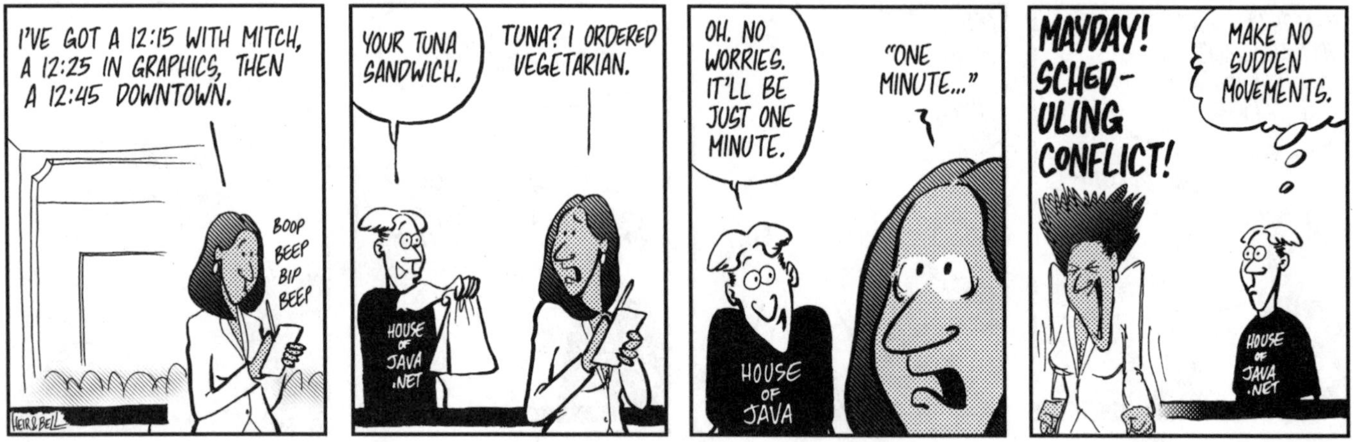
I'VE GOT A 12:15 WITH MITCH, A 12:25 IN GRAPHICS, THEN A 12:45 DOWNTOWN.
BOOP BEEP BIP BEEP
HEIR & BELL
YOUR TUNA SANDWICH.
TUNA? I ORDERED VEGETARIAN.
HOUSE OF JAVA .NET
OH. NO WORRIES. IT'LL BE JUST ONE MINUTE.
"ONE MINUTE..."
HOUSE OF JAVA
MAYDAY! SCHED-ULING CONFLICT!
MAKE NO SUDDEN MOVEMENTS.
HOUSE OF JAVA .NET

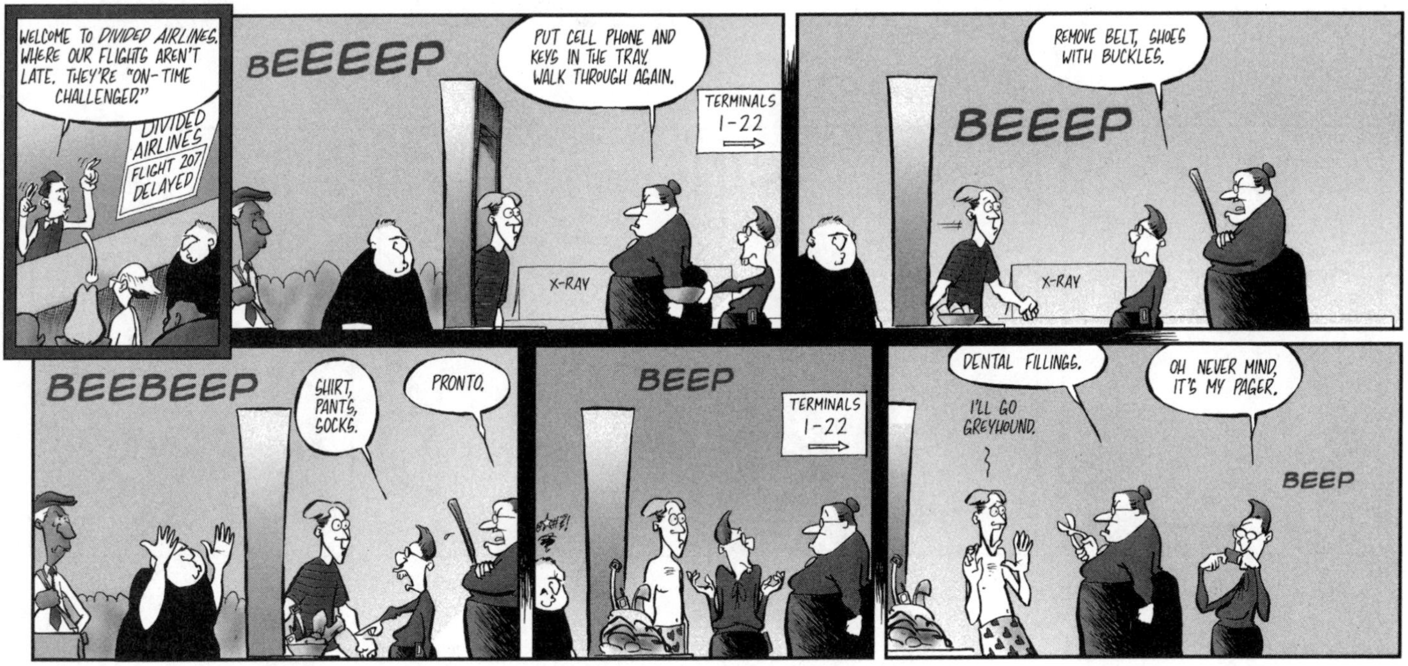
WELCOME TO DIVIDED AIRLINES. WHERE OUR FLIGHTS AREN'T LATE. THEY'RE "ON-TIME CHALLENGED."
DIVIDED AIRLINES
FLIGHT 207 DELAYED
BEEEEEP
PUT CELL PHONE AND KEYS IN THE TRAY. WALK THROUGH AGAIN.
TERMINALS 1-22
X-RAY
REMOVE BELT, SHOES WITH BUCKLES.
BEEEP
X-RAY
BEEBEEP
SHIRT, PANTS, SOCKS.
PRONTO.
BEEP
TERMINALS 1-22
DENTAL FILLINGS.
I'LL GO GREYHOUND.
OH NEVER MIND, IT'S MY PAGER.
BEEP

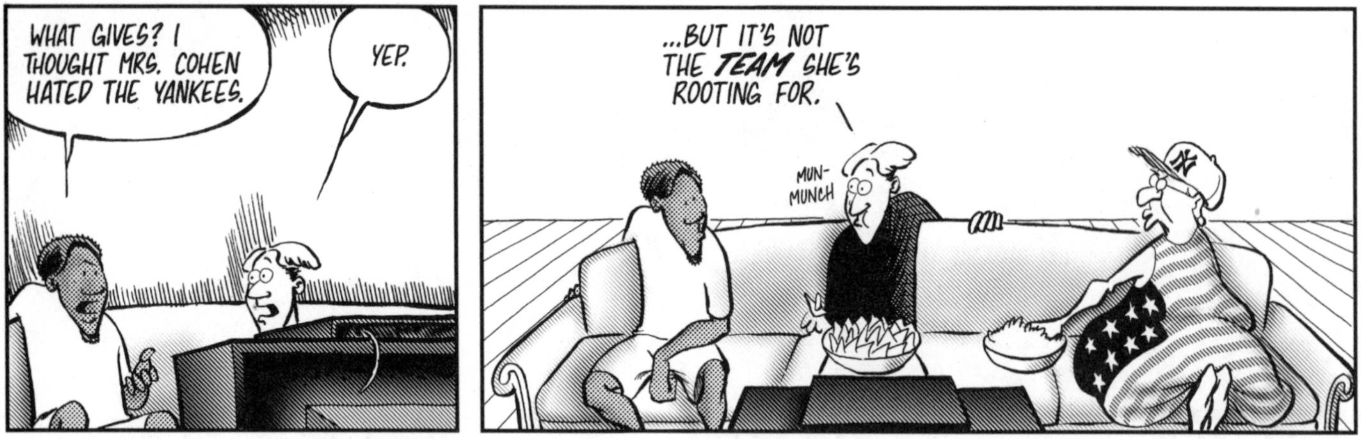
WHAT GIVES? I THOUGHT MRS. COHEN HATED THE YANKEES.
YEP.
...BUT IT'S NOT THE *TEAM* SHE'S ROOTING FOR.
MUN-MUNCH

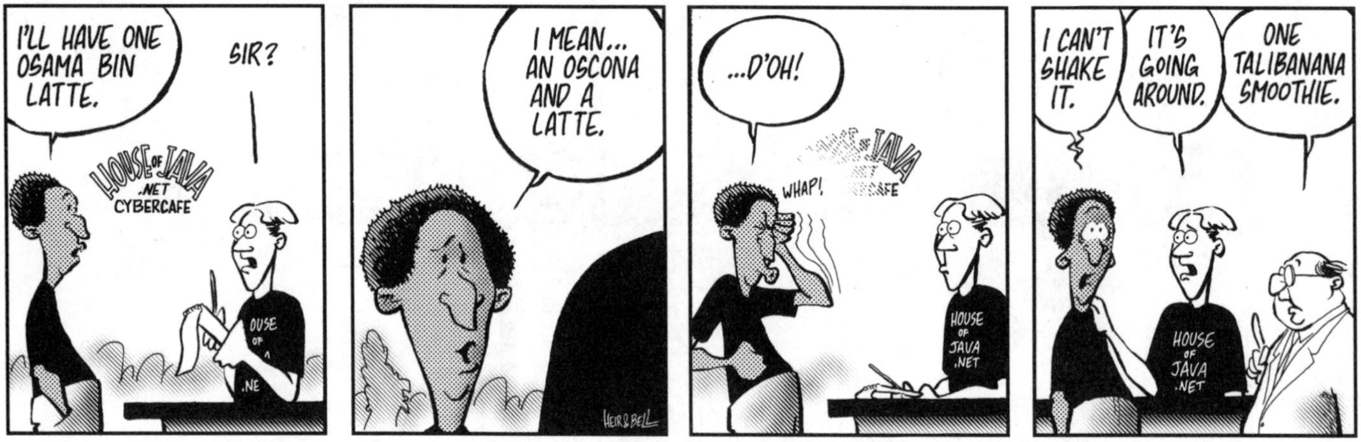
I'LL HAVE ONE OSAMA BIN LATTE.
HOUSE OF JAVA .NET CYBERCAFE
SIR?
I MEAN... AN OSCONA AND A LATTE.
HEIR & BELL
...D'OH!
WHAP!
HOUSE OF JAVA .NET
I CAN'T SHAKE IT.
IT'S GOING AROUND.
ONE TALIBANANA SMOOTHIE.
HOUSE OF JAVA .NET

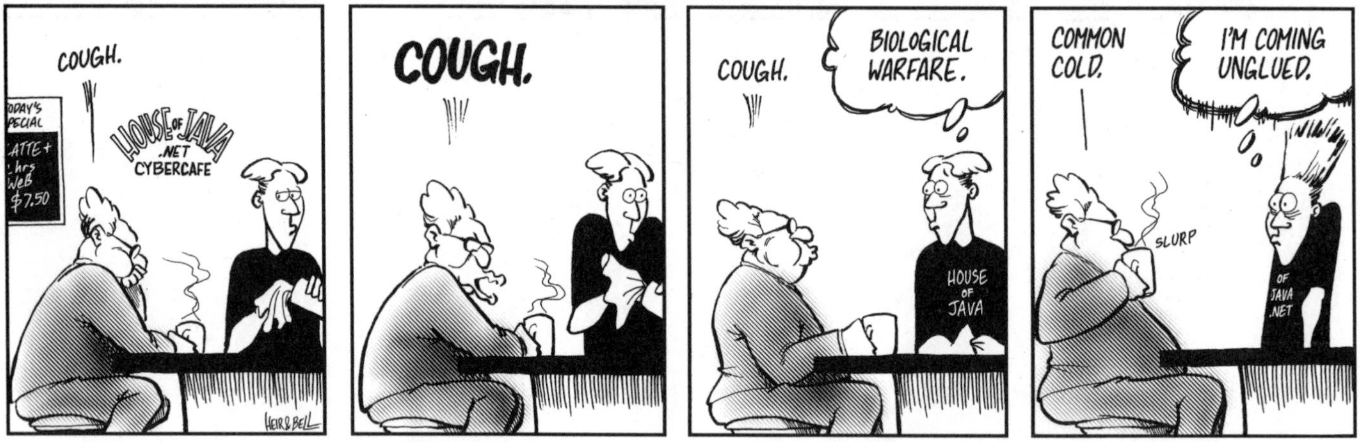
COUGH.
HOUSE OF JAVA .NET CYBERCAFE
$7.50
HEIR & BELL
COUGH.
COUGH.
BIOLOGICAL WARFARE.
HOUSE OF JAVA
COMMON COLD.
I'M COMING UNGLUED.
SLURP
OF JAVA .NET

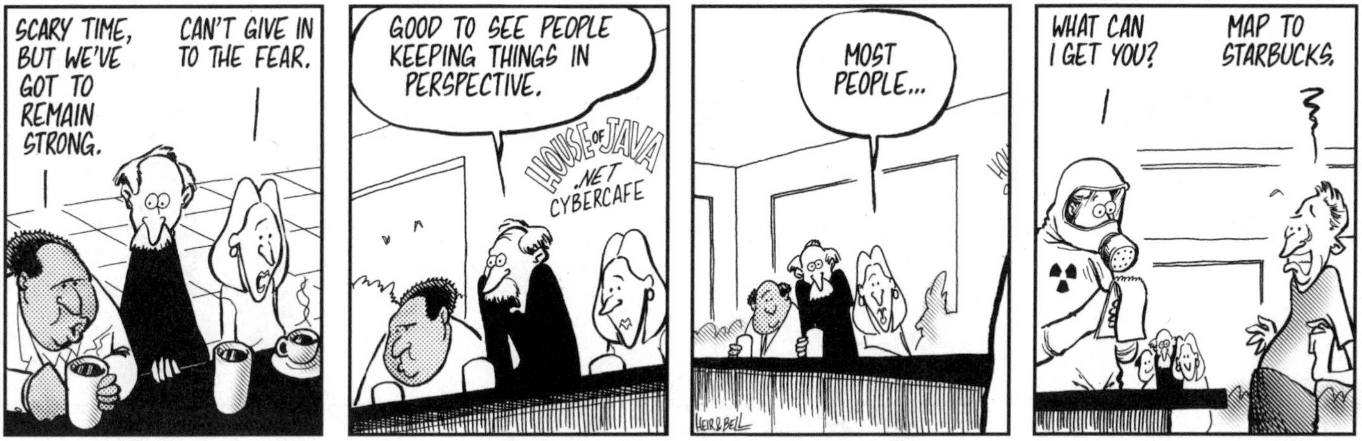
SCARY TIME, BUT WE'VE GOT TO REMAIN STRONG.
CAN'T GIVE IN TO THE FEAR.
GOOD TO SEE PEOPLE KEEPING THINGS IN PERSPECTIVE.
HOUSE OF JAVA .NET CYBERCAFE
MOST PEOPLE...
WHAT CAN I GET YOU?
MAP TO STARBUCKS.
HEIR&BELL

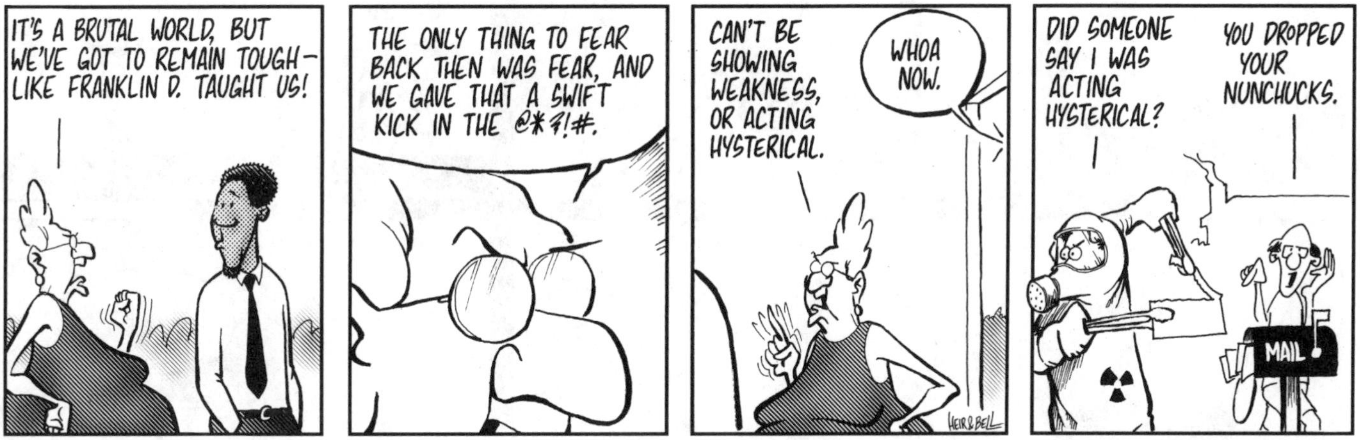
IT'S A BRUTAL WORLD, BUT WE'VE GOT TO REMAIN TOUGH—LIKE FRANKLIN D. TAUGHT US!
THE ONLY THING TO FEAR BACK THEN WAS FEAR, AND WE GAVE THAT A SWIFT KICK IN THE @*?!#.
CAN'T BE SHOWING WEAKNESS, OR ACTING HYSTERICAL.
WHOA NOW.
HEIR&BELL
DID SOMEONE SAY I WAS ACTING HYSTERICAL?
YOU DROPPED YOUR NUNCHUCKS.
MAIL

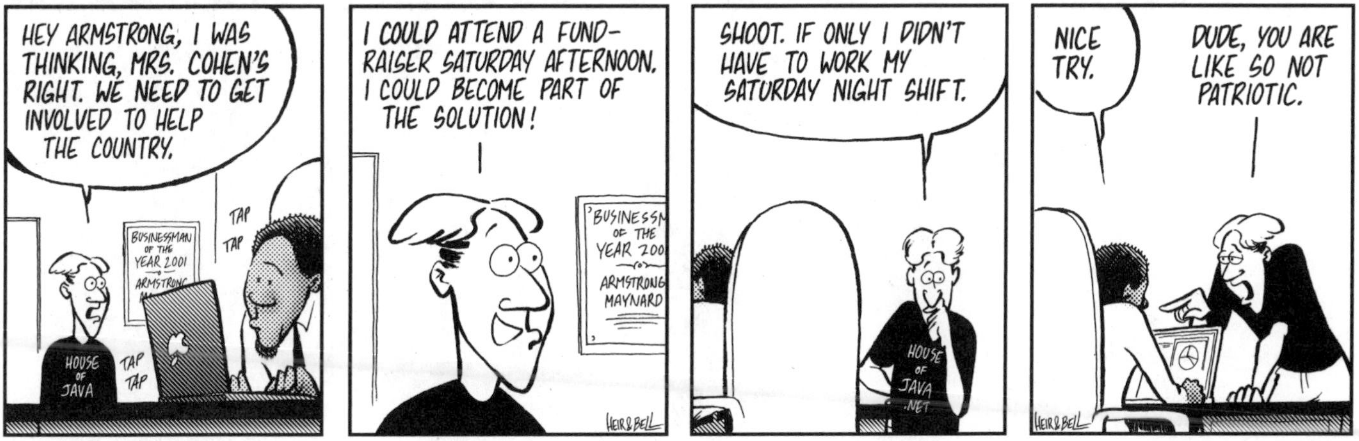
HEY ARMSTRONG, I WAS THINKING, MRS. COHEN'S RIGHT. WE NEED TO GET INVOLVED TO HELP THE COUNTRY.
BUSINESSMAN OF THE YEAR 2001 ARMSTRONG
TAP TAP
TAP TAP
HOUSE OF JAVA
I COULD ATTEND A FUND-RAISER SATURDAY AFTERNOON. I COULD BECOME PART OF THE SOLUTION!
BUSINESSM OF THE YEAR 200 ARMSTRONG MAYNARD
HEIR&BELL
SHOOT. IF ONLY I DIDN'T HAVE TO WORK MY SATURDAY NIGHT SHIFT.
HOUSE OF JAVA .NET
NICE TRY.
DUDE, YOU ARE LIKE SO NOT PATRIOTIC.
HEIR&BELL

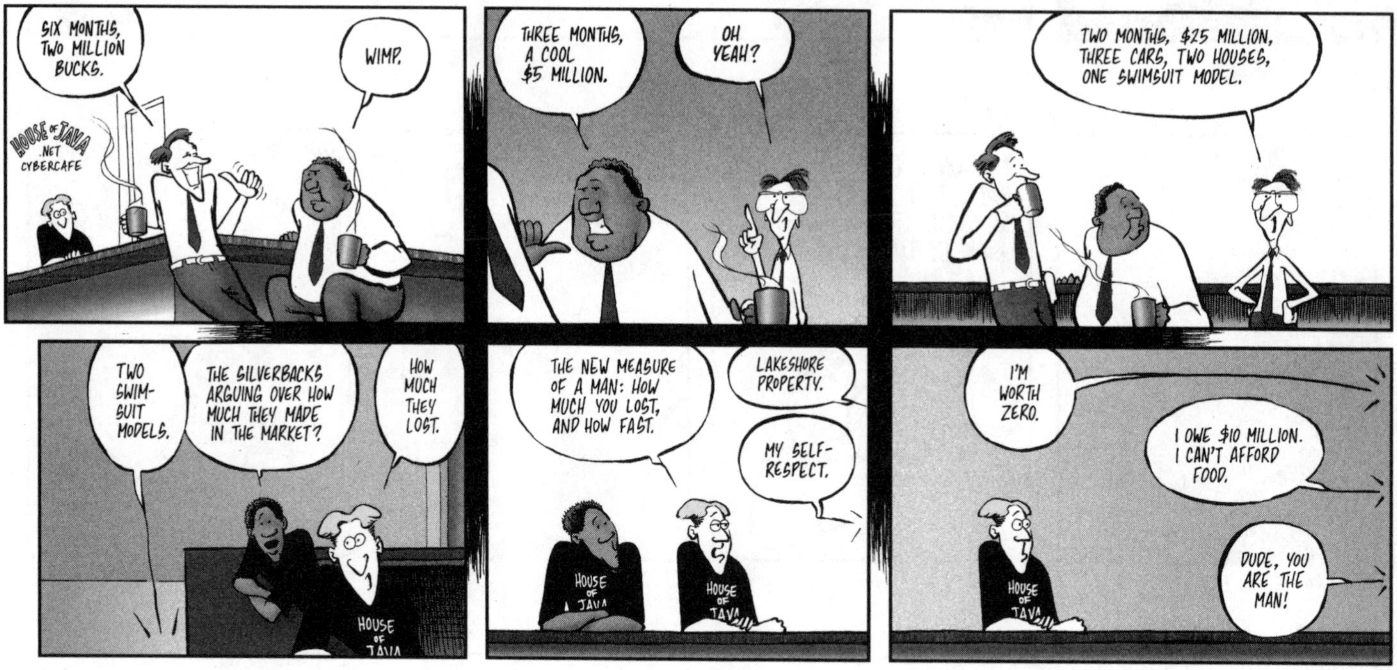
SIX MONTHS, TWO MILLION BUCKS.
WIMP.
HOUSE OF JAVA .NET CYBERCAFE
THREE MONTHS, A COOL $5 MILLION.
OH YEAH?
TWO MONTHS, $25 MILLION, THREE CARS, TWO HOUSES, ONE SWIMSUIT MODEL.
TWO SWIM-SUIT MODELS.
THE SILVERBACKS ARGUING OVER HOW MUCH THEY MADE IN THE MARKET?
HOW MUCH THEY LOST.
THE NEW MEASURE OF A MAN: HOW MUCH YOU LOST, AND HOW FAST.
LAKESHORE PROPERTY.
MY SELF-RESPECT.
I'M WORTH ZERO.
I OWE $10 MILLION. I CAN'T AFFORD FOOD.
DUDE, YOU ARE THE MAN!

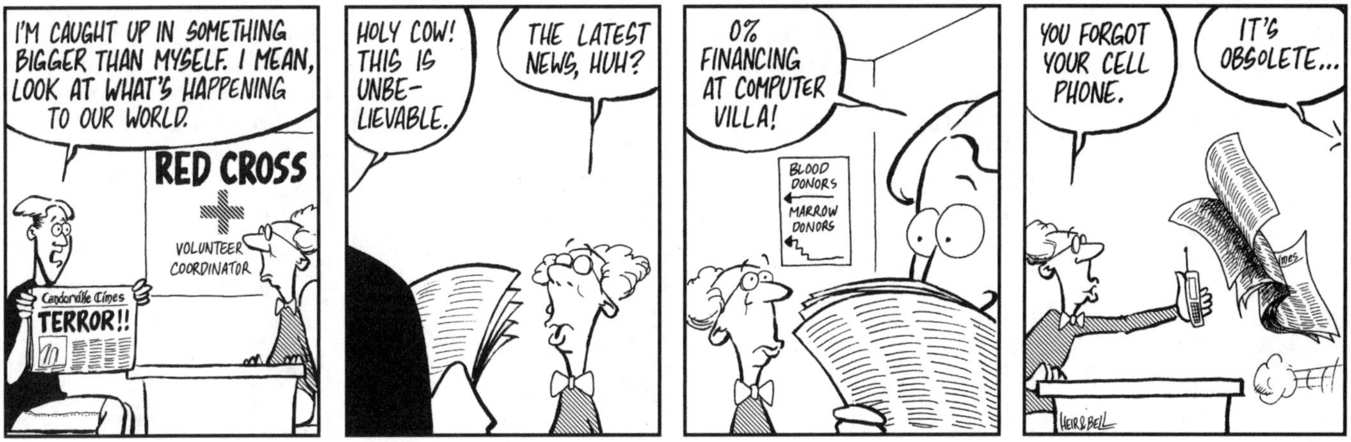
I'M CAUGHT UP IN SOMETHING BIGGER THAN MYSELF. I MEAN, LOOK AT WHAT'S HAPPENING TO OUR WORLD.
RED CROSS
VOLUNTEER COORDINATOR
Candorville Times
TERROR!!
HOLY COW! THIS IS UNBE-LIEVABLE.
THE LATEST NEWS, HUH?
0% FINANCING AT COMPUTER VILLA!
BLOOD DONORS
MARROW DONORS
YOU FORGOT YOUR CELL PHONE.
IT'S OBSOLETE...
HEIR & BELL

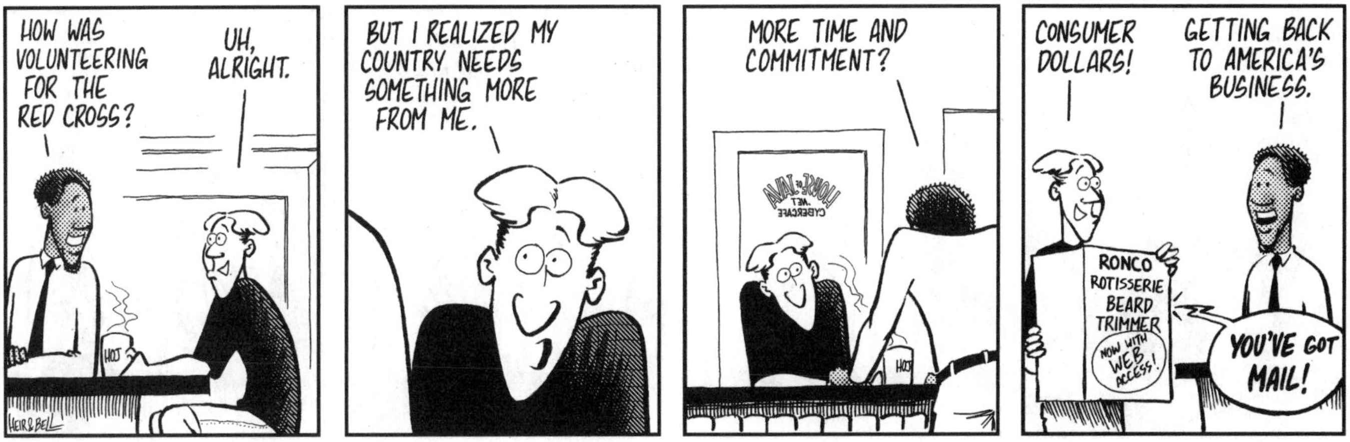
HOW WAS VOLUNTEERING FOR THE RED CROSS?
UH, ALRIGHT.
HEIR & BELL
BUT I REALIZED MY COUNTRY NEEDS SOMETHING MORE FROM ME.
MORE TIME AND COMMITMENT?
CONSUMER DOLLARS!
GETTING BACK TO AMERICA'S BUSINESS.
RONCO ROTISSERIE BEARD TRIMMER
NOW WITH WEB ACCESS!
YOU'VE GOT MAIL!

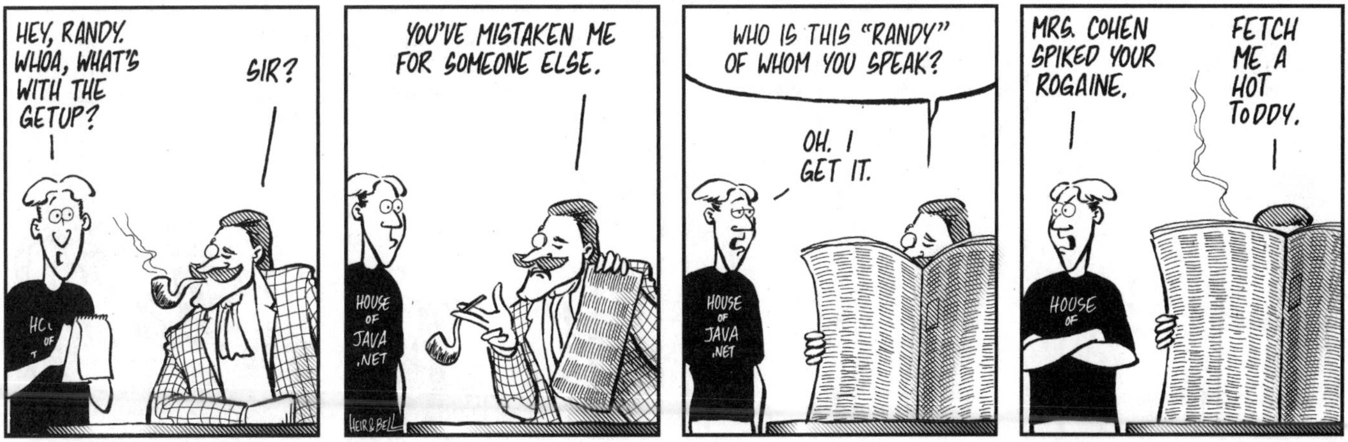
HEY, RANDY. WHOA, WHAT'S WITH THE GETUP?
SIR?
YOU'VE MISTAKEN ME FOR SOMEONE ELSE.
HOUSE OF JAVA .NET
HEIR & BELL
WHO IS THIS "RANDY" OF WHOM YOU SPEAK?
OH. I GET IT.
HOUSE OF JAVA .NET
MRS. COHEN SPIKED YOUR ROGAINE.
FETCH ME A HOT TODDY.
HOUSE OF

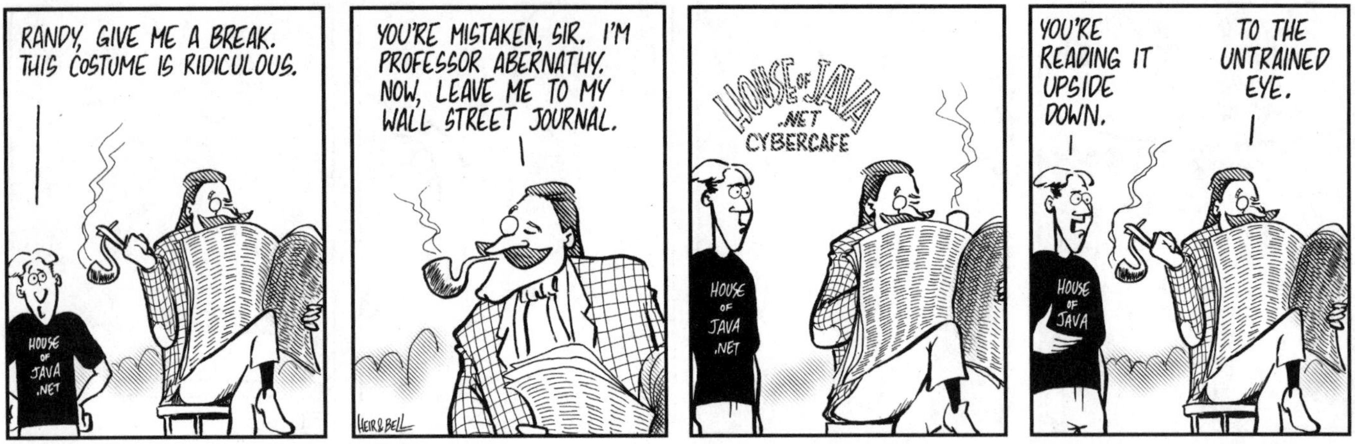
RANDY, GIVE ME A BREAK. THIS COSTUME IS RIDICULOUS.
YOU'RE MISTAKEN, SIR. I'M PROFESSOR ABERNATHY. NOW, LEAVE ME TO MY WALL STREET JOURNAL.
HOUSE OF JAVA .NET CYBERCAFE
YOU'RE READING IT UPSIDE DOWN.
TO THE UNTRAINED EYE.

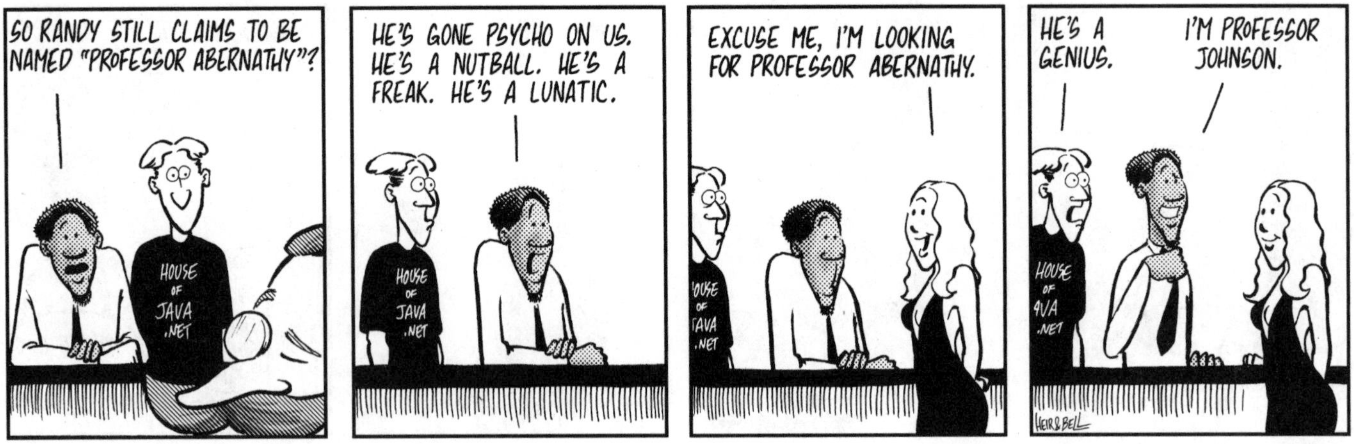
SO RANDY STILL CLAIMS TO BE NAMED "PROFESSOR ABERNATHY"?
HE'S GONE PSYCHO ON US. HE'S A NUTBALL. HE'S A FREAK. HE'S A LUNATIC.
EXCUSE ME, I'M LOOKING FOR PROFESSOR ABERNATHY.
HE'S A GENIUS.
I'M PROFESSOR JOHNSON.

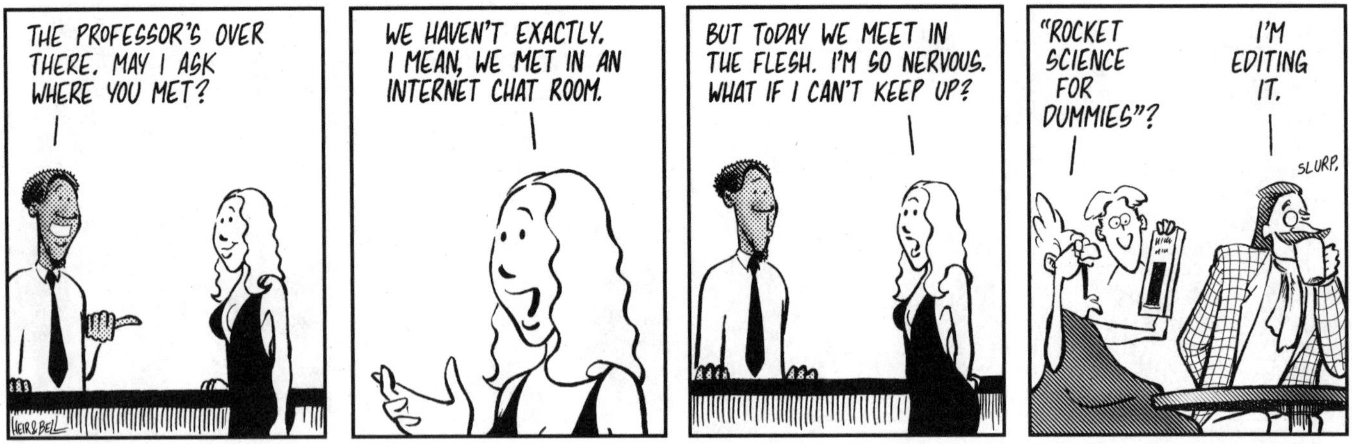
THE PROFESSOR'S OVER THERE. MAY I ASK WHERE YOU MET?
WE HAVEN'T EXACTLY. I MEAN, WE MET IN AN INTERNET CHAT ROOM.
BUT TODAY WE MEET IN THE FLESH. I'M SO NERVOUS. WHAT IF I CAN'T KEEP UP?
"ROCKET SCIENCE FOR DUMMIES"?
I'M EDITING IT.
SLURP.

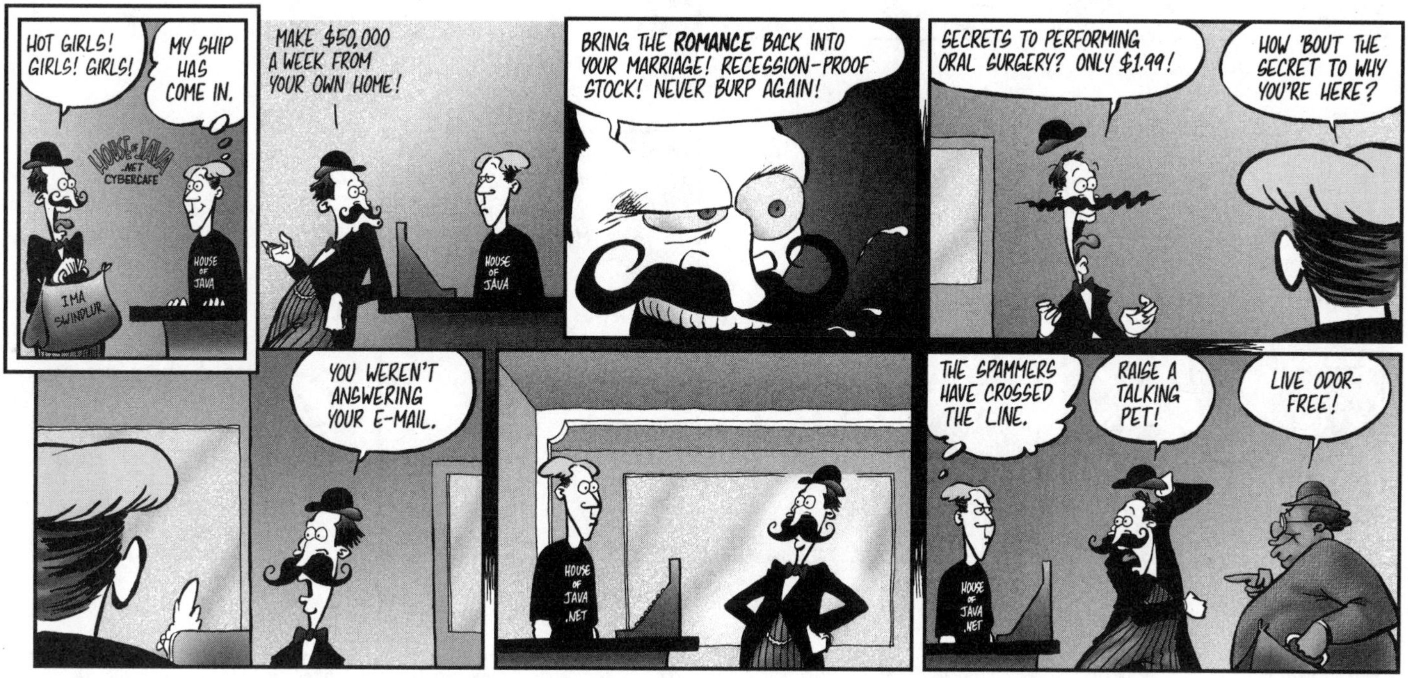
HOT GIRLS! GIRLS! GIRLS!
MY SHIP HAS COME IN.
HOUSE OF JAVA .NET CYBERCAFE
IMA SWINDLUR
HOUSE OF JAVA
MAKE $50,000 A WEEK FROM YOUR OWN HOME!
HOUSE OF JAVA
BRING THE **ROMANCE** BACK INTO YOUR MARRIAGE! RECESSION-PROOF STOCK! NEVER BURP AGAIN!
SECRETS TO PERFORMING ORAL SURGERY? ONLY $1.99!
HOW 'BOUT THE SECRET TO WHY YOU'RE HERE?
YOU WEREN'T ANSWERING YOUR E-MAIL.
HOUSE OF JAVA .NET
THE SPAMMERS HAVE CROSSED THE LINE.
RAISE A TALKING PET!
LIVE ODOR-FREE!
HOUSE OF JAVA .NET

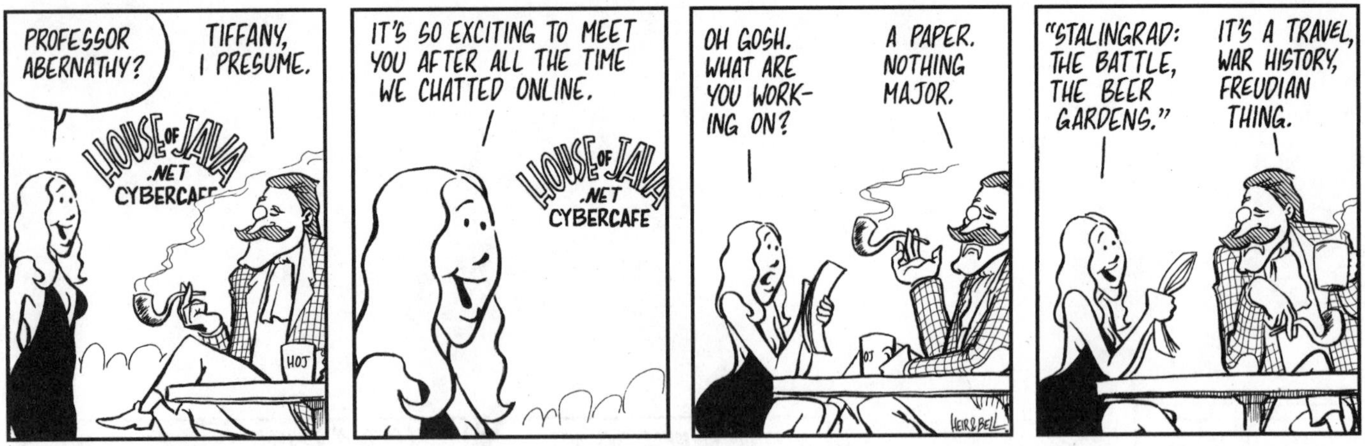
PROFESSOR ABERNATHY?
TIFFANY, I PRESUME.
HOUSE OF JAVA .NET CYBERCAFE
IT'S SO EXCITING TO MEET YOU AFTER ALL THE TIME WE CHATTED ONLINE.
OH GOSH. WHAT ARE YOU WORKING ON?
A PAPER. NOTHING MAJOR.
"STALINGRAD: THE BATTLE, THE BEER GARDENS."
IT'S A TRAVEL, WAR HISTORY, FREUDIAN THING.

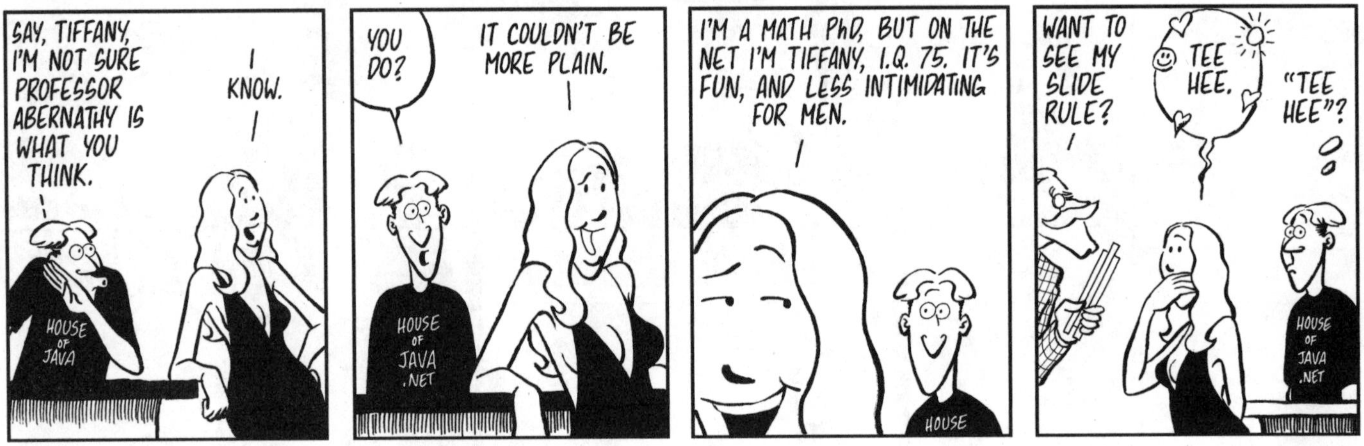
SAY, TIFFANY, I'M NOT SURE PROFESSOR ABERNATHY IS WHAT YOU THINK.
I KNOW.
YOU DO?
IT COULDN'T BE MORE PLAIN.
I'M A MATH PhD, BUT ON THE NET I'M TIFFANY, I.Q. 75. IT'S FUN, AND LESS INTIMIDATING FOR MEN.
WANT TO SEE MY SLIDE RULE?
TEE HEE.
"TEE HEE"?

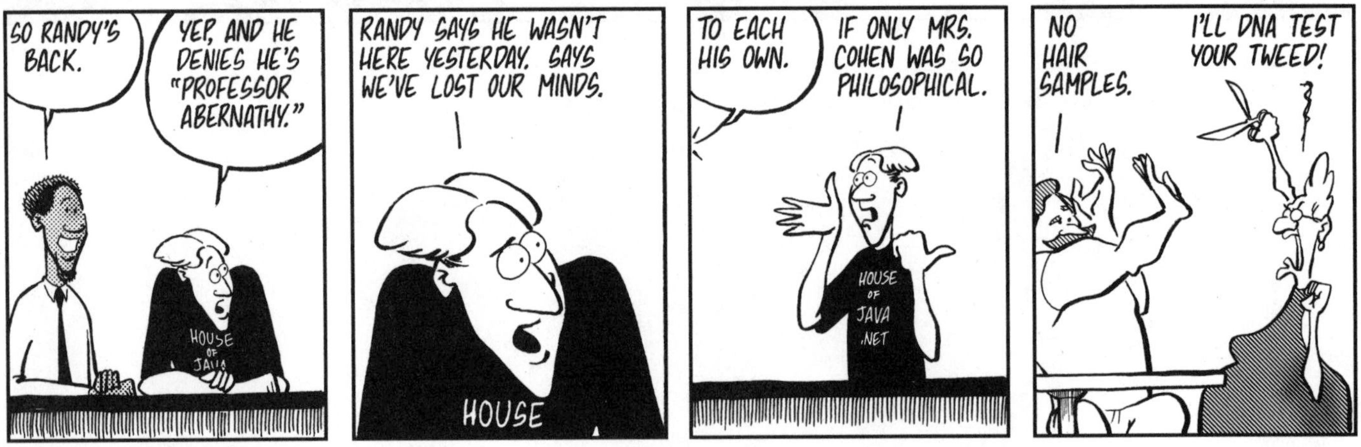
SO RANDY'S BACK.
YEP, AND HE DENIES HE'S "PROFESSOR ABERNATHY."
RANDY SAYS HE WASN'T HERE YESTERDAY. SAYS WE'VE LOST OUR MINDS.
TO EACH HIS OWN.
IF ONLY MRS. COHEN WAS SO PHILOSOPHICAL.
NO HAIR SAMPLES.
I'LL DNA TEST YOUR TWEED!

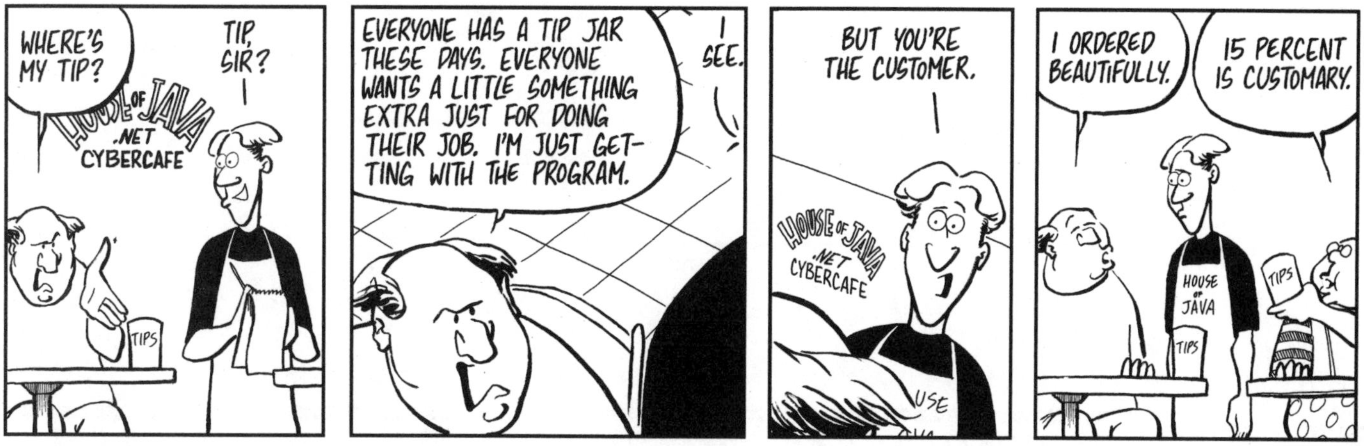
WHERE'S MY TIP?
TIP, SIR?
HOUSE OF JAVA .NET CYBERCAFE
TIPS
EVERYONE HAS A TIP JAR THESE DAYS. EVERYONE WANTS A LITTLE SOMETHING EXTRA JUST FOR DOING THEIR JOB. I'M JUST GETTING WITH THE PROGRAM.
I SEE.
BUT YOU'RE THE CUSTOMER.
HOUSE OF JAVA .NET CYBERCAFE
I ORDERED BEAUTIFULLY.
15 PERCENT IS CUSTOMARY.
HOUSE OF JAVA
TIPS

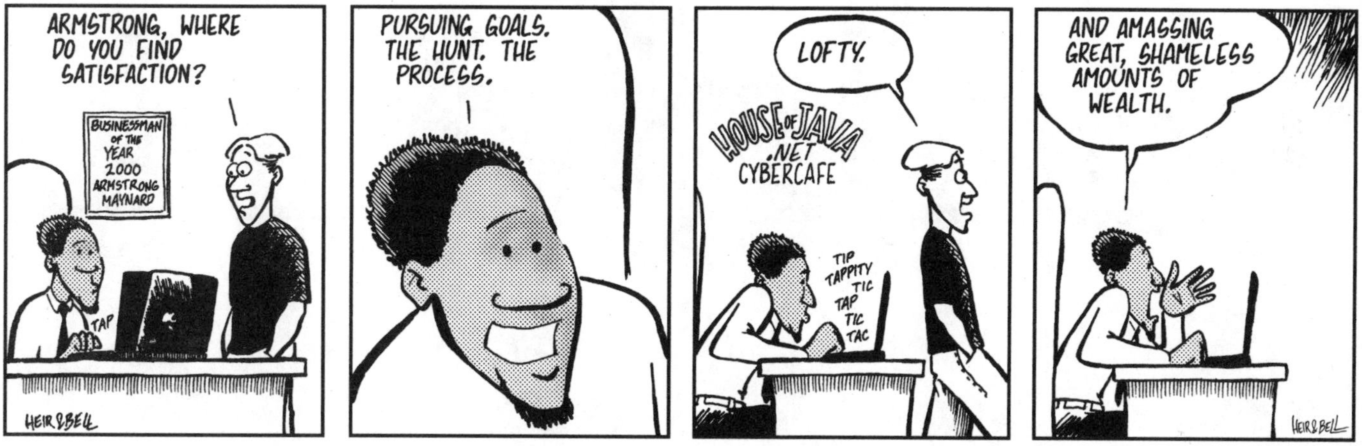
ARMSTRONG, WHERE DO YOU FIND SATISFACTION?
BUSINESSMAN OF THE YEAR 2000 ARMSTRONG MAYNARD
TAP
HEIR & BELL
PURSUING GOALS. THE HUNT. THE PROCESS.
LOFTY.
HOUSE OF JAVA .NET CYBERCAFE
TIP TAPPITY TIC TAP TIC TAC
AND AMASSING GREAT, SHAMELESS AMOUNTS OF WEALTH.
HEIR & BELL

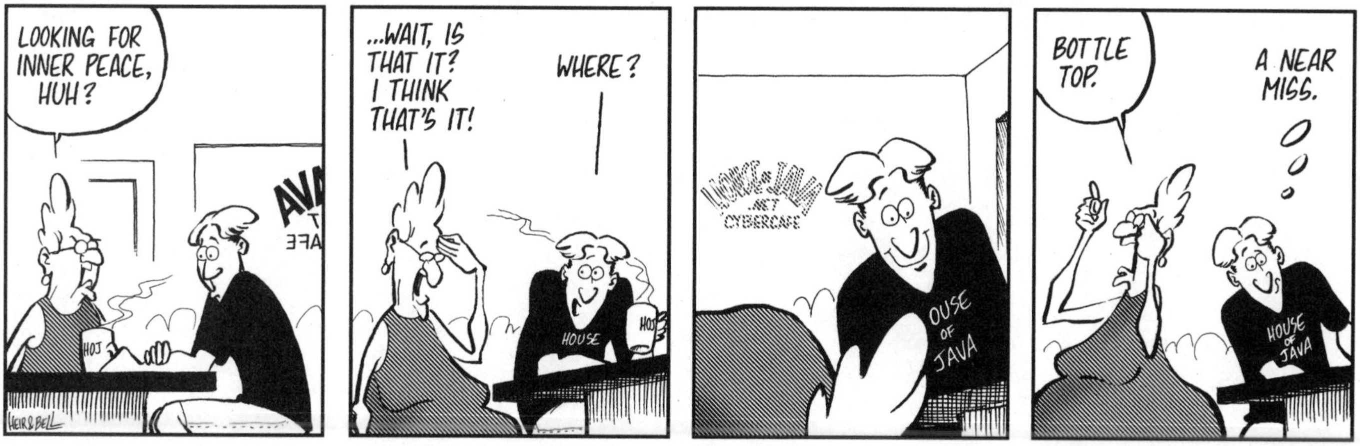
LOOKING FOR INNER PEACE, HUH?
HOJ
HEIR & BELL
...WAIT, IS THAT IT? I THINK THAT'S IT!
WHERE?
HOUSE
HOUSE OF JAVA .NET CYBERCAFE
OUSE OF JAVA
BOTTLE TOP.
A NEAR MISS.
HOUSE OF JAVA

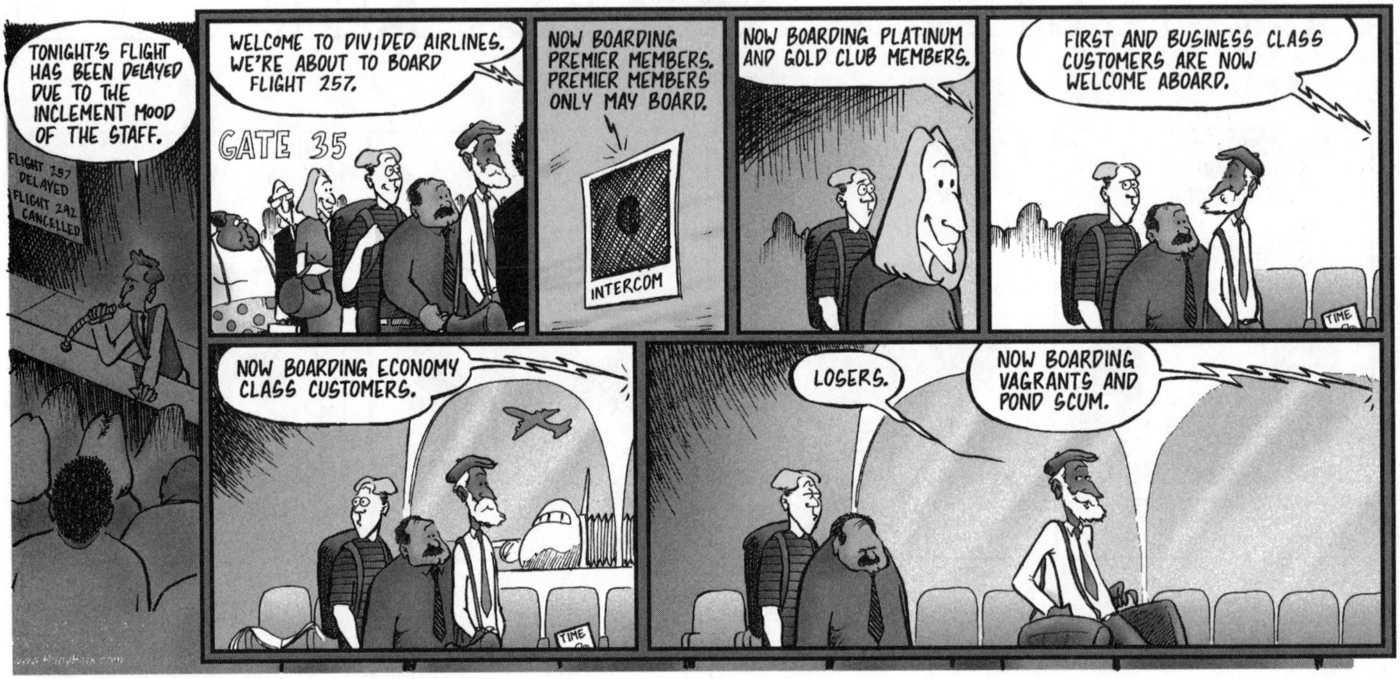
TONIGHT'S FLIGHT HAS BEEN DELAYED DUE TO THE INCLEMENT MOOD OF THE STAFF.
FLIGHT 257 DELAYED FLIGHT 292 CANCELLED
WELCOME TO DIVIDED AIRLINES. WE'RE ABOUT TO BOARD FLIGHT 257.
GATE 35
NOW BOARDING PREMIER MEMBERS. PREMIER MEMBERS ONLY MAY BOARD.
INTERCOM
NOW BOARDING PLATINUM AND GOLD CLUB MEMBERS.
FIRST AND BUSINESS CLASS CUSTOMERS ARE NOW WELCOME ABOARD.
TIME
NOW BOARDING ECONOMY CLASS CUSTOMERS.
TIME
LOSERS.
NOW BOARDING VAGRANTS AND POND SCUM.

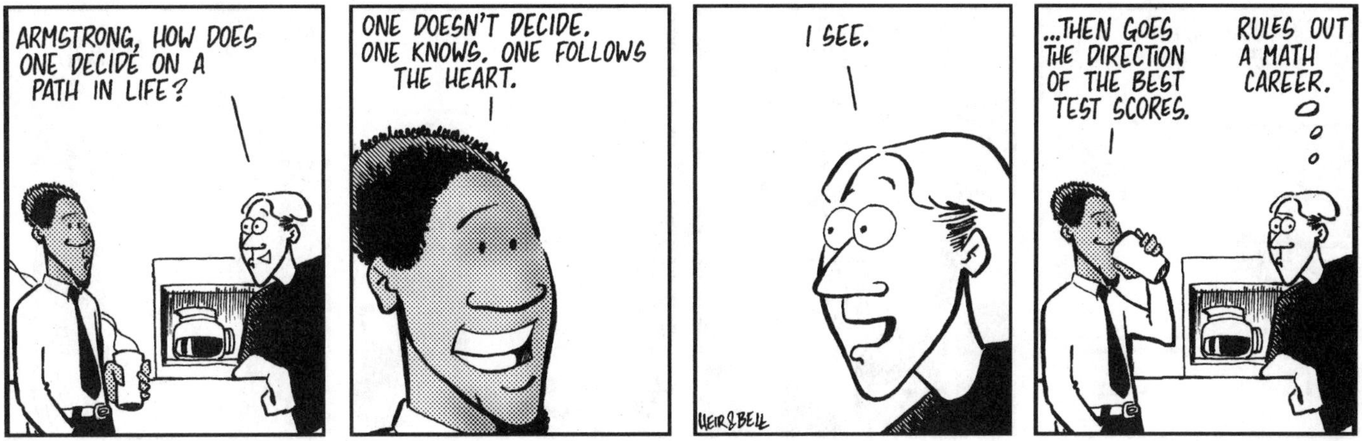
ARMSTRONG, HOW DOES ONE DECIDE ON A PATH IN LIFE?
ONE DOESN'T DECIDE. ONE KNOWS. ONE FOLLOWS THE HEART.
I SEE.
...THEN GOES THE DIRECTION OF THE BEST TEST SCORES.
RULES OUT A MATH CAREER.

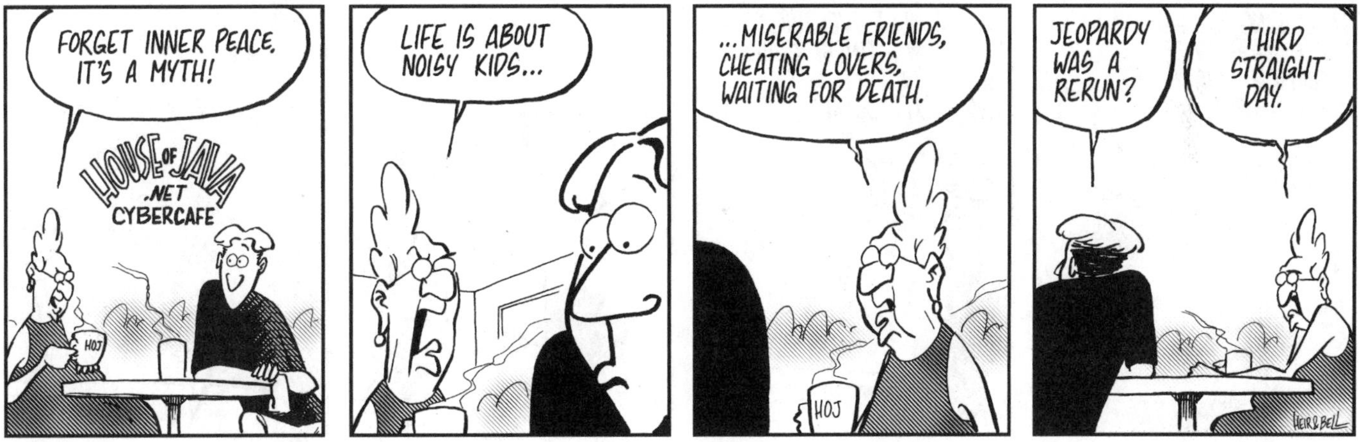
FORGET INNER PEACE. IT'S A MYTH!
HOUSE OF JAVA .NET CYBERCAFE
HOJ
LIFE IS ABOUT NOISY KIDS...
...MISERABLE FRIENDS, CHEATING LOVERS, WAITING FOR DEATH.
HOJ
JEOPARDY WAS A RERUN?
THIRD STRAIGHT DAY.

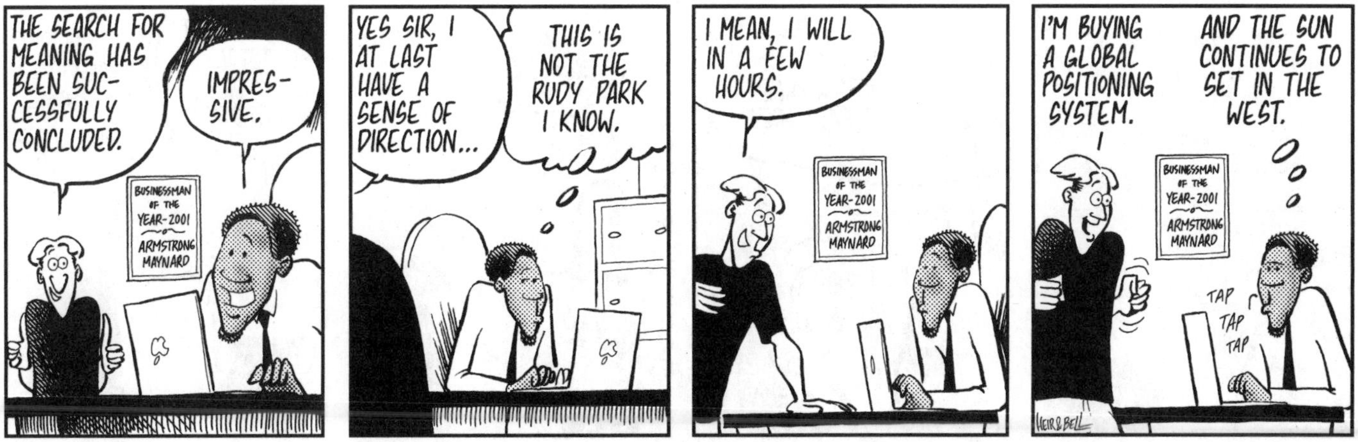
THE SEARCH FOR MEANING HAS BEEN SUCCESSFULLY CONCLUDED.
IMPRESSIVE.
BUSINESSMAN OF THE YEAR-2001 ARMSTRONG MAYNARD
YES SIR, I AT LAST HAVE A SENSE OF DIRECTION...
THIS IS NOT THE RUDY PARK I KNOW.
I MEAN, I WILL IN A FEW HOURS.
BUSINESSMAN OF THE YEAR-2001 ARMSTRONG MAYNARD
I'M BUYING A GLOBAL POSITIONING SYSTEM.
AND THE SUN CONTINUES TO SET IN THE WEST.
BUSINESSMAN OF THE YEAR-2001 ARMSTRONG MAYNARD
TAP TAP TAP

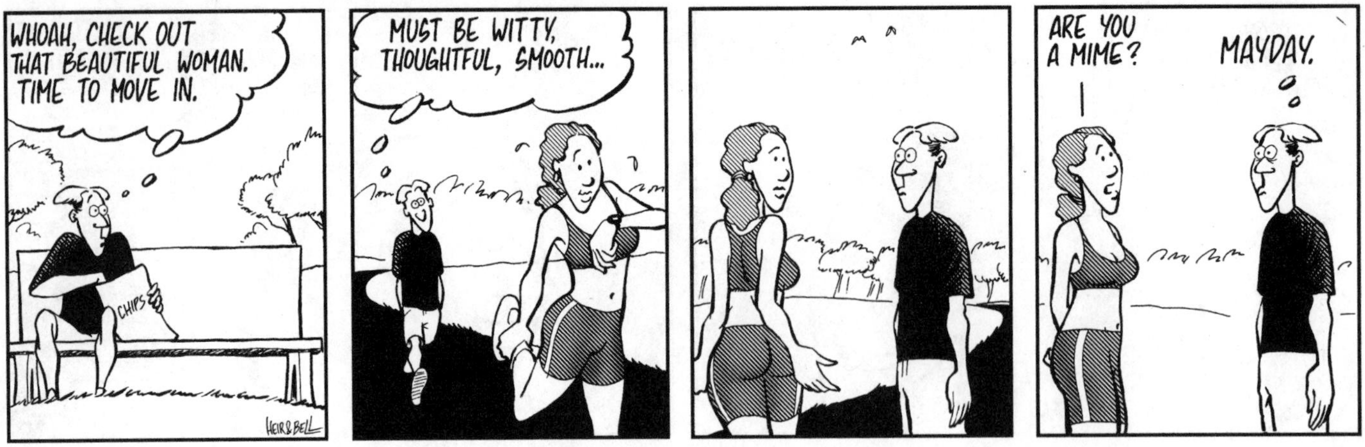
WHOAH, CHECK OUT THAT BEAUTIFUL WOMAN. TIME TO MOVE IN.
CHIPS
HEIR&BELL
MUST BE WITTY, THOUGHTFUL, SMOOTH...
ARE YOU A MIME?
MAYDAY.

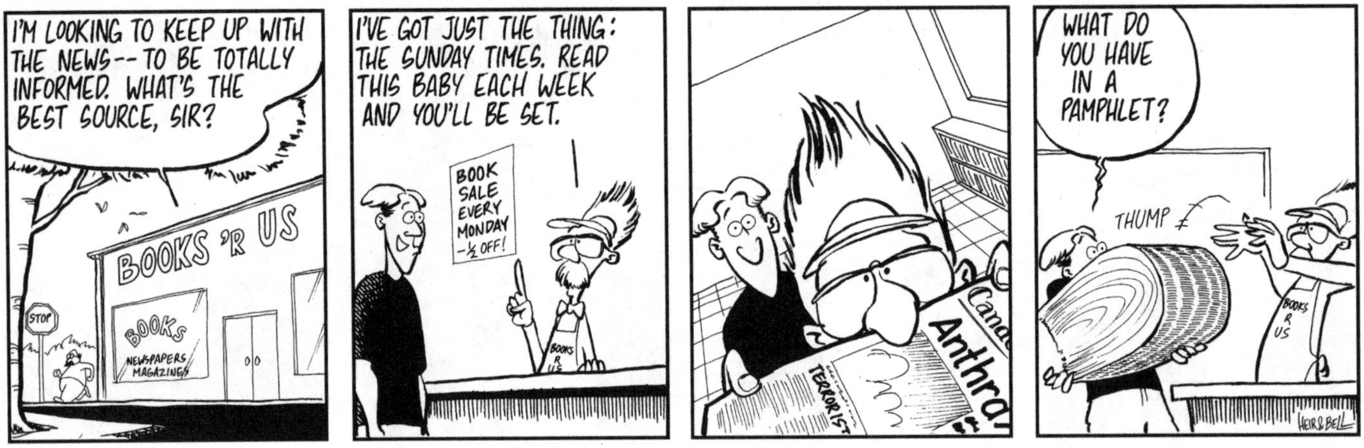
I'M LOOKING TO KEEP UP WITH THE NEWS--TO BE TOTALLY INFORMED. WHAT'S THE BEST SOURCE, SIR?
BOOKS 'R US
STOP
BOOKS
NEWSPAPERS MAGAZINES
I'VE GOT JUST THE THING: THE SUNDAY TIMES. READ THIS BABY EACH WEEK AND YOU'LL BE SET.
BOOK SALE EVERY MONDAY -½ OFF!
BOOKS R US
TERRORIST
WHAT DO YOU HAVE IN A PAMPHLET?
THUMP
BOOKS R US
HEIR&BELL

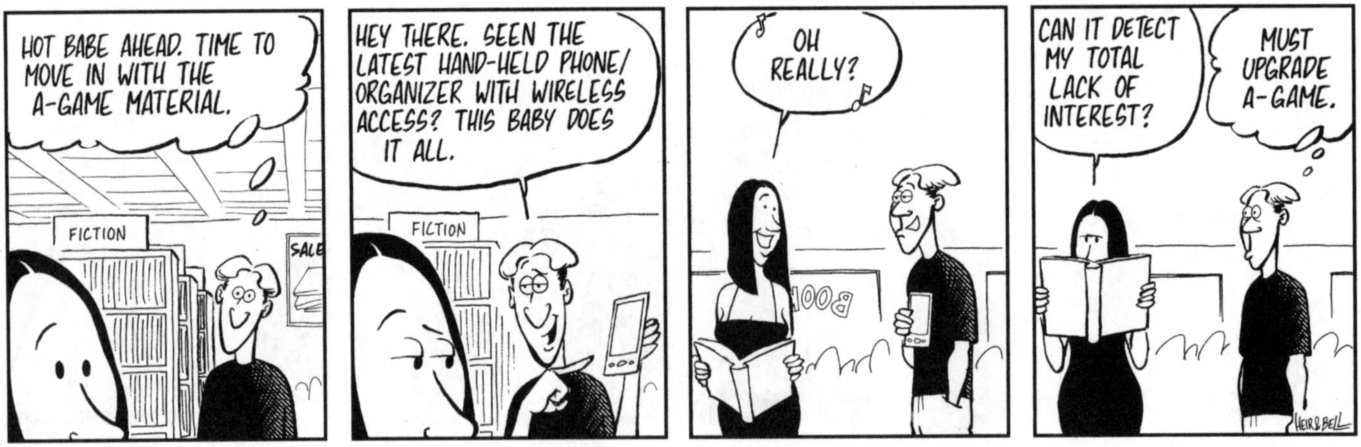
HOT BABE AHEAD. TIME TO MOVE IN WITH THE A-GAME MATERIAL.
FICTION
SALE
HEY THERE. SEEN THE LATEST HAND-HELD PHONE/ ORGANIZER WITH WIRELESS ACCESS? THIS BABY DOES IT ALL.
FICTION
OH REALLY?
CAN IT DETECT MY TOTAL LACK OF INTEREST?
MUST UPGRADE A-GAME.
HEIR&BELL

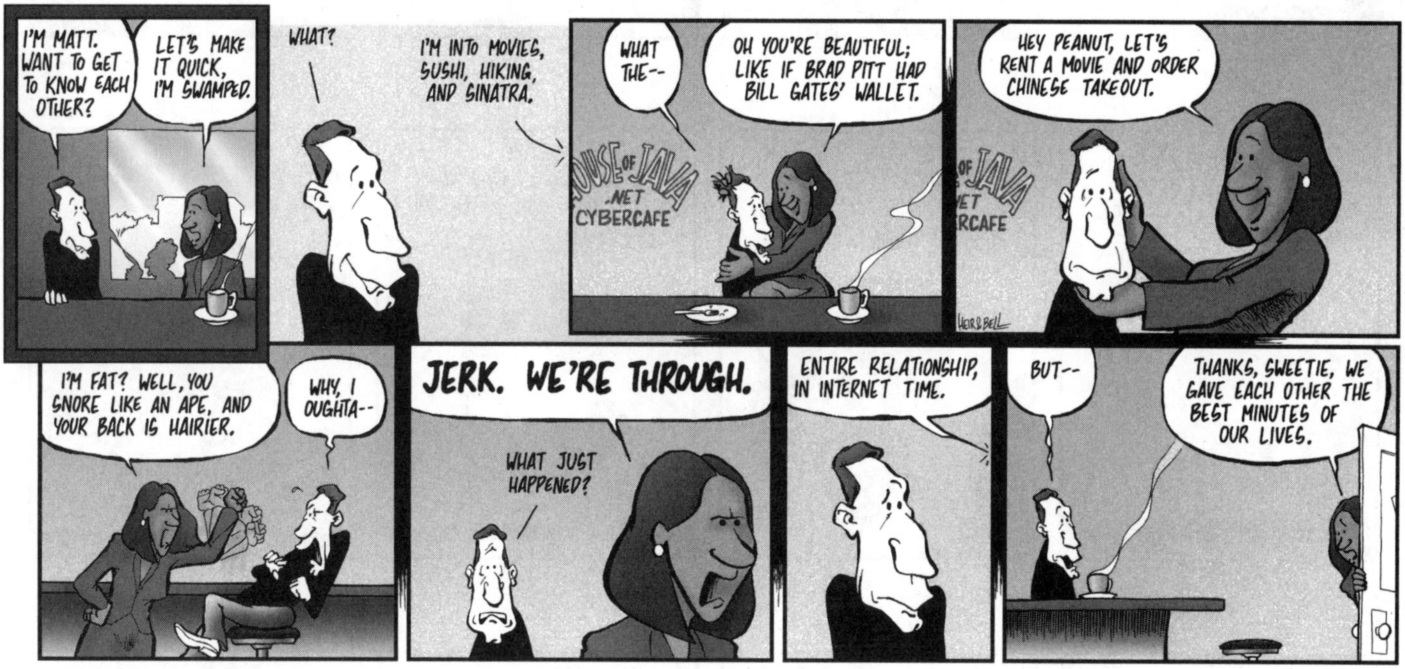
I'M MATT. WANT TO GET TO KNOW EACH OTHER?
LET'S MAKE IT QUICK, I'M SWAMPED.
WHAT?
I'M INTO MOVIES, SUSHI, HIKING, AND SINATRA.
WHAT THE--
OH YOU'RE BEAUTIFUL; LIKE IF BRAD PITT HAD BILL GATES' WALLET.
HOUSE OF JAVA .NET CYBERCAFE
HEY PEANUT, LET'S RENT A MOVIE AND ORDER CHINESE TAKEOUT.
I'M FAT? WELL, YOU SNORE LIKE AN APE, AND YOUR BACK IS HAIRIER.
WHY, I OUGHTA--
JERK. WE'RE THROUGH.
WHAT JUST HAPPENED?
ENTIRE RELATIONSHIP, IN INTERNET TIME.
BUT--
THANKS, SWEETIE, WE GAVE EACH OTHER THE BEST MINUTES OF OUR LIVES.

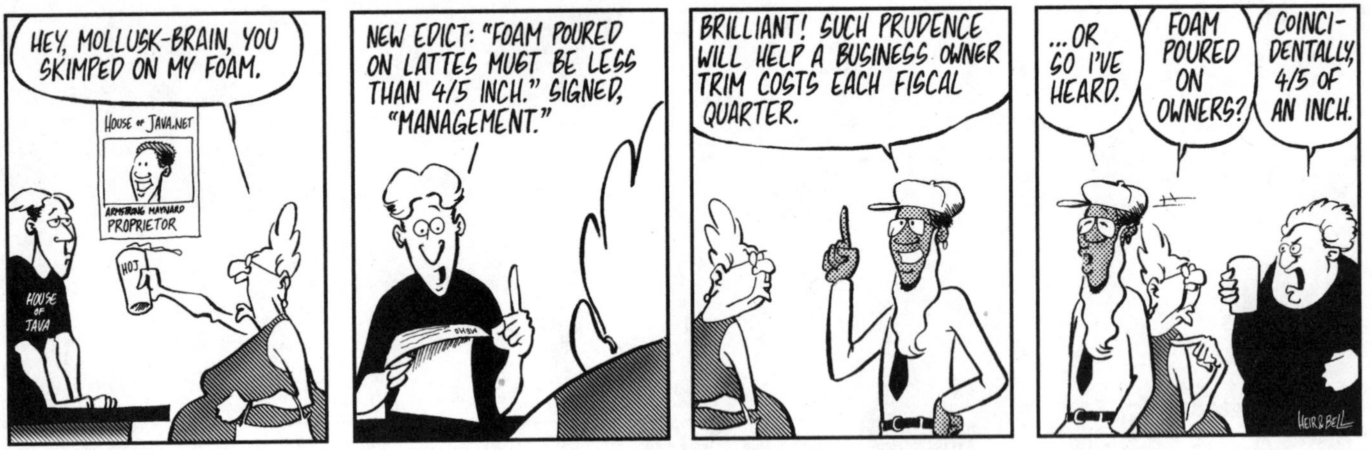
HEY, MOLLUSK-BRAIN, YOU SKIMPED ON MY FOAM.
HOUSE of JAVA.NET
ARMSTRONG MAYNARD
PROPRIETOR
HOJ
HOUSE OF JAVA
NEW EDICT: "FOAM POURED ON LATTES MUST BE LESS THAN 4/5 INCH." SIGNED, "MANAGEMENT."
BRILLIANT! SUCH PRUDENCE WILL HELP A BUSINESS OWNER TRIM COSTS EACH FISCAL QUARTER.
...OR SO I'VE HEARD.
FOAM POURED ON OWNERS?
COINCI-DENTALLY, 4/5 OF AN INCH.
HEIR & BELL

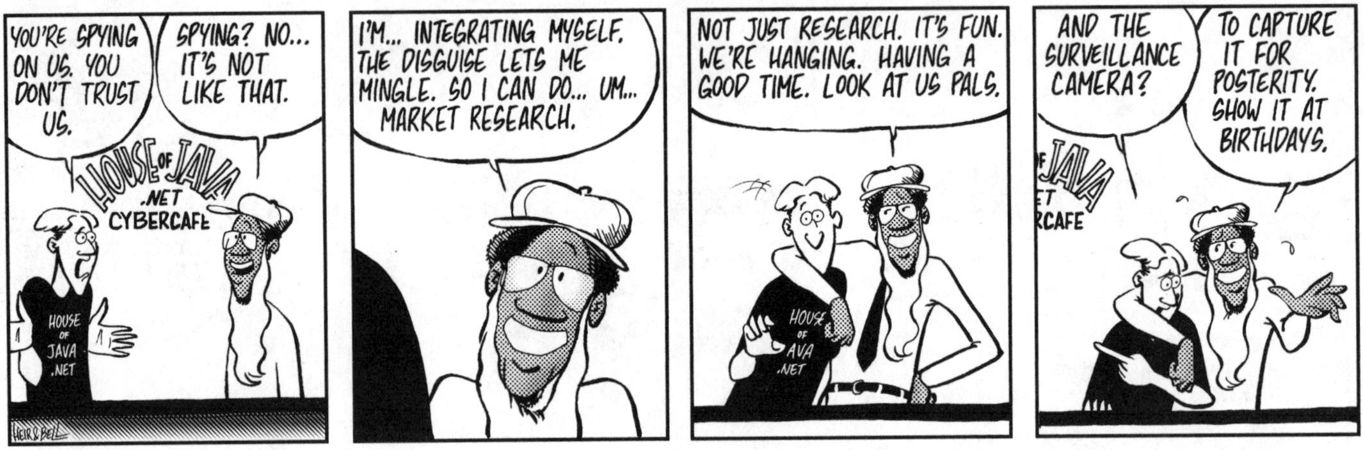
YOU'RE SPYING ON US. YOU DON'T TRUST US.
SPYING? NO... IT'S NOT LIKE THAT.
HOUSE OF JAVA .NET CYBERCAFE
HOUSE OF JAVA .NET
HEIR & BELL
I'M... INTEGRATING MYSELF. THE DISGUISE LETS ME MINGLE. SO I CAN DO... UM... MARKET RESEARCH.
NOT JUST RESEARCH. IT'S FUN. WE'RE HANGING. HAVING A GOOD TIME. LOOK AT US PALS.
AND THE SURVEILLANCE CAMERA?
TO CAPTURE IT FOR POSTERITY. SHOW IT AT BIRTHDAYS.

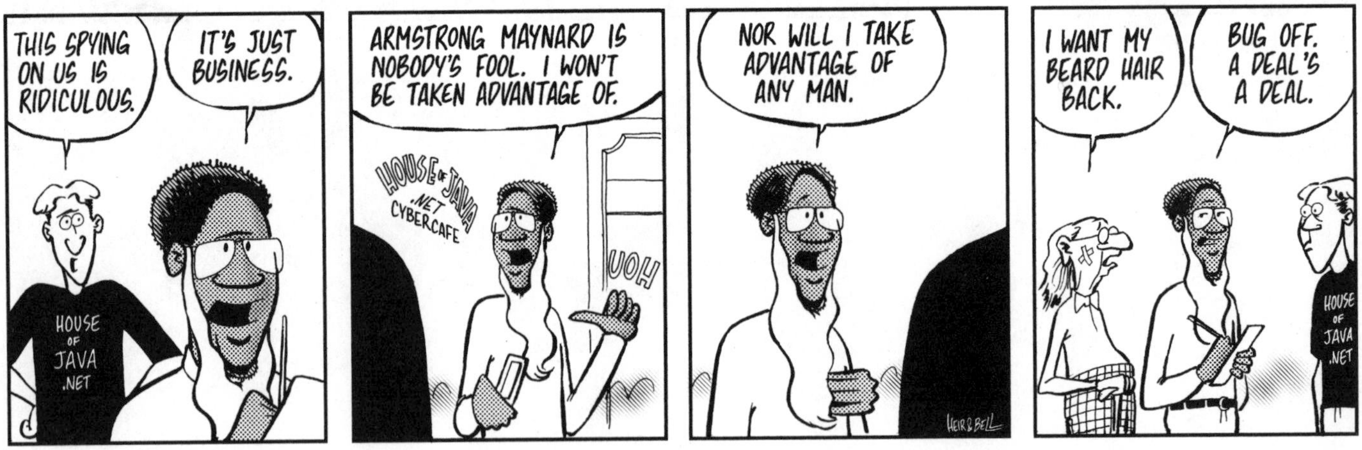
THIS SPYING ON US IS RIDICULOUS.
IT'S JUST BUSINESS.
HOUSE OF JAVA .NET
ARMSTRONG MAYNARD IS NOBODY'S FOOL. I WON'T BE TAKEN ADVANTAGE OF.
HOUSE OF JAVA .NET CYBERCAFE
NOR WILL I TAKE ADVANTAGE OF ANY MAN.
HEIR & BELL
I WANT MY BEARD HAIR BACK.
BUG OFF. A DEAL'S A DEAL.
HOUSE OF JAVA .NET

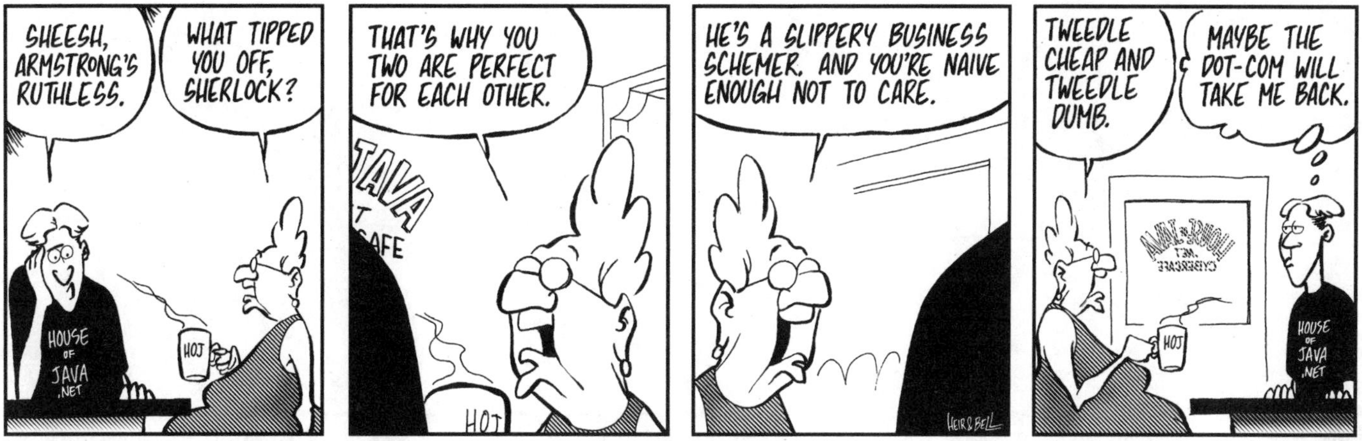
SHEESH, ARMSTRONG'S RUTHLESS.
WHAT TIPPED YOU OFF, SHERLOCK?
HOUSE OF JAVA .NET
HOJ
THAT'S WHY YOU TWO ARE PERFECT FOR EACH OTHER.
HE'S A SLIPPERY BUSINESS SCHEMER. AND YOU'RE NAIVE ENOUGH NOT TO CARE.
HEIR & BELL
TWEEDLE CHEAP AND TWEEDLE DUMB.
MAYBE THE DOT-COM WILL TAKE ME BACK.
HOUSE OF JAVA .NET

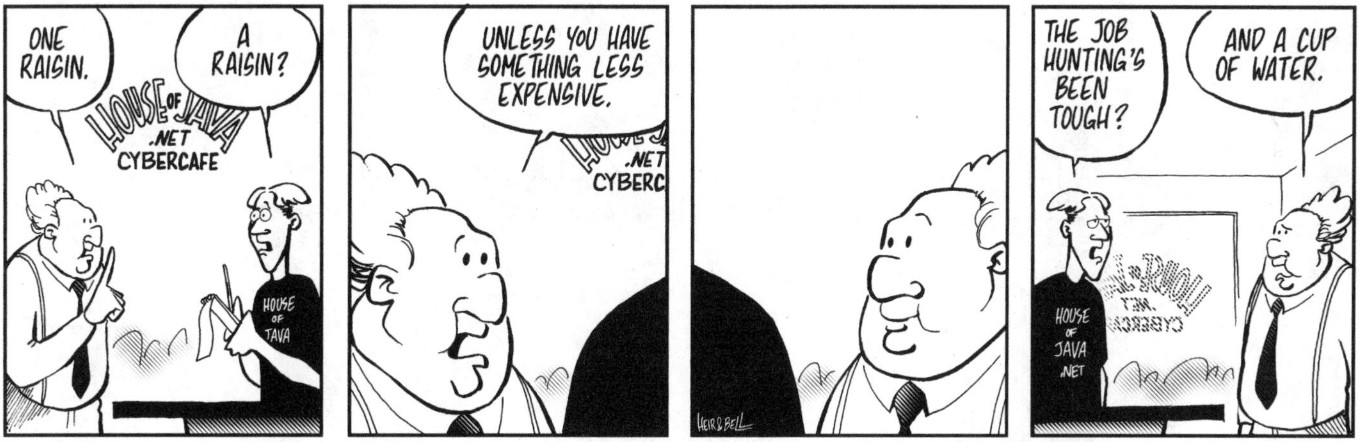
ONE RAISIN.
A RAISIN?
HOUSE OF JAVA .NET CYBERCAFE
HOUSE OF JAVA
UNLESS YOU HAVE SOMETHING LESS EXPENSIVE.
HEIR & BELL
THE JOB HUNTING'S BEEN TOUGH?
AND A CUP OF WATER.
HOUSE OF JAVA .NET

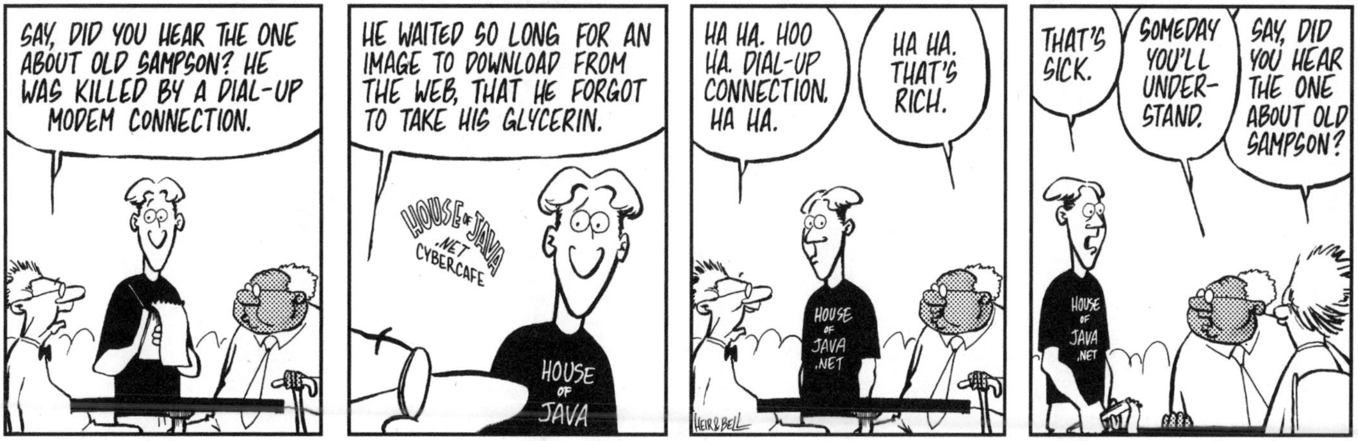
SAY, DID YOU HEAR THE ONE ABOUT OLD SAMPSON? HE WAS KILLED BY A DIAL-UP MODEM CONNECTION.
HE WAITED SO LONG FOR AN IMAGE TO DOWNLOAD FROM THE WEB, THAT HE FORGOT TO TAKE HIS GLYCERIN.
HOUSE OF JAVA .NET CYBERCAFE
HOUSE OF JAVA
HA HA. HOO HA. DIAL-UP CONNECTION. HA HA.
HA HA. THAT'S RICH.
HOUSE OF JAVA .NET
HEIR & BELL
THAT'S SICK.
SOMEDAY YOU'LL UNDERSTAND.
SAY, DID YOU HEAR THE ONE ABOUT OLD SAMPSON?
HOUSE OF JAVA .NET

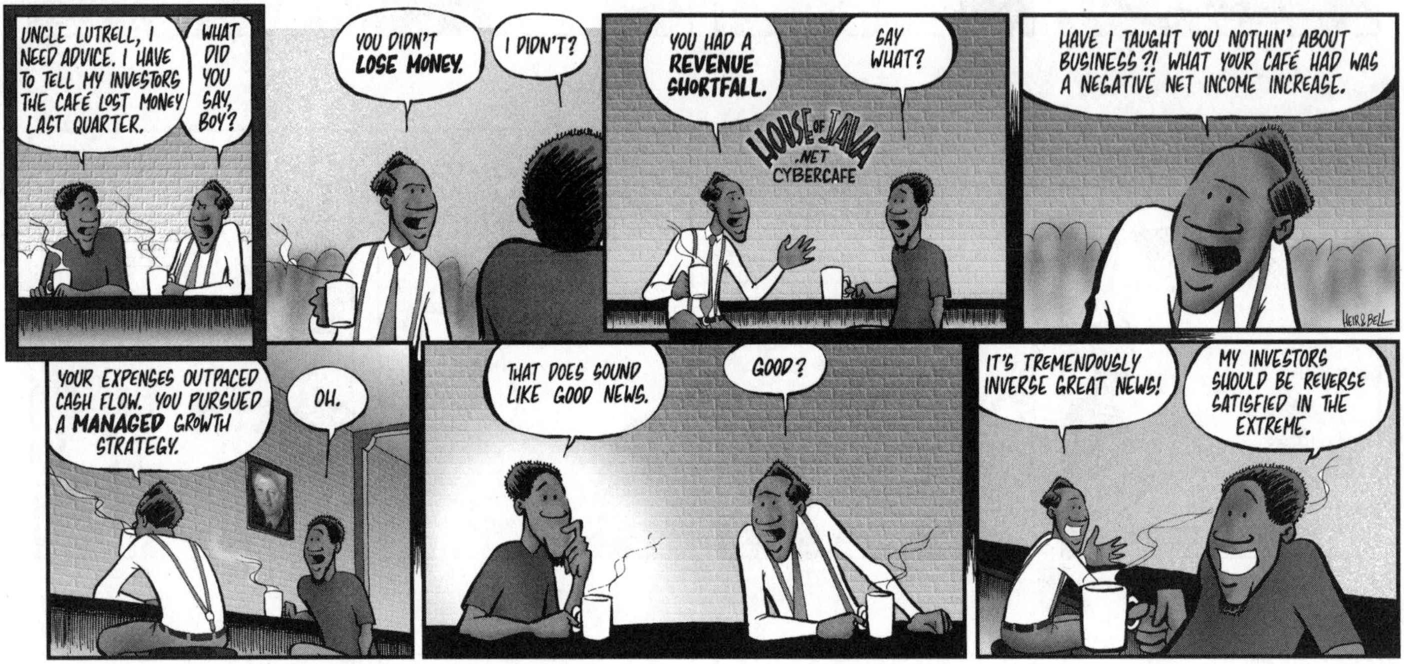
UNCLE LUTRELL, I NEED ADVICE. I HAVE TO TELL MY INVESTORS THE CAFÉ LOST MONEY LAST QUARTER.
WHAT DID YOU SAY, BOY?
YOU DIDN'T **LOSE MONEY.**
I DIDN'T?
YOU HAD A **REVENUE SHORTFALL.**
HOUSE OF JAVA .NET CYBERCAFE
SAY WHAT?
HAVE I TAUGHT YOU NOTHIN' ABOUT BUSINESS?! WHAT YOUR CAFÉ HAD WAS A NEGATIVE NET INCOME INCREASE.
HEIR & BELL
YOUR EXPENSES OUTPACED CASH FLOW. YOU PURSUED A **MANAGED** GROWTH STRATEGY.
OH.
THAT DOES SOUND LIKE GOOD NEWS.
GOOD?
IT'S TREMENDOUSLY INVERSE GREAT NEWS!
MY INVESTORS SHOULD BE REVERSE SATISFIED IN THE EXTREME.

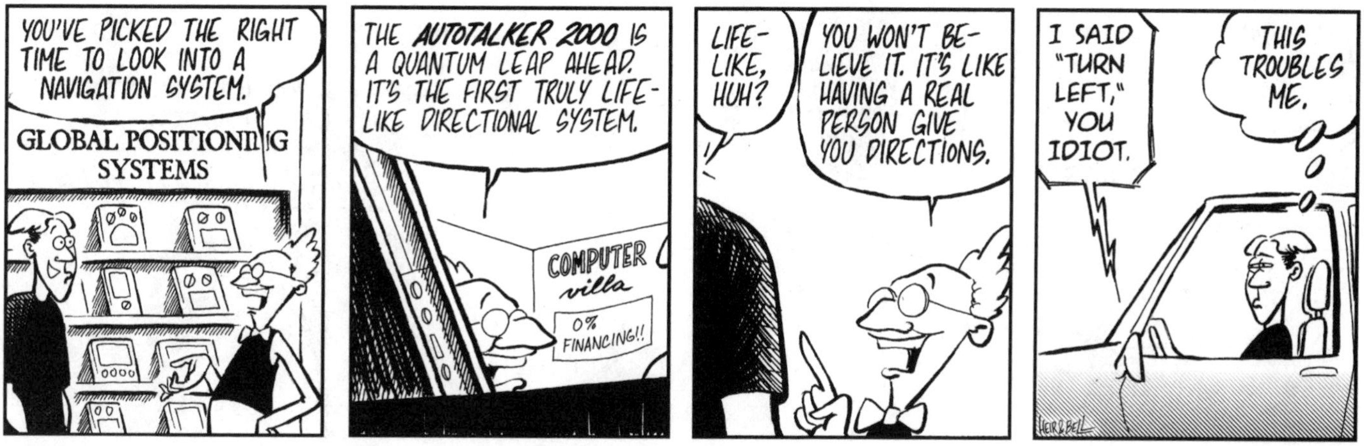
YOU'VE PICKED THE RIGHT TIME TO LOOK INTO A NAVIGATION SYSTEM.
GLOBAL POSITIONING SYSTEMS
THE AUTOTALKER 2000 IS A QUANTUM LEAP AHEAD. IT'S THE FIRST TRULY LIFE-LIKE DIRECTIONAL SYSTEM.
COMPUTER villa
0% FINANCING!!
LIFE-LIKE, HUH?
YOU WON'T BELIEVE IT. IT'S LIKE HAVING A REAL PERSON GIVE YOU DIRECTIONS.
I SAID "TURN LEFT," YOU IDIOT.
THIS TROUBLES ME.
HEIR & BELL

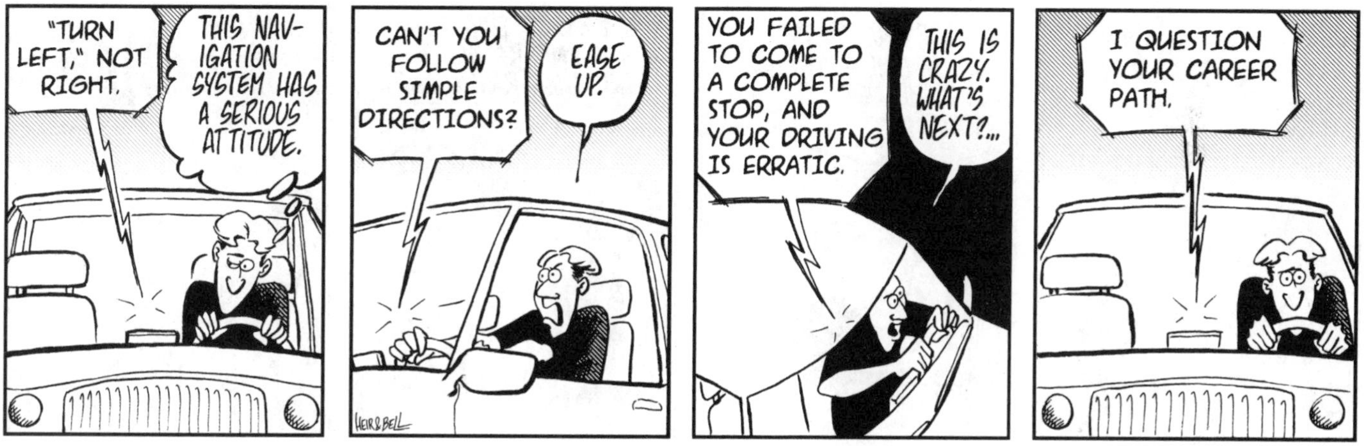
"TURN LEFT," NOT RIGHT.
THIS NAVIGATION SYSTEM HAS A SERIOUS ATTITUDE.
CAN'T YOU FOLLOW SIMPLE DIRECTIONS?
EASE UP.
HEIR & BELL
YOU FAILED TO COME TO A COMPLETE STOP, AND YOUR DRIVING IS ERRATIC.
THIS IS CRAZY. WHAT'S NEXT?...
I QUESTION YOUR CAREER PATH.

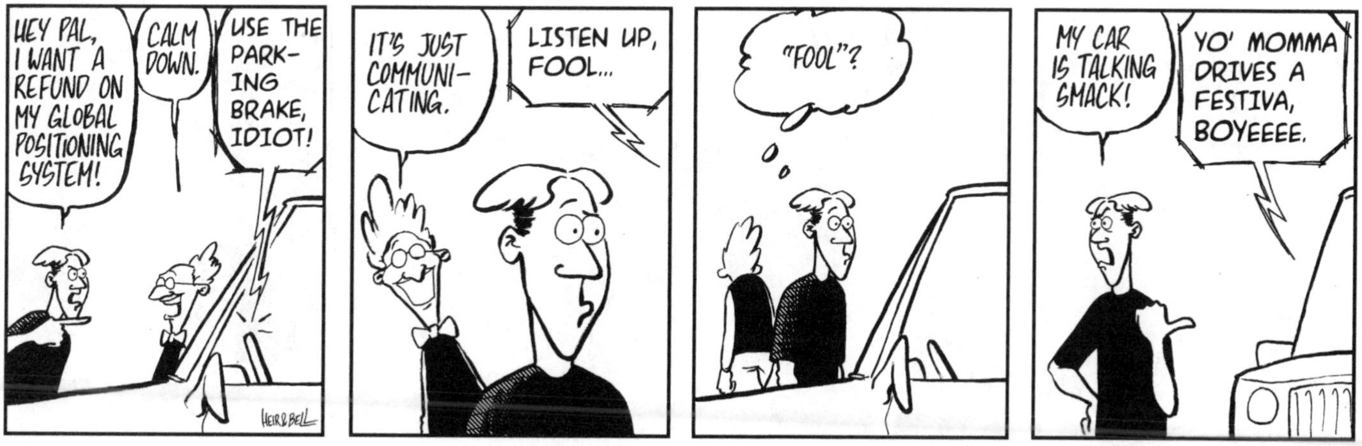
HEY PAL, I WANT A REFUND ON MY GLOBAL POSITIONING SYSTEM!
CALM DOWN.
USE THE PARKING BRAKE, IDIOT!
HEIR & BELL
IT'S JUST COMMUNICATING.
LISTEN UP, FOOL...
"FOOL"?
MY CAR IS TALKING SMACK!
YO' MOMMA DRIVES A FESTIVA, BOYEEEE.

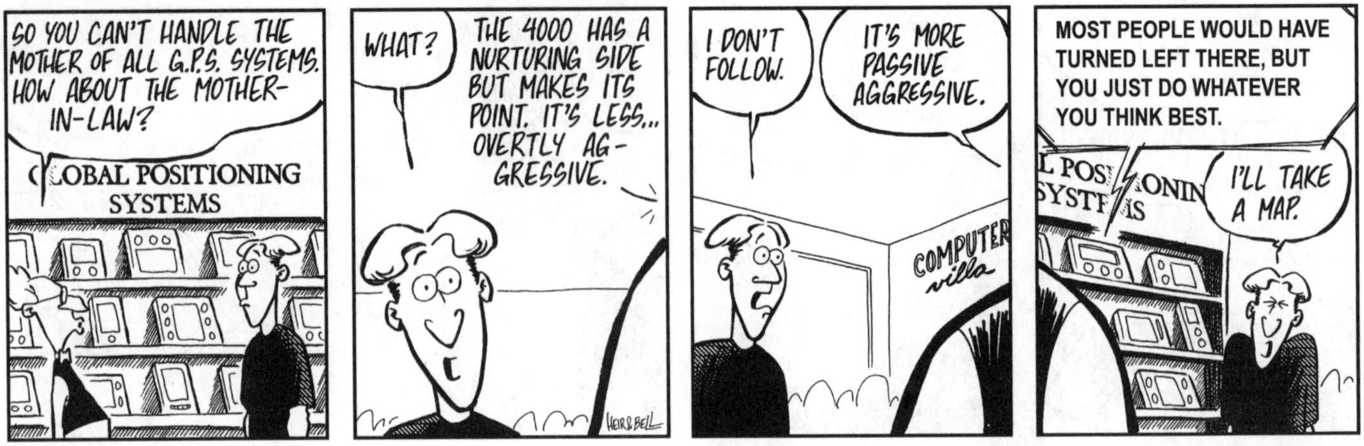
SO YOU CAN'T HANDLE THE MOTHER OF ALL G.P.S. SYSTEMS. HOW ABOUT THE MOTHER-IN-LAW?
GLOBAL POSITIONING SYSTEMS
WHAT?
THE 4000 HAS A NURTURING SIDE BUT MAKES ITS POINT. IT'S LESS... OVERTLY AGGRESSIVE.
HEIR & BELL
I DON'T FOLLOW.
IT'S MORE PASSIVE AGGRESSIVE.
COMPUTER villa
MOST PEOPLE WOULD HAVE TURNED LEFT THERE, BUT YOU JUST DO WHATEVER YOU THINK BEST.
I'LL TAKE A MAP.

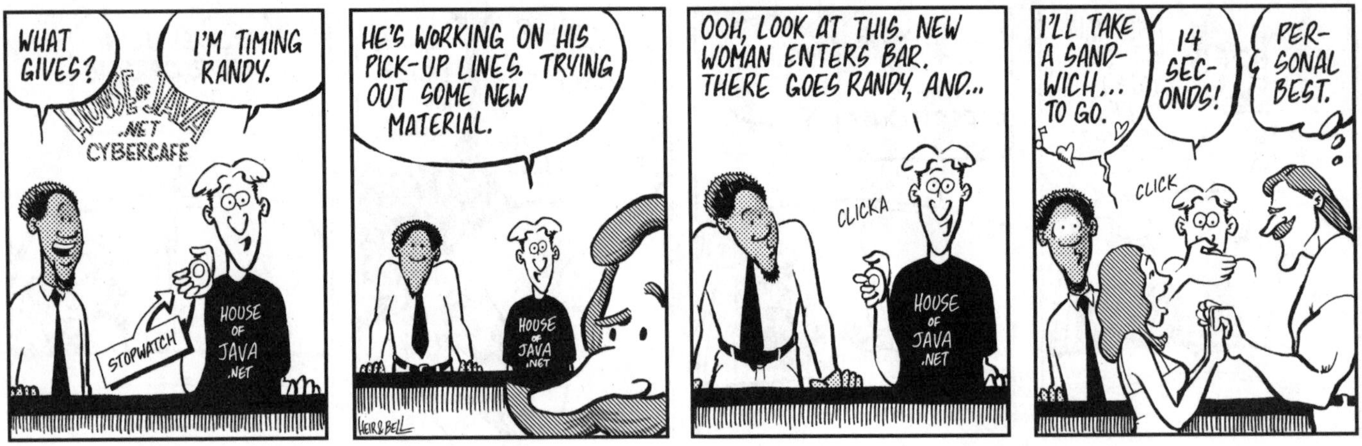
WHAT GIVES?
I'M TIMING RANDY.
HOUSE OF JAVA .NET CYBERCAFE
STOPWATCH
HOUSE OF JAVA .NET
HE'S WORKING ON HIS PICK-UP LINES. TRYING OUT SOME NEW MATERIAL.
HEIR & BELL
OOH, LOOK AT THIS. NEW WOMAN ENTERS BAR. THERE GOES RANDY, AND...
CLICKA
I'LL TAKE A SANDWICH... TO GO.
14 SECONDS!
PERSONAL BEST.
CLICK

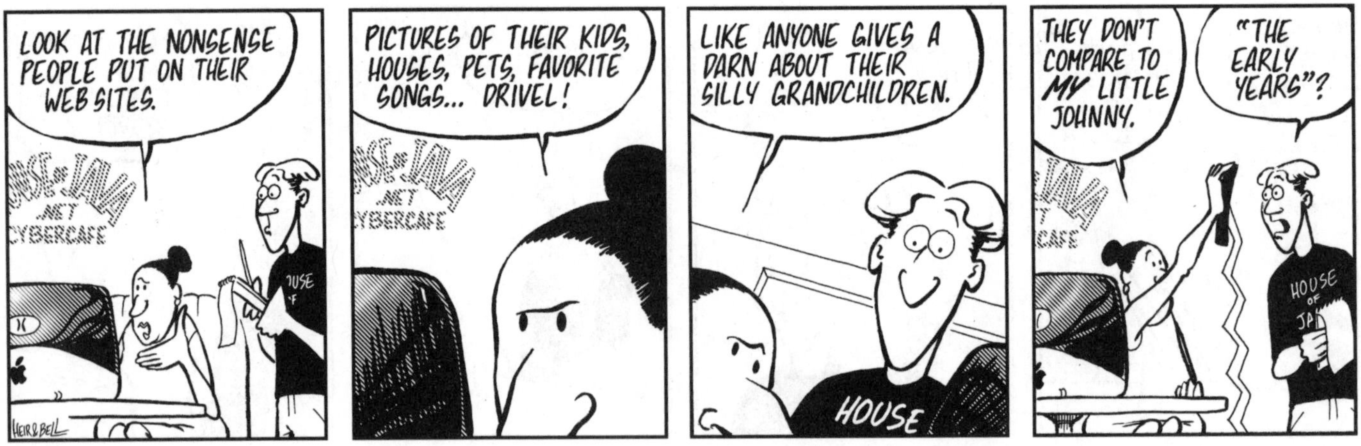
LOOK AT THE NONSENSE PEOPLE PUT ON THEIR WEB SITES.
HEIR & BELL
PICTURES OF THEIR KIDS, HOUSES, PETS, FAVORITE SONGS... DRIVEL!
LIKE ANYONE GIVES A DARN ABOUT THEIR SILLY GRANDCHILDREN.
HOUSE
THEY DON'T COMPARE TO MY LITTLE JOHNNY.
"THE EARLY YEARS"?

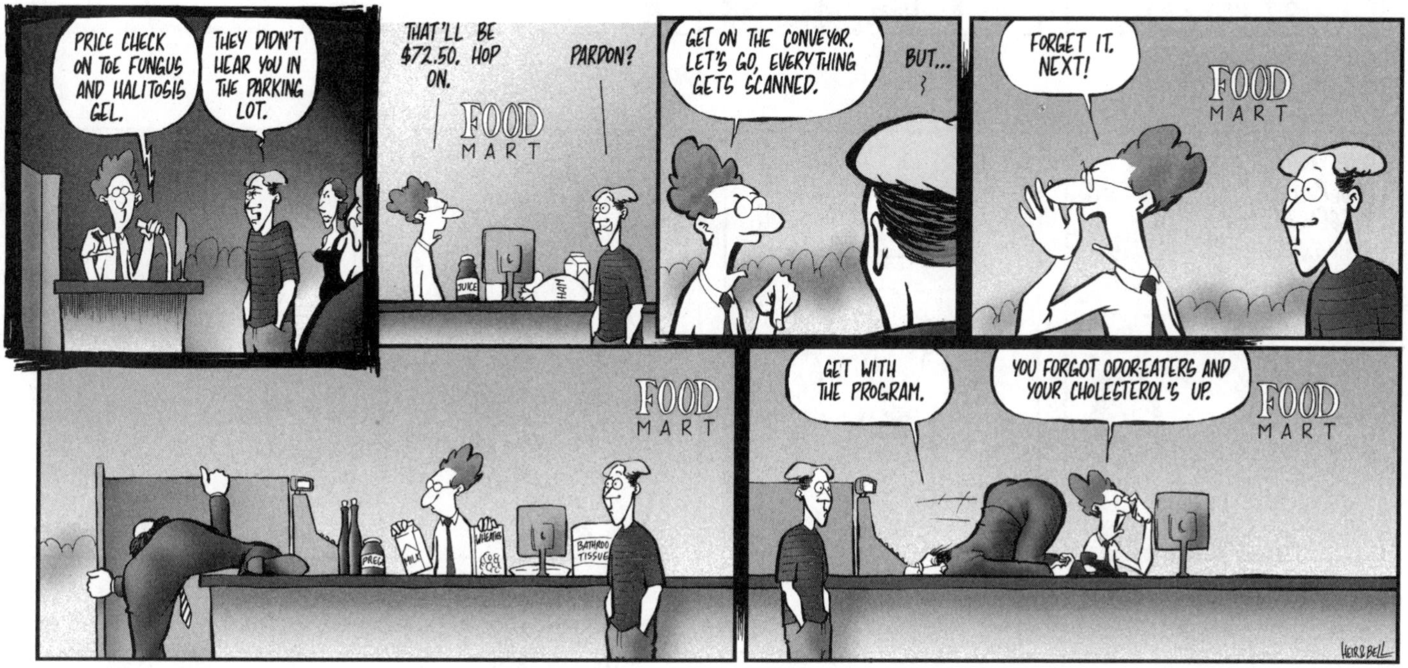
PRICE CHECK ON TOE FUNGUS AND HALITOSIS GEL.
THEY DIDN'T HEAR YOU IN THE PARKING LOT.
THAT'LL BE $72.50. HOP ON.
PARDON?
FOOD MART
GET ON THE CONVEYOR. LET'S GO, EVERYTHING GETS SCANNED.
BUT...
FORGET IT. NEXT!
FOOD MART
FOOD MART
GET WITH THE PROGRAM.
YOU FORGOT ODOR-EATERS AND YOUR CHOLESTEROL'S UP.
FOOD MART

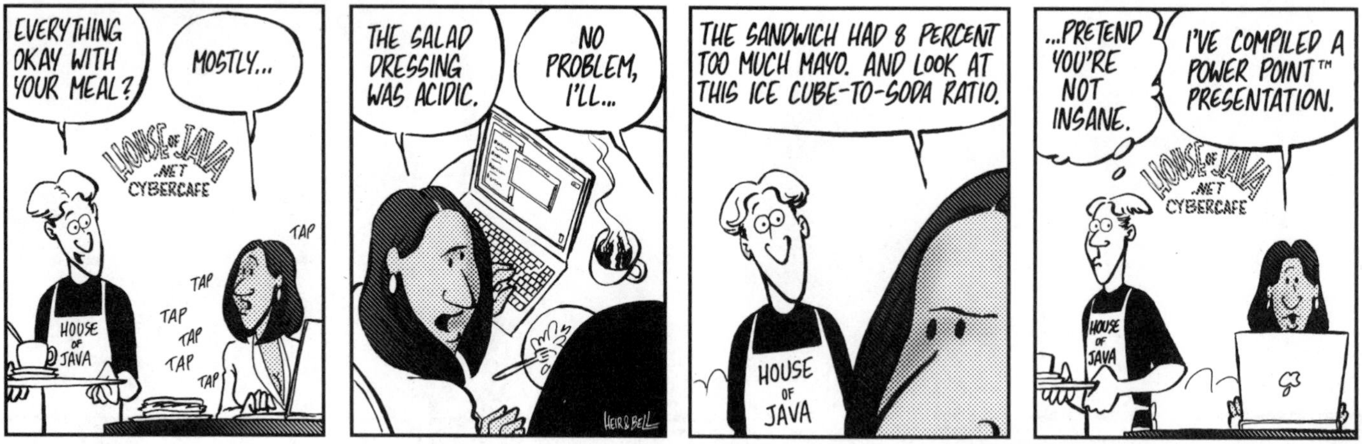
EVERYTHING OKAY WITH YOUR MEAL?
MOSTLY...
HOUSE OF JAVA .NET CYBERCAFE
TAP TAP TAP TAP TAP TAP
HOUSE OF JAVA
THE SALAD DRESSING WAS ACIDIC.
NO PROBLEM, I'LL...
THE SANDWICH HAD 8 PERCENT TOO MUCH MAYO. AND LOOK AT THIS ICE CUBE-TO-SODA RATIO.
HOUSE OF JAVA
...PRETEND YOU'RE NOT INSANE.
I'VE COMPILED A POWER POINT™ PRESENTATION.
HOUSE OF JAVA .NET CYBERCAFE
HOUSE OF JAVA

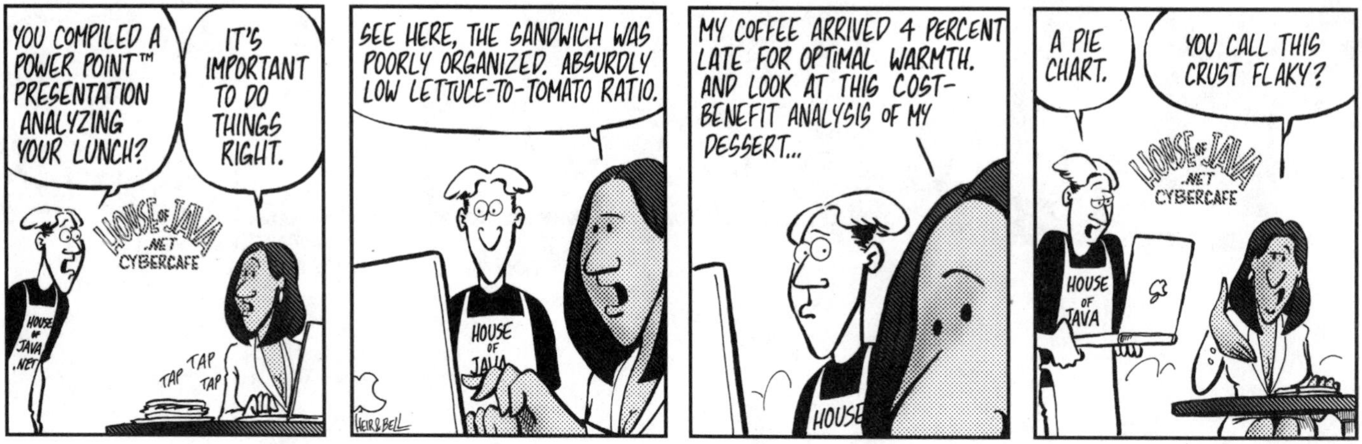
YOU COMPILED A POWER POINT™ PRESENTATION ANALYZING YOUR LUNCH?
IT'S IMPORTANT TO DO THINGS RIGHT.
HOUSE OF JAVA .NET CYBERCAFE
HOUSE OF JAVA .NET
TAP TAP TAP
SEE HERE, THE SANDWICH WAS POORLY ORGANIZED. ABSURDLY LOW LETTUCE-TO-TOMATO RATIO.
HOUSE OF JAVA
MY COFFEE ARRIVED 4 PERCENT LATE FOR OPTIMAL WARMTH. AND LOOK AT THIS COST-BENEFIT ANALYSIS OF MY DESSERT...
HOUSE
A PIE CHART.
YOU CALL THIS CRUST FLAKY?
HOUSE OF JAVA .NET CYBERCAFE
HOUSE OF JAVA

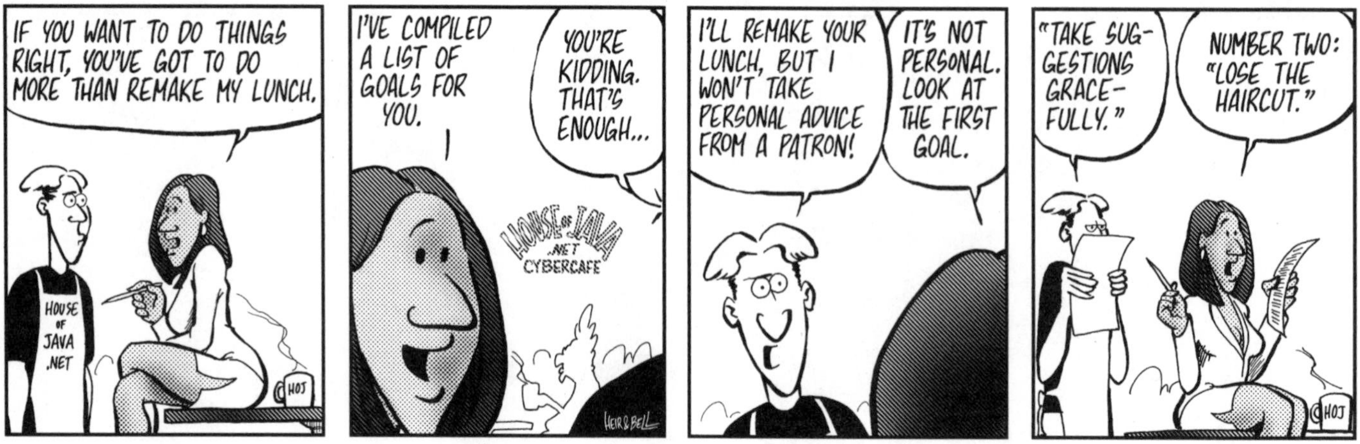
IF YOU WANT TO DO THINGS RIGHT, YOU'VE GOT TO DO MORE THAN REMAKE MY LUNCH.
HOUSE OF JAVA .NET
HOJ
I'VE COMPILED A LIST OF GOALS FOR YOU.
YOU'RE KIDDING. THAT'S ENOUGH...
HOUSE OF JAVA .NET CYBERCAFE
I'LL REMAKE YOUR LUNCH, BUT I WON'T TAKE PERSONAL ADVICE FROM A PATRON!
IT'S NOT PERSONAL. LOOK AT THE FIRST GOAL.
"TAKE SUGGESTIONS GRACEFULLY."
NUMBER TWO: "LOSE THE HAIRCUT."
HOJ

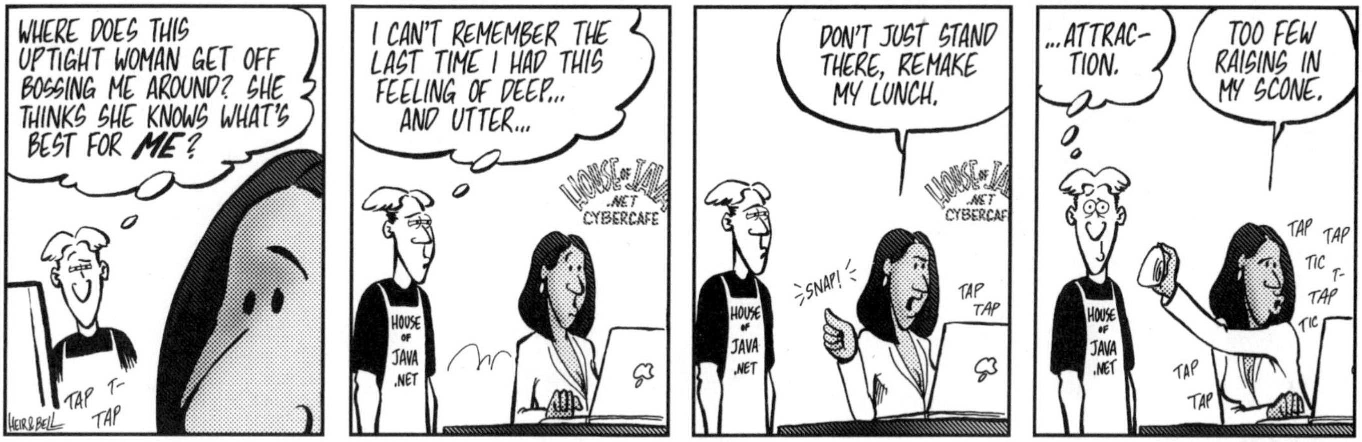
WHERE DOES THIS UPTIGHT WOMAN GET OFF BOSSING ME AROUND? SHE THINKS SHE KNOWS WHAT'S BEST FOR **ME**?
TAP T-TAP
HEIR & BELL
I CAN'T REMEMBER THE LAST TIME I HAD THIS FEELING OF DEEP... AND UTTER...
HOUSE OF JAVA .NET CYBERCAFE
HOUSE OF JAVA .NET
DON'T JUST STAND THERE, REMAKE MY LUNCH.
SNAP!
TAP TAP
HOUSE OF JAVA .NET CYBERCAFE
HOUSE OF JAVA .NET
...ATTRACTION.
TOO FEW RAISINS IN MY SCONE.
TAP TAP TIC T-TAP TIC
TAP TAP
HOUSE OF JAVA .NET

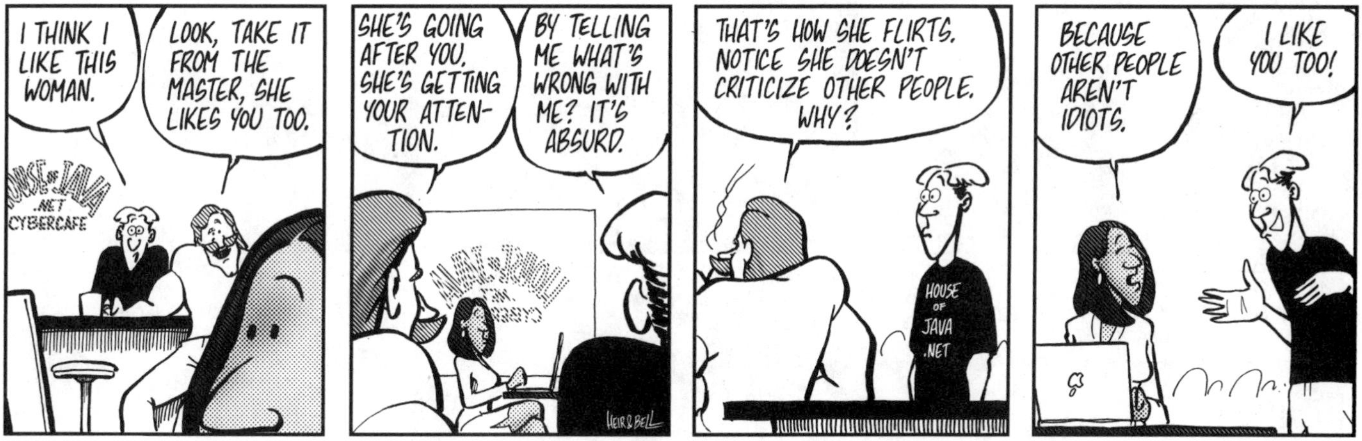
I THINK I LIKE THIS WOMAN.
LOOK, TAKE IT FROM THE MASTER, SHE LIKES YOU TOO.
HOUSE OF JAVA .NET CYBERCAFE
SHE'S GOING AFTER YOU. SHE'S GETTING YOUR ATTENTION.
BY TELLING ME WHAT'S WRONG WITH ME? IT'S ABSURD.
HEIR & BELL
THAT'S HOW SHE FLIRTS. NOTICE SHE DOESN'T CRITICIZE OTHER PEOPLE. WHY?
HOUSE OF JAVA .NET
BECAUSE OTHER PEOPLE AREN'T IDIOTS.
I LIKE YOU TOO!

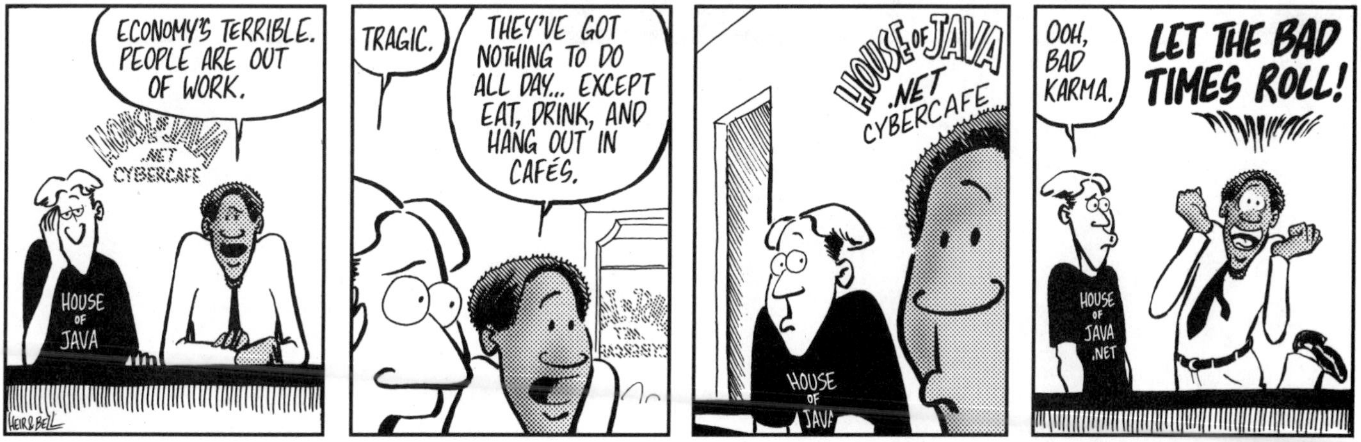
ECONOMY'S TERRIBLE. PEOPLE ARE OUT OF WORK.
HOUSE OF JAVA .NET CYBERCAFE
HOUSE OF JAVA
HEIR & BELL
TRAGIC.
THEY'VE GOT NOTHING TO DO ALL DAY... EXCEPT EAT, DRINK, AND HANG OUT IN CAFÉS.
HOUSE OF JAVA .NET CYBERCAFE
HOUSE OF JAVA
OOH, BAD KARMA.
LET THE BAD TIMES ROLL!
HOUSE OF JAVA .NET

NOW PLAYING
CROUCHING RUDY HIDDEN COHEN
A RUDY PARK PRODUCTION
COPYRIGHT 2001 DARRIN BELL & THERON HEIR
IN LIGHT OF MINOR OVERSTATEMENTS IN MOVIE ADS, THE HONESTY IN ADVERTISING COALITION OFFERS A PUBLIC SERVICE NOTE FROM OUR HOLLYWOOD FRIENDS:
H.A.C.
AN AD FOR THE FILM "BIRDS OF PREY" QUOTED A REVIEWER CALLING THE MOVIE "A TRIUMPH."
TECHNICALLY, THE REVIEWER HAD WRITTEN IT WAS A "TRIUMPH OF MEDIOCRITY."
AN AD FOR "NIGHT FRIGHT" SCREAMED "TRULY HORRIFYING!" THE ACTUAL REVIEW WAS "TRULY HORRIFYING ACTING!"
FRUITY POPS
AN AD CALLING "HEARTS OF MEN" THE "DATE MOVIE OF THE YEAR" EXAGGERATED THE ACTUAL REVIEW: "PURE TRASH. SHE'LL HATE YOU!"
H.A.C.
HOLLYWOOD REGRETS ANY INCONVENIENCE.
JERK.
OOH, "BIRDS OF PREY" LOOKS GOOD.
HEART OF ME

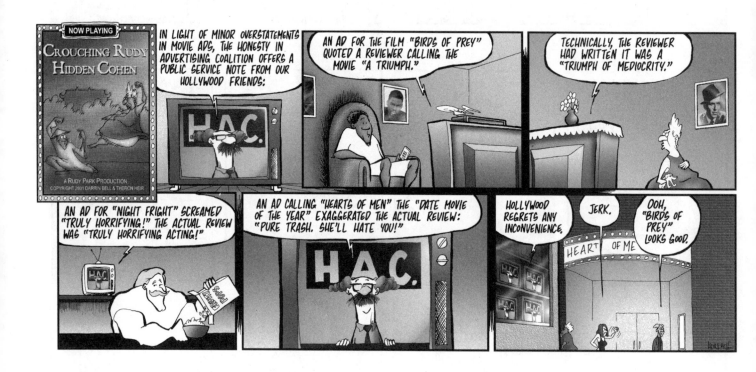

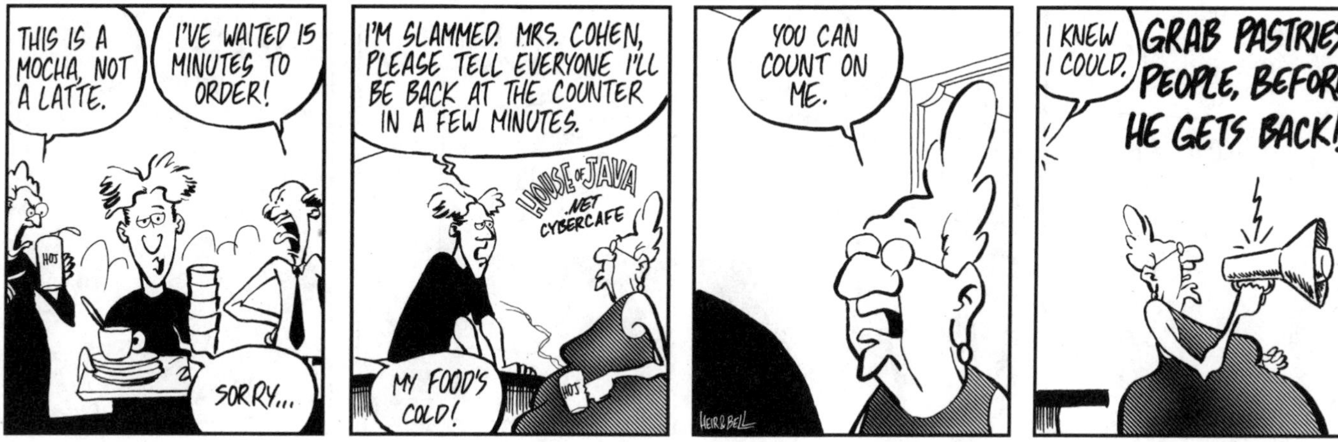
THIS IS A MOCHA, NOT A LATTE.
I'VE WAITED 15 MINUTES TO ORDER!
HOJ
SORRY...
I'M SLAMMED. MRS. COHEN, PLEASE TELL EVERYONE I'LL BE BACK AT THE COUNTER IN A FEW MINUTES.
HOUSE OF JAVA .NET CYBERCAFE
MY FOOD'S COLD!
YOU CAN COUNT ON ME.
I KNEW I COULD.
GRAB PASTRIES, PEOPLE, BEFORE HE GETS BACK!
HEIR & BELL

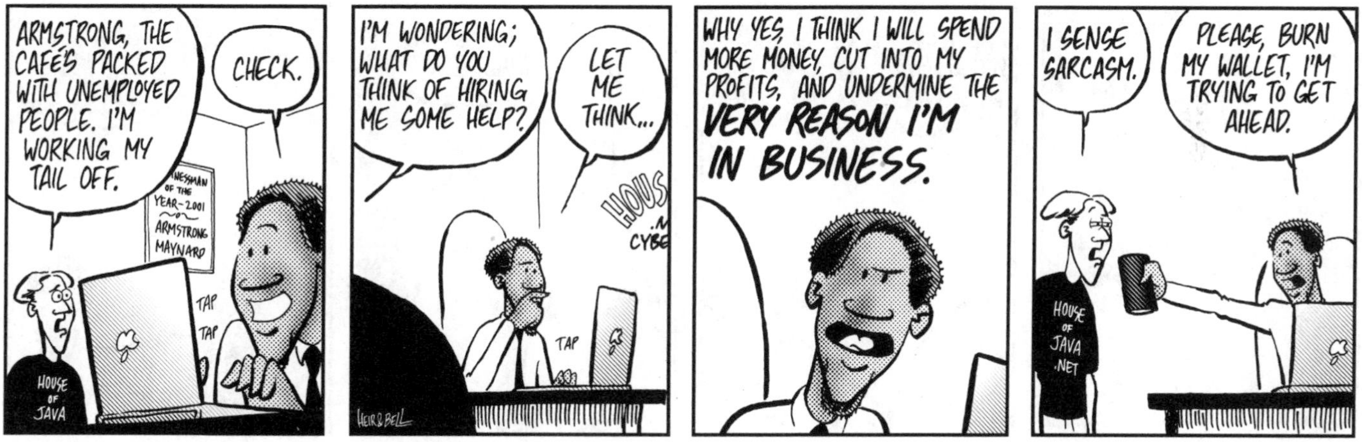
ARMSTRONG, THE CAFÉ'S PACKED WITH UNEMPLOYED PEOPLE. I'M WORKING MY TAIL OFF.
CHECK.
BUSINESSMAN OF THE YEAR-2001 ARMSTRONG MAYNARD
TAP TAP
HOUSE OF JAVA
I'M WONDERING; WHAT DO YOU THINK OF HIRING ME SOME HELP?
LET ME THINK...
TAP
HEIR & BELL
WHY YES, I THINK I WILL SPEND MORE MONEY, CUT INTO MY PROFITS, AND UNDERMINE THE VERY REASON I'M IN BUSINESS.
I SENSE SARCASM.
PLEASE, BURN MY WALLET, I'M TRYING TO GET AHEAD.
HOUSE OF JAVA .NET

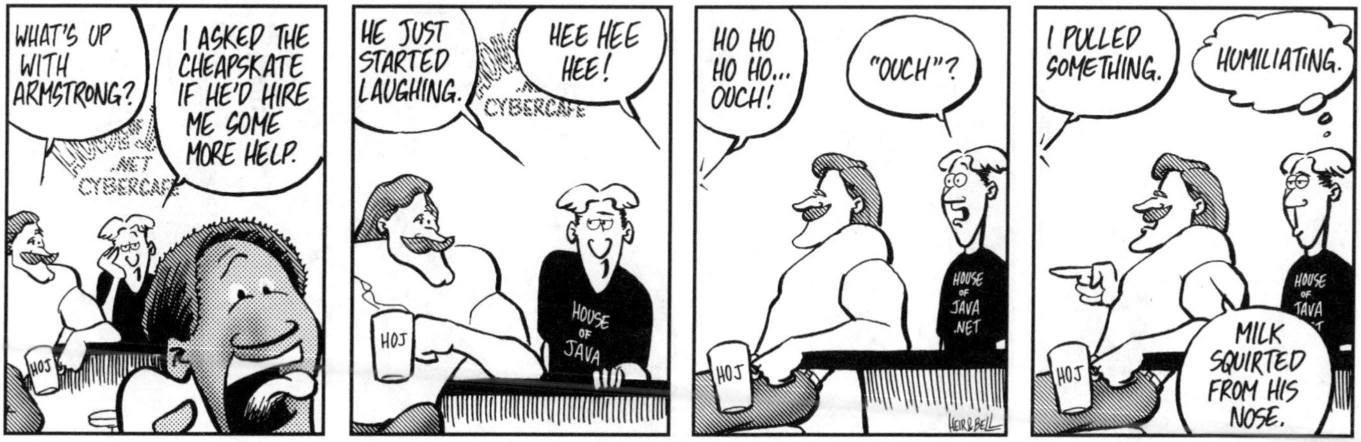
WHAT'S UP WITH ARMSTRONG?
I ASKED THE CHEAPSKATE IF HE'D HIRE ME SOME MORE HELP.
HOJ
HE JUST STARTED LAUGHING.
HEE HEE HEE!
HOUSE OF JAVA
HO HO HO HO... OUCH!
"OUCH"?
HOUSE OF JAVA .NET
HEIR & BELL
I PULLED SOMETHING.
HUMILIATING.
MILK SQUIRTED FROM HIS NOSE.

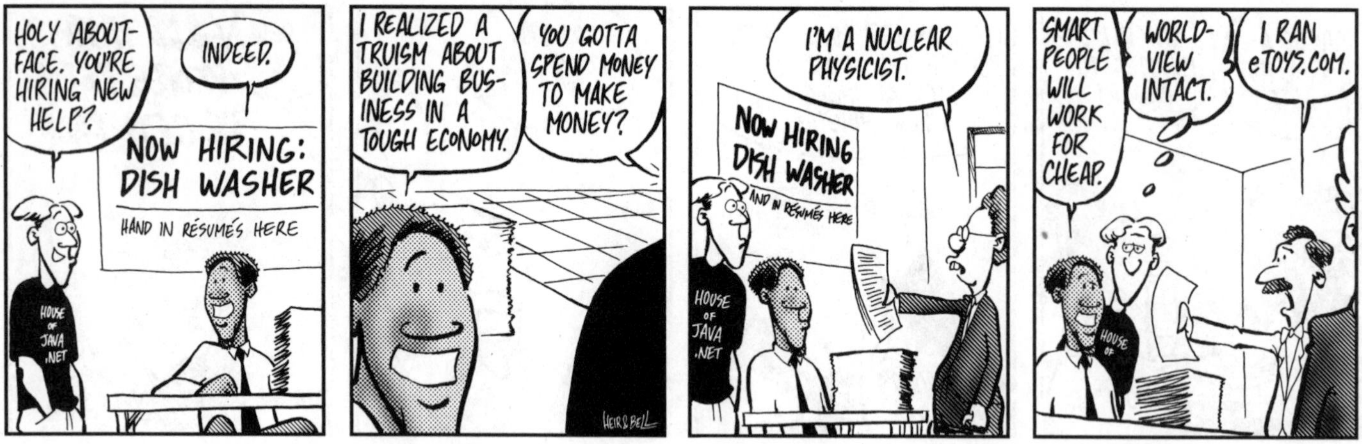
HOLY ABOUT-FACE. YOU'RE HIRING NEW HELP?
INDEED.
NOW HIRING: DISH WASHER
HAND IN RÉSUMÉS HERE
HOUSE OF JAVA .NET
I REALIZED A TRUISM ABOUT BUILDING BUSINESS IN A TOUGH ECONOMY.
YOU GOTTA SPEND MONEY TO MAKE MONEY?
HEIR & BELL
I'M A NUCLEAR PHYSICIST.
NOW HIRING DISH WASHER
AND IN RÉSUMÉS HERE
HOUSE OF JAVA .NET
SMART PEOPLE WILL WORK FOR CHEAP.
WORLD-VIEW INTACT.
I RAN eTOYS.COM.
HOUSE OF

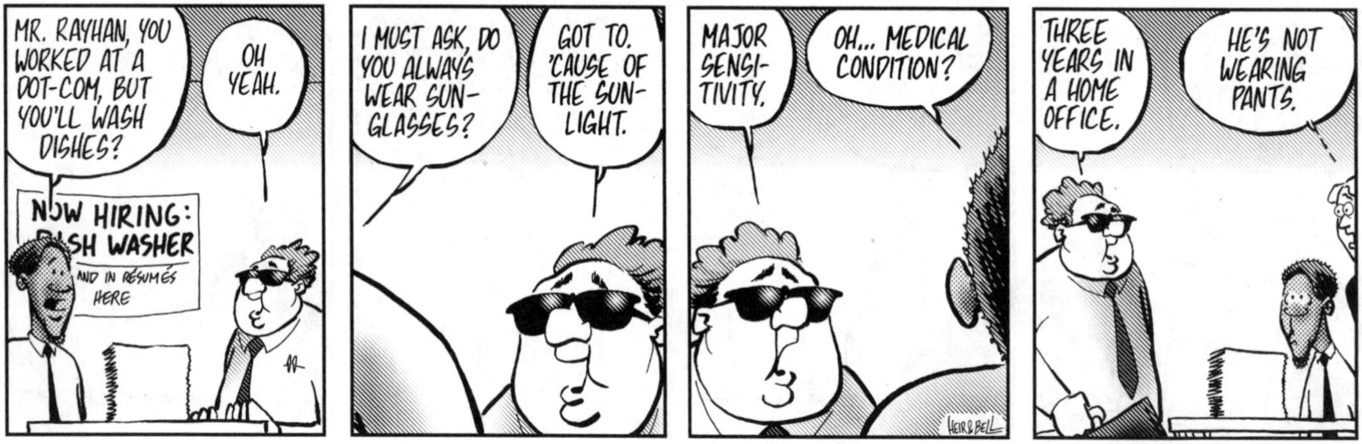
MR. RAYHAN, YOU WORKED AT A DOT-COM, BUT YOU'LL WASH DISHES?
OH YEAH.
NOW HIRING: DISH WASHER
AND IN RÉSUMÉS HERE
I MUST ASK, DO YOU ALWAYS WEAR SUNGLASSES?
GOT TO. 'CAUSE OF THE SUNLIGHT.
MAJOR SENSITIVITY.
OH... MEDICAL CONDITION?
HEIR & BELL
THREE YEARS IN A HOME OFFICE.
HE'S NOT WEARING PANTS.

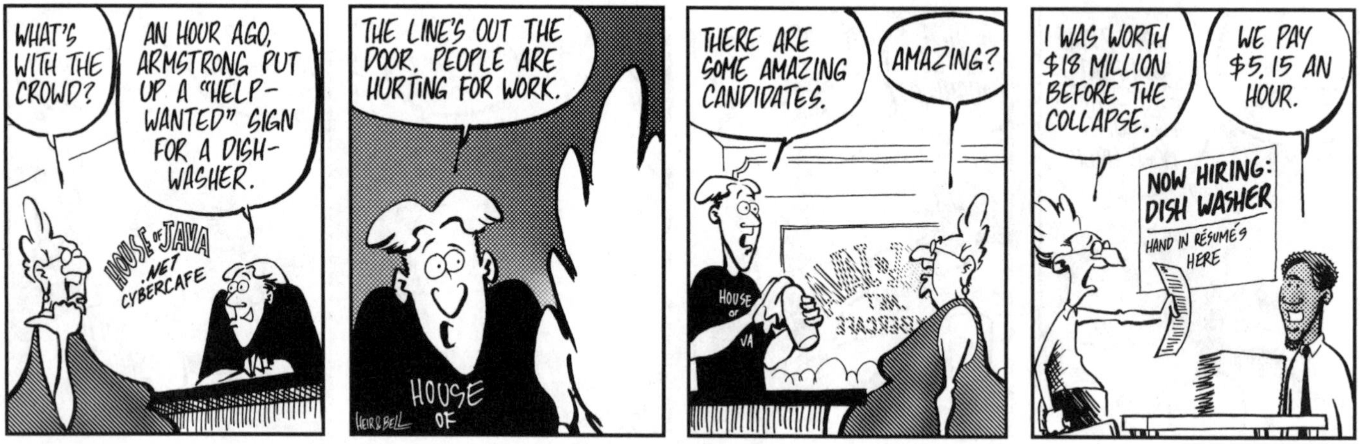
WHAT'S WITH THE CROWD?
AN HOUR AGO, ARMSTRONG PUT UP A "HELP-WANTED" SIGN FOR A DISHWASHER.
HOUSE OF JAVA .NET CYBERCAFE
THE LINE'S OUT THE DOOR. PEOPLE ARE HURTING FOR WORK.
HOUSE OF
HEIR & BELL
THERE ARE SOME AMAZING CANDIDATES.
AMAZING?
I WAS WORTH $18 MILLION BEFORE THE COLLAPSE.
WE PAY $5.15 AN HOUR.
NOW HIRING: DISH WASHER
HAND IN RÉSUMÉS HERE

I'M OF TWO MINDS ABOUT THIS WHOLE MICROSOFT ISSUE.
NELVO, WHAT HAVE YOU LEARNED ABOUT THE EARTHLING SPECIMENS?
WE HAVE WHAT APPEARS TO BE A MONOGAMOUS COUPLE.
LIKE MANY SUCH PAIRS ON EARTH, THEY ARE VIRTUALLY INSEPARABLE.
IT SEEMS THE BIGGER ONE DOES THE HEAVY LIFTING, WHILE THE SMALLER ONE IS THE MORE ADVANCED THINKER.
ON THE OTHER HAND, THE SMALLER ONE FLIPS OUT SOMETIMES AND JUST SHUTS DOWN. THEN THE BIG ONE GETS CONFUSED AND ANGRY.
WHAT ABOUT MATING?
SAY CHEESE
HARD TO SAY. HOWEVER, FROM WHAT WE'VE OBSERVED...
...WE BELIEVE THEY REFER TO MATING AS "TOMB RAIDER."
HIGH SCORE, BABY. HIGH SCORE.
INTERESTING. AND NOT THE SLIGHTEST BIT OF SHAME.

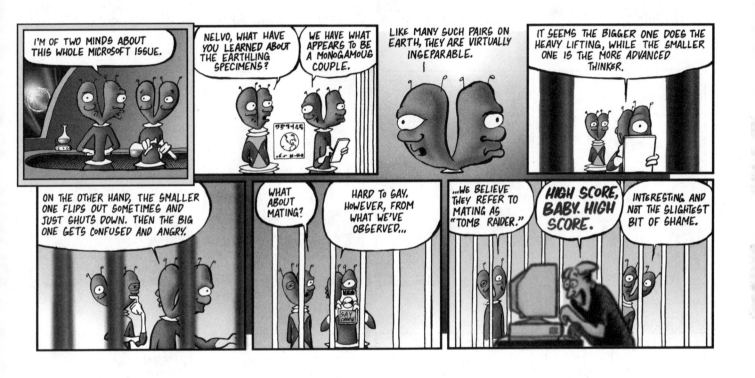

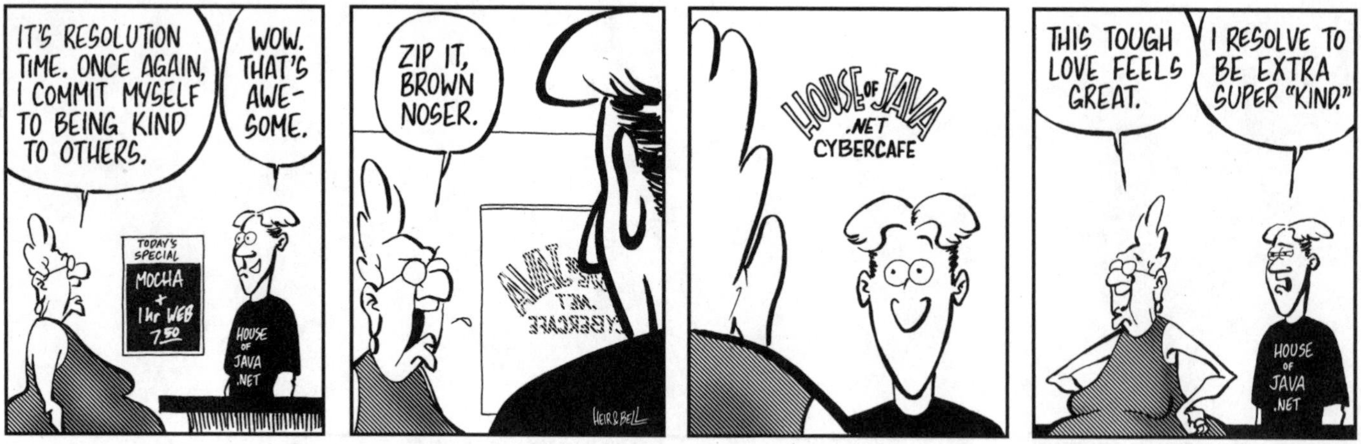

IT'S RESOLUTION TIME. ONCE AGAIN, I COMMIT MYSELF TO BEING KIND TO OTHERS.
WOW. THAT'S AWE-SOME.
TODAY'S SPECIAL MOCHA + 1 hr WEB 7.50
HOUSE OF JAVA .NET
ZIP IT, BROWN NOSER.
HOUSE OF JAVA .NET CYBERCAFE
THIS TOUGH LOVE FEELS GREAT.
I RESOLVE TO BE EXTRA SUPER "KIND."
HOUSE OF JAVA .NET
HEIR & BELL

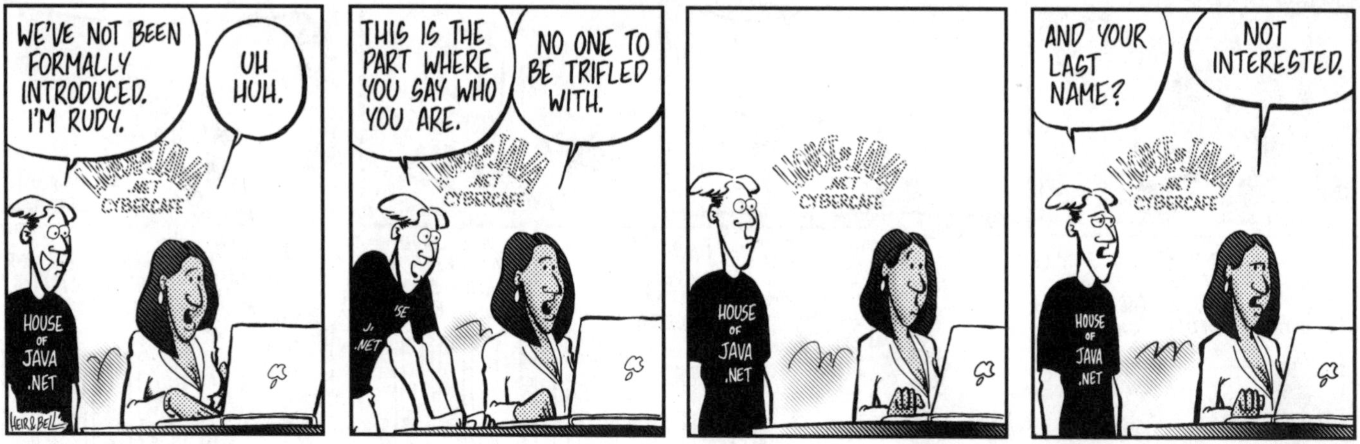

WE'VE NOT BEEN FORMALLY INTRODUCED. I'M RUDY.
UH HUH.
HOUSE OF JAVA .NET CYBERCAFE
HOUSE OF JAVA .NET
THIS IS THE PART WHERE YOU SAY WHO YOU ARE.
NO ONE TO BE TRIFLED WITH.
AND YOUR LAST NAME?
NOT INTERESTED.
HEIR & BELL

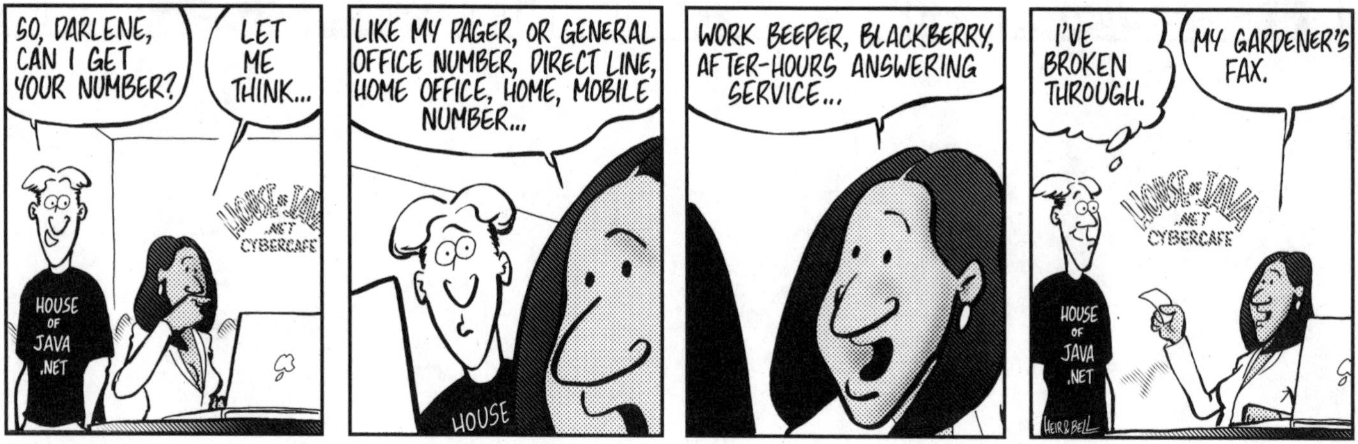

SO, DARLENE, CAN I GET YOUR NUMBER?
LET ME THINK...
HOUSE OF JAVA .NET CYBERCAFE
HOUSE OF JAVA .NET
LIKE MY PAGER, OR GENERAL OFFICE NUMBER, DIRECT LINE, HOME OFFICE, HOME, MOBILE NUMBER...
HOUSE
WORK BEEPER, BLACKBERRY, AFTER-HOURS ANSWERING SERVICE...
I'VE BROKEN THROUGH.
MY GARDENER'S FAX.
HEIR & BELL

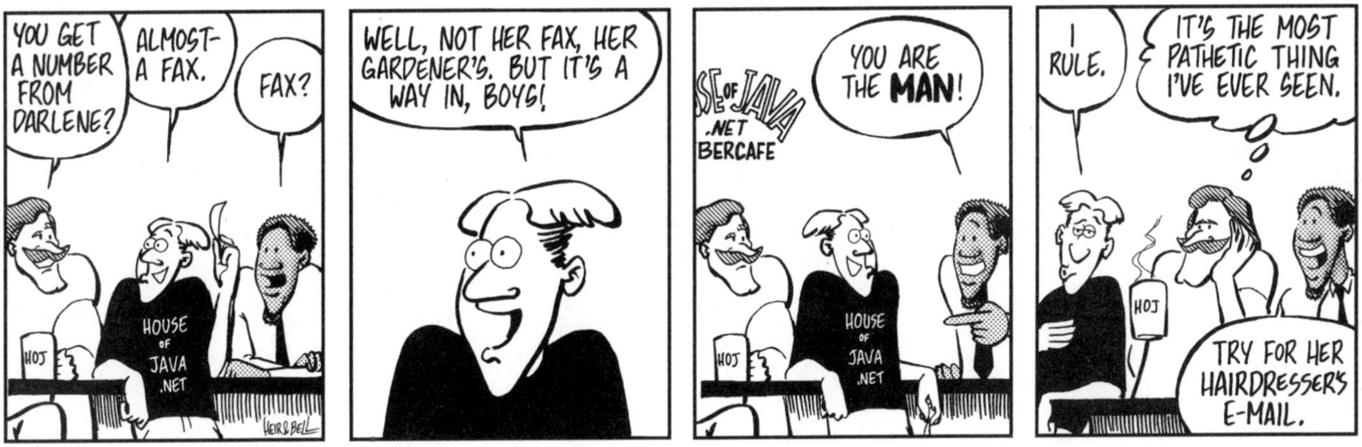
YOU GET A NUMBER FROM DARLENE?
ALMOST-A FAX.
FAX?
HOUSE OF JAVA .NET
HOJ
HEIR & BELL
WELL, NOT HER FAX, HER GARDENER'S. BUT IT'S A WAY IN, BOYS!
YOU ARE THE **MAN**!
SE OF JAVA .NET BERCAFE
HOUSE OF JAVA .NET
HOJ
I RULE.
IT'S THE MOST PATHETIC THING I'VE EVER SEEN.
HOJ
TRY FOR HER HAIRDRESSER'S E-MAIL.

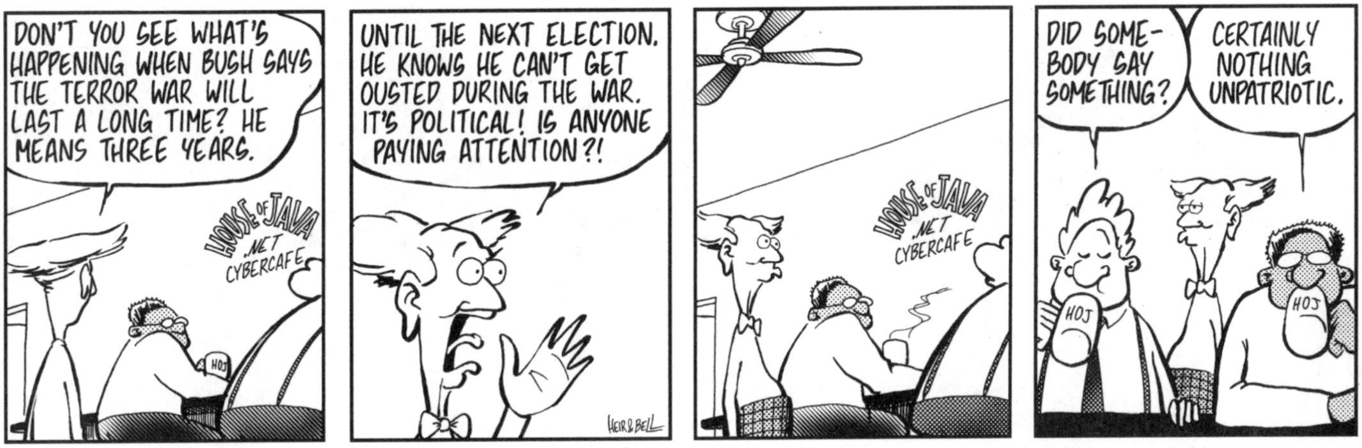
DON'T YOU SEE WHAT'S HAPPENING WHEN BUSH SAYS THE TERROR WAR WILL LAST A LONG TIME? HE MEANS THREE YEARS.
HOUSE OF JAVA .NET CYBERCAFE
HOJ
UNTIL THE NEXT ELECTION. HE KNOWS HE CAN'T GET OUSTED DURING THE WAR. IT'S POLITICAL! IS ANYONE PAYING ATTENTION?!
HEIR & BELL
HOUSE OF JAVA .NET CYBERCAFE
DID SOMEBODY SAY SOMETHING?
CERTAINLY NOTHING UNPATRIOTIC.
HOJ
HOJ

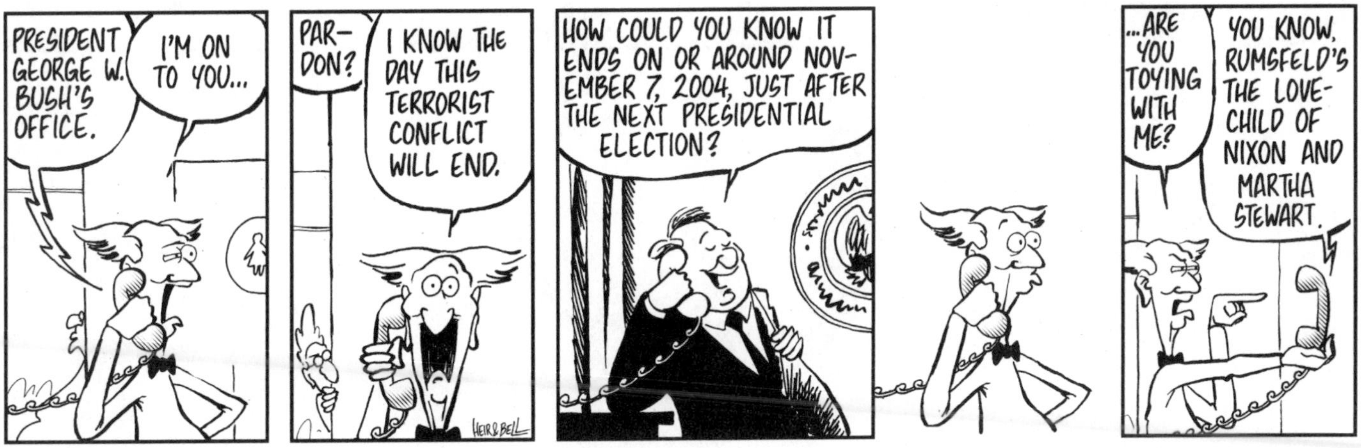
PRESIDENT GEORGE W. BUSH'S OFFICE.
I'M ON TO YOU...
PARDON?
I KNOW THE DAY THIS TERRORIST CONFLICT WILL END.
HEIR & BELL
HOW COULD YOU KNOW IT ENDS ON OR AROUND NOVEMBER 7, 2004, JUST AFTER THE NEXT PRESIDENTIAL ELECTION?
...ARE YOU TOYING WITH ME?
YOU KNOW, RUMSFELD'S THE LOVE-CHILD OF NIXON AND MARTHA STEWART.

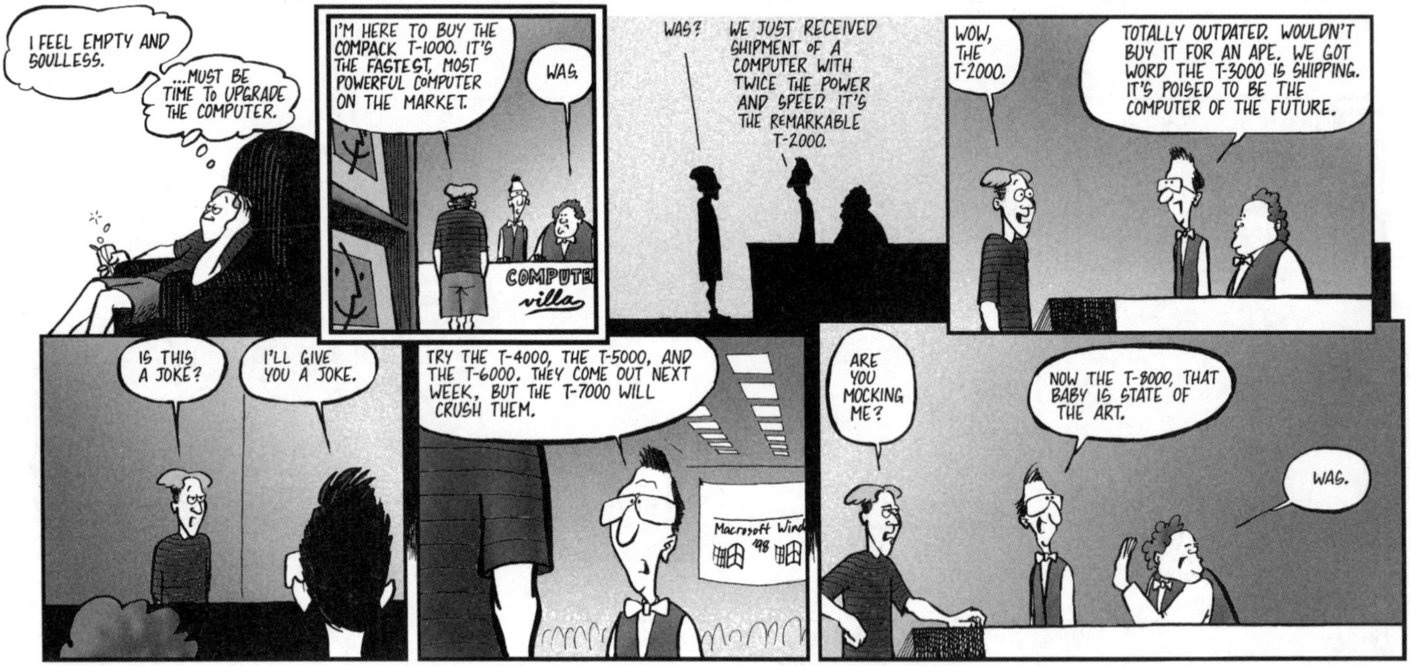

I FEEL EMPTY AND SOULLESS.
...MUST BE TIME TO UPGRADE THE COMPUTER.
I'M HERE TO BUY THE COMPACK T-1000. IT'S THE FASTEST, MOST POWERFUL COMPUTER ON THE MARKET.
WAS.
COMPUTER villa
WAS?
WE JUST RECEIVED SHIPMENT OF A COMPUTER WITH TWICE THE POWER AND SPEED. IT'S THE REMARKABLE T-2000.
WOW, THE T-2000.
TOTALLY OUTDATED. WOULDN'T BUY IT FOR AN APE. WE GOT WORD THE T-3000 IS SHIPPING. IT'S POISED TO BE THE COMPUTER OF THE FUTURE.
IS THIS A JOKE?
I'LL GIVE YOU A JOKE.
TRY THE T-4000, THE T-5000, AND THE T-6000. THEY COME OUT NEXT WEEK, BUT THE T-7000 WILL CRUSH THEM.
Macrosoft Wind '98
ARE YOU MOCKING ME?
NOW THE T-8000, THAT BABY IS STATE OF THE ART.
WAS.

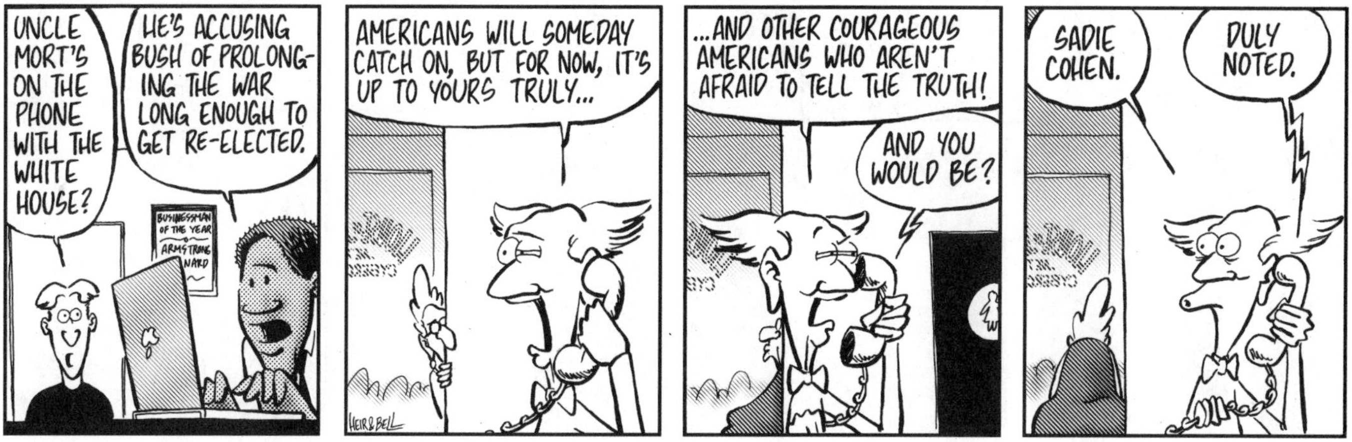
UNCLE MORT'S ON THE PHONE WITH THE WHITE HOUSE?
HE'S ACCUSING BUSH OF PROLONGING THE WAR LONG ENOUGH TO GET RE-ELECTED.
AMERICANS WILL SOMEDAY CATCH ON, BUT FOR NOW, IT'S UP TO YOURS TRULY...
...AND OTHER COURAGEOUS AMERICANS WHO AREN'T AFRAID TO TELL THE TRUTH!
AND YOU WOULD BE?
SADIE COHEN.
DULY NOTED.
HEIR & BELL

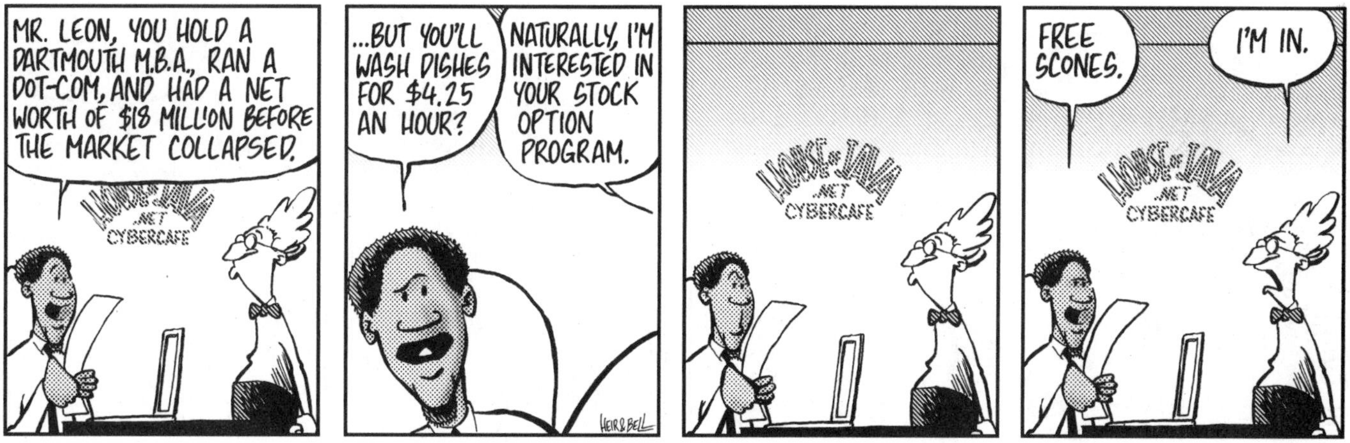
MR. LEON, YOU HOLD A DARTMOUTH M.B.A., RAN A DOT-COM, AND HAD A NET WORTH OF $18 MILLION BEFORE THE MARKET COLLAPSED.
HOUSE OF JAVA .NET CYBERCAFE
...BUT YOU'LL WASH DISHES FOR $4.25 AN HOUR?
NATURALLY, I'M INTERESTED IN YOUR STOCK OPTION PROGRAM.
HEIR & BELL
FREE SCONES.
I'M IN.

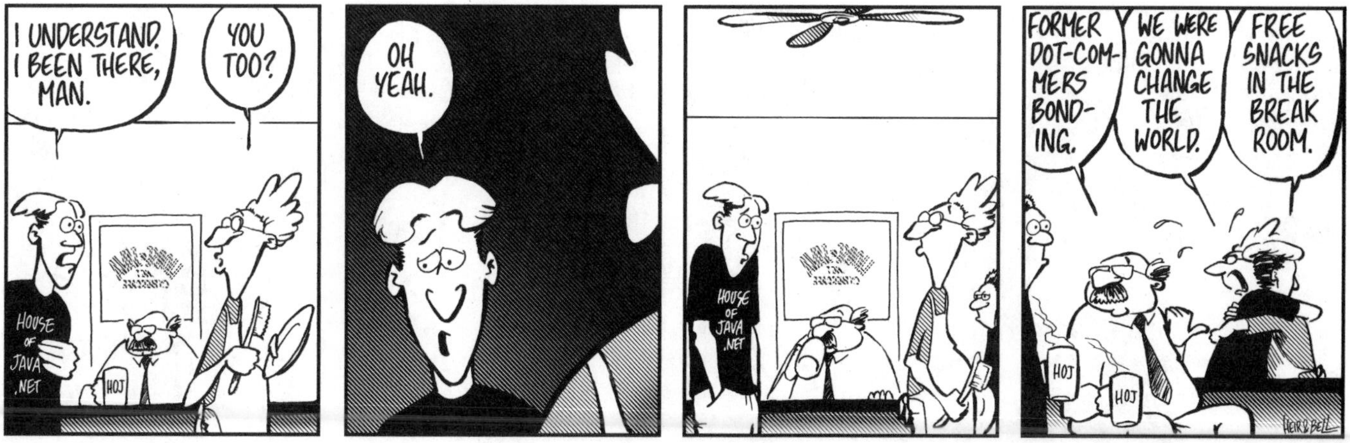
I UNDERSTAND. I BEEN THERE, MAN.
YOU TOO?
HOUSE OF JAVA .NET
HOJ
OH YEAH.
FORMER DOT-COMMERS BONDING.
WE WERE GONNA CHANGE THE WORLD.
FREE SNACKS IN THE BREAK ROOM.
HEIR & BELL

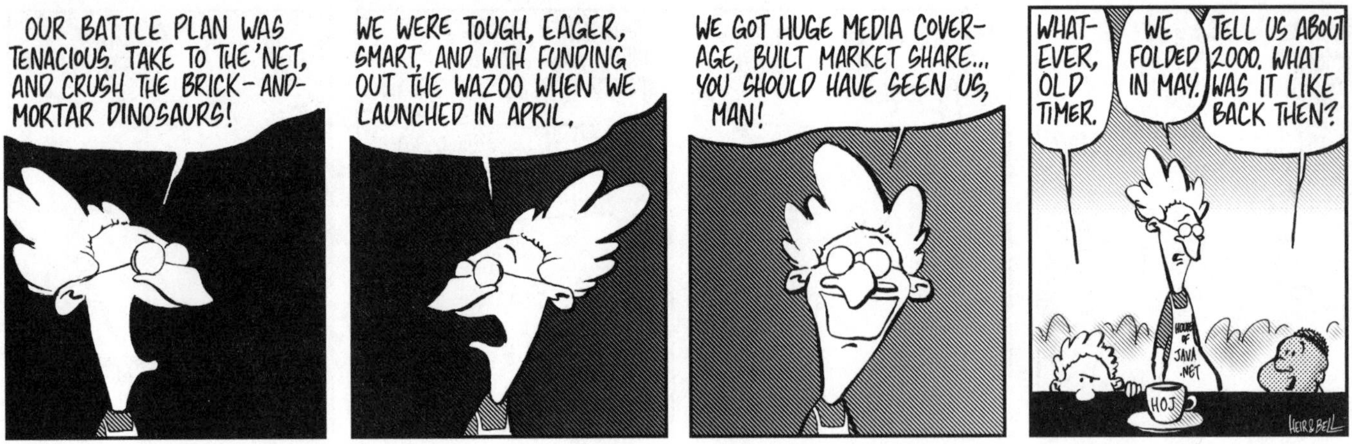
OUR BATTLE PLAN WAS TENACIOUS. TAKE TO THE 'NET, AND CRUSH THE BRICK-AND-MORTAR DINOSAURS!
WE WERE TOUGH, EAGER, SMART, AND WITH FUNDING OUT THE WAZOO WHEN WE LAUNCHED IN APRIL.
WE GOT HUGE MEDIA COVERAGE, BUILT MARKET SHARE... YOU SHOULD HAVE SEEN US, MAN!
WHATEVER, OLD TIMER.
WE FOLDED IN MAY.
TELL US ABOUT 2000. WHAT WAS IT LIKE BACK THEN?

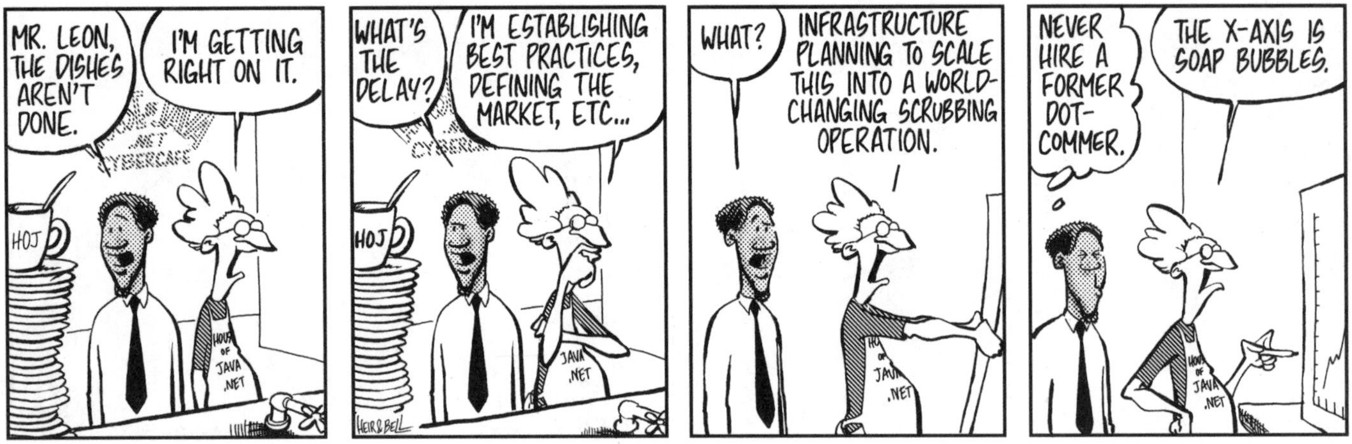
MR. LEON, THE DISHES AREN'T DONE.
I'M GETTING RIGHT ON IT.
WHAT'S THE DELAY?
I'M ESTABLISHING BEST PRACTICES, DEFINING THE MARKET, ETC...
WHAT?
INFRASTRUCTURE PLANNING TO SCALE THIS INTO A WORLD-CHANGING SCRUBBING OPERATION.
NEVER HIRE A FORMER DOT-COMMER.
THE X-AXIS IS SOAP BUBBLES.

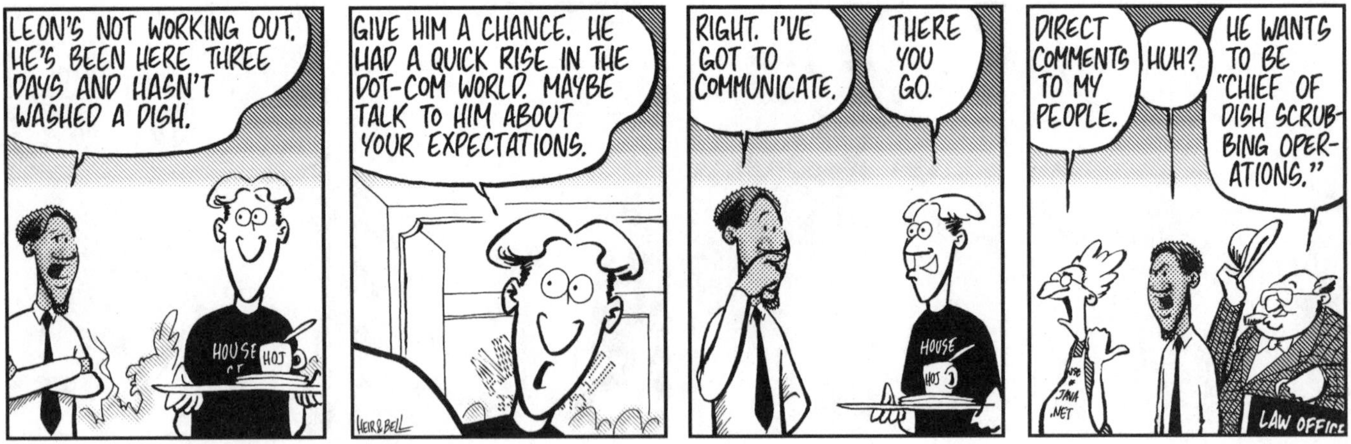
LEON'S NOT WORKING OUT. HE'S BEEN HERE THREE DAYS AND HASN'T WASHED A DISH.
GIVE HIM A CHANCE. HE HAD A QUICK RISE IN THE DOT-COM WORLD. MAYBE TALK TO HIM ABOUT YOUR EXPECTATIONS.
RIGHT. I'VE GOT TO COMMUNICATE.
THERE YOU GO.
DIRECT COMMENTS TO MY PEOPLE.
HUH?
HE WANTS TO BE "CHIEF OF DISH SCRUBBING OPERATIONS."

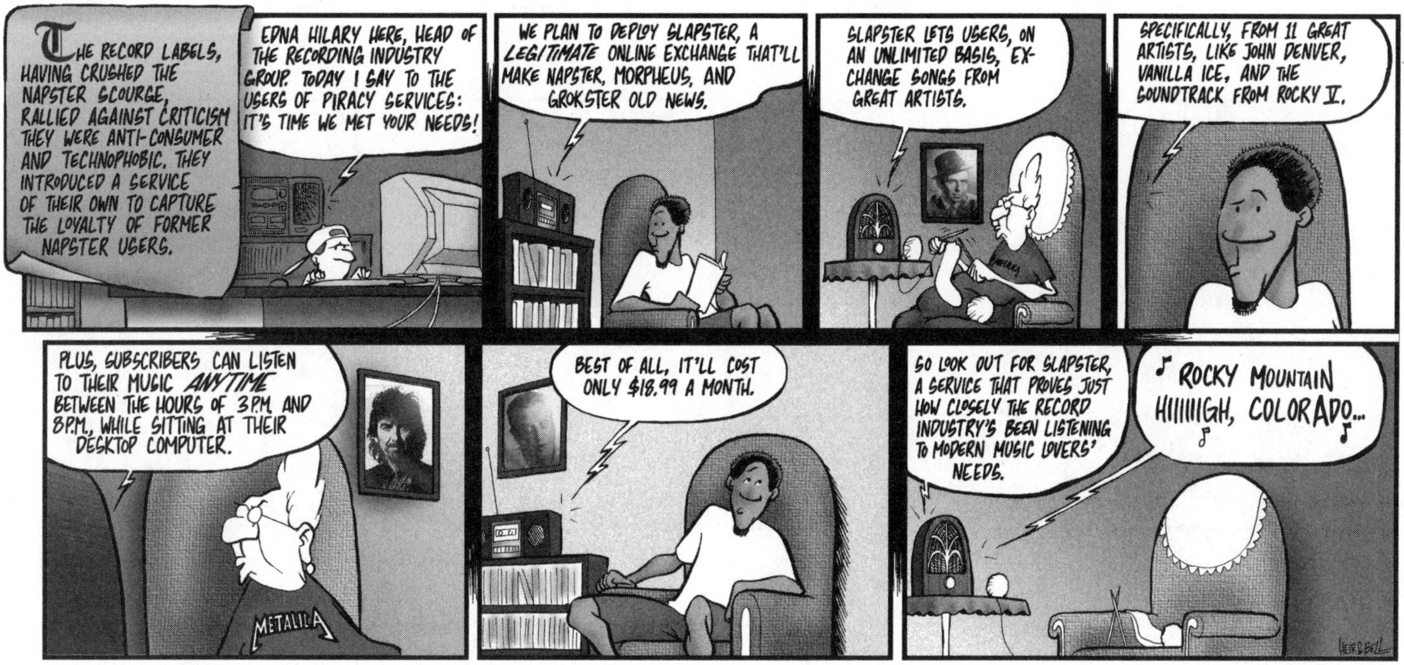
THE RECORD LABELS, HAVING CRUSHED THE NAPSTER SCOURGE, RALLIED AGAINST CRITICISM THEY WERE ANTI-CONSUMER AND TECHNOPHOBIC. THEY INTRODUCED A SERVICE OF THEIR OWN TO CAPTURE THE LOYALTY OF FORMER NAPSTER USERS.
EDNA HILARY HERE, HEAD OF THE RECORDING INDUSTRY GROUP. TODAY I SAY TO THE USERS OF PIRACY SERVICES: IT'S TIME WE MET YOUR NEEDS!
WE PLAN TO DEPLOY SLAPSTER, A LEGITIMATE ONLINE EXCHANGE THAT'LL MAKE NAPSTER, MORPHEUS, AND GROKSTER OLD NEWS.
SLAPSTER LETS USERS, ON AN UNLIMITED BASIS, EXCHANGE SONGS FROM GREAT ARTISTS.
SPECIFICALLY, FROM 11 GREAT ARTISTS, LIKE JOHN DENVER, VANILLA ICE, AND THE SOUNDTRACK FROM ROCKY V.
PLUS, SUBSCRIBERS CAN LISTEN TO THEIR MUSIC ANYTIME BETWEEN THE HOURS OF 3P.M. AND 8P.M., WHILE SITTING AT THEIR DESKTOP COMPUTER.
METALLICA
BEST OF ALL, IT'LL COST ONLY $18.99 A MONTH.
SO LOOK OUT FOR SLAPSTER, A SERVICE THAT PROVES JUST HOW CLOSELY THE RECORD INDUSTRY'S BEEN LISTENING TO MODERN MUSIC LOVERS' NEEDS.
ROCKY MOUNTAIN HIIIIIGH, COLORADO...

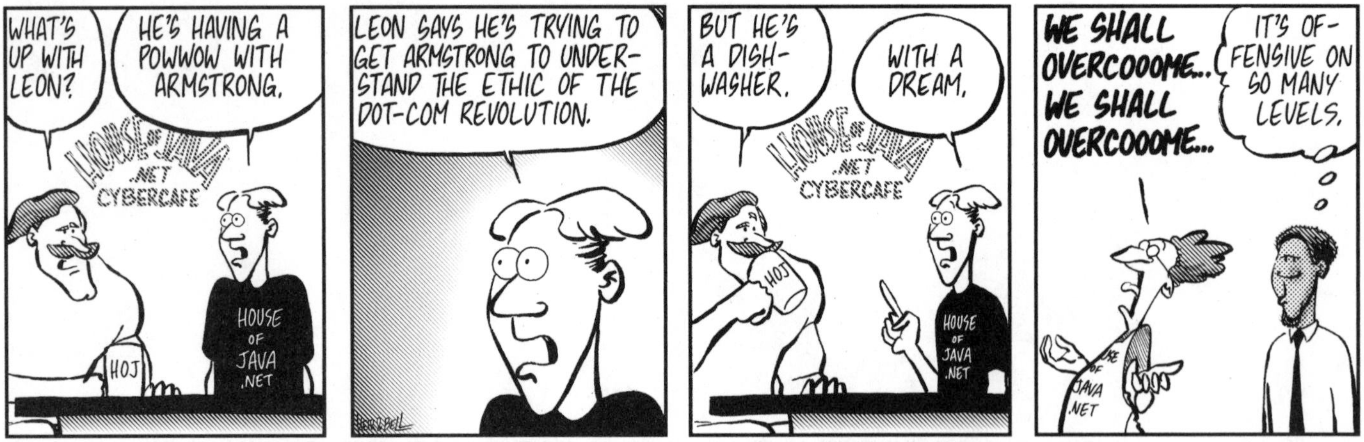

WHAT'S UP WITH LEON?
HE'S HAVING A POWWOW WITH ARMSTRONG.
HOUSE OF JAVA .NET CYBERCAFE
HOJ
HOUSE OF JAVA .NET
LEON SAYS HE'S TRYING TO GET ARMSTRONG TO UNDERSTAND THE ETHIC OF THE DOT-COM REVOLUTION.
BUT HE'S A DISHWASHER.
WITH A DREAM.
HOUSE OF JAVA .NET CYBERCAFE
HOJ
HOUSE OF JAVA .NET
WE SHALL OVERCOOOME... WE SHALL OVERCOOOME...
IT'S OFFENSIVE ON SO MANY LEVELS.

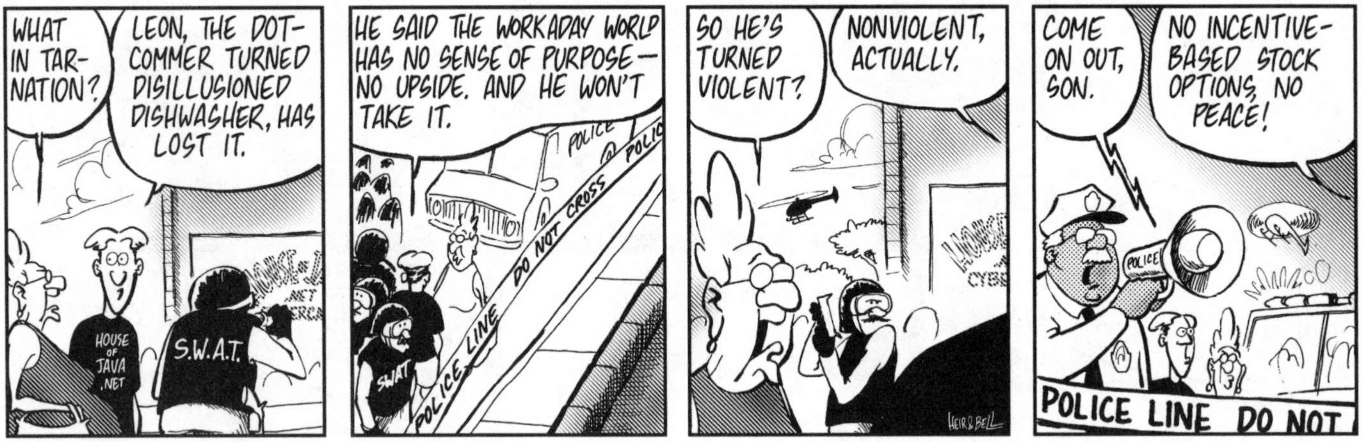

WHAT IN TARNATION?
LEON, THE DOT-COMMER TURNED DISILLUSIONED DISHWASHER, HAS LOST IT.
HOUSE OF JAVA .NET
S.W.A.T.
HE SAID THE WORKADAY WORLD HAS NO SENSE OF PURPOSE— NO UPSIDE. AND HE WON'T TAKE IT.
POLICE
DO NOT CROSS
POLICE LINE
SWAT
SO HE'S TURNED VIOLENT?
NONVIOLENT, ACTUALLY.
COME ON OUT, SON.
NO INCENTIVE-BASED STOCK OPTIONS, NO PEACE!
POLICE
POLICE LINE DO NOT

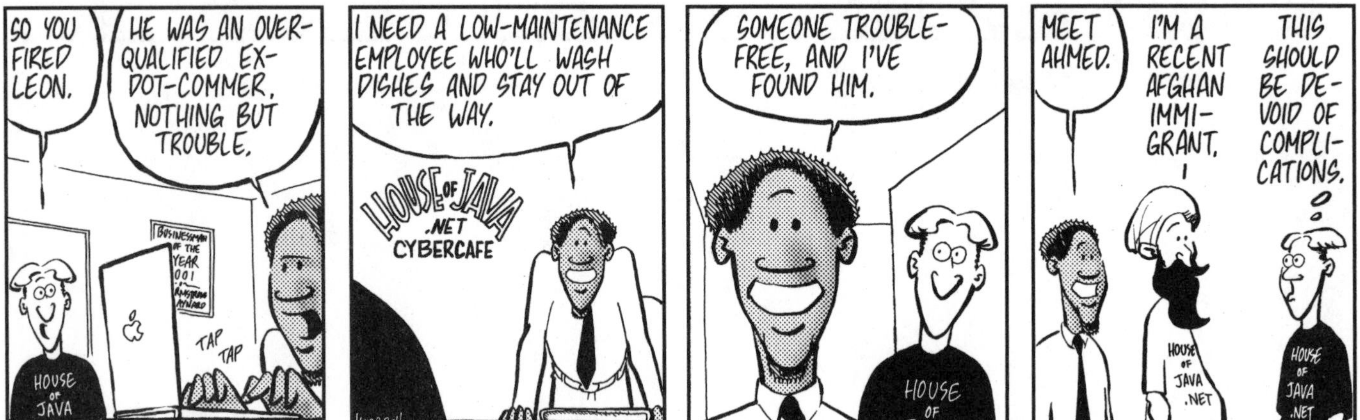

SO YOU FIRED LEON.
HE WAS AN OVERQUALIFIED EX-DOT-COMMER, NOTHING BUT TROUBLE.
HOUSE OF JAVA
TAP TAP
I NEED A LOW-MAINTENANCE EMPLOYEE WHO'LL WASH DISHES AND STAY OUT OF THE WAY.
HOUSE OF JAVA .NET CYBERCAFE
SOMEONE TROUBLE-FREE, AND I'VE FOUND HIM.
HOUSE OF
MEET AHMED.
I'M A RECENT AFGHAN IMMIGRANT.
THIS SHOULD BE DEVOID OF COMPLICATIONS.
HOUSE OF JAVA .NET
HOUSE OF JAVA .NET

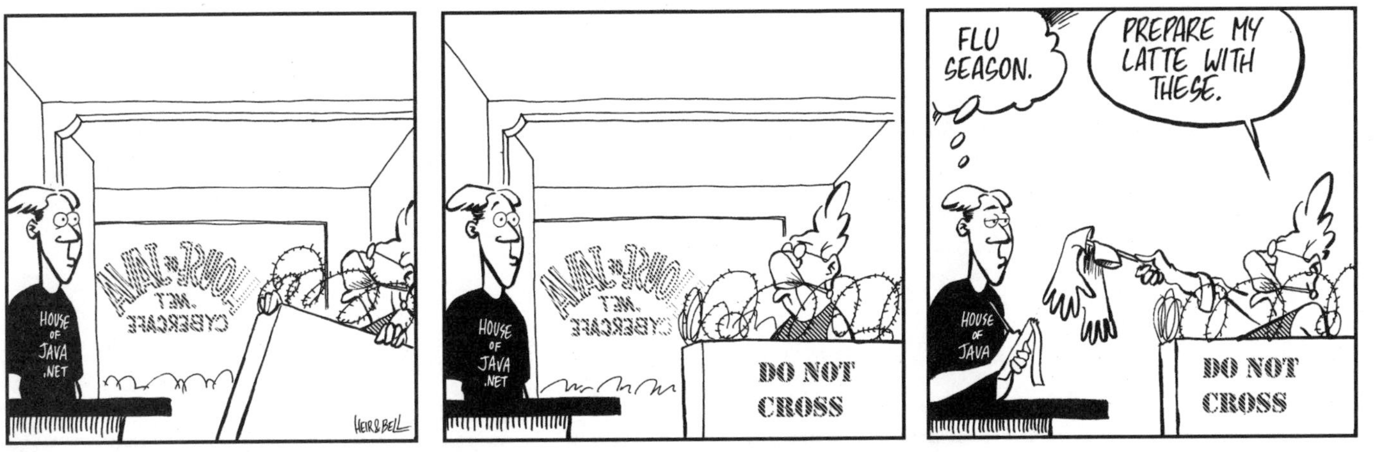
HOUSE OF JAVA .NET
HOUSE OF JAVA .NET CYBERCAFE
HEIR & BELL
DO NOT CROSS
FLU SEASON.
PREPARE MY LATTE WITH THESE.
HOUSE OF JAVA

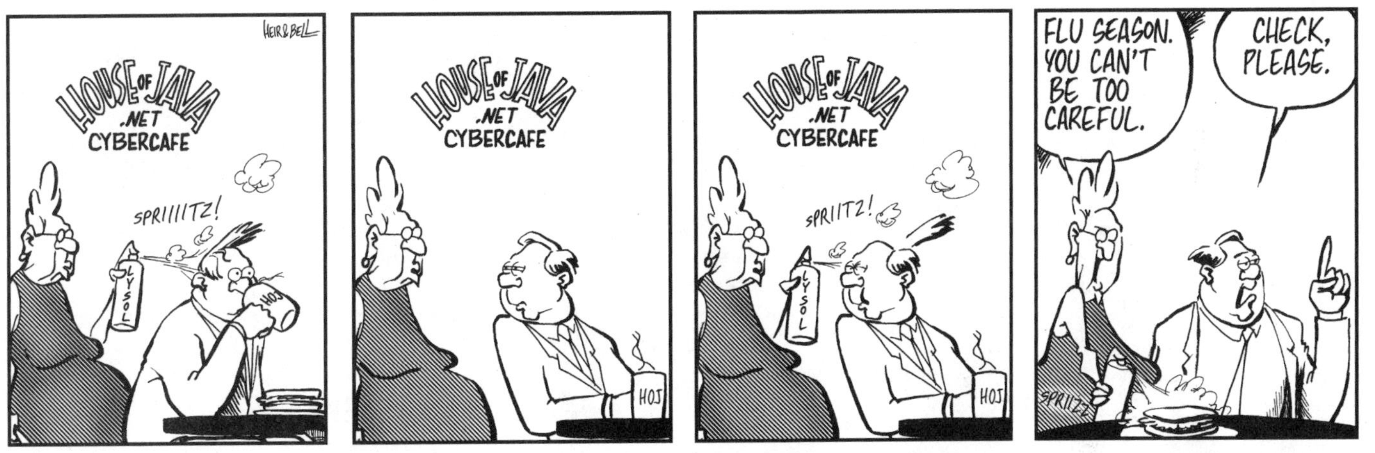
HEIR & BELL
HOUSE OF JAVA .NET CYBERCAFE
SPRIIIIITZ!
LYSOL
HOJ
SPRIITZ!
FLU SEASON. YOU CAN'T BE TOO CAREFUL.
CHECK, PLEASE.
SPRIIZZ

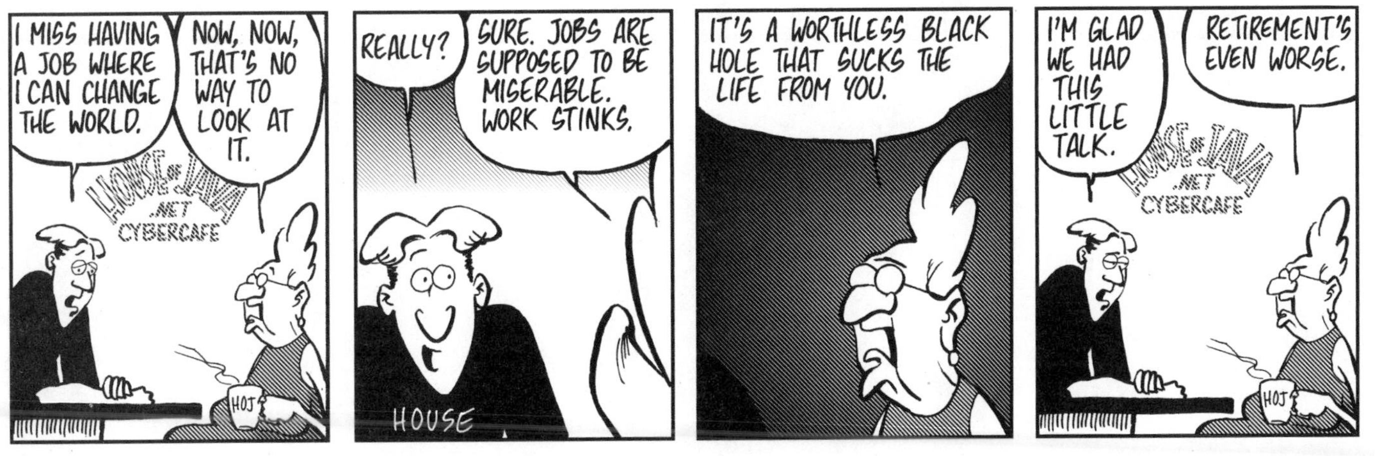
I MISS HAVING A JOB WHERE I CAN CHANGE THE WORLD.
NOW, NOW, THAT'S NO WAY TO LOOK AT IT.
HOUSE OF JAVA .NET CYBERCAFE
HOJ
REALLY?
SURE. JOBS ARE SUPPOSED TO BE MISERABLE. WORK STINKS.
HOUSE
IT'S A WORTHLESS BLACK HOLE THAT SUCKS THE LIFE FROM YOU.
I'M GLAD WE HAD THIS LITTLE TALK.
RETIREMENT'S EVEN WORSE.

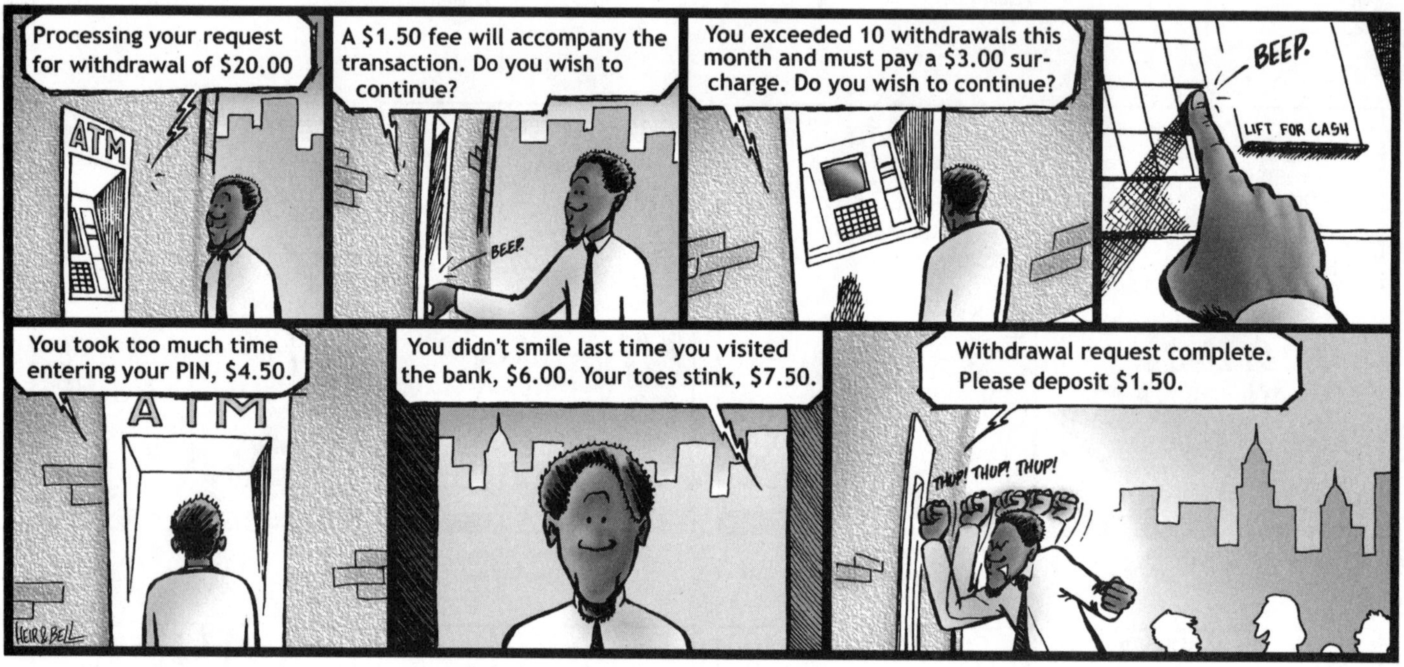
Processing your request for withdrawal of $20.00
A $1.50 fee will accompany the transaction. Do you wish to continue?
BEEP
You exceeded 10 withdrawals this month and must pay a $3.00 surcharge. Do you wish to continue?
BEEP.
LIFT FOR CASH
You took too much time entering your PIN, $4.50.
ATM
You didn't smile last time you visited the bank, $6.00. Your toes stink, $7.50.
Withdrawal request complete. Please deposit $1.50.
THUP! THUP! THUP!
HEIR & BELL

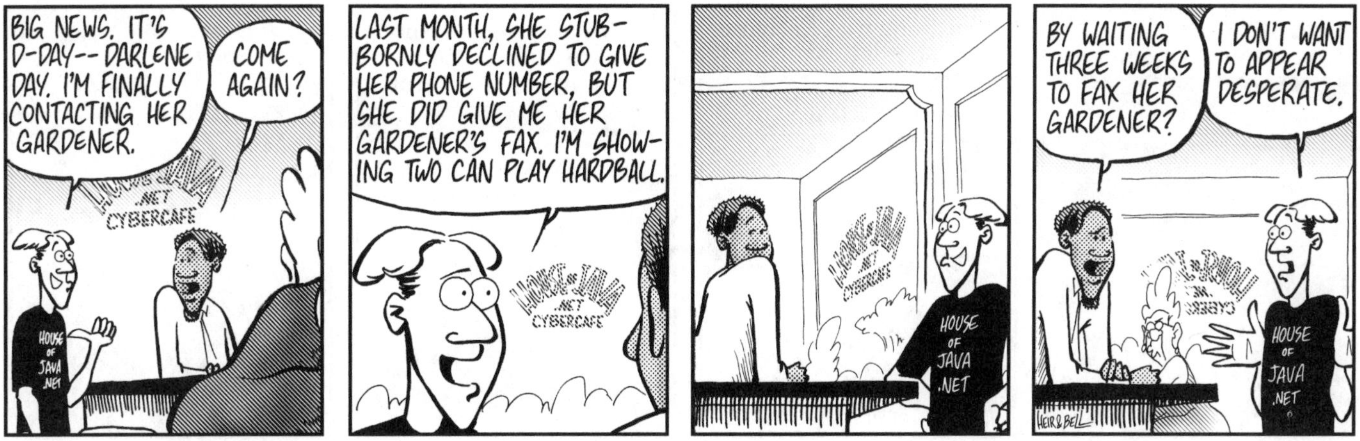
BIG NEWS. IT'S D-DAY--DARLENE DAY. I'M FINALLY CONTACTING HER GARDENER.
COME AGAIN?
LAST MONTH, SHE STUBBORNLY DECLINED TO GIVE HER PHONE NUMBER, BUT SHE DID GIVE ME HER GARDENER'S FAX. I'M SHOWING TWO CAN PLAY HARDBALL.
BY WAITING THREE WEEKS TO FAX HER GARDENER?
I DON'T WANT TO APPEAR DESPERATE.

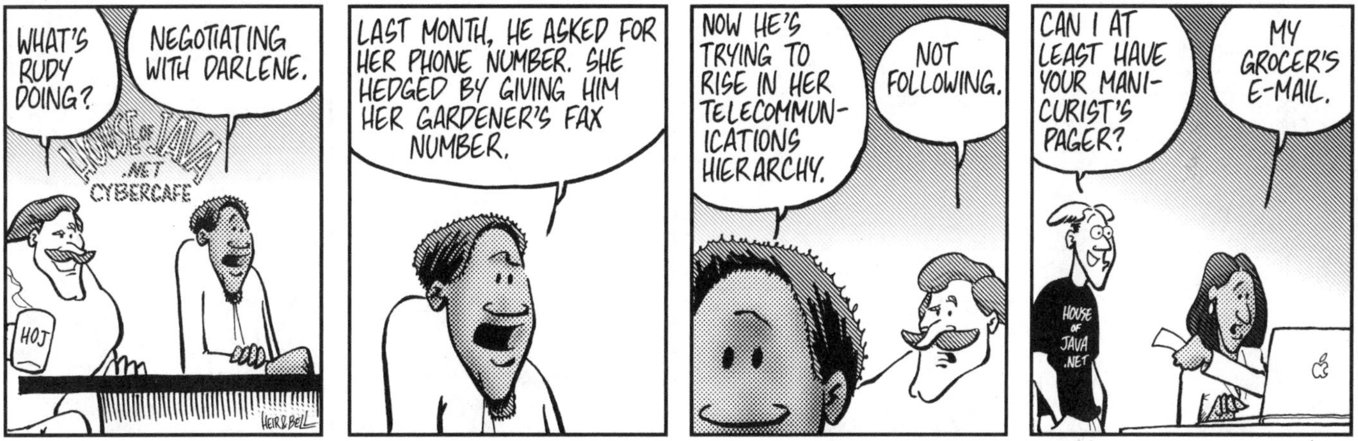
WHAT'S RUDY DOING?
NEGOTIATING WITH DARLENE.
LAST MONTH, HE ASKED FOR HER PHONE NUMBER. SHE HEDGED BY GIVING HIM HER GARDENER'S FAX NUMBER.
NOW HE'S TRYING TO RISE IN HER TELECOMMUNICATIONS HIERARCHY.
NOT FOLLOWING.
CAN I AT LEAST HAVE YOUR MANICURIST'S PAGER?
MY GROCER'S E-MAIL.

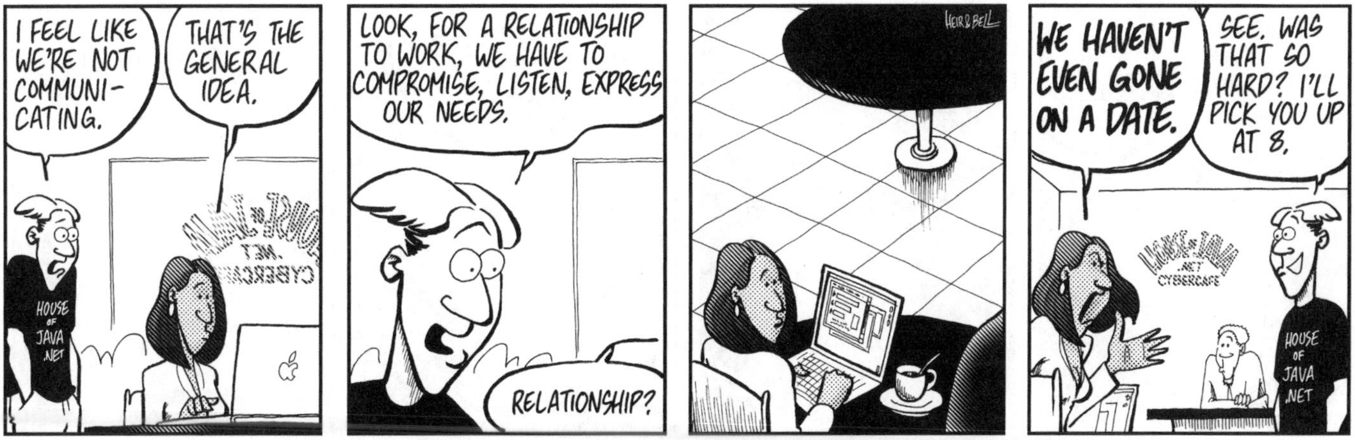
I FEEL LIKE WE'RE NOT COMMUNICATING.
THAT'S THE GENERAL IDEA.
LOOK, FOR A RELATIONSHIP TO WORK, WE HAVE TO COMPROMISE, LISTEN, EXPRESS OUR NEEDS.
RELATIONSHIP?
WE HAVEN'T EVEN GONE ON A DATE.
SEE. WAS THAT SO HARD? I'LL PICK YOU UP AT 8.

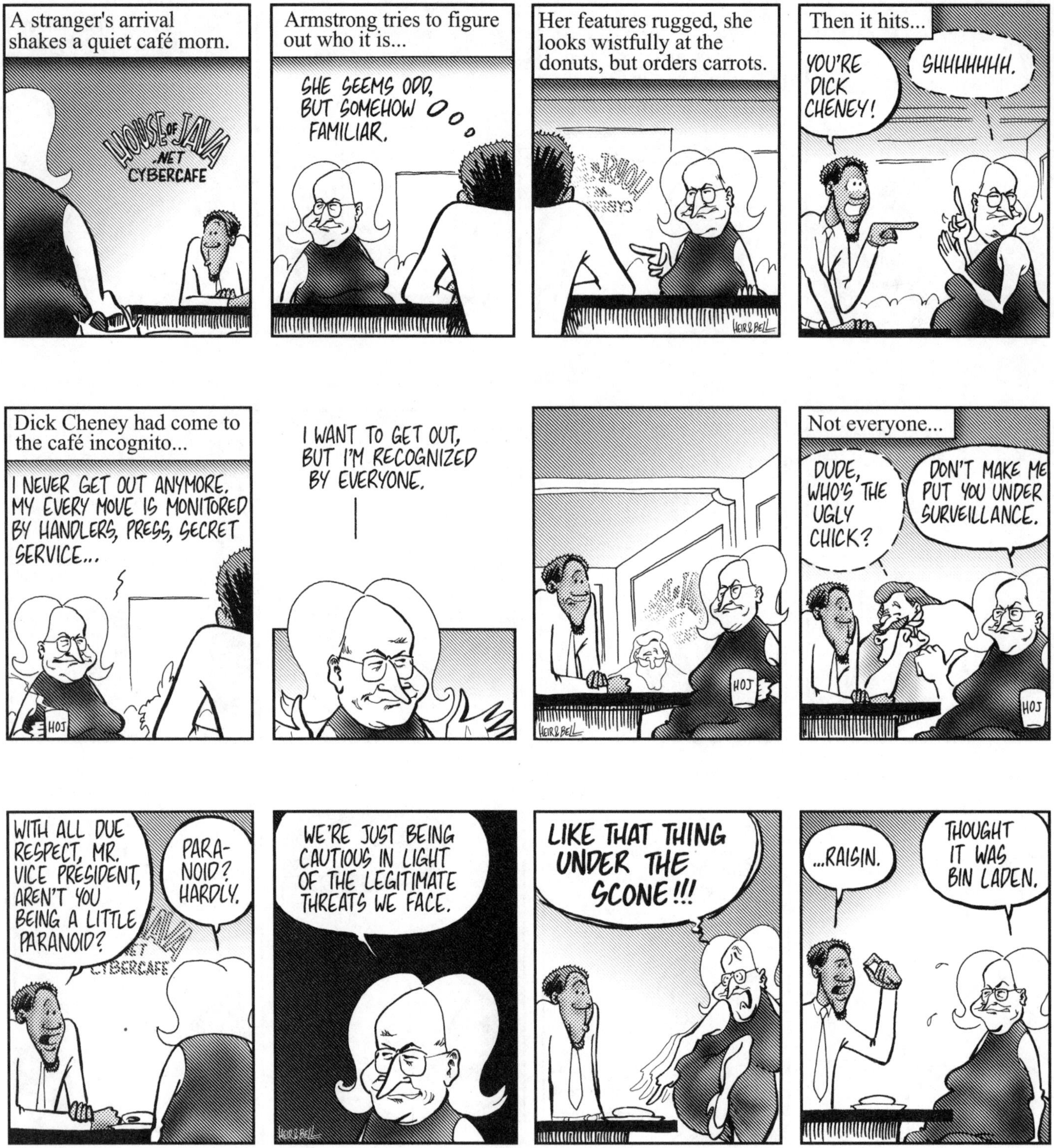
A stranger's arrival shakes a quiet café morn.
HOUSE OF JAVA .NET CYBERCAFE
Armstrong tries to figure out who it is...
SHE SEEMS ODD, BUT SOMEHOW FAMILIAR.
Her features rugged, she looks wistfully at the donuts, but orders carrots.
Then it hits...
YOU'RE DICK CHENEY!
SHHHHHHH.
HEIR & BELL
Dick Cheney had come to the café incognito...
I NEVER GET OUT ANYMORE. MY EVERY MOVE IS MONITORED BY HANDLERS, PRESS, SECRET SERVICE...
HOJ
I WANT TO GET OUT, BUT I'M RECOGNIZED BY EVERYONE.
HOJ
HEIR & BELL
Not everyone...
DUDE, WHO'S THE UGLY CHICK?
DON'T MAKE ME PUT YOU UNDER SURVEILLANCE.
HOJ
WITH ALL DUE RESPECT, MR. VICE PRESIDENT, AREN'T YOU BEING A LITTLE PARANOID?
PARA-NOID? HARDLY.
CYBERCAFE
WE'RE JUST BEING CAUTIOUS IN LIGHT OF THE LEGITIMATE THREATS WE FACE.
HEIR & BELL
LIKE THAT THING UNDER THE SCONE!!!
...RAISIN.
THOUGHT IT WAS BIN LADEN.

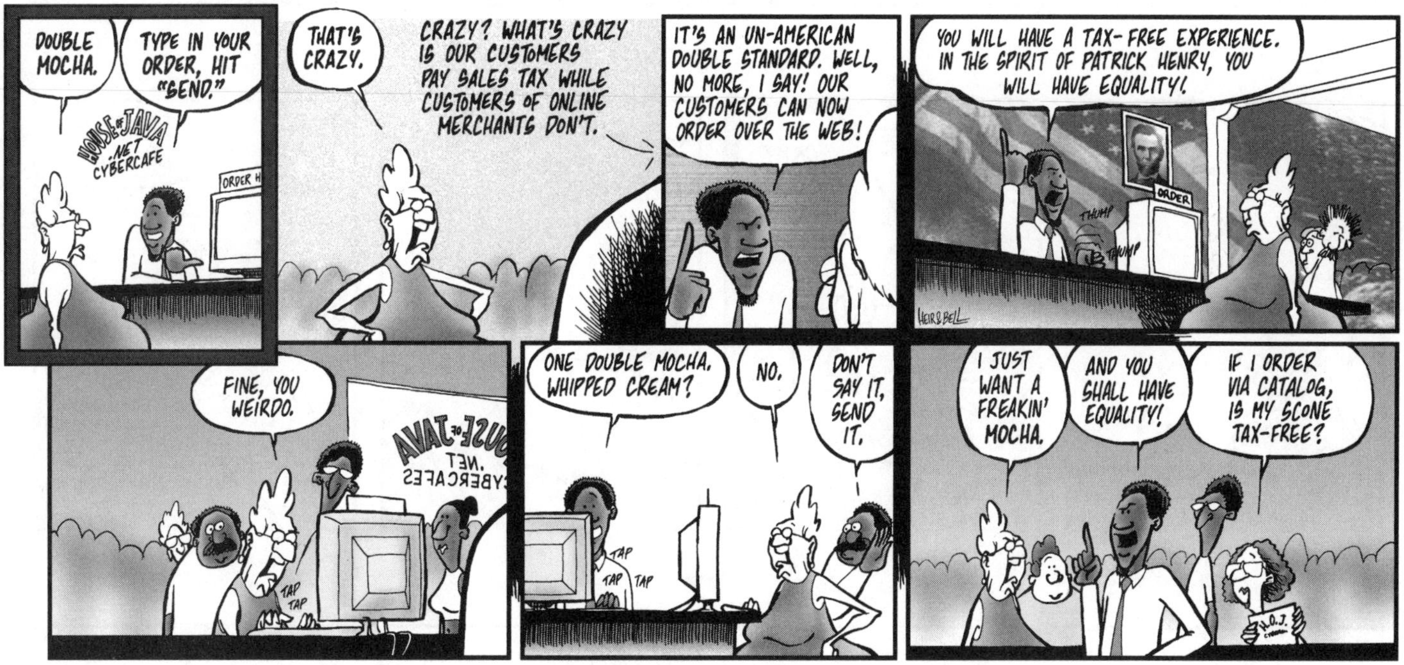
DOUBLE MOCHA.
TYPE IN YOUR ORDER, HIT "SEND."
HOUSE of JAVA .NET CYBERCAFE
THAT'S CRAZY.
CRAZY? WHAT'S CRAZY IS OUR CUSTOMERS PAY SALES TAX WHILE CUSTOMERS OF ONLINE MERCHANTS DON'T.
IT'S AN UN-AMERICAN DOUBLE STANDARD. WELL, NO MORE, I SAY! OUR CUSTOMERS CAN NOW ORDER OVER THE WEB!
YOU WILL HAVE A TAX-FREE EXPERIENCE. IN THE SPIRIT OF PATRICK HENRY, YOU WILL HAVE EQUALITY!
ORDER
THUMP
THUMP
HEIR & BELL
FINE, YOU WEIRDO.
TAP TAP
ONE DOUBLE MOCHA. WHIPPED CREAM?
NO.
DON'T SAY IT, SEND IT.
TAP
TAP TAP
I JUST WANT A FREAKIN' MOCHA.
AND YOU SHALL HAVE EQUALITY!
IF I ORDER VIA CATALOG, IS MY SCONE TAX-FREE?

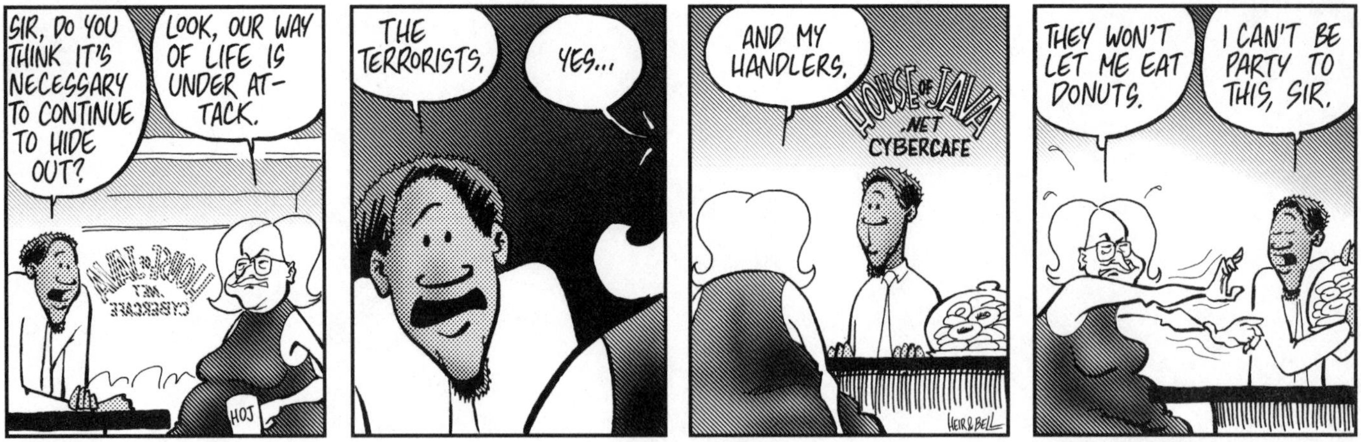
SIR, DO YOU THINK IT'S NECESSARY TO CONTINUE TO HIDE OUT?
LOOK, OUR WAY OF LIFE IS UNDER AT-TACK.
THE TERRORISTS.
YES...
AND MY HANDLERS.
HOUSE OF JAVA .NET CYBERCAFE
THEY WON'T LET ME EAT DONUTS.
I CAN'T BE PARTY TO THIS, SIR.
HEIR & BELL

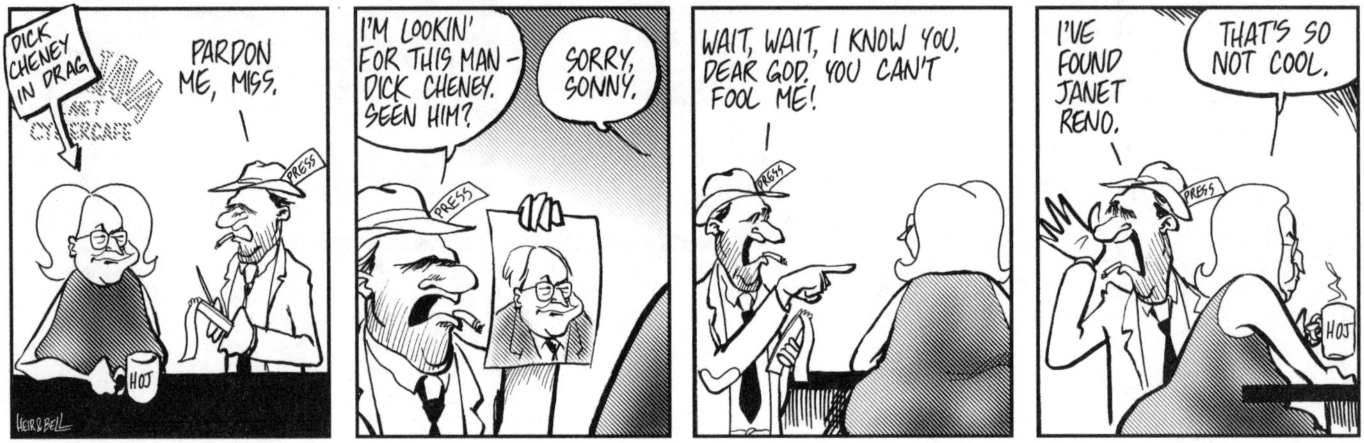
DICK CHENEY IN DRAG
PARDON ME, MISS.
PRESS
HOJ
I'M LOOKIN' FOR THIS MAN - DICK CHENEY. SEEN HIM?
SORRY, SONNY.
WAIT, WAIT, I KNOW YOU. DEAR GOD. YOU CAN'T FOOL ME!
I'VE FOUND JANET RENO.
THAT'S SO NOT COOL.
HEIR & BELL

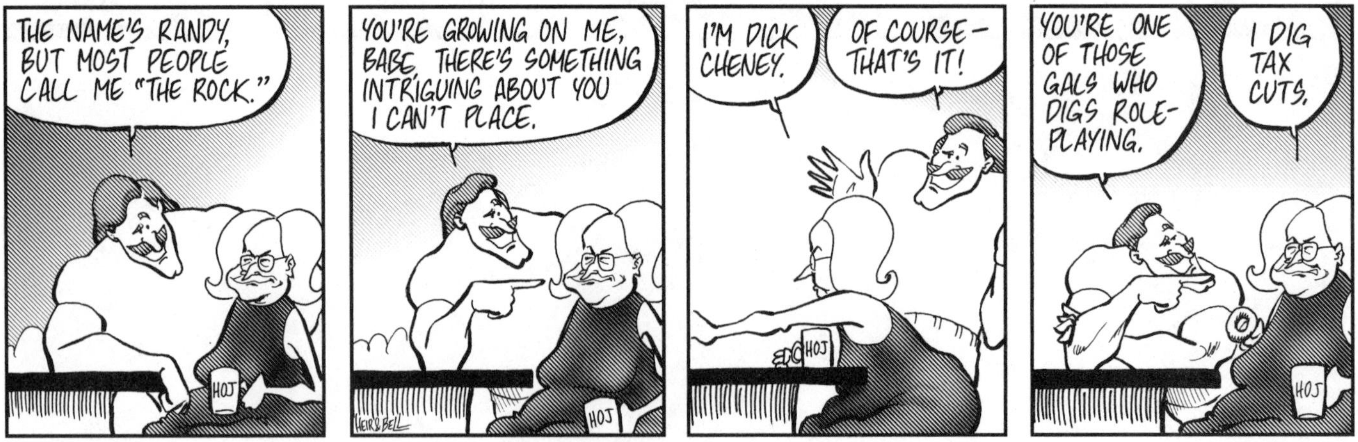
THE NAME'S RANDY, BUT MOST PEOPLE CALL ME "THE ROCK."
YOU'RE GROWING ON ME, BABE. THERE'S SOMETHING INTRIGUING ABOUT YOU I CAN'T PLACE.
I'M DICK CHENEY.
OF COURSE - THAT'S IT!
YOU'RE ONE OF THOSE GALS WHO DIGS ROLE-PLAYING.
I DIG TAX CUTS.
HOJ
HEIR & BELL

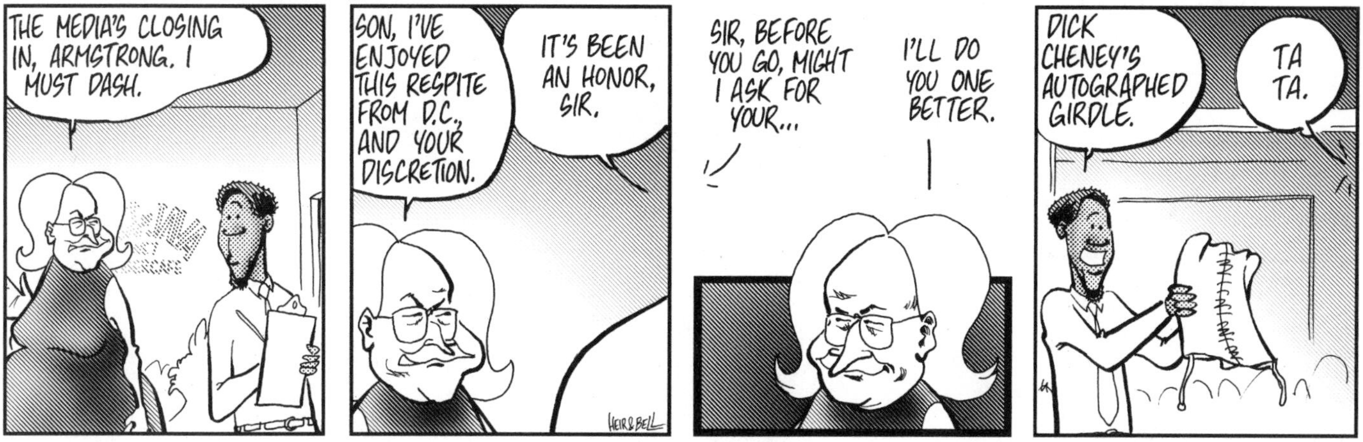
THE MEDIA'S CLOSING IN, ARMSTRONG. I MUST DASH.
SON, I'VE ENJOYED THIS RESPITE FROM D.C., AND YOUR DISCRETION.
IT'S BEEN AN HONOR, SIR.
SIR, BEFORE YOU GO, MIGHT I ASK FOR YOUR...
I'LL DO YOU ONE BETTER.
DICK CHENEY'S AUTOGRAPHED GIRDLE.
TA TA.
HEIR&BELL

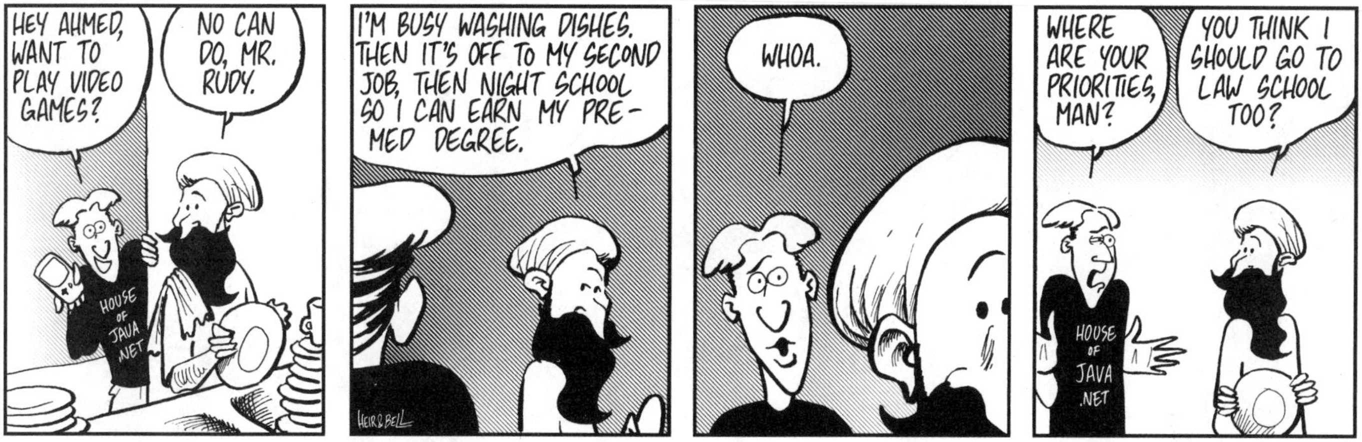
HEY AHMED, WANT TO PLAY VIDEO GAMES?
NO CAN DO, MR. RUDY.
HOUSE OF JAVA .NET
I'M BUSY WASHING DISHES. THEN IT'S OFF TO MY SECOND JOB, THEN NIGHT SCHOOL SO I CAN EARN MY PRE-MED DEGREE.
HEIR&BELL
WHOA.
WHERE ARE YOUR PRIORITIES, MAN?
YOU THINK I SHOULD GO TO LAW SCHOOL TOO?
HOUSE OF JAVA .NET

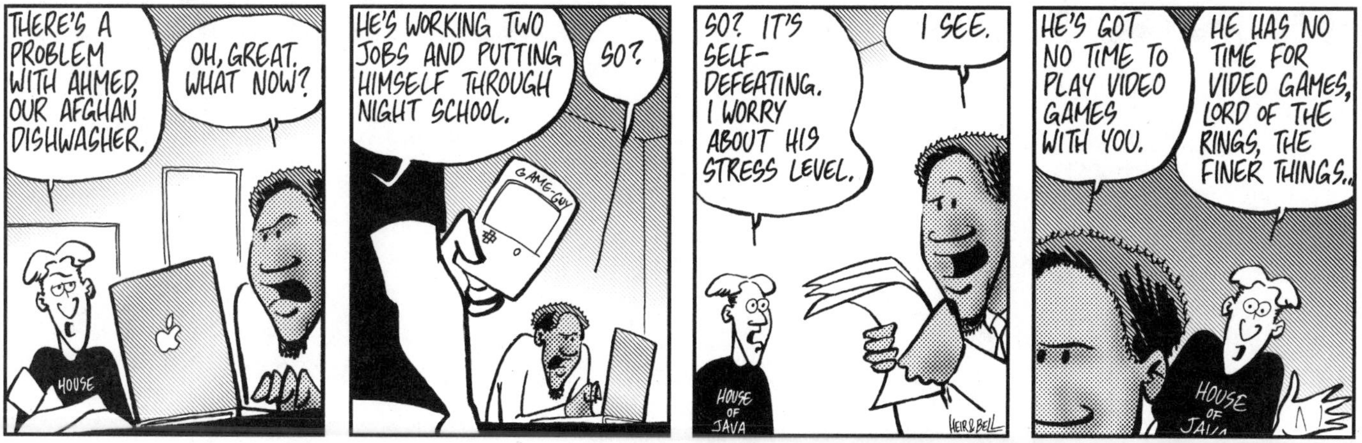
THERE'S A PROBLEM WITH AHMED, OUR AFGHAN DISHWASHER.
OH, GREAT. WHAT NOW?
HOUSE
HE'S WORKING TWO JOBS AND PUTTING HIMSELF THROUGH NIGHT SCHOOL.
SO?
GAME-GUY
SO? IT'S SELF-DEFEATING. I WORRY ABOUT HIS STRESS LEVEL.
I SEE.
HOUSE OF JAVA
HEIR&BELL
HE'S GOT NO TIME TO PLAY VIDEO GAMES WITH YOU.
HE HAS NO TIME FOR VIDEO GAMES, LORD OF THE RINGS, THE FINER THINGS...
HOUSE OF

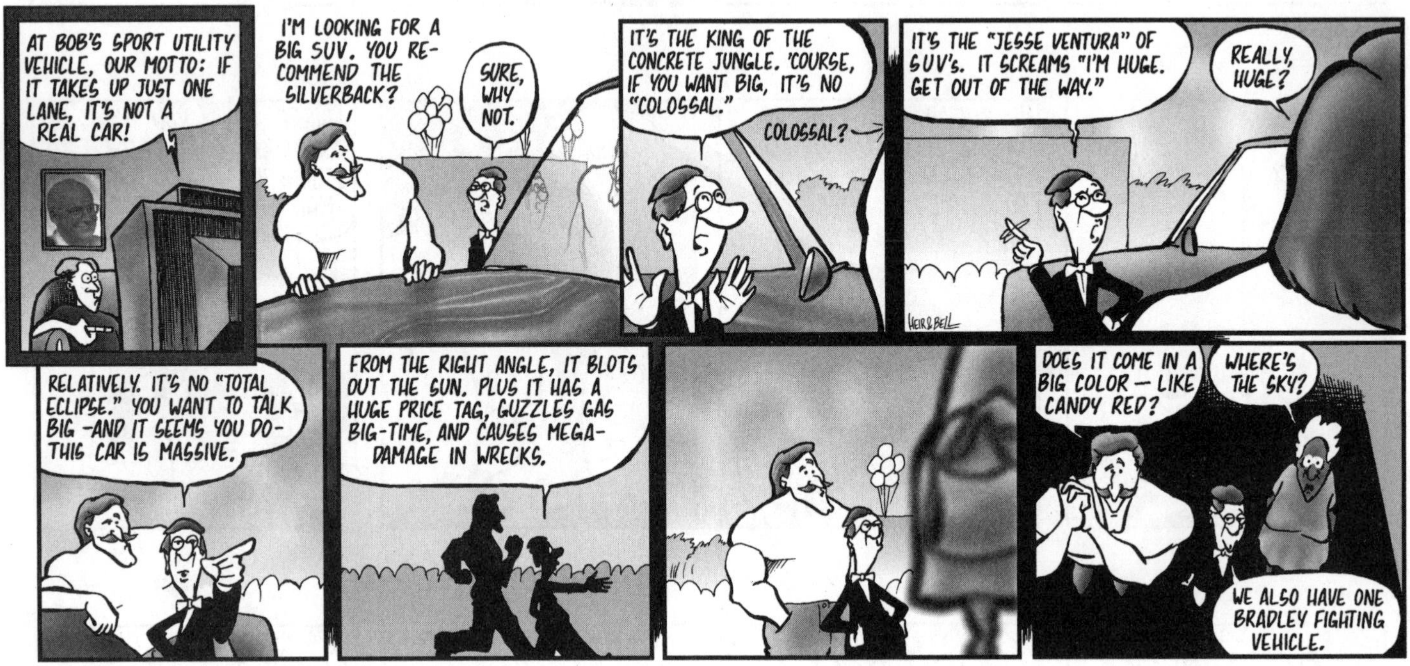
AT BOB'S SPORT UTILITY VEHICLE, OUR MOTTO: IF IT TAKES UP JUST ONE LANE, IT'S NOT A REAL CAR!
I'M LOOKING FOR A BIG SUV. YOU RECOMMEND THE SILVERBACK?
SURE, WHY NOT.
IT'S THE KING OF THE CONCRETE JUNGLE. 'COURSE, IF YOU WANT BIG, IT'S NO "COLOSSAL."
COLOSSAL?
IT'S THE "JESSE VENTURA" OF SUV's. IT SCREAMS "I'M HUGE. GET OUT OF THE WAY."
REALLY, HUGE?
HEIR & BELL
RELATIVELY. IT'S NO "TOTAL ECLIPSE." YOU WANT TO TALK BIG -AND IT SEEMS YOU DO- THIS CAR IS MASSIVE.
FROM THE RIGHT ANGLE, IT BLOTS OUT THE SUN. PLUS IT HAS A HUGE PRICE TAG, GUZZLES GAS BIG-TIME, AND CAUSES MEGA-DAMAGE IN WRECKS.
DOES IT COME IN A BIG COLOR — LIKE CANDY RED?
WHERE'S THE SKY?
WE ALSO HAVE ONE BRADLEY FIGHTING VEHICLE.

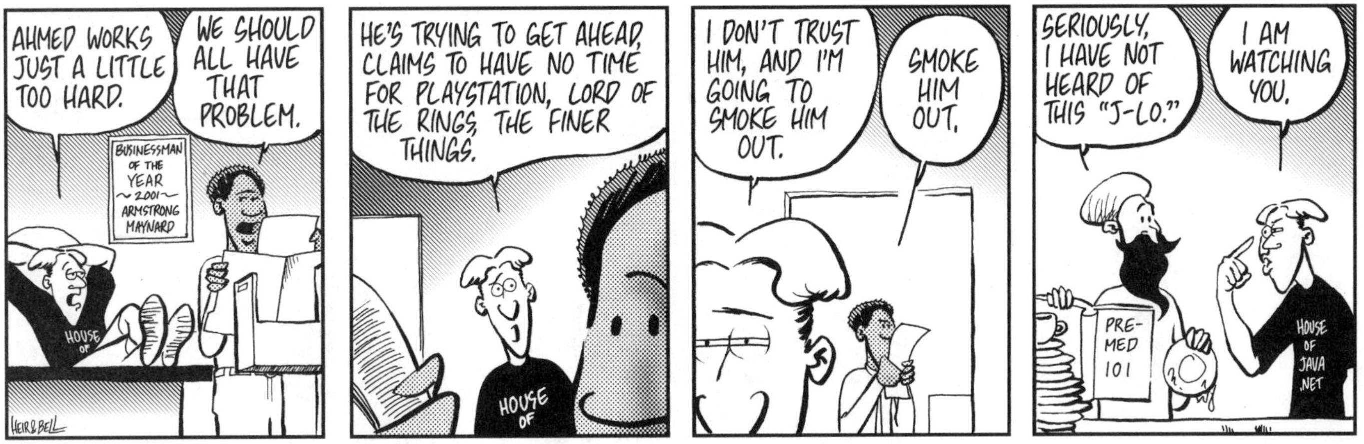
AHMED WORKS JUST A LITTLE TOO HARD.
WE SHOULD ALL HAVE THAT PROBLEM.
BUSINESSMAN OF THE YEAR 2001 ARMSTRONG MAYNARD
HOUSE OF
HEIR & BELL
HE'S TRYING TO GET AHEAD, CLAIMS TO HAVE NO TIME FOR PLAYSTATION, LORD OF THE RINGS, THE FINER THINGS.
HOUSE OF
I DON'T TRUST HIM, AND I'M GOING TO SMOKE HIM OUT.
SMOKE HIM OUT.
SERIOUSLY, I HAVE NOT HEARD OF THIS "J-LO."
I AM WATCHING YOU.
PRE-MED 101
HOUSE OF JAVA .NET

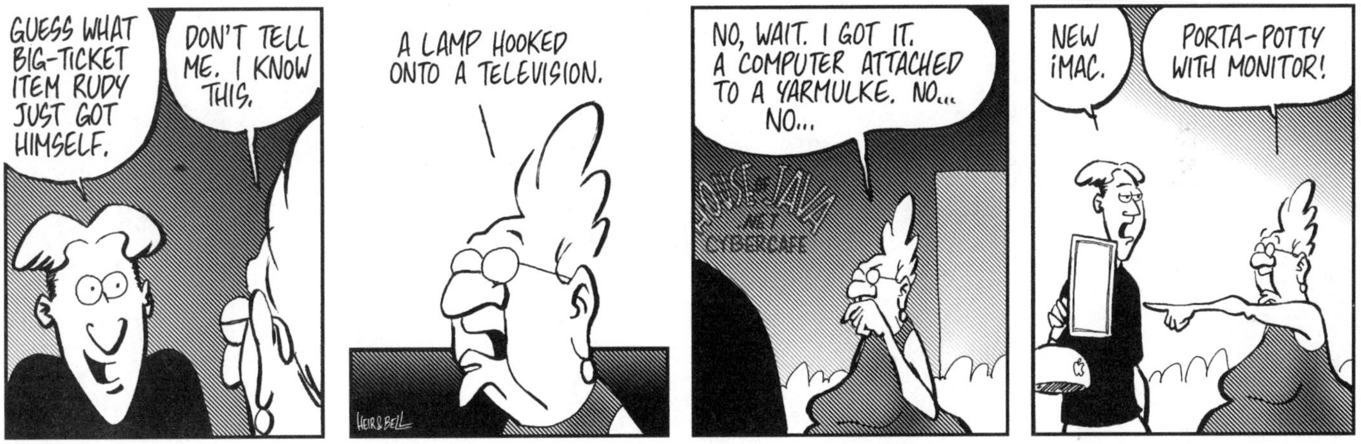
GUESS WHAT BIG-TICKET ITEM RUDY JUST GOT HIMSELF.
DON'T TELL ME. I KNOW THIS.
A LAMP HOOKED ONTO A TELEVISION.
HEIR & BELL
NO, WAIT. I GOT IT. A COMPUTER ATTACHED TO A YARMULKE. NO... NO...
HOUSE of JAVA .NET CYBERCAFE
NEW iMAC.
PORTA-POTTY WITH MONITOR!

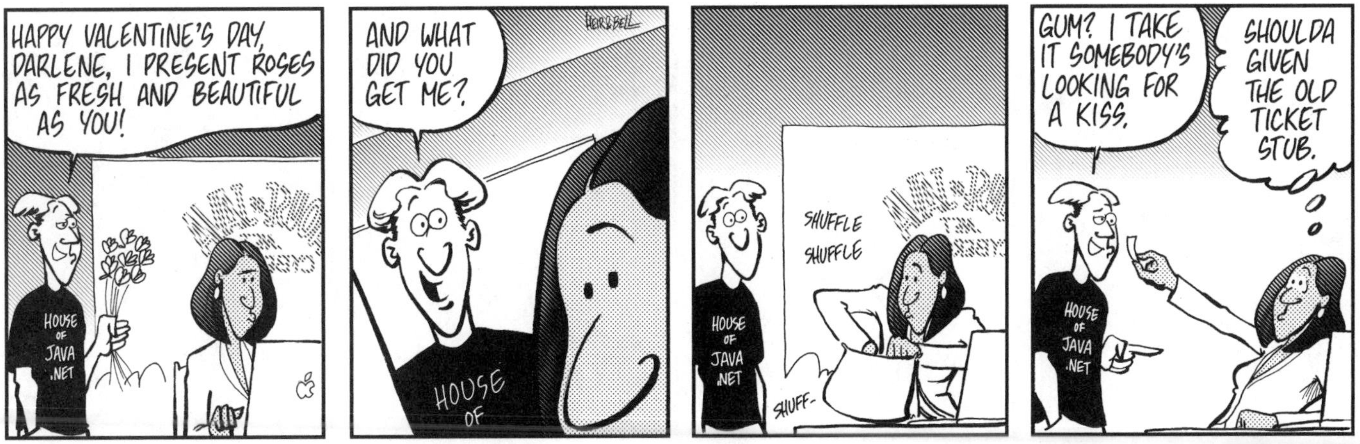
HAPPY VALENTINE'S DAY, DARLENE, I PRESENT ROSES AS FRESH AND BEAUTIFUL AS YOU!
HOUSE OF JAVA .NET
HEIR & BELL
AND WHAT DID YOU GET ME?
HOUSE OF
SHUFFLE
SHUFFLE
SHUFF-
HOUSE OF JAVA .NET
GUM? I TAKE IT SOMEBODY'S LOOKING FOR A KISS.
SHOULDA GIVEN THE OLD TICKET STUB.
HOUSE OF JAVA .NET

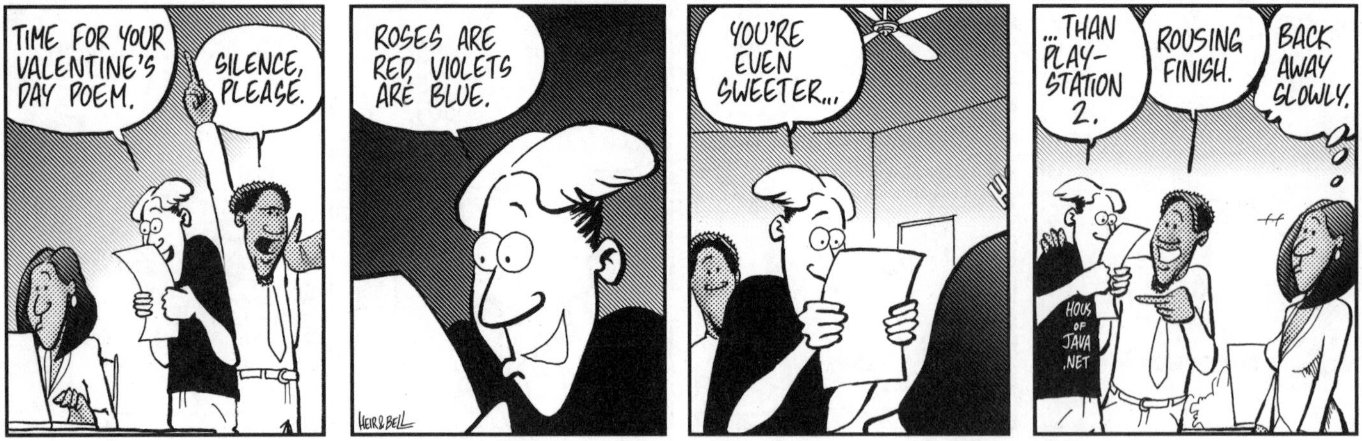
TIME FOR YOUR VALENTINE'S DAY POEM.
SILENCE, PLEASE.
ROSES ARE RED, VIOLETS ARE BLUE.
HEIR&BELL
YOU'RE EVEN SWEETER...
...THAN PLAY-STATION 2.
ROUSING FINISH.
BACK AWAY SLOWLY.
HOUS OF JAVA .NET

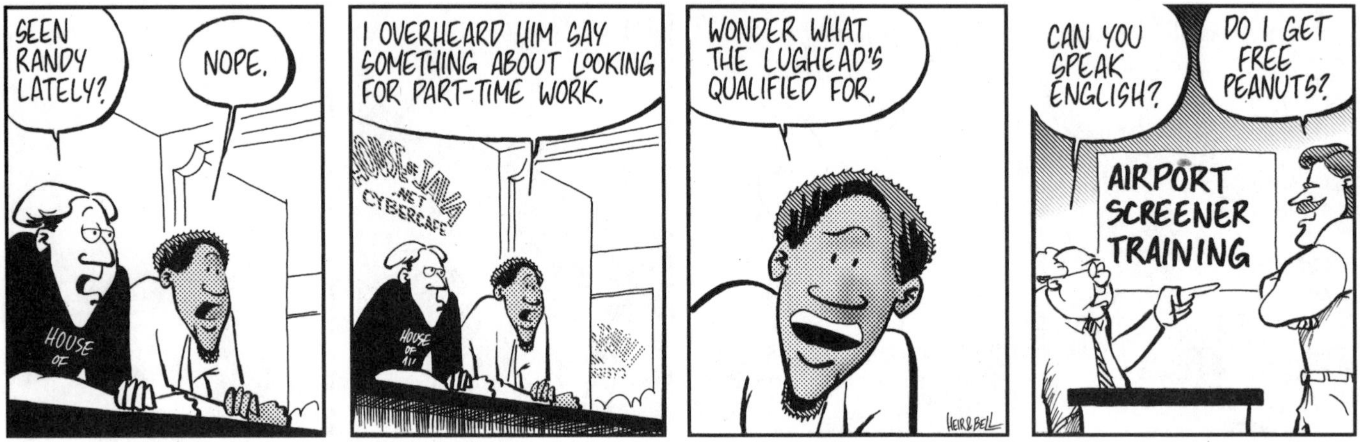
SEEN RANDY LATELY?
NOPE.
HOUSE OF
I OVERHEARD HIM SAY SOMETHING ABOUT LOOKING FOR PART-TIME WORK.
HOUSE OF JAVA .NET CYBERCAFE
WONDER WHAT THE LUGHEAD'S QUALIFIED FOR.
HEIR&BELL
CAN YOU SPEAK ENGLISH?
DO I GET FREE PEANUTS?
AIRPORT SCREENER TRAINING

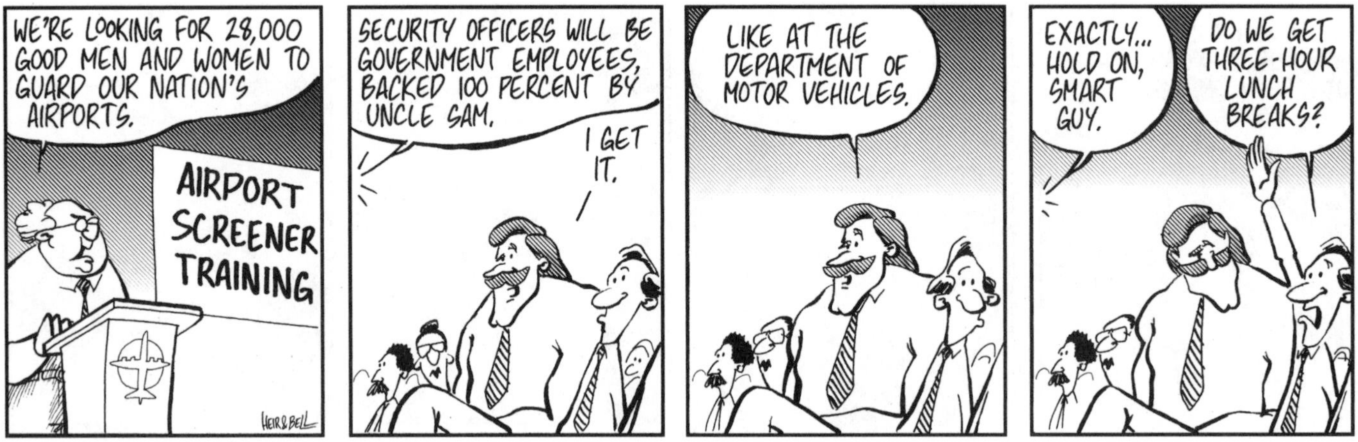
WE'RE LOOKING FOR 28,000 GOOD MEN AND WOMEN TO GUARD OUR NATION'S AIRPORTS.
AIRPORT SCREENER TRAINING
HEIR&BELL
SECURITY OFFICERS WILL BE GOVERNMENT EMPLOYEES, BACKED 100 PERCENT BY UNCLE SAM.
I GET IT.
LIKE AT THE DEPARTMENT OF MOTOR VEHICLES.
EXACTLY... HOLD ON, SMART GUY.
DO WE GET THREE-HOUR LUNCH BREAKS?

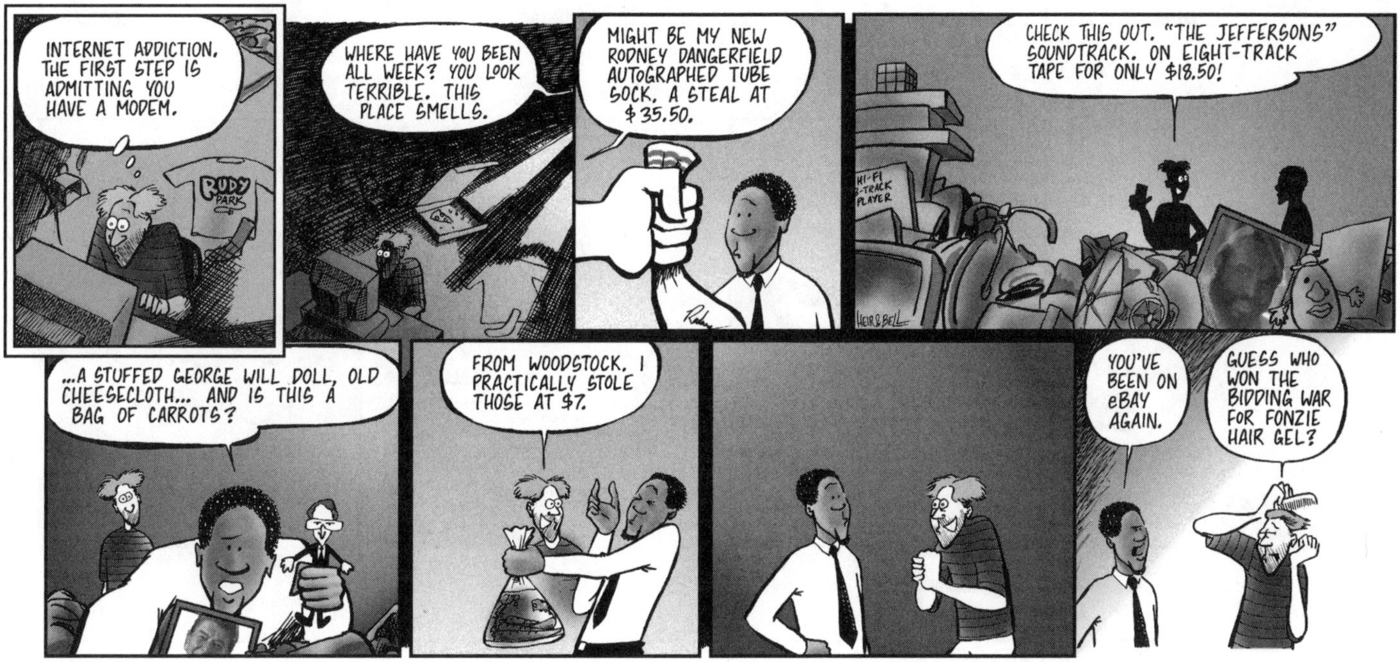

INTERNET ADDICTION. THE FIRST STEP IS ADMITTING YOU HAVE A MODEM.
WHERE HAVE YOU BEEN ALL WEEK? YOU LOOK TERRIBLE. THIS PLACE SMELLS.
MIGHT BE MY NEW RODNEY DANGERFIELD AUTOGRAPHED TUBE SOCK. A STEAL AT $35.50.
CHECK THIS OUT. "THE JEFFERSONS" SOUNDTRACK. ON EIGHT-TRACK TAPE FOR ONLY $18.50!
...A STUFFED GEORGE WILL DOLL, OLD CHEESECLOTH... AND IS THIS A BAG OF CARROTS?
FROM WOODSTOCK. I PRACTICALLY STOLE THOSE AT $7.
YOU'VE BEEN ON eBAY AGAIN.
GUESS WHO WON THE BIDDING WAR FOR FONZIE HAIR GEL?

RANDY HASN'T BEEN AROUND MUCH AT ALL.

I KNOW IT.

WONDER WHAT HE'S UP TO.

WHATEVER IT IS, YOU CAN REST ASSURED OF ONE THING...

SOME HOT BABE'S LOOKING FOR HIS ATTENTIONS.

YOU SURE YOU DON'T WANT TO FRISK ME?

TRUST ME, YOU'RE CLEAR, MA'AM.

Charles M. Schulz SONOMA COUNTY **AIRPORT**

X-RAY

I LOVE TOM CRUISE. HE'S SUCH A HUNK. IT JUST BREAKS MY HEART THAT HE'S GAY.

HE IS?

2-HEADED BOY FOUND!

ENQUIRER TOM CRUISE GAY!

HOJ

JAVA

THE EVIDENCE IS INCONTROVERTIBLE: HE WAS MARRIED, HAD TWO KIDS, AND NOW HE DATES A BEAUTIFUL STARLET!

ENQUIRER TOM CRUISE GAY

HOUSE OF JAVA .NET CYBERCAFE

HOUSE OF JAVA .NET

ENQUIRER TOM CRUISE GAY

SEEMS TO ADD RIGHT UP.

JOHN TRAVOLTA'S AN ALIEN.

HOUSE OF JAVA .NET CYBERCAFE

ENQUIRER TOM CRUISE GAY

HEADS UP, IT'S HERB, THE "LATE ADOPTER."

WHO?

GUY IS ALWAYS A COUPLE YEARS BEHIND THE TIMES,

LET YOU BOYS IN ON A LITTLE SECRET...

YOU MUST CHECK OUT THE FUNKY FRESH "WHO WANTS TO BE A MILLIONAIRE."

RIGHT ON TIME, HERB.

THAT REGIS IS DA BOMB!

HOUSE OF JAVA .NET

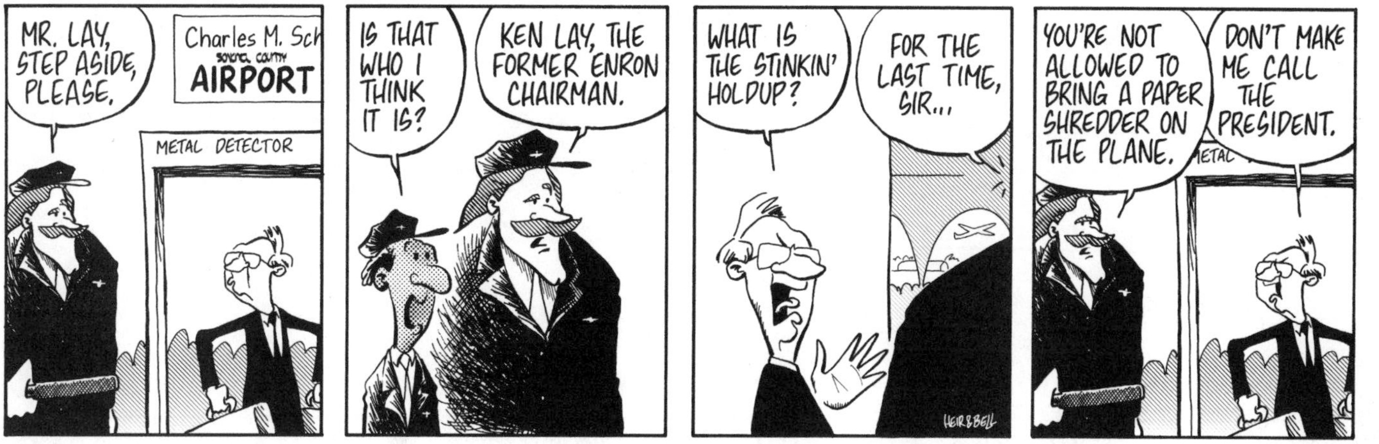
MR. LAY, STEP ASIDE, PLEASE.
Charles M. Sch
AIRPORT
METAL DETECTOR
IS THAT WHO I THINK IT IS?
KEN LAY, THE FORMER ENRON CHAIRMAN.
WHAT IS THE STINKIN' HOLDUP?
FOR THE LAST TIME, SIR...
YOU'RE NOT ALLOWED TO BRING A PAPER SHREDDER ON THE PLANE.
DON'T MAKE ME CALL THE PRESIDENT.

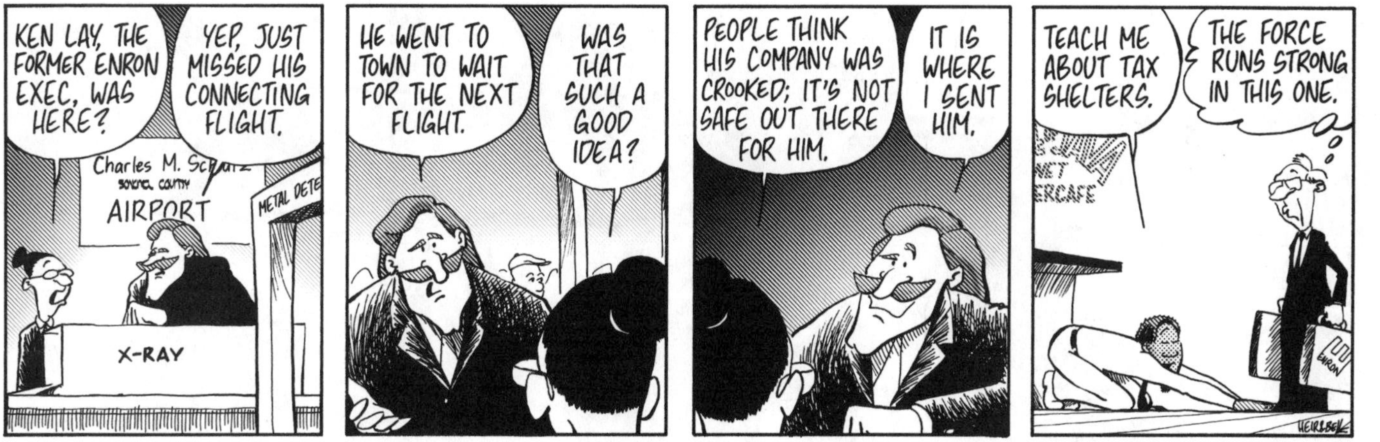
KEN LAY, THE FORMER ENRON EXEC, WAS HERE?
YEP, JUST MISSED HIS CONNECTING FLIGHT.
AIRPORT
X-RAY
HE WENT TO TOWN TO WAIT FOR THE NEXT FLIGHT.
WAS THAT SUCH A GOOD IDEA?
PEOPLE THINK HIS COMPANY WAS CROOKED; IT'S NOT SAFE OUT THERE FOR HIM.
IT IS WHERE I SENT HIM.
TEACH ME ABOUT TAX SHELTERS.
THE FORCE RUNS STRONG IN THIS ONE.
ENRON

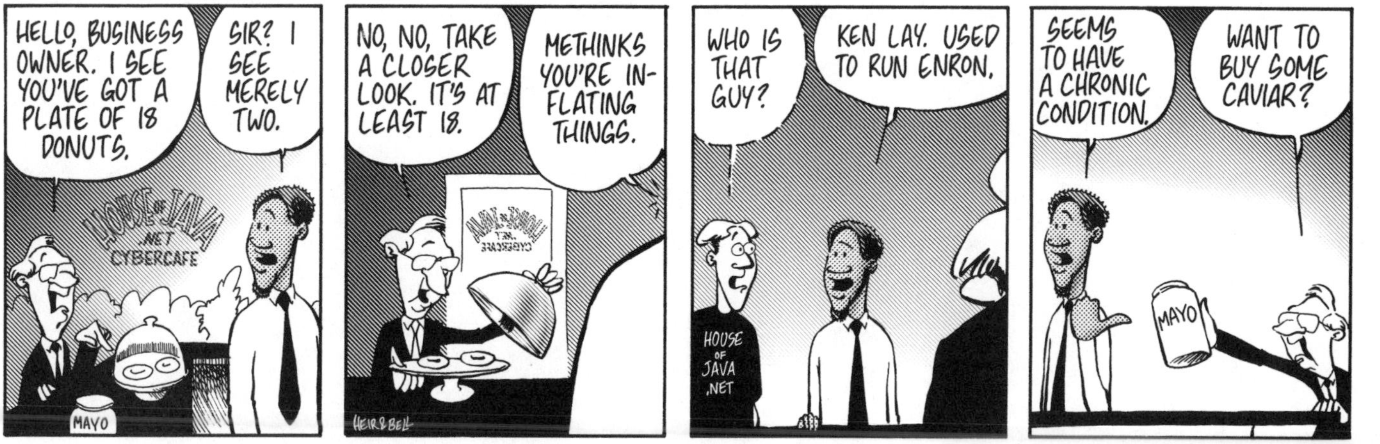
HELLO, BUSINESS OWNER. I SEE YOU'VE GOT A PLATE OF 18 DONUTS.
SIR? I SEE MERELY TWO.
HOUSE OF JAVA .NET CYBERCAFE
MAYO
NO, NO, TAKE A CLOSER LOOK. IT'S AT LEAST 18.
METHINKS YOU'RE IN-FLATING THINGS.
WHO IS THAT GUY?
KEN LAY. USED TO RUN ENRON.
HOUSE OF JAVA .NET
SEEMS TO HAVE A CHRONIC CONDITION.
WANT TO BUY SOME CAVIAR?
MAYO

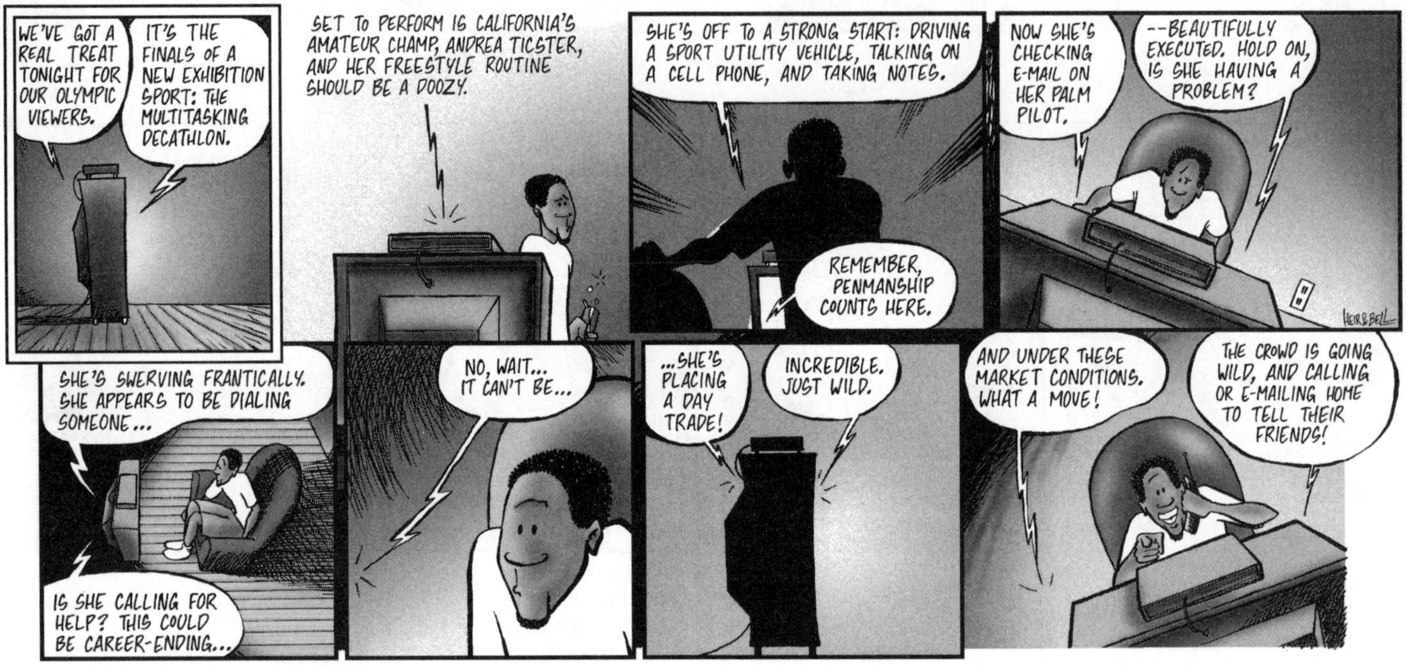
WE'VE GOT A REAL TREAT TONIGHT FOR OUR OLYMPIC VIEWERS.
IT'S THE FINALS OF A NEW EXHIBITION SPORT: THE MULTITASKING DECATHLON.
SET TO PERFORM IS CALIFORNIA'S AMATEUR CHAMP, ANDREA TICSTER, AND HER FREESTYLE ROUTINE SHOULD BE A DOOZY.
SHE'S OFF TO A STRONG START: DRIVING A SPORT UTILITY VEHICLE, TALKING ON A CELL PHONE, AND TAKING NOTES.
REMEMBER, PENMANSHIP COUNTS HERE.
NOW SHE'S CHECKING E-MAIL ON HER PALM PILOT.
--BEAUTIFULLY EXECUTED. HOLD ON, IS SHE HAVING A PROBLEM?
HEIR & BELL
SHE'S SWERVING FRANTICALLY. SHE APPEARS TO BE DIALING SOMEONE...
IS SHE CALLING FOR HELP? THIS COULD BE CAREER-ENDING...
NO, WAIT... IT CAN'T BE...
...SHE'S PLACING A DAY TRADE!
INCREDIBLE. JUST WILD.
AND UNDER THESE MARKET CONDITIONS. WHAT A MOVE!
THE CROWD IS GOING WILD, AND CALLING OR E-MAILING HOME TO TELL THEIR FRIENDS!

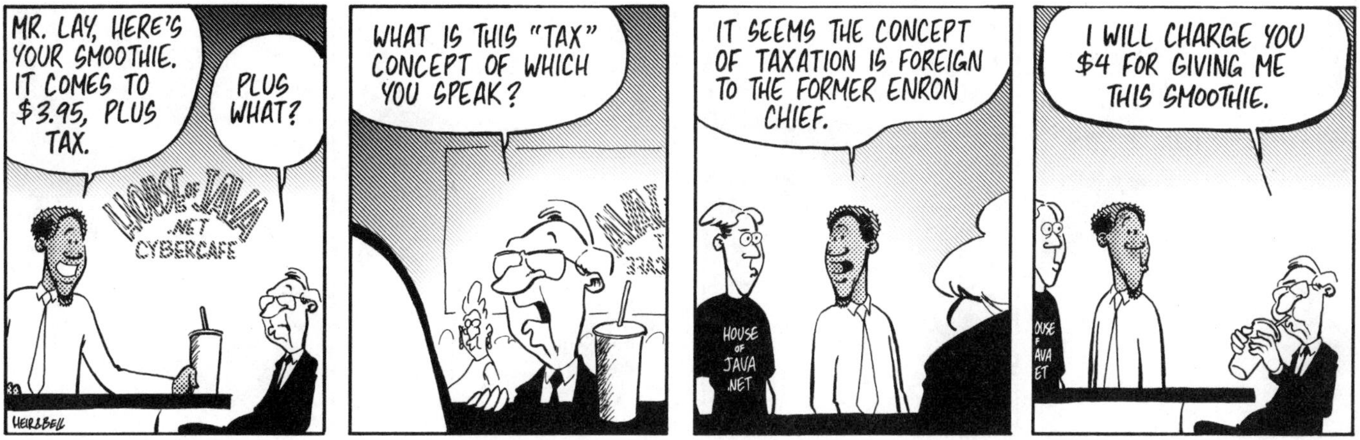
MR. LAY, HERE'S YOUR SMOOTHIE. IT COMES TO $3.95, PLUS TAX.
PLUS WHAT?
HOUSE of JAVA .NET CYBERCAFE
WHAT IS THIS "TAX" CONCEPT OF WHICH YOU SPEAK?
IT SEEMS THE CONCEPT OF TAXATION IS FOREIGN TO THE FORMER ENRON CHIEF.
HOUSE OF JAVA .NET
I WILL CHARGE YOU $4 FOR GIVING ME THIS SMOOTHIE.
HEIR&BELL

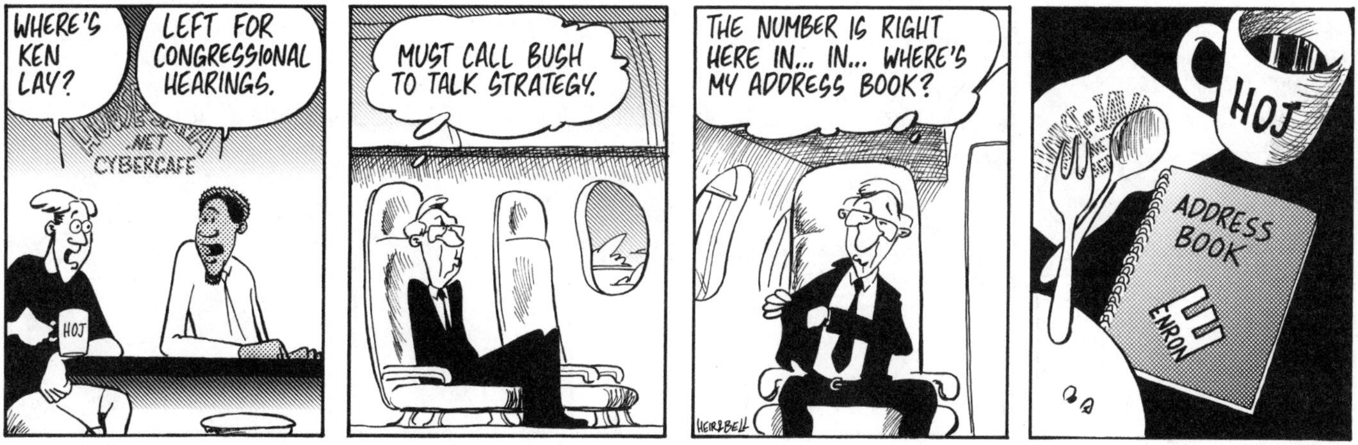
WHERE'S KEN LAY?
LEFT FOR CONGRESSIONAL HEARINGS.
.NET CYBERCAFE
HOJ
MUST CALL BUSH TO TALK STRATEGY.
THE NUMBER IS RIGHT HERE IN... IN... WHERE'S MY ADDRESS BOOK?
HEIR&BELL
HOJ
ADDRESS BOOK
ENRON

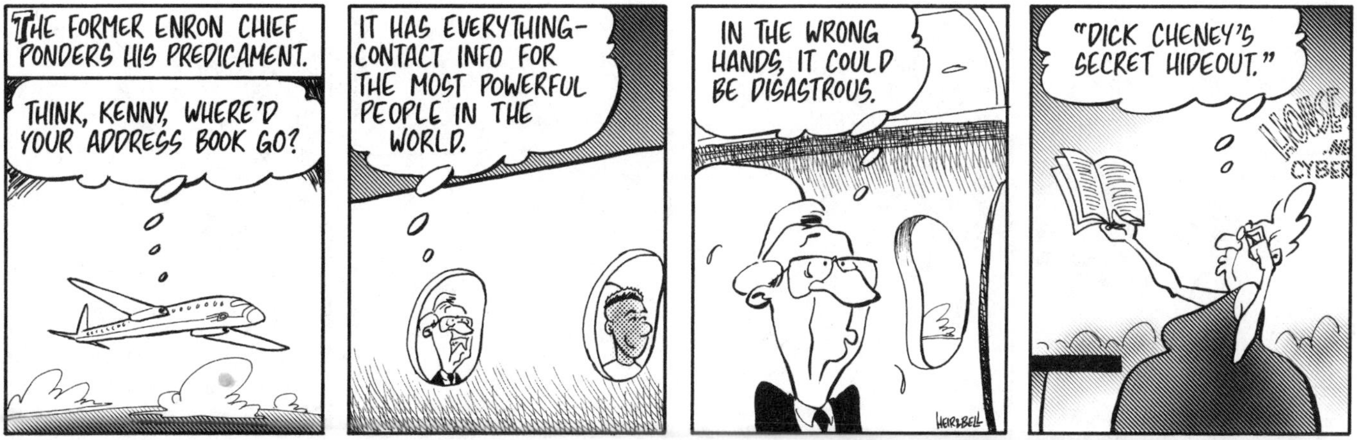
THE FORMER ENRON CHIEF PONDERS HIS PREDICAMENT.
THINK, KENNY, WHERE'D YOUR ADDRESS BOOK GO?
IT HAS EVERYTHING- CONTACT INFO FOR THE MOST POWERFUL PEOPLE IN THE WORLD.
IN THE WRONG HANDS, IT COULD BE DISASTROUS.
HEIR&BELL
"DICK CHENEY'S SECRET HIDEOUT."

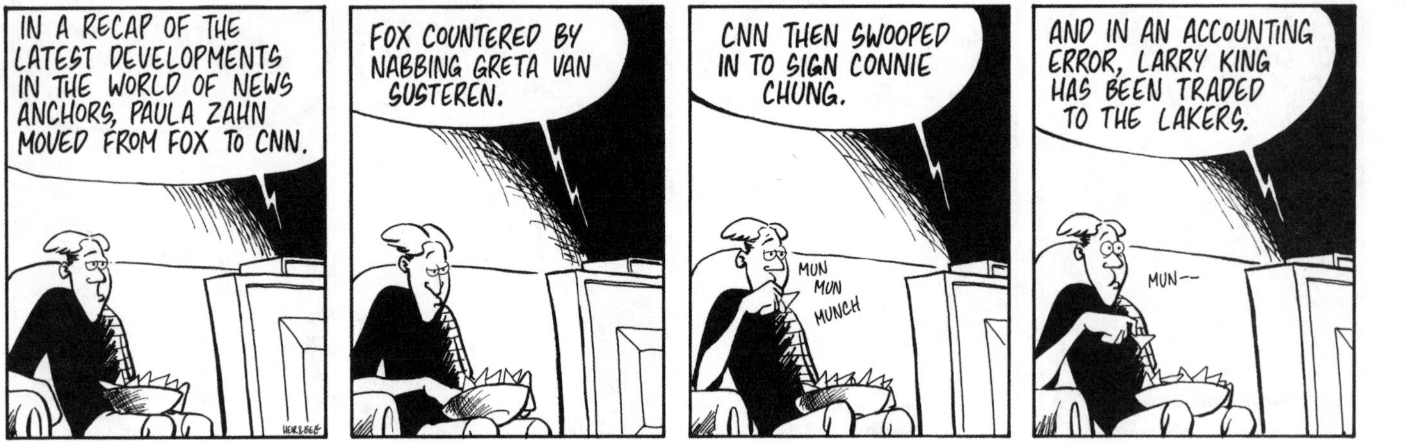
IN A RECAP OF THE LATEST DEVELOPMENTS IN THE WORLD OF NEWS ANCHORS, PAULA ZAHN MOVED FROM FOX TO CNN.
FOX COUNTERED BY NABBING GRETA VAN SUSTEREN.
CNN THEN SWOOPED IN TO SIGN CONNIE CHUNG.
MUN MUN MUNCH
AND IN AN ACCOUNTING ERROR, LARRY KING HAS BEEN TRADED TO THE LAKERS.
MUN--

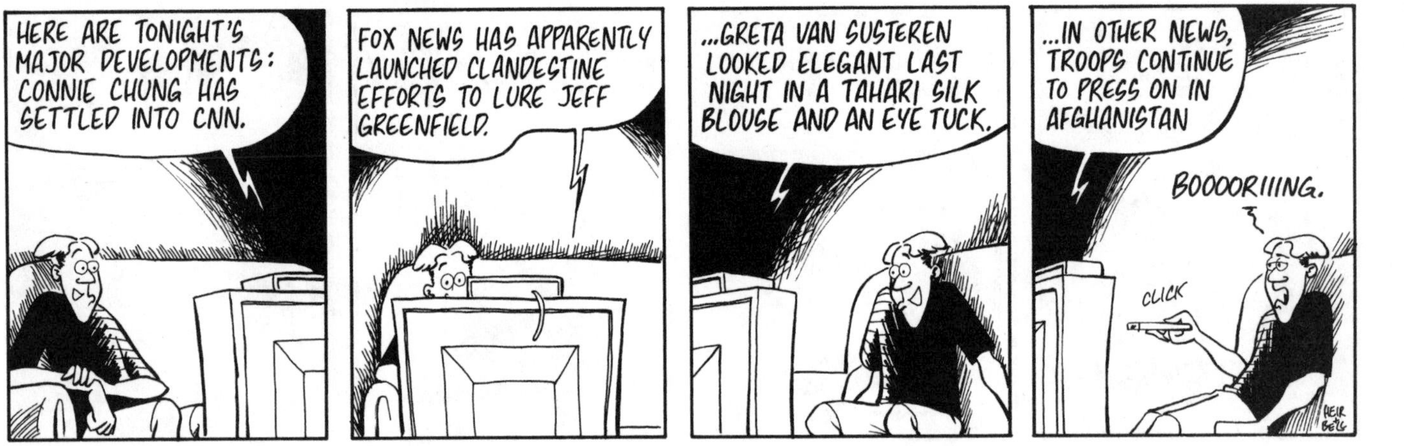
HERE ARE TONIGHT'S MAJOR DEVELOPMENTS: CONNIE CHUNG HAS SETTLED INTO CNN.
FOX NEWS HAS APPARENTLY LAUNCHED CLANDESTINE EFFORTS TO LURE JEFF GREENFIELD.
...GRETA VAN SUSTEREN LOOKED ELEGANT LAST NIGHT IN A TAHARI SILK BLOUSE AND AN EYE TUCK.
...IN OTHER NEWS, TROOPS CONTINUE TO PRESS ON IN AFGHANISTAN
BOOOORIIING.
CLICK

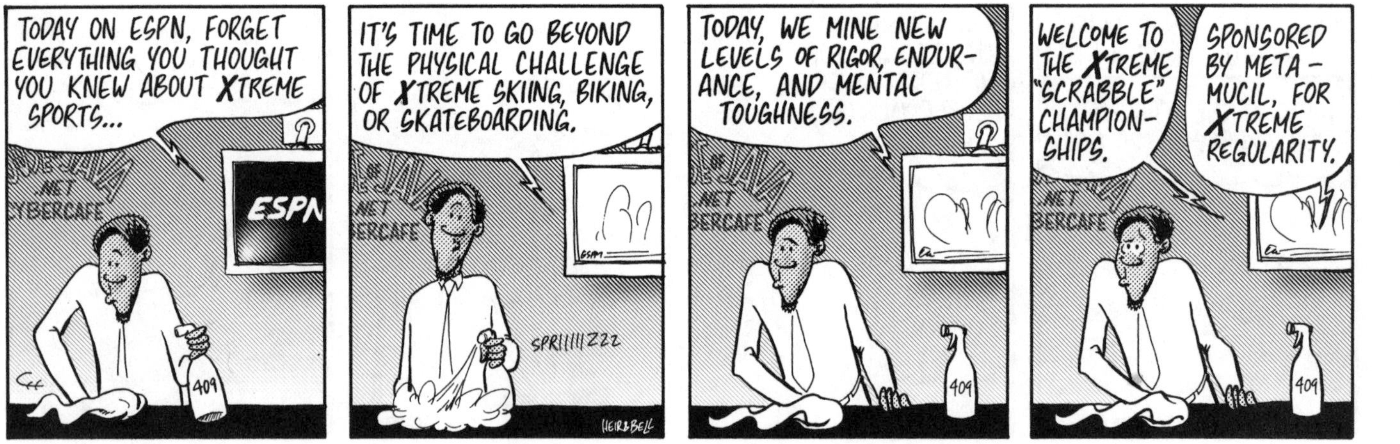
TODAY ON ESPN, FORGET EVERYTHING YOU THOUGHT YOU KNEW ABOUT XTREME SPORTS...
ESPN
409
IT'S TIME TO GO BEYOND THE PHYSICAL CHALLENGE OF XTREME SKIING, BIKING, OR SKATEBOARDING.
SPRIIIIIZZZ
TODAY, WE MINE NEW LEVELS OF RIGOR, ENDURANCE, AND MENTAL TOUGHNESS.
409
WELCOME TO THE XTREME "SCRABBLE" CHAMPIONSHIPS.
SPONSORED BY METAMUCIL, FOR XTREME REGULARITY.
409

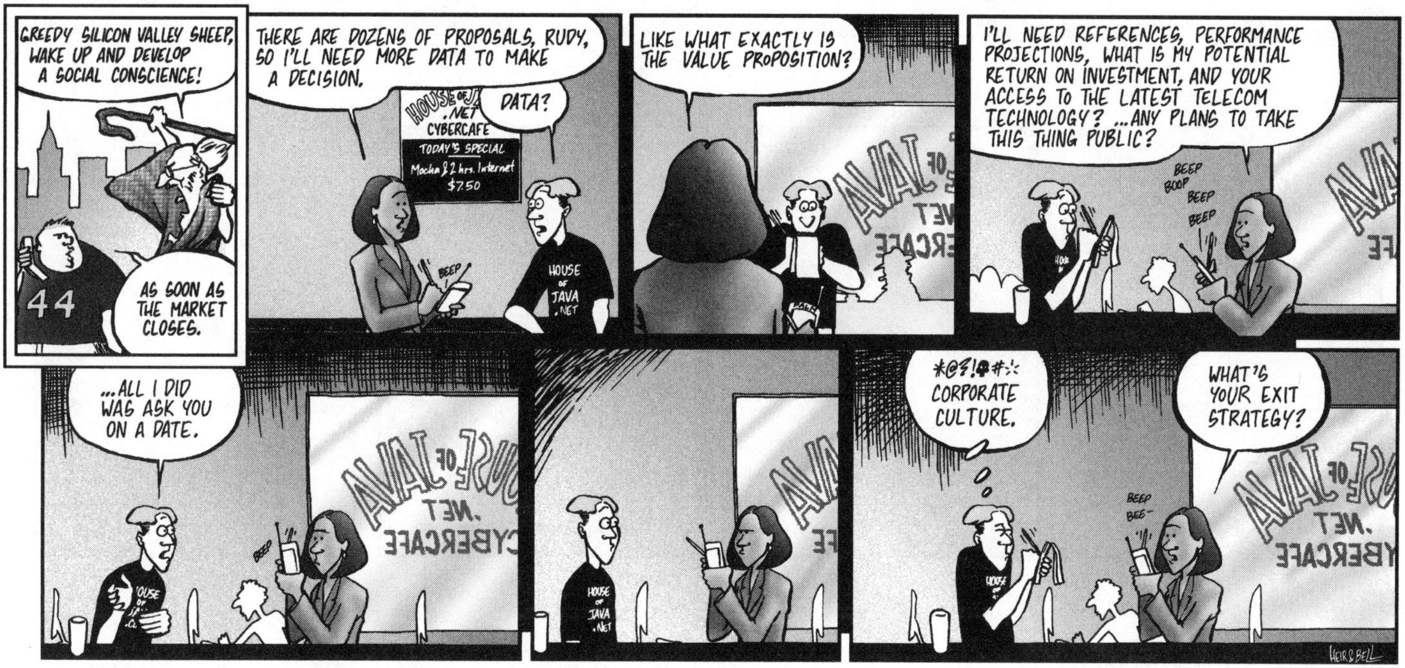
GREEDY SILICON VALLEY SHEEP, WAKE UP AND DEVELOP A SOCIAL CONSCIENCE!
AS SOON AS THE MARKET CLOSES.
44
THERE ARE DOZENS OF PROPOSALS, RUDY, SO I'LL NEED MORE DATA TO MAKE A DECISION.
DATA?
CYBERCAFE
TODAY'S SPECIAL
Mocha & 2 hrs. Internet $7.50
BEEP
HOUSE OF JAVA .NET
LIKE WHAT EXACTLY IS THE VALUE PROPOSITION?
I'LL NEED REFERENCES, PERFORMANCE PROJECTIONS, WHAT IS MY POTENTIAL RETURN ON INVESTMENT, AND YOUR ACCESS TO THE LATEST TELECOM TECHNOLOGY? ...ANY PLANS TO TAKE THIS THING PUBLIC?
BEEP BOOP BEEP BEEP
...ALL I DID WAS ASK YOU ON A DATE.
BEEP
HOUSE OF JAVA .NET
*@?!#
CORPORATE CULTURE.
WHAT'S YOUR EXIT STRATEGY?
BEEP BEE-
HEIR & BELL

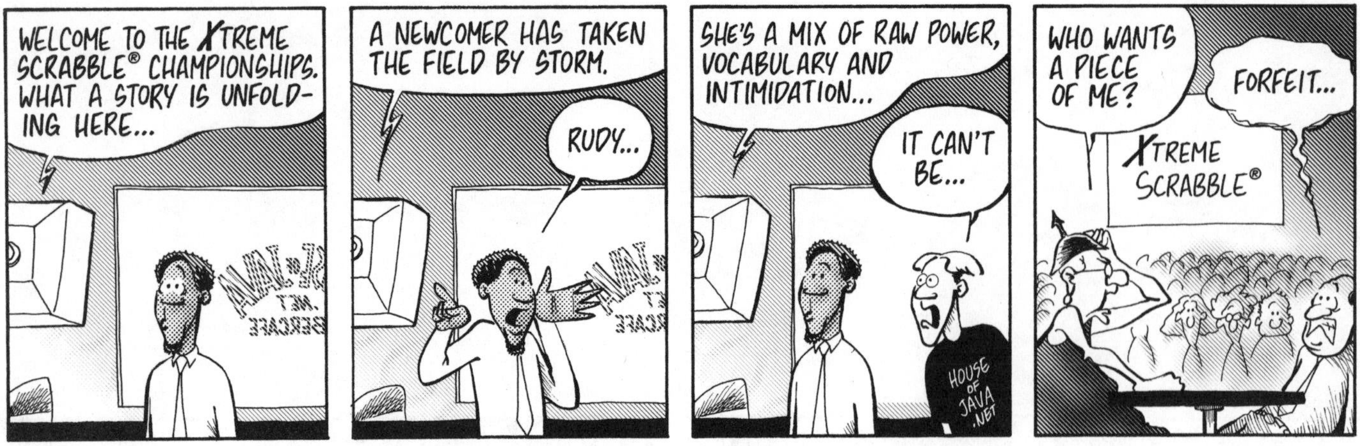
WELCOME TO THE XTREME SCRABBLE® CHAMPIONSHIPS. WHAT A STORY IS UNFOLDING HERE...
A NEWCOMER HAS TAKEN THE FIELD BY STORM.
RUDY...
SHE'S A MIX OF RAW POWER, VOCABULARY AND INTIMIDATION...
IT CAN'T BE...
HOUSE OF JAVA .NET
WHO WANTS A PIECE OF ME?
FORFEIT...
XTREME SCRABBLE®

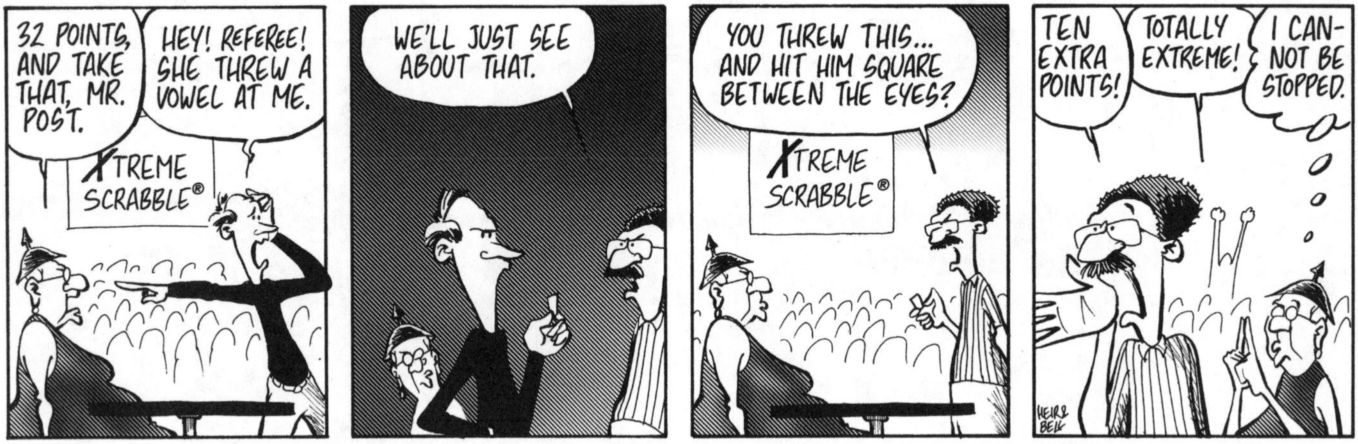
32 POINTS, AND TAKE THAT, MR. POST.
HEY! REFEREE! SHE THREW A VOWEL AT ME.
XTREME SCRABBLE®
WE'LL JUST SEE ABOUT THAT.
YOU THREW THIS... AND HIT HIM SQUARE BETWEEN THE EYES?
XTREME SCRABBLE®
TEN EXTRA POINTS!
TOTALLY EXTREME!
I CANNOT BE STOPPED.
HEIR & BELL

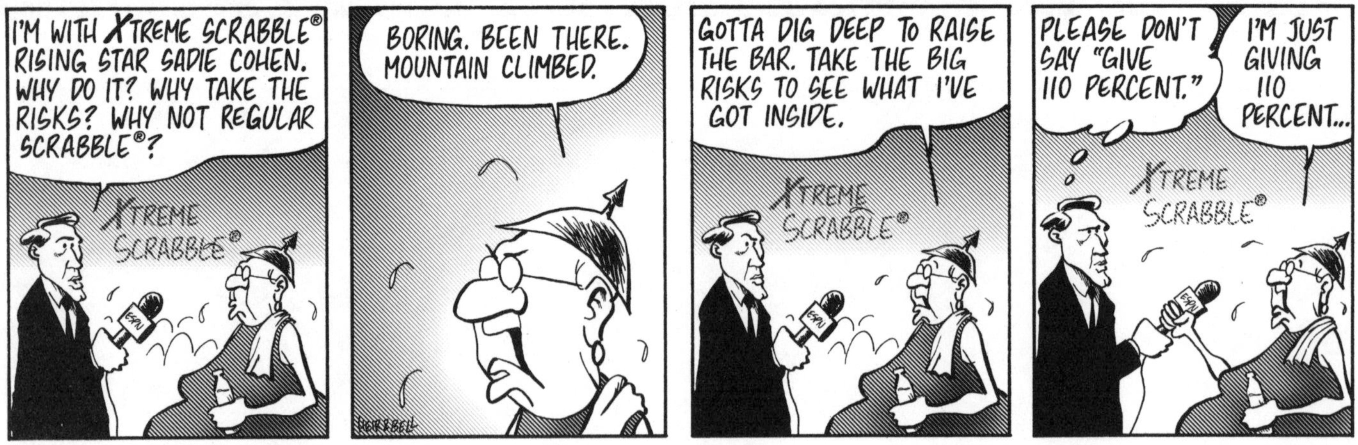
I'M WITH XTREME SCRABBLE® RISING STAR SADIE COHEN. WHY DO IT? WHY TAKE THE RISKS? WHY NOT REGULAR SCRABBLE®?
XTREME SCRABBLE®
BORING. BEEN THERE. MOUNTAIN CLIMBED.
HEIR & BELL
GOTTA DIG DEEP TO RAISE THE BAR. TAKE THE BIG RISKS TO SEE WHAT I'VE GOT INSIDE.
XTREME SCRABBLE®
PLEASE DON'T SAY "GIVE 110 PERCENT."
I'M JUST GIVING 110 PERCENT...
XTREME SCRABBLE®

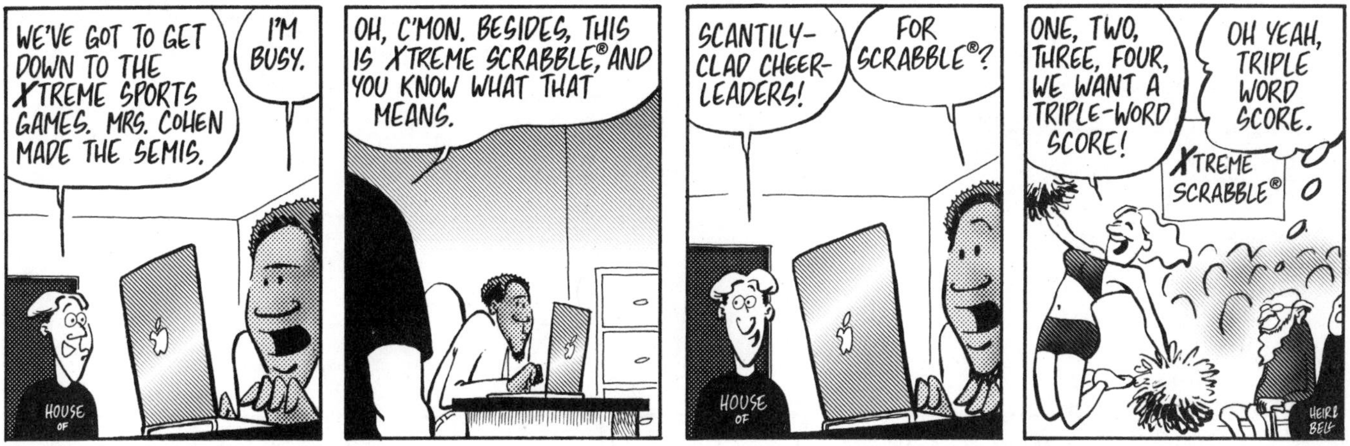
WE'VE GOT TO GET DOWN TO THE XTREME SPORTS GAMES. MRS. COHEN MADE THE SEMIS.
I'M BUSY.
HOUSE OF
OH, C'MON. BESIDES, THIS IS XTREME SCRABBLE,® AND YOU KNOW WHAT THAT MEANS.
SCANTILY-CLAD CHEER-LEADERS!
FOR SCRABBLE®?
HOUSE OF
ONE, TWO, THREE, FOUR, WE WANT A TRIPLE-WORD SCORE!
OH YEAH, TRIPLE WORD SCORE.
XTREME SCRABBLE®
HEIR & BELL

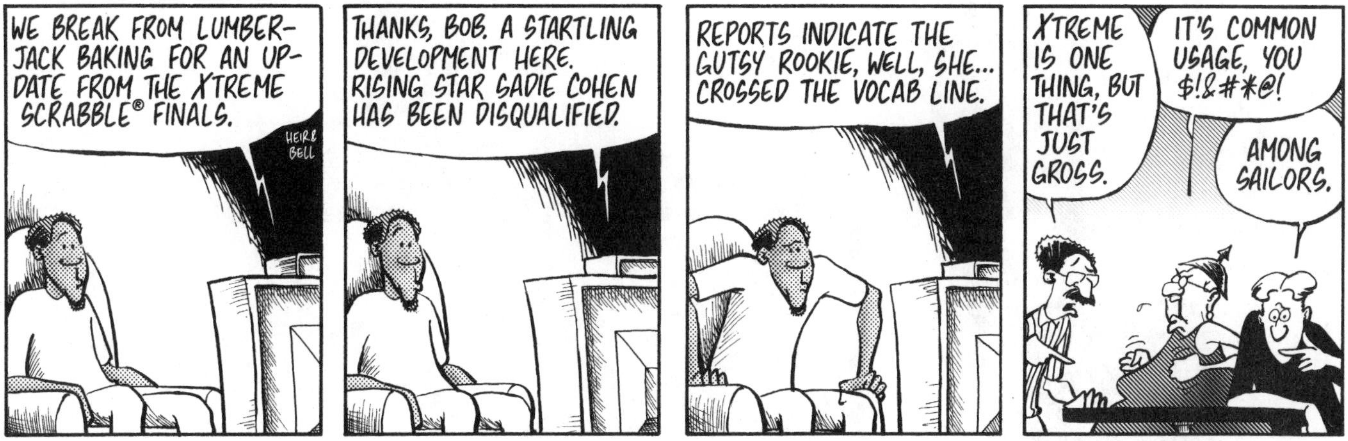
WE BREAK FROM LUMBER-JACK BAKING FOR AN UP-DATE FROM THE XTREME SCRABBLE® FINALS.
HEIR & BELL
THANKS, BOB. A STARTLING DEVELOPMENT HERE. RISING STAR SADIE COHEN HAS BEEN DISQUALIFIED.
REPORTS INDICATE THE GUTSY ROOKIE, WELL, SHE... CROSSED THE VOCAB LINE.
XTREME IS ONE THING, BUT THAT'S JUST GROSS.
IT'S COMMON USAGE, YOU $!&#*@!
AMONG SAILORS.

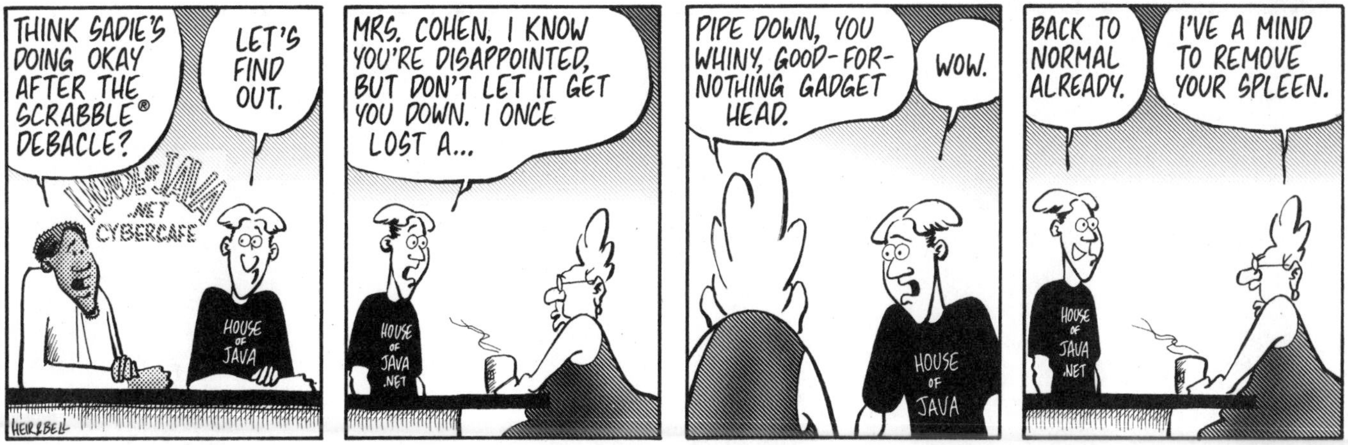
THINK SADIE'S DOING OKAY AFTER THE SCRABBLE® DEBACLE?
LET'S FIND OUT.
HOUSE OF JAVA .NET CYBERCAFE
HOUSE OF JAVA
HEIR & BELL
MRS. COHEN, I KNOW YOU'RE DISAPPOINTED, BUT DON'T LET IT GET YOU DOWN. I ONCE LOST A...
HOUSE OF JAVA .NET
PIPE DOWN, YOU WHINY, GOOD-FOR-NOTHING GADGET HEAD.
WOW.
HOUSE OF JAVA
BACK TO NORMAL ALREADY.
I'VE A MIND TO REMOVE YOUR SPLEEN.
HOUSE OF JAVA .NET

MAY I ASK A FEW QUESTIONS?
SURE, DEAR, BUT I'VE BEEN "UN-DECIDED" SINCE THE 1970s.
WE LIVE IN MATERIALISTIC, APOLITICAL TIMES, BUT A LARGE ILLITERATE UNDER-CLASS STILL EXISTS IN THE U.S.
HOW OFTEN DO YOU THINK ABOUT THE PLIGHT OF THIS GROUP? (A) "OFTEN"
(B) "SOMETIMES" (C) "RARELY"
...OR (D) "WAY COOL PALM PILOT. CAN I CHECK IT OUT?"
CAREFUL, HONEY, IT MAY BE A TRICK.
"D" AGAIN.
DOES THIS "UNDERCLASS" HAVE COOL PALM PILOTS?
HEIR & BELL

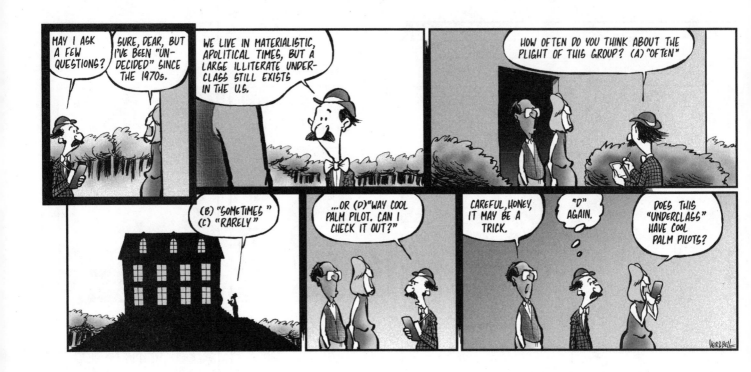

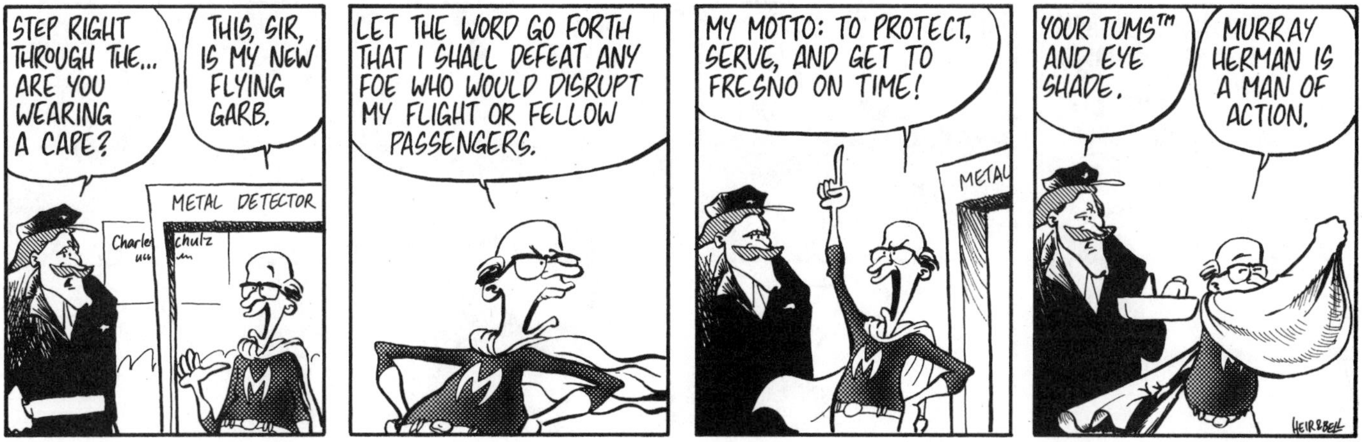
STEP RIGHT THROUGH THE... ARE YOU WEARING A CAPE?
THIS, SIR, IS MY NEW FLYING GARB.
METAL DETECTOR
LET THE WORD GO FORTH THAT I SHALL DEFEAT ANY FOE WHO WOULD DISRUPT MY FLIGHT OR FELLOW PASSENGERS.
MY MOTTO: TO PROTECT, SERVE, AND GET TO FRESNO ON TIME!
METAL
YOUR TUMS™ AND EYE SHADE.
MURRAY HERMAN IS A MAN OF ACTION.
HEIR&BELL

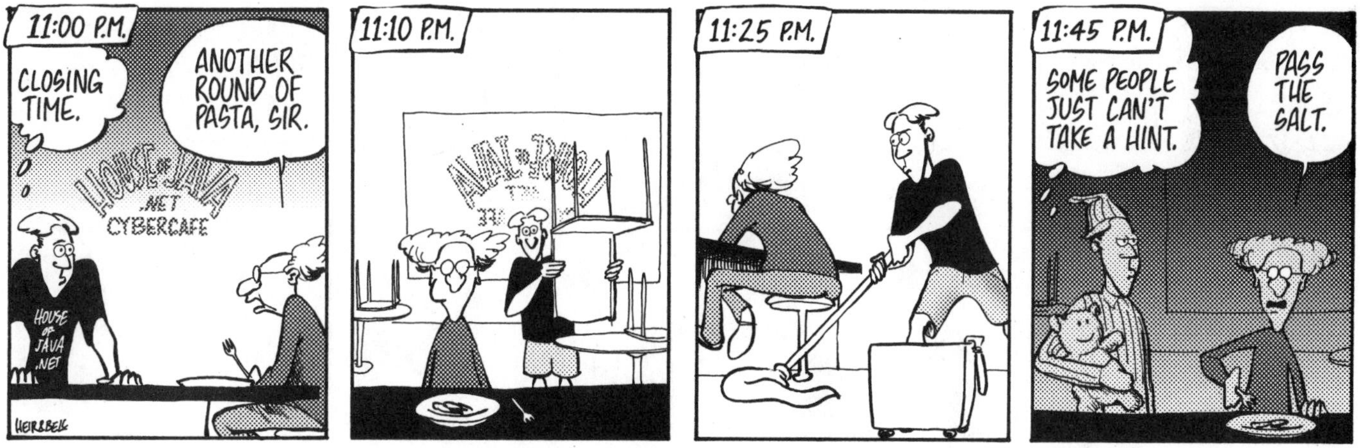
11:00 P.M.
CLOSING TIME.
ANOTHER ROUND OF PASTA, SIR.
HOUSE OF JAVA .NET CYBERCAFE
HOUSE OF JAVA .NET
HEIR&BELL
11:10 P.M.
11:25 P.M.
11:45 P.M.
SOME PEOPLE JUST CAN'T TAKE A HINT.
PASS THE SALT.

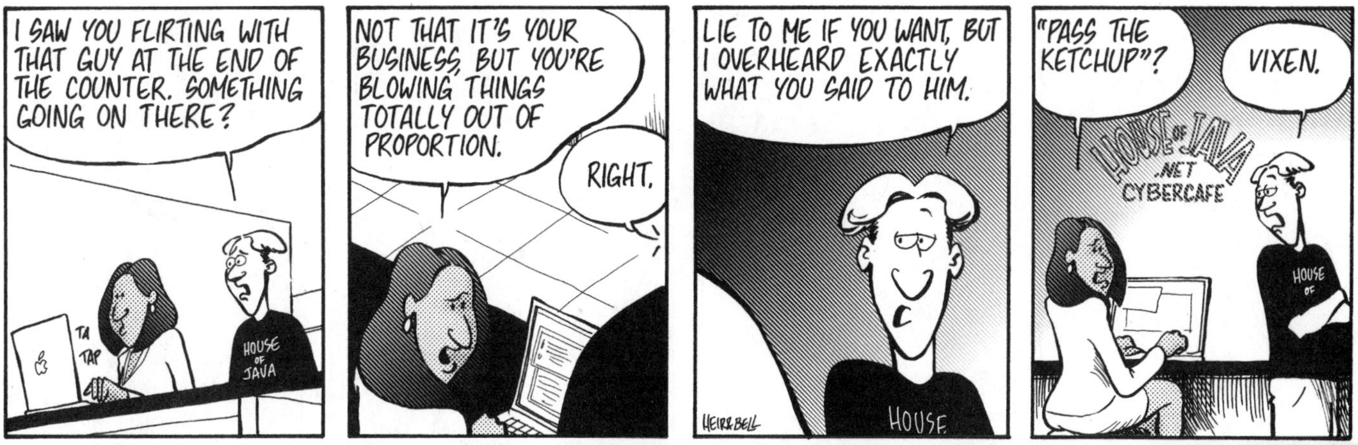
I SAW YOU FLIRTING WITH THAT GUY AT THE END OF THE COUNTER. SOMETHING GOING ON THERE?
TA TAP
HOUSE OF JAVA
NOT THAT IT'S YOUR BUSINESS, BUT YOU'RE BLOWING THINGS TOTALLY OUT OF PROPORTION.
RIGHT.
LIE TO ME IF YOU WANT, BUT I OVERHEARD EXACTLY WHAT YOU SAID TO HIM.
HOUSE
HEIR&BELL
"PASS THE KETCHUP"?
VIXEN.
HOUSE OF JAVA .NET CYBERCAFE
HOUSE OF

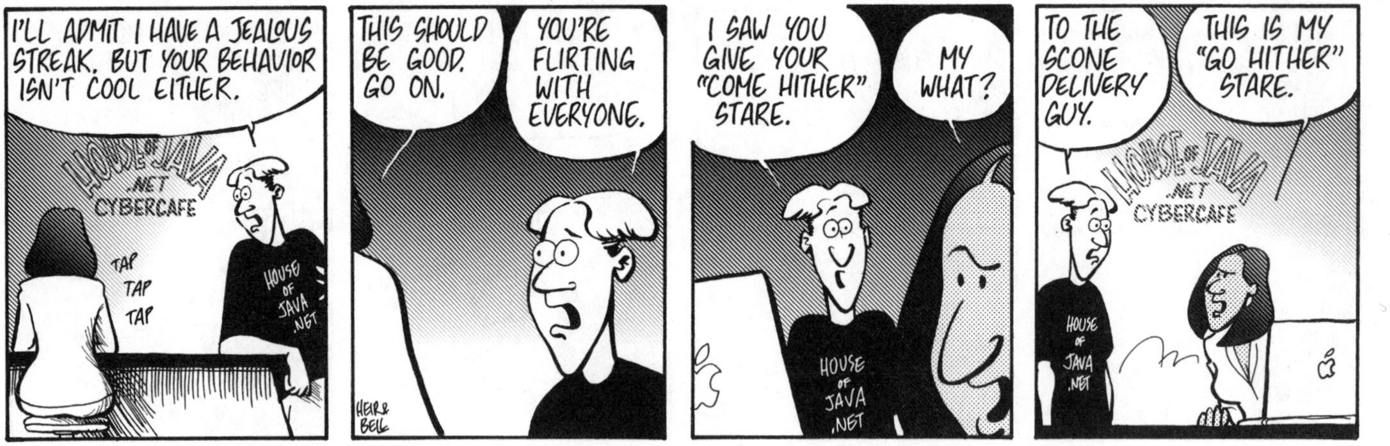
I'LL ADMIT I HAVE A JEALOUS STREAK. BUT YOUR BEHAVIOR ISN'T COOL EITHER.
HOUSE OF JAVA .NET CYBERCAFE
TAP TAP TAP
HOUSE OF JAVA .NET
THIS SHOULD BE GOOD. GO ON.
YOU'RE FLIRTING WITH EVERYONE.
I SAW YOU GIVE YOUR "COME HITHER" STARE.
MY WHAT?
HOUSE OF JAVA .NET
TO THE SCONE DELIVERY GUY.
THIS IS MY "GO HITHER" STARE.
HOUSE OF JAVA .NET CYBERCAFE
HOUSE OF JAVA .NET

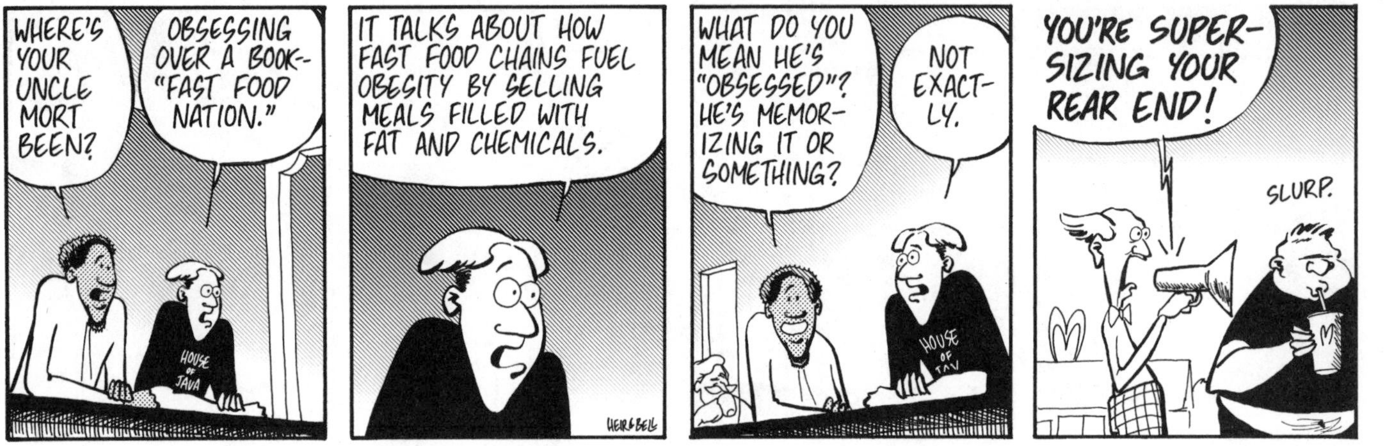
WHERE'S YOUR UNCLE MORT BEEN?
OBSESSING OVER A BOOK-- "FAST FOOD NATION."
HOUSE OF JAVA
IT TALKS ABOUT HOW FAST FOOD CHAINS FUEL OBESITY BY SELLING MEALS FILLED WITH FAT AND CHEMICALS.
WHAT DO YOU MEAN HE'S "OBSESSED"? HE'S MEMORIZING IT OR SOMETHING?
NOT EXACT-LY.
YOU'RE SUPER-SIZING YOUR REAR END!
SLURP.

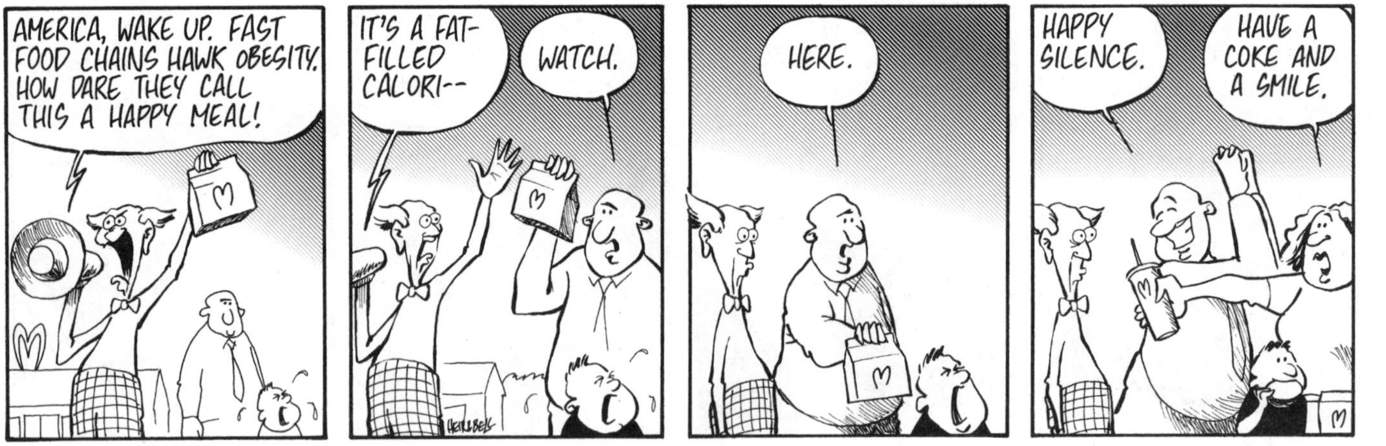
AMERICA, WAKE UP. FAST FOOD CHAINS HAWK OBESITY. HOW DARE THEY CALL THIS A HAPPY MEAL!
IT'S A FAT-FILLED CALORI--
WATCH.
HERE.
HAPPY SILENCE.
HAVE A COKE AND A SMILE.

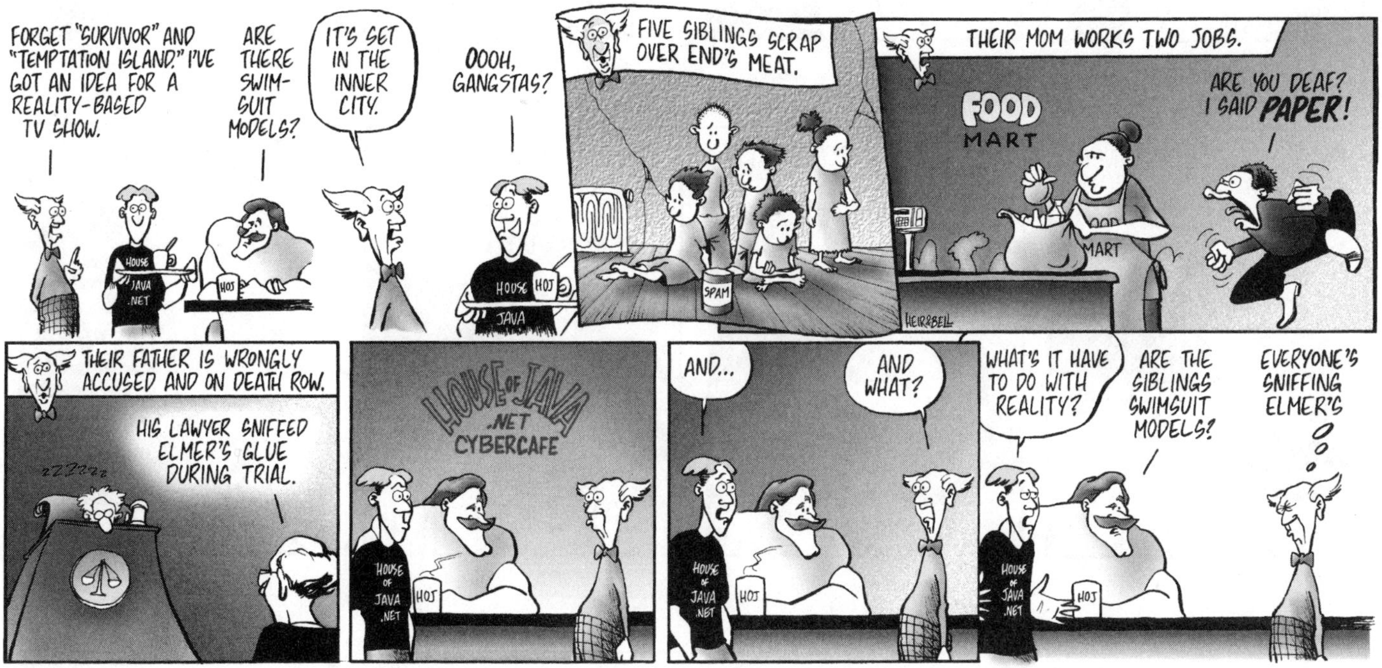

FORGET "SURVIVOR" AND "TEMPTATION ISLAND." I'VE GOT AN IDEA FOR A REALITY-BASED TV SHOW.
ARE THERE SWIM-SUIT MODELS?
IT'S SET IN THE INNER CITY.
OOOH, GANGSTAS?
FIVE SIBLINGS SCRAP OVER END'S MEAT.
SPAM
THEIR MOM WORKS TWO JOBS.
FOOD MART
ARE YOU DEAF? I SAID PAPER!
HEIR&BELL
THEIR FATHER IS WRONGLY ACCUSED AND ON DEATH ROW.
HIS LAWYER SNIFFED ELMER'S GLUE DURING TRIAL.
HOUSE OF JAVA .NET CYBERCAFE
AND...
AND WHAT?
WHAT'S IT HAVE TO DO WITH REALITY?
ARE THE SIBLINGS SWIMSUIT MODELS?
EVERYONE'S SNIFFING ELMER'S

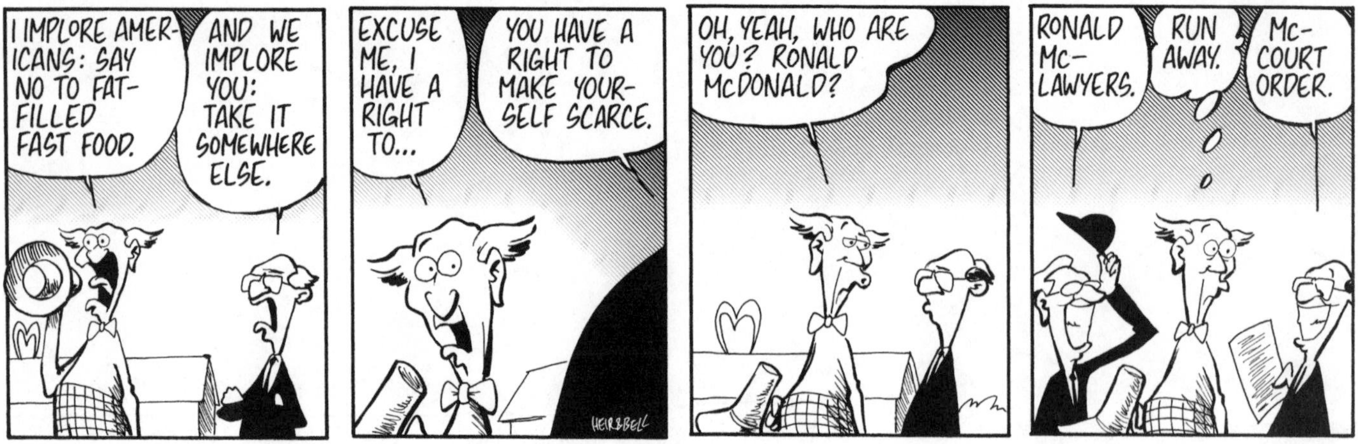
I IMPLORE AMERICANS: SAY NO TO FAT-FILLED FAST FOOD.
AND WE IMPLORE YOU: TAKE IT SOMEWHERE ELSE.
EXCUSE ME, I HAVE A RIGHT TO...
YOU HAVE A RIGHT TO MAKE YOURSELF SCARCE.
HEIR&BELL
OH, YEAH, WHO ARE YOU? RONALD McDONALD?
RONALD Mc-LAWYERS.
RUN AWAY.
Mc-COURT ORDER.

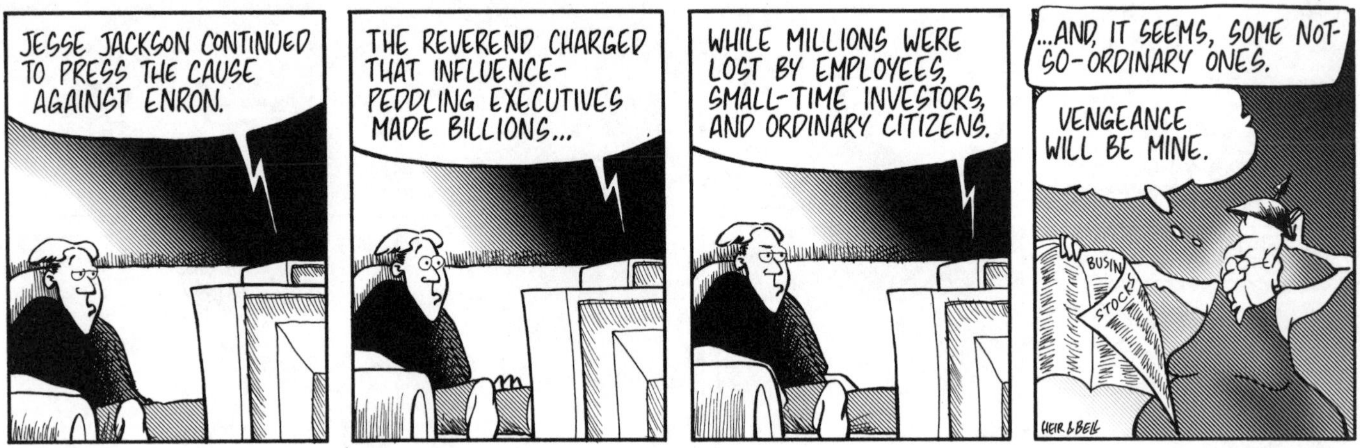
JESSE JACKSON CONTINUED TO PRESS THE CAUSE AGAINST ENRON.
THE REVEREND CHARGED THAT INFLUENCE-PEDDLING EXECUTIVES MADE BILLIONS...
WHILE MILLIONS WERE LOST BY EMPLOYEES, SMALL-TIME INVESTORS, AND ORDINARY CITIZENS.
...AND, IT SEEMS, SOME NOT-SO-ORDINARY ONES.
VENGEANCE WILL BE MINE.
BUSIN
STOCKS
HEIR&BELL

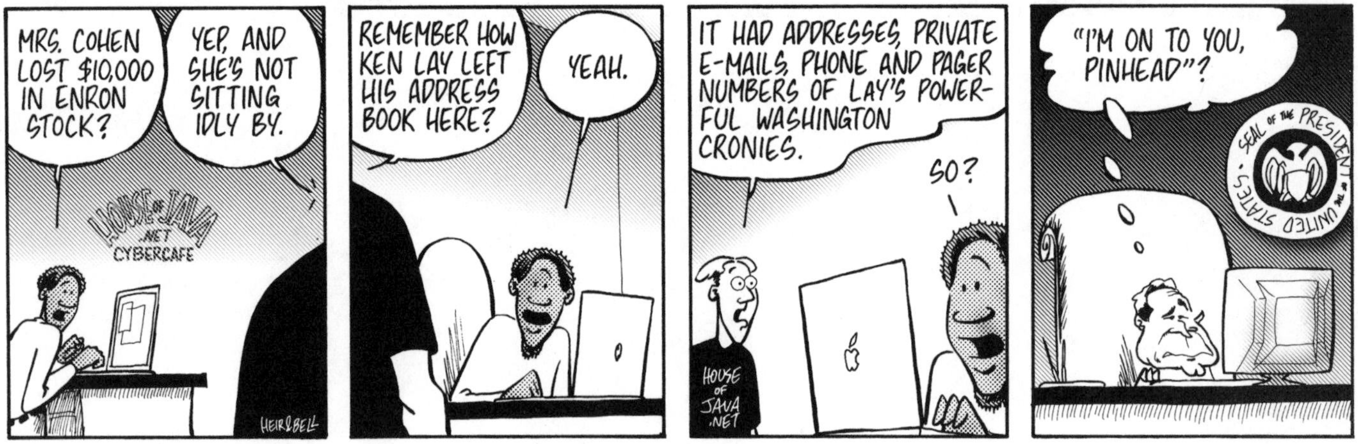
MRS. COHEN LOST $10,000 IN ENRON STOCK?
YEP, AND SHE'S NOT SITTING IDLY BY.
HOUSE OF JAVA .NET CYBERCAFE
HEIR&BELL
REMEMBER HOW KEN LAY LEFT HIS ADDRESS BOOK HERE?
YEAH.
IT HAD ADDRESSES, PRIVATE E-MAILS, PHONE AND PAGER NUMBERS OF LAY'S POWERFUL WASHINGTON CRONIES.
SO?
HOUSE OF JAVA .NET
"I'M ON TO YOU, PINHEAD"?
SEAL OF THE PRESIDENT OF THE UNITED STATES

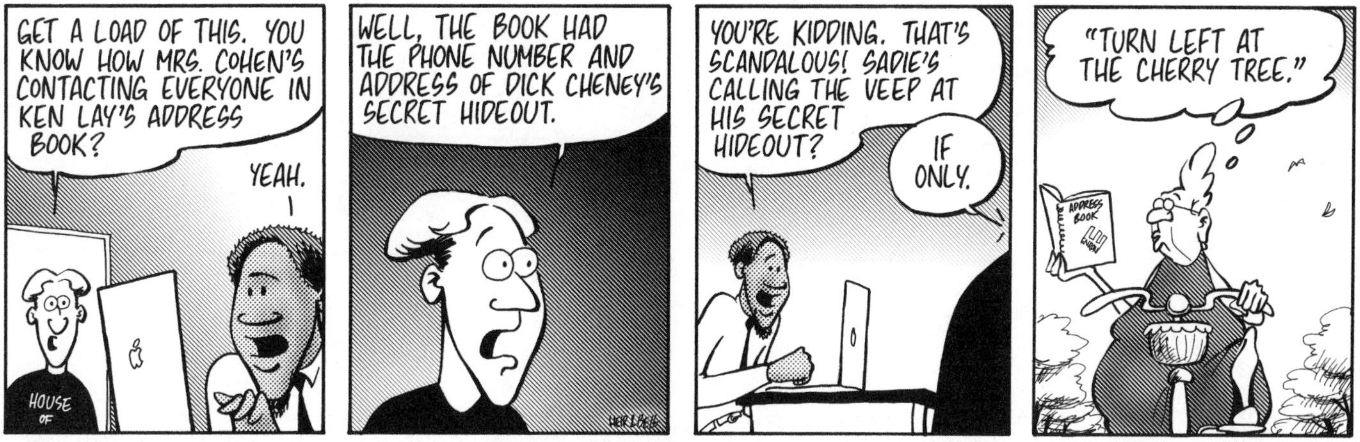
GET A LOAD OF THIS. YOU KNOW HOW MRS. COHEN'S CONTACTING EVERYONE IN KEN LAY'S ADDRESS BOOK?
YEAH.
HOUSE OF
WELL, THE BOOK HAD THE PHONE NUMBER AND ADDRESS OF DICK CHENEY'S SECRET HIDEOUT.
HEIR&BELL
YOU'RE KIDDING. THAT'S SCANDALOUS! SADIE'S CALLING THE VEEP AT HIS SECRET HIDEOUT?
IF ONLY.
"TURN LEFT AT THE CHERRY TREE."
ADDRESS BOOK

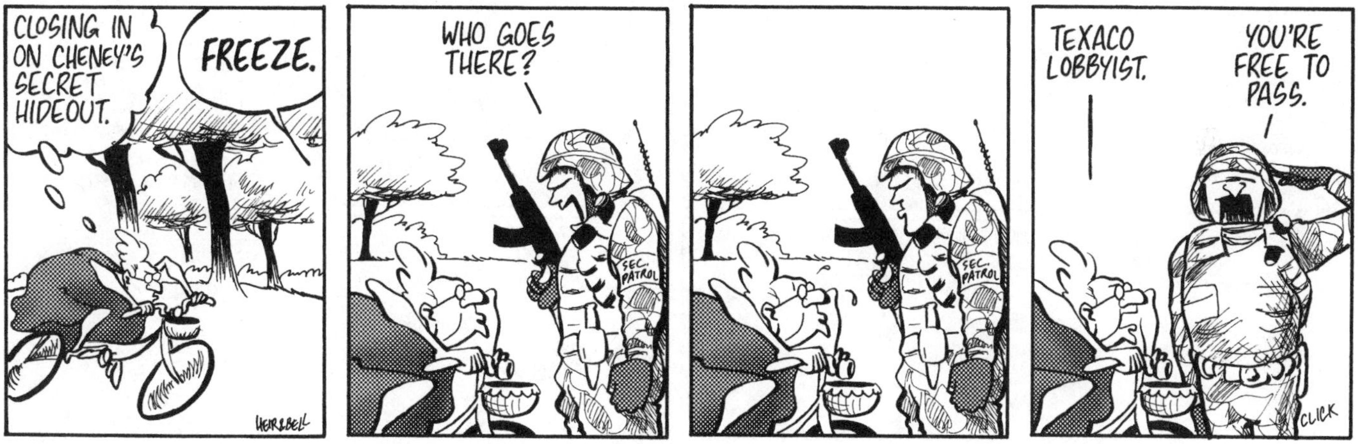
CLOSING IN ON CHENEY'S SECRET HIDEOUT.
FREEZE.
HEIR&BELL
WHO GOES THERE?
SEC. PATROL
SEC. PATROL
TEXACO LOBBYIST.
YOU'RE FREE TO PASS.
CLICK

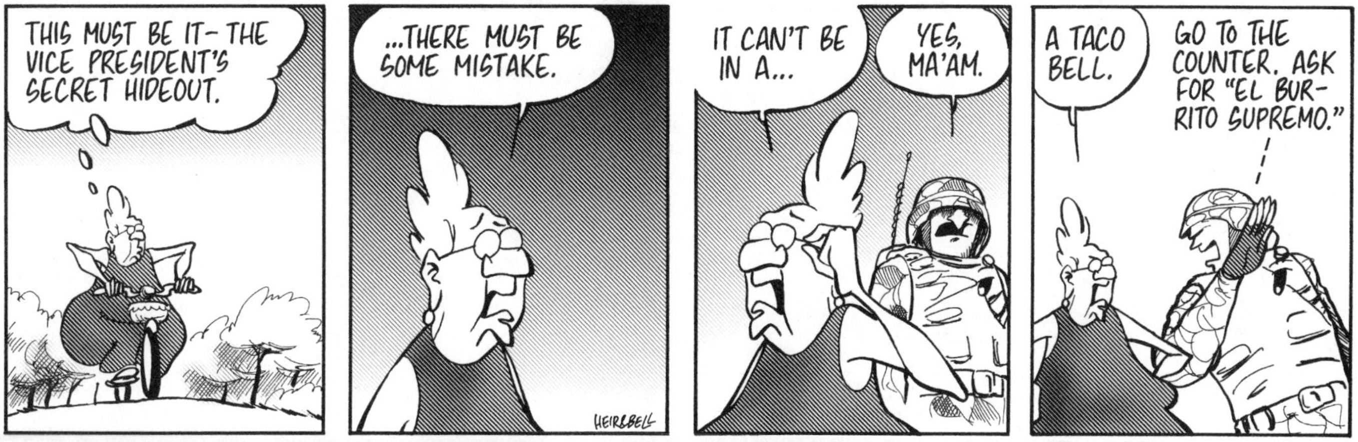
THIS MUST BE IT- THE VICE PRESIDENT'S SECRET HIDEOUT.
...THERE MUST BE SOME MISTAKE.
HEIR&BELL
IT CAN'T BE IN A...
YES, MA'AM.
A TACO BELL.
GO TO THE COUNTER. ASK FOR "EL BURRITO SUPREMO."

21ST CENTURY MEDIA CHALLENGE!
IN A NOD TO 24-HOUR TV NEWS SHOWS, RUDY TODAY INTRODUCES AN ENHANCED FORMAT. HERE'S WHERE YOU COME IN. GLANCE AT THE STRIP FOR 20 SECONDS, THEN SEE HOW MUCH YOU CAN RETAIN. IT'S JUST LIKE TV! BONUS POINTS FOR FINDING GERALDO.

THIS JUST IN: BRAD PITT TO WED ASHCROFT... LINCOLN BEDROOM CONTRACTS ANTHRAX... BIN LADEN LOOKS ELEGANT AT 35... JULIA ROBERTS STILL MISSING...

NEWS IN BRIEF
HAGAR INDICTED FOR PILLAGING, LOOTING
LOCKHORN CAUGHT WITH INTERN

GPS GERALDO POSITIONING SYSTEM
GERALDO IS CURRENTLY IN KANDAHAR... WAIT... WE MEAN FRESNO.

HOUSE OF JAVA

BREAKING NEWS
TRUDEAU EATS SANDWICH

STARKIST — TUNA BELIEVED TO BE INVOLVED

THIS DAY IN HISTORY, 1978
Mrs. Cohen slaps George Steinbrenner for firing Billy Martin. Fisticuffs ensue.

WEATHER FORECAST

SHERMAN'S LAGOON	CONTINUED WET	
THE BOONDOCKS	COLD AND ANGRY	
BLONDIE	EXPECT SANDWICHES	

NEWS OVERLOAD. HE WAS WATCHING CNN AGAIN, AND GOT HIS DATA STREAMS CONFUSED.

RUDY PARK BREAKING DIALOGUE

BUSH EATS NASDAQ GERALDO WEATHER!

MEDIC!

NOTHING A BLOW TO THE HEAD WITH A NEWSPAPER CAN'T FIX.

RCCI RUDY CONSUMER CONFIDENCE INDEX

RUDY PARK

(RUDY) *What can I get you, my little petunia?* (DARLENE) *Latte and a little peace and quiet* (RANDY) *Look at my biceps* (MRS. COHE

GARFIELD NEWS TICKER .. GARFIELD HATES MONDAYS... JON GETS SCRATCHED... DOGS ARE SLOBBERING IDIOTS... GARFIELD HATES MONDAYS... JO

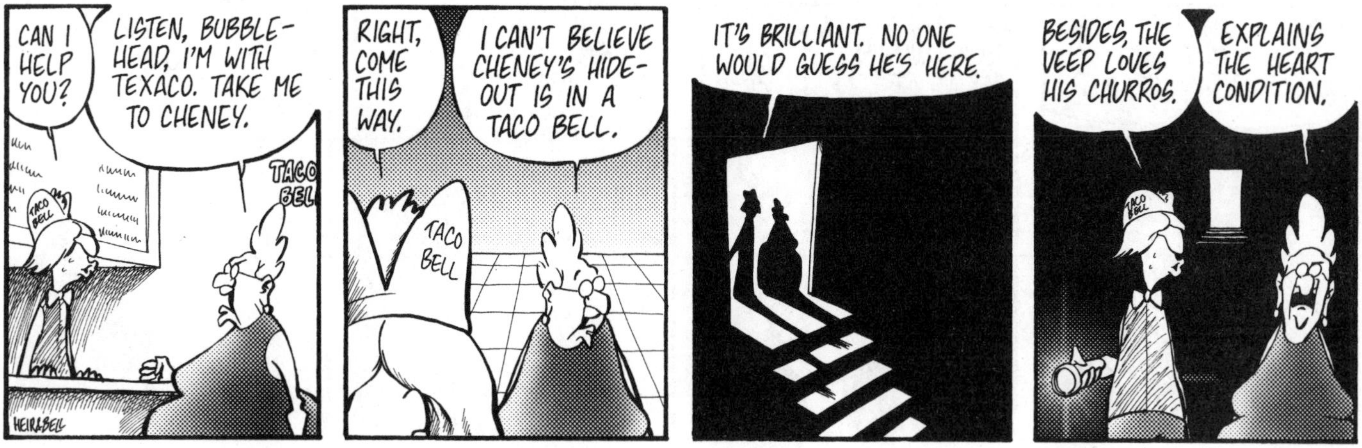
CAN I HELP YOU?
LISTEN, BUBBLE-HEAD, I'M WITH TEXACO. TAKE ME TO CHENEY.
TACO BELL
TACO BELL
HEIR & BELL
RIGHT, COME THIS WAY.
I CAN'T BELIEVE CHENEY'S HIDE-OUT IS IN A TACO BELL.
TACO BELL
IT'S BRILLIANT. NO ONE WOULD GUESS HE'S HERE.
BESIDES, THE VEEP LOVES HIS CHURROS.
EXPLAINS THE HEART CONDITION.
TACO BELL

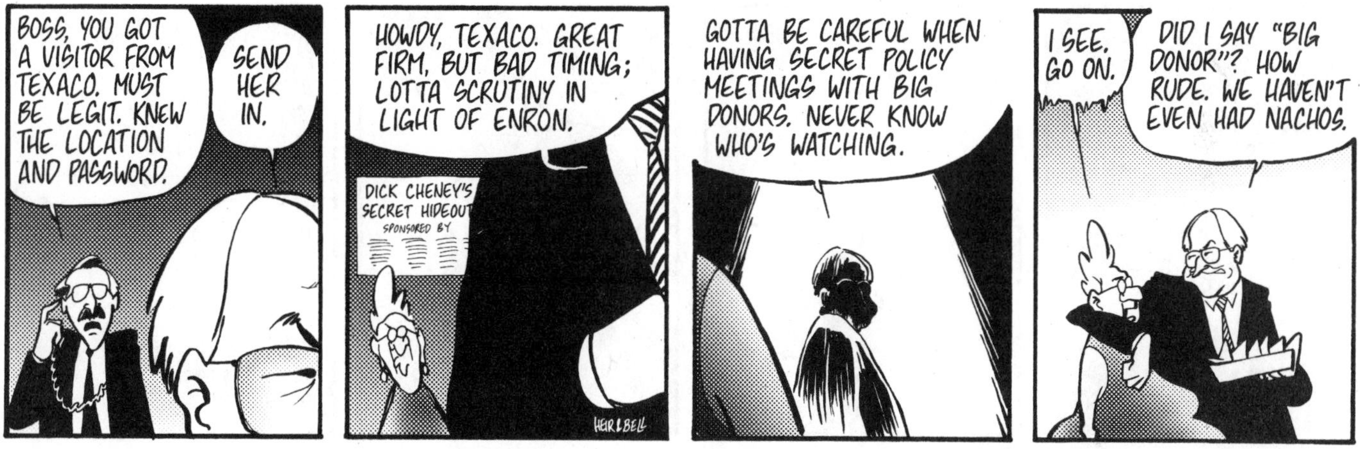
BOSS, YOU GOT A VISITOR FROM TEXACO. MUST BE LEGIT. KNEW THE LOCATION AND PASSWORD.
SEND HER IN.
HOWDY, TEXACO. GREAT FIRM, BUT BAD TIMING; LOTTA SCRUTINY IN LIGHT OF ENRON.
DICK CHENEY'S SECRET HIDEOUT SPONSORED BY
HEIR & BELL
GOTTA BE CAREFUL WHEN HAVING SECRET POLICY MEETINGS WITH BIG DONORS. NEVER KNOW WHO'S WATCHING.
I SEE. GO ON.
DID I SAY "BIG DONOR"? HOW RUDE. WE HAVEN'T EVEN HAD NACHOS.

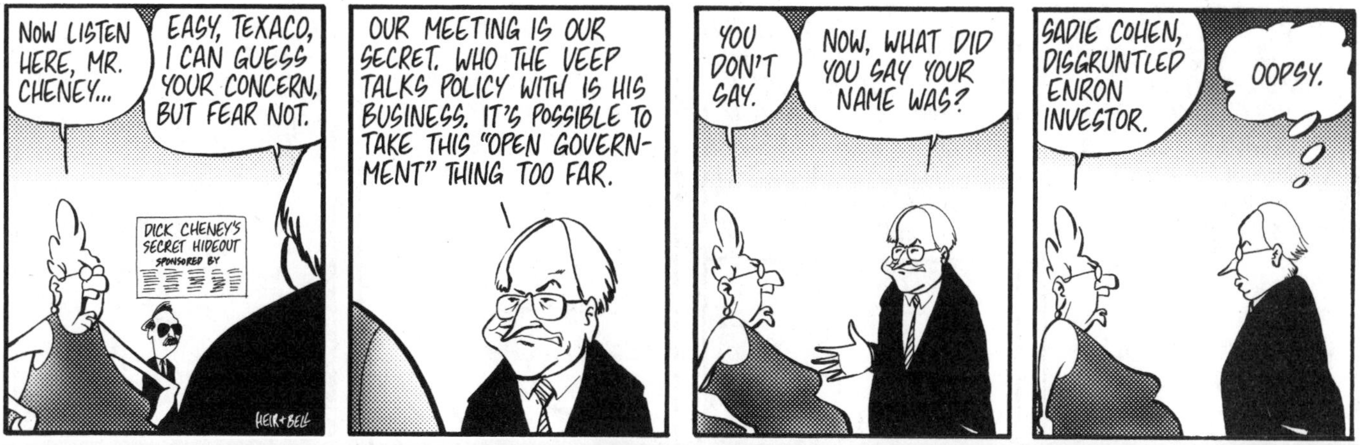
NOW LISTEN HERE, MR. CHENEY...
EASY, TEXACO, I CAN GUESS YOUR CONCERN, BUT FEAR NOT.
DICK CHENEY'S SECRET HIDEOUT SPONSORED BY
HEIR + BELL
OUR MEETING IS OUR SECRET. WHO THE VEEP TALKS POLICY WITH IS HIS BUSINESS. IT'S POSSIBLE TO TAKE THIS "OPEN GOVERNMENT" THING TOO FAR.
YOU DON'T SAY.
NOW, WHAT DID YOU SAY YOUR NAME WAS?
SADIE COHEN, DISGRUNTLED ENRON INVESTOR.
OOPSY.

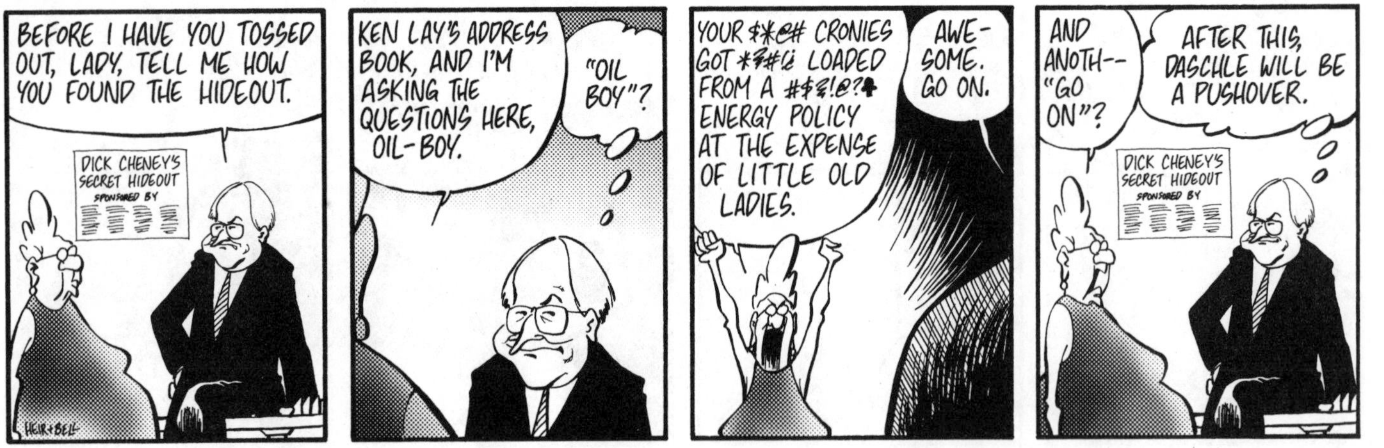
BEFORE I HAVE YOU TOSSED OUT, LADY, TELL ME HOW YOU FOUND THE HIDEOUT.
DICK CHENEY'S SECRET HIDEOUT SPONSORED BY
HEIR+BELL
KEN LAY'S ADDRESS BOOK, AND I'M ASKING THE QUESTIONS HERE, OIL-BOY.
"OIL BOY"?
YOUR $*@# CRONIES GOT *#%¿ LOADED FROM A #$%!@?♣ ENERGY POLICY AT THE EXPENSE OF LITTLE OLD LADIES.
AWE-SOME. GO ON.
AND ANOTH-- "GO ON"?
AFTER THIS, DASCHLE WILL BE A PUSHOVER.
DICK CHENEY'S SECRET HIDEOUT SPONSORED BY

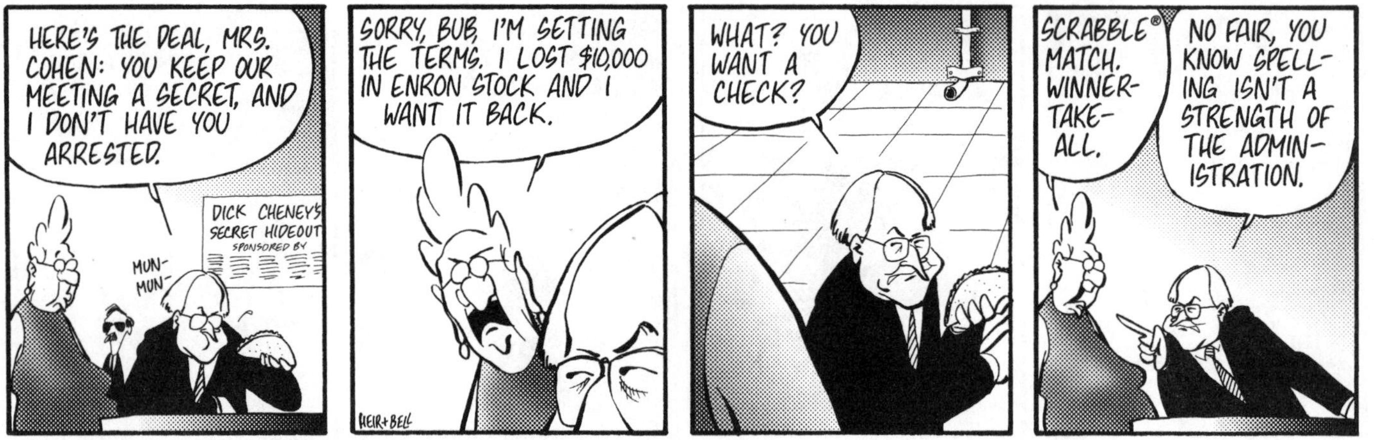
HERE'S THE DEAL, MRS. COHEN: YOU KEEP OUR MEETING A SECRET, AND I DON'T HAVE YOU ARRESTED.
DICK CHENEY'S SECRET HIDEOUT SPONSORED BY
MUN-MUN-
SORRY, BUB, I'M SETTING THE TERMS. I LOST $10,000 IN ENRON STOCK AND I WANT IT BACK.
HEIR+BELL
WHAT? YOU WANT A CHECK?
SCRABBLE® MATCH. WINNER-TAKE-ALL.
NO FAIR, YOU KNOW SPELL-ING ISN'T A STRENGTH OF THE ADMIN-ISTRATION.

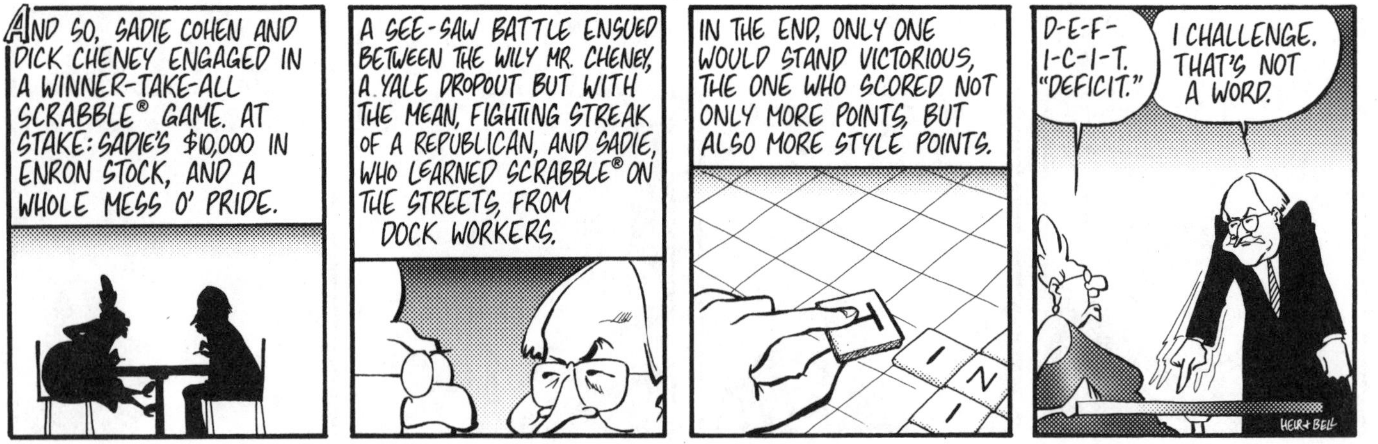
AND SO, SADIE COHEN AND DICK CHENEY ENGAGED IN A WINNER-TAKE-ALL SCRABBLE® GAME. AT STAKE: SADIE'S $10,000 IN ENRON STOCK, AND A WHOLE MESS O' PRIDE.
A SEE-SAW BATTLE ENSUED BETWEEN THE WILY MR. CHENEY, A YALE DROPOUT BUT WITH THE MEAN, FIGHTING STREAK OF A REPUBLICAN, AND SADIE, WHO LEARNED SCRABBLE® ON THE STREETS, FROM DOCK WORKERS.
IN THE END, ONLY ONE WOULD STAND VICTORIOUS, THE ONE WHO SCORED NOT ONLY MORE POINTS, BUT ALSO MORE STYLE POINTS.
T
I N I
D-E-F-I-C-I-T. "DEFICIT."
I CHALLENGE. THAT'S NOT A WORD.
HEIR+BELL

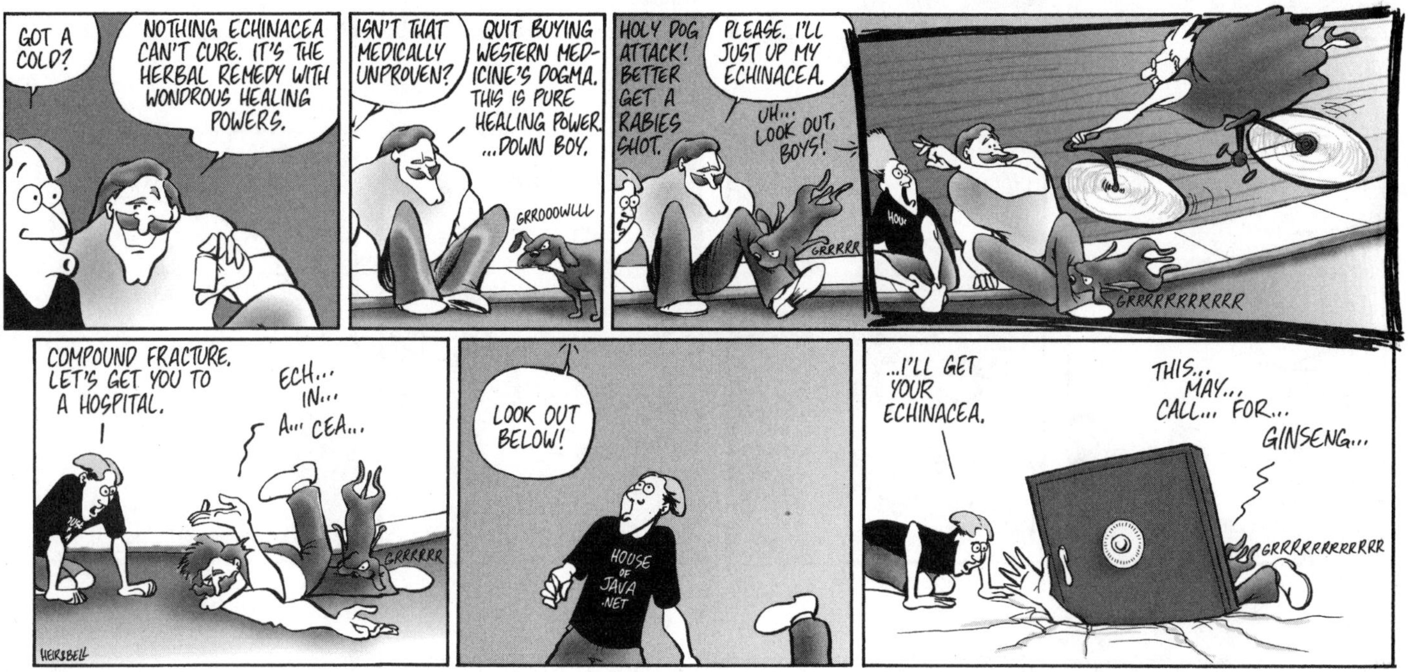
GOT A COLD?
NOTHING ECHINACEA CAN'T CURE. IT'S THE HERBAL REMEDY WITH WONDROUS HEALING POWERS.
ISN'T THAT MEDICALLY UNPROVEN?
QUIT BUYING WESTERN MED-ICINE'S DOGMA. THIS IS PURE HEALING POWER. ...DOWN BOY.
GRROOOWLLL
HOLY DOG ATTACK! BETTER GET A RABIES SHOT.
PLEASE. I'LL JUST UP MY ECHINACEA.
UH... LOOK OUT, BOYS!
GRRRRR
GRRRRRRRRRRR
COMPOUND FRACTURE. LET'S GET YOU TO A HOSPITAL.
ECH... IN... A... CEA...
GRRRRRR
HEIR&BELL
LOOK OUT BELOW!
HOUSE OF JAVA .NET
...I'LL GET YOUR ECHINACEA.
THIS... MAY... CALL... FOR... GINSENG...
GRRRRRRRRRRRR

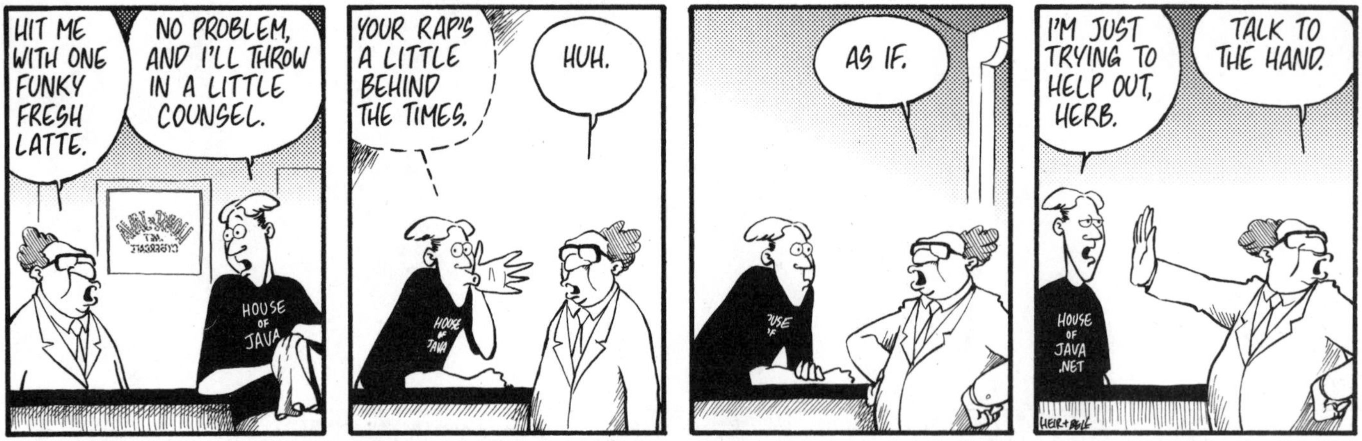
HIT ME WITH ONE FUNKY FRESH LATTE.
NO PROBLEM, AND I'LL THROW IN A LITTLE COUNSEL.
YOUR RAP'S A LITTLE BEHIND THE TIMES.
HUH.
AS IF.
I'M JUST TRYING TO HELP OUT, HERB.
TALK TO THE HAND.
HOUSE OF JAVA .NET
HEIR+BELL

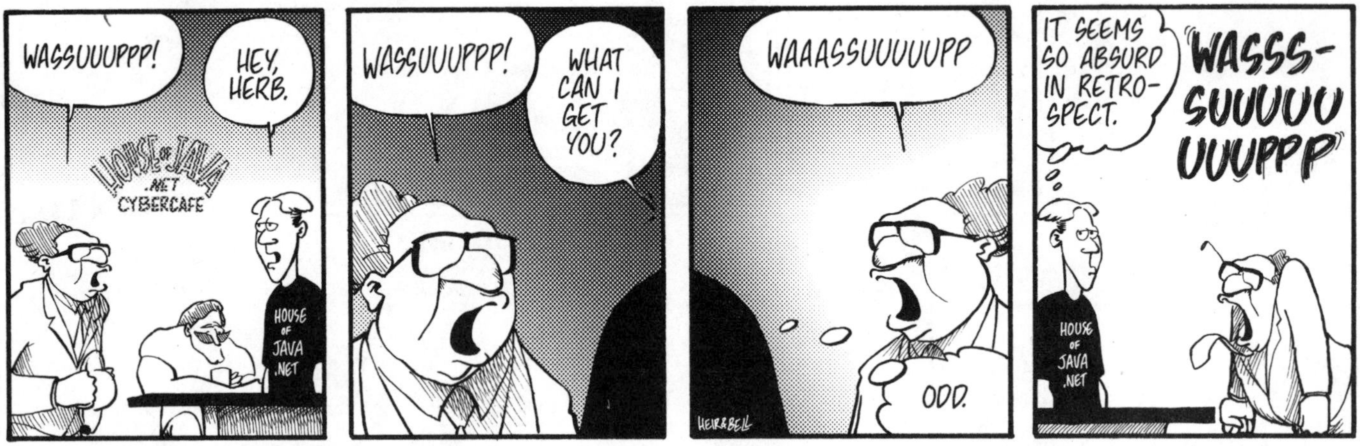
WASSUUUPPP!
HEY, HERB.
HOUSE OF JAVA .NET CYBERCAFE
WASSUUUPPP!
WHAT CAN I GET YOU?
WAAASSUUUUUPP
ODD.
HEIR&BELL
IT SEEMS SO ABSURD IN RETRO-SPECT.
"WASSS-SUUUUU UUUPPP"
HOUSE OF JAVA .NET

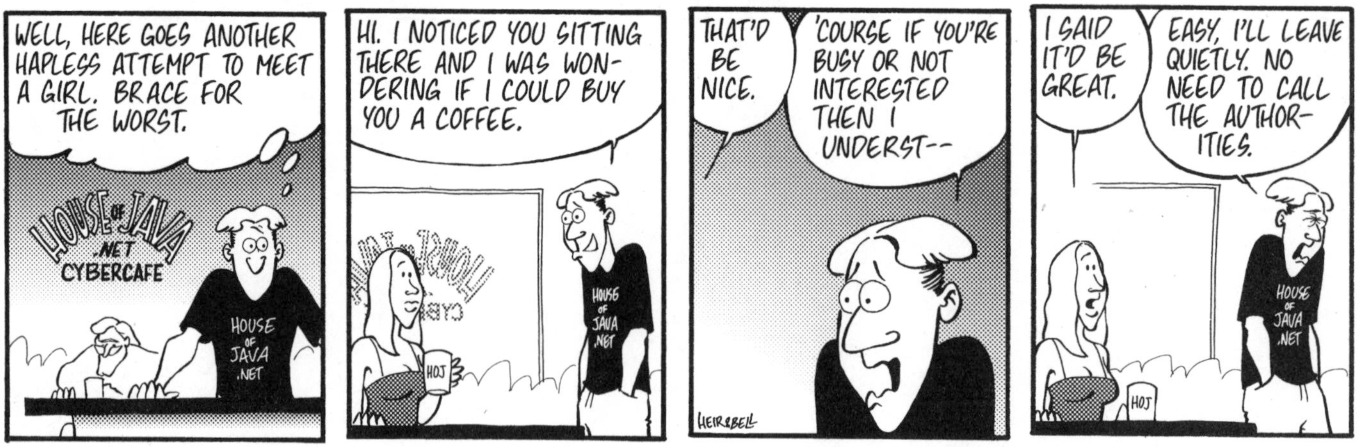
WELL, HERE GOES ANOTHER HAPLESS ATTEMPT TO MEET A GIRL. BRACE FOR THE WORST.
HOUSE OF JAVA .NET CYBERCAFE
HI. I NOTICED YOU SITTING THERE AND I WAS WON-DERING IF I COULD BUY YOU A COFFEE.
HOJ
THAT'D BE NICE.
'COURSE IF YOU'RE BUSY OR NOT INTERESTED THEN I UNDERST--
HEIR&BELL
I SAID IT'D BE GREAT.
EASY, I'LL LEAVE QUIETLY. NO NEED TO CALL THE AUTHOR-ITIES.
HOUSE OF JAVA .NET

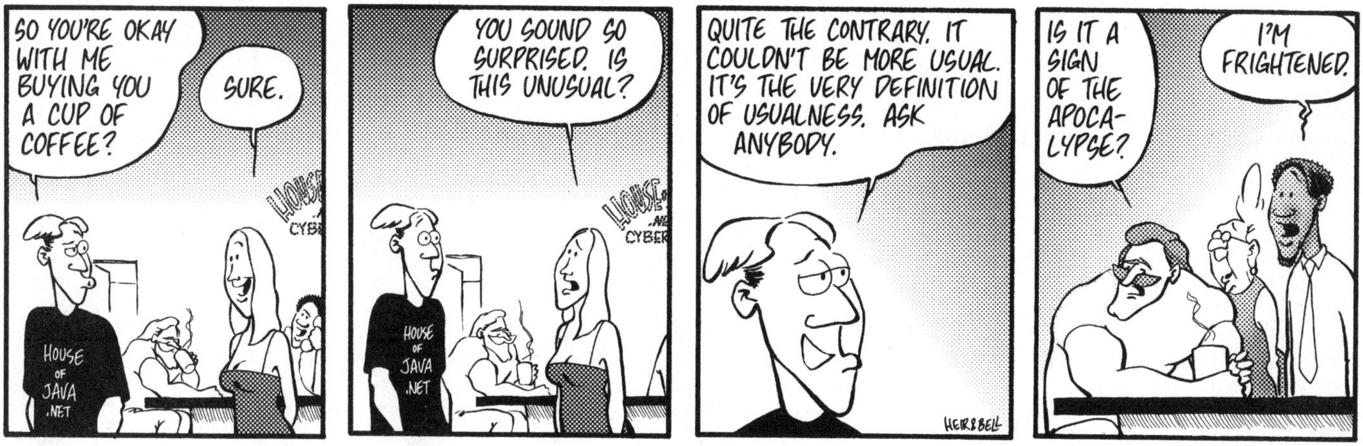
SO YOU'RE OKAY WITH ME BUYING YOU A CUP OF COFFEE?
SURE.
YOU SOUND SO SURPRISED. IS THIS UNUSUAL?
QUITE THE CONTRARY. IT COULDN'T BE MORE USUAL. IT'S THE VERY DEFINITION OF USUALNESS. ASK ANYBODY.
IS IT A SIGN OF THE APOCALYPSE?
I'M FRIGHTENED.

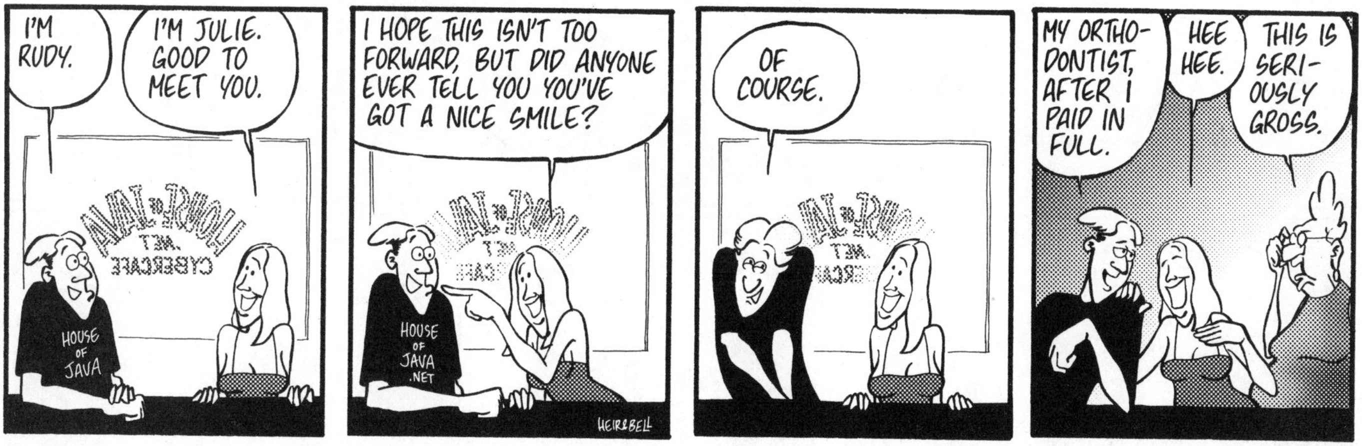
I'M RUDY.
I'M JULIE. GOOD TO MEET YOU.
I HOPE THIS ISN'T TOO FORWARD, BUT DID ANYONE EVER TELL YOU YOU'VE GOT A NICE SMILE?
OF COURSE.
MY ORTHODONTIST, AFTER I PAID IN FULL.
HEE HEE.
THIS IS SERIOUSLY GROSS.

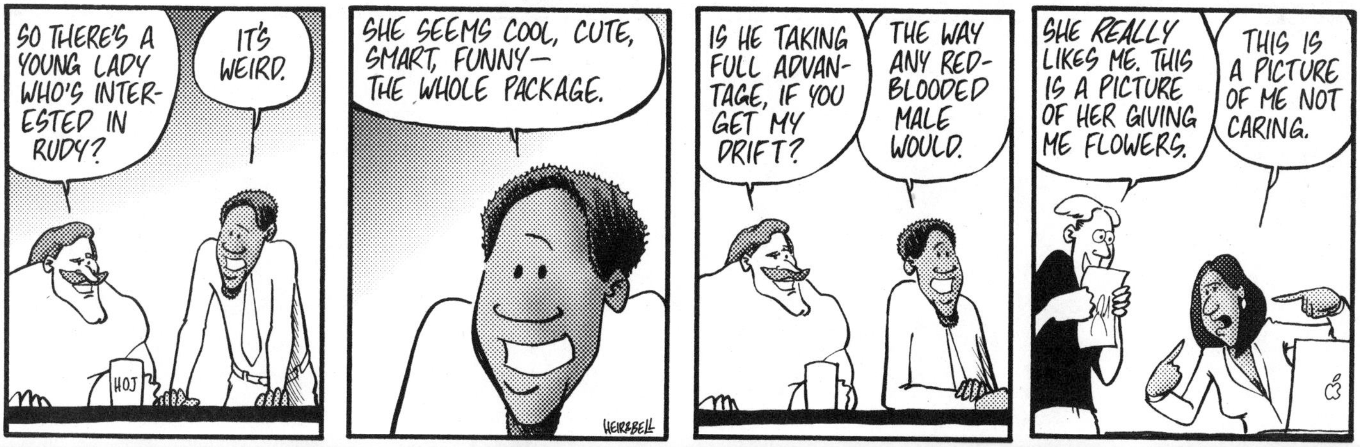
SO THERE'S A YOUNG LADY WHO'S INTERESTED IN RUDY?
IT'S WEIRD.
SHE SEEMS COOL, CUTE, SMART, FUNNY— THE WHOLE PACKAGE.
IS HE TAKING FULL ADVANTAGE, IF YOU GET MY DRIFT?
THE WAY ANY RED-BLOODED MALE WOULD.
SHE *REALLY* LIKES ME. THIS IS A PICTURE OF HER GIVING ME FLOWERS.
THIS IS A PICTURE OF ME NOT CARING.

ONE LATTE, EXTRA FOAM.
WOW. ALAN GREENSPAN? IT'S AN HONOR, YOUR EMINENCE.
.NET CYBERCAFE
SHHH. YOU'LL ATTRACT AN ENTOURAGE.
ENTOU-RAGE?
HERE HE IS!
YOUR LATTE, MR. GREEN-SPAN.
LATTE!
LATTE! LATTE! HE GOT A LATTE!
UM... IS THE FOAM HIGH ENOUGH?
HIGHER.
HOLY COW. HE SAID HIGHER!
HIGHER! IT CAN MEAN ONE THING!
HE'S PESSIMISTIC!
HE'S OPTIMISTIC!
SELL! SELL!
BUY! BUY!
ONE JELLY DONUT.
HOLY COW! HE'S CHANGING COURSE!

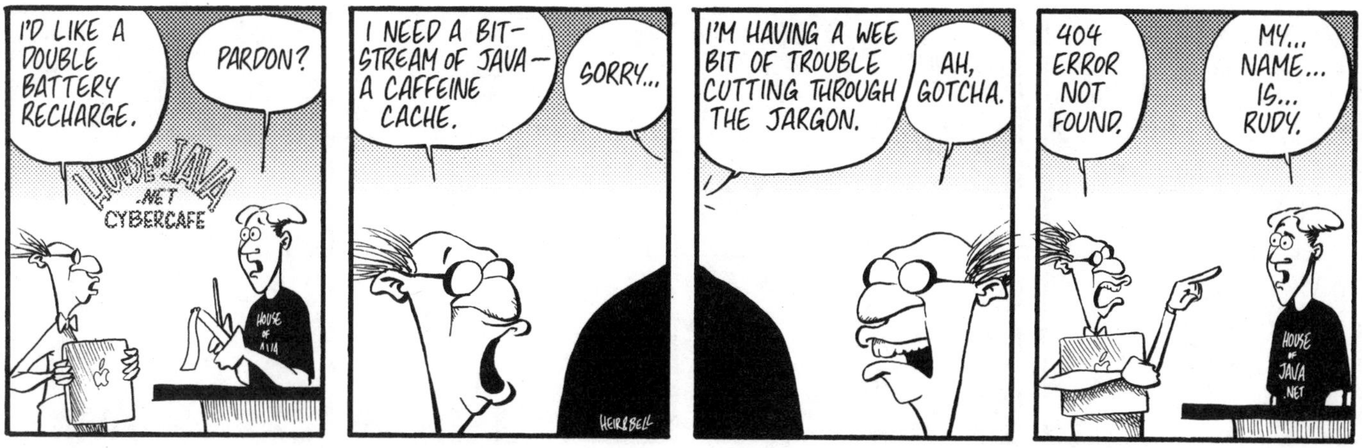
I'D LIKE A DOUBLE BATTERY RECHARGE.
PARDON?
HOUSE OF JAVA .NET CYBERCAFE
I NEED A BIT-STREAM OF JAVA— A CAFFEINE CACHE.
SORRY...
I'M HAVING A WEE BIT OF TROUBLE CUTTING THROUGH THE JARGON.
AH, GOTCHA.
404 ERROR NOT FOUND.
MY... NAME... IS... RUDY.

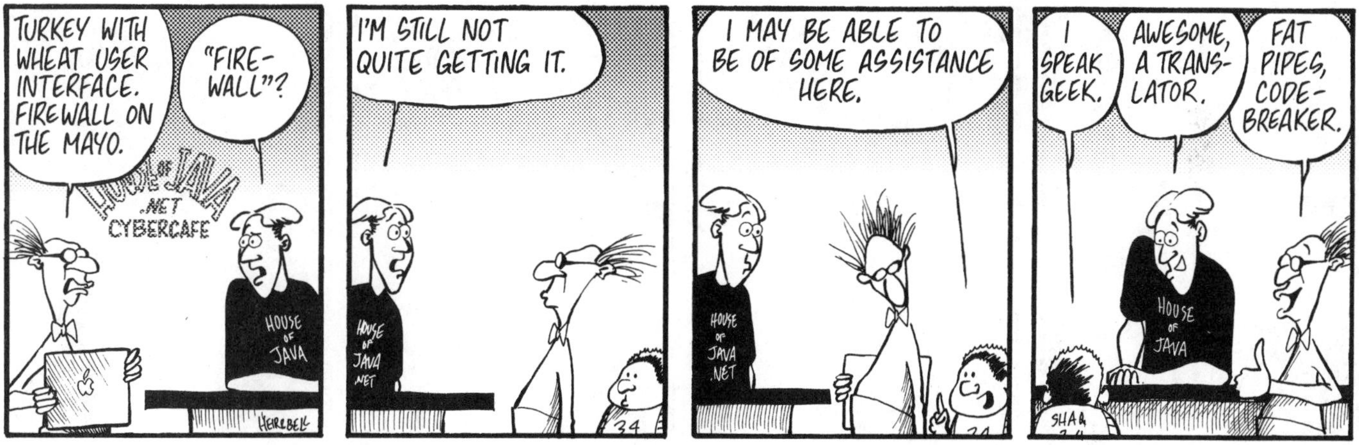
TURKEY WITH WHEAT USER INTERFACE. FIREWALL ON THE MAYO.
"FIRE-WALL"?
HOUSE OF JAVA .NET CYBERCAFE
I'M STILL NOT QUITE GETTING IT.
I MAY BE ABLE TO BE OF SOME ASSISTANCE HERE.
I SPEAK GEEK.
AWESOME, A TRANSLATOR.
FAT PIPES, CODE-BREAKER.

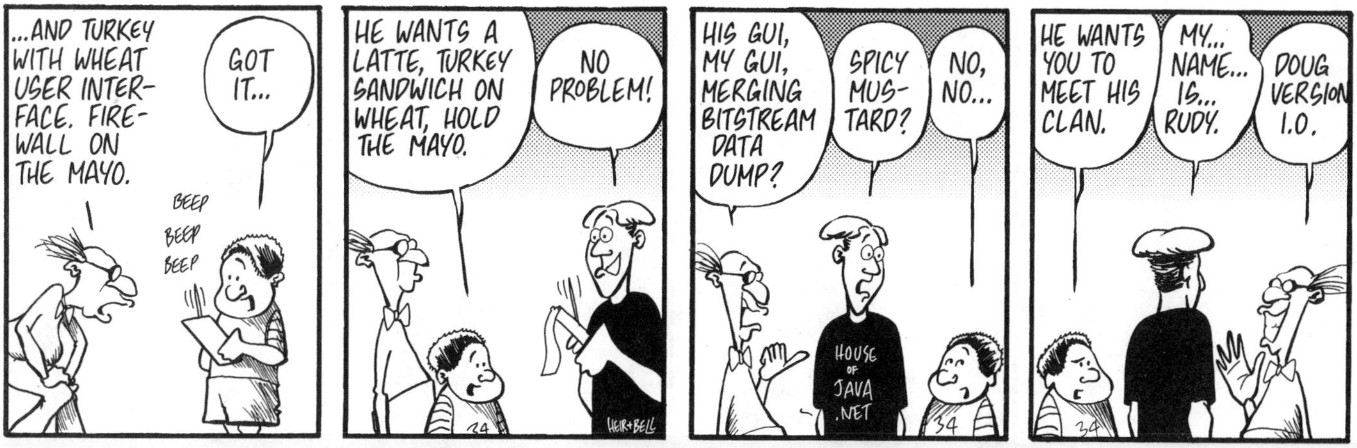
...AND TURKEY WITH WHEAT USER INTERFACE. FIREWALL ON THE MAYO.
GOT IT...
BEEP
BEEP
BEEP
HE WANTS A LATTE, TURKEY SANDWICH ON WHEAT, HOLD THE MAYO.
NO PROBLEM!
HIS GUI, MY GUI, MERGING BITSTREAM DATA DUMP?
SPICY MUSTARD?
NO, NO...
HE WANTS YOU TO MEET HIS CLAN.
MY... NAME... IS... RUDY.
DOUG VERSION 1.0.

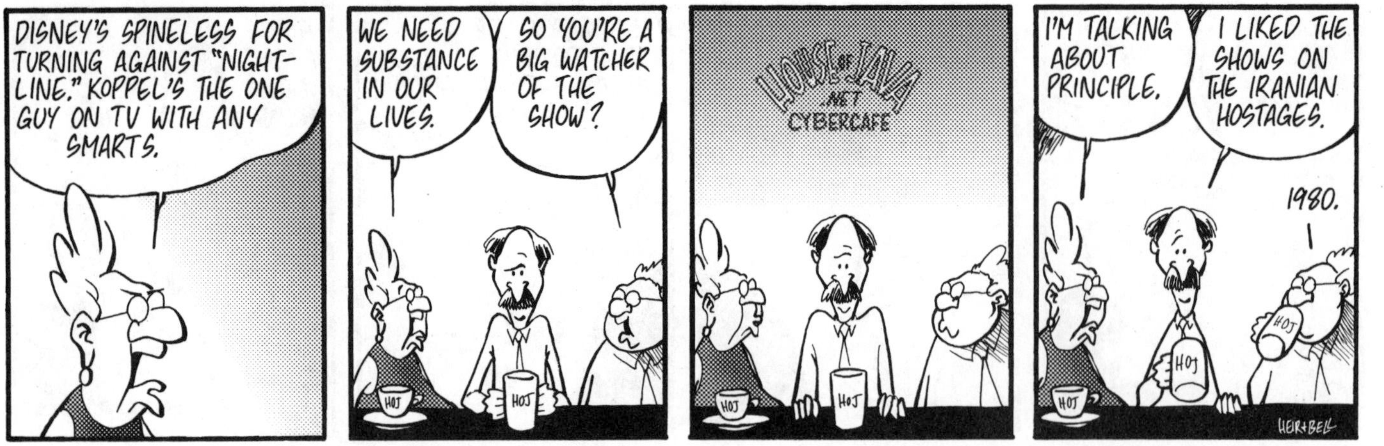
DISNEY'S SPINELESS FOR TURNING AGAINST "NIGHTLINE." KOPPEL'S THE ONE GUY ON TV WITH ANY SMARTS.
HOUSE OF JAVA .NET CYBERCAFE
WE NEED SUBSTANCE IN OUR LIVES.
SO YOU'RE A BIG WATCHER OF THE SHOW?
I'M TALKING ABOUT PRINCIPLE.
I LIKED THE SHOWS ON THE IRANIAN HOSTAGES.
1980.
HEIR+BELL

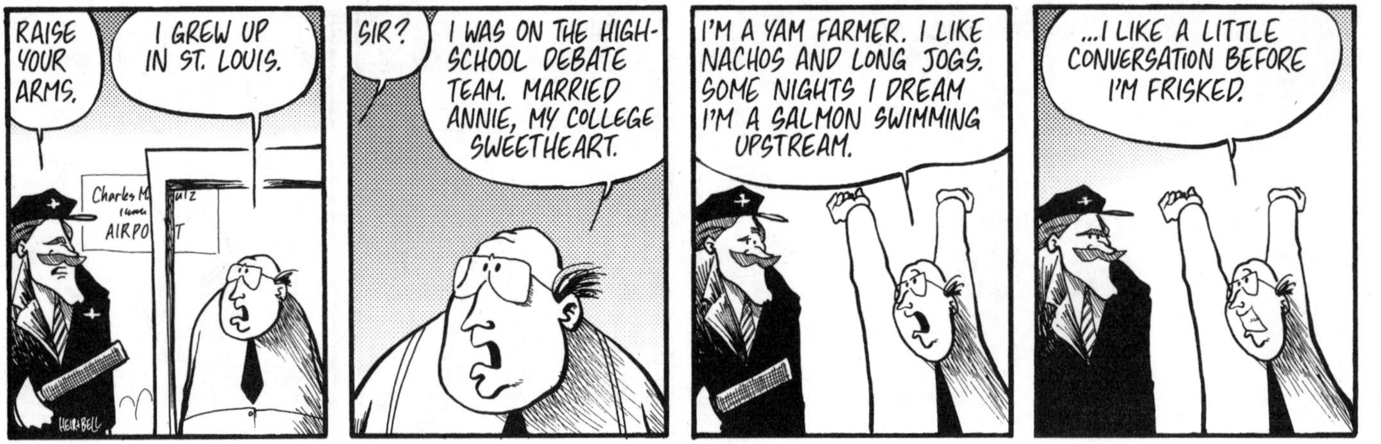
RAISE YOUR ARMS.
I GREW UP IN ST. LOUIS.
SIR?
I WAS ON THE HIGH-SCHOOL DEBATE TEAM. MARRIED ANNIE, MY COLLEGE SWEETHEART.
I'M A YAM FARMER. I LIKE NACHOS AND LONG JOGS. SOME NIGHTS I DREAM I'M A SALMON SWIMMING UPSTREAM.
...I LIKE A LITTLE CONVERSATION BEFORE I'M FRISKED.
HEIR+BELL

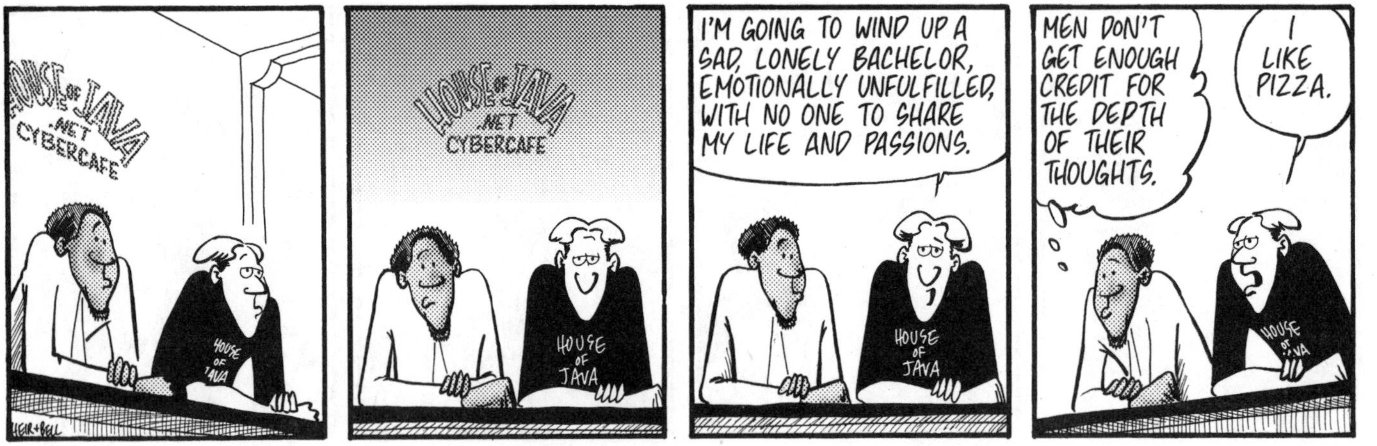
HOUSE OF JAVA .NET CYBERCAFE
I'M GOING TO WIND UP A SAD, LONELY BACHELOR, EMOTIONALLY UNFULFILLED, WITH NO ONE TO SHARE MY LIFE AND PASSIONS.
MEN DON'T GET ENOUGH CREDIT FOR THE DEPTH OF THEIR THOUGHTS.
I LIKE PIZZA.
HEIR+BELL

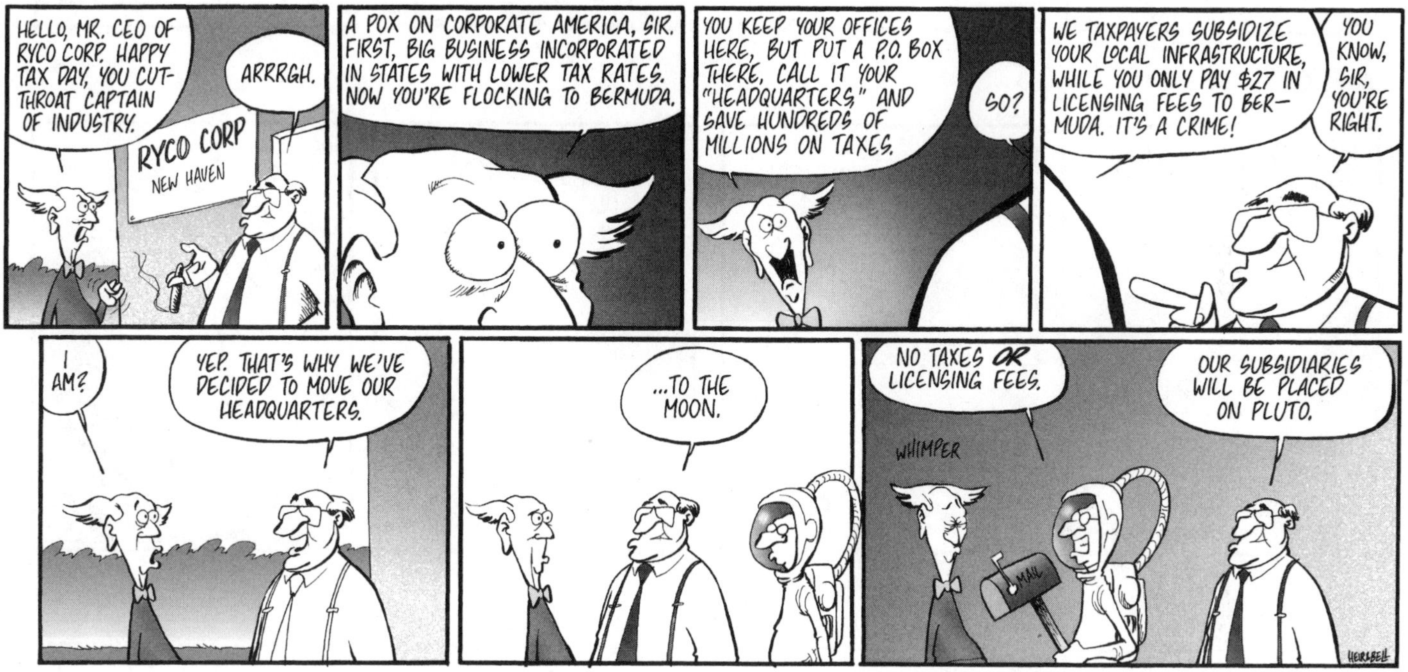
HELLO, MR. CEO OF RYCO CORP. HAPPY TAX DAY, YOU CUT-THROAT CAPTAIN OF INDUSTRY.
ARRRGH.
RYCO CORP
NEW HAVEN
A POX ON CORPORATE AMERICA, SIR. FIRST, BIG BUSINESS INCORPORATED IN STATES WITH LOWER TAX RATES. NOW YOU'RE FLOCKING TO BERMUDA.
YOU KEEP YOUR OFFICES HERE, BUT PUT A P.O. BOX THERE, CALL IT YOUR "HEADQUARTERS," AND SAVE HUNDREDS OF MILLIONS ON TAXES.
SO?
WE TAXPAYERS SUBSIDIZE YOUR LOCAL INFRASTRUCTURE, WHILE YOU ONLY PAY $27 IN LICENSING FEES TO BER-MUDA. IT'S A CRIME!
YOU KNOW, SIR, YOU'RE RIGHT.
I AM?
YEP. THAT'S WHY WE'VE DECIDED TO MOVE OUR HEADQUARTERS.
...TO THE MOON.
NO TAXES OR LICENSING FEES.
WHIMPER
MAIL
OUR SUBSIDIARIES WILL BE PLACED ON PLUTO.

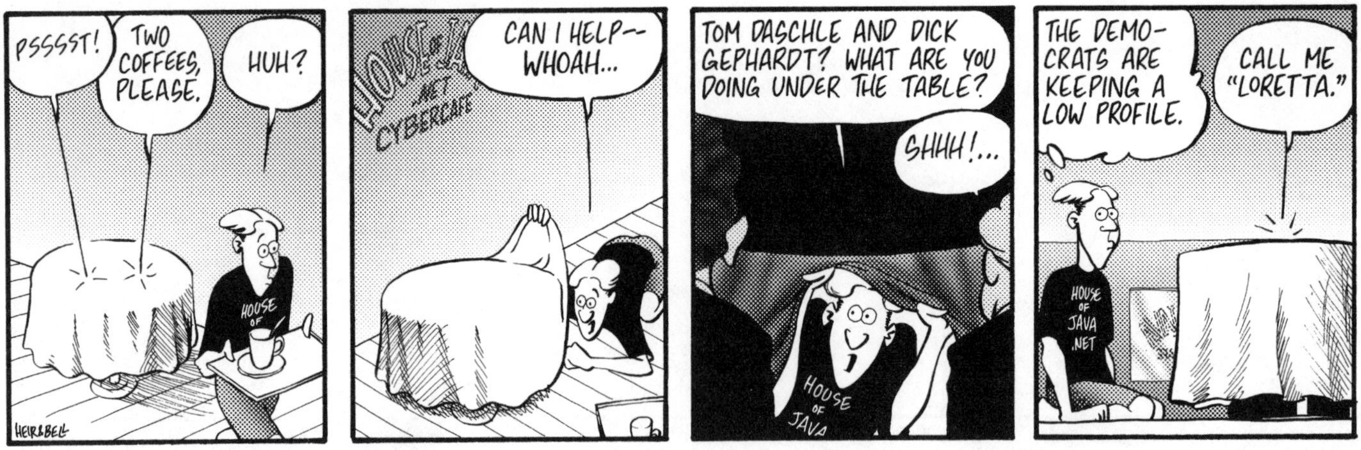
PSSSST!
TWO COFFEES, PLEASE.
HUH?
HEIR&BELL
HOUSE OF
HOUSE OF JAVA .NET CYBERCAFE
CAN I HELP-- WHOAH...
TOM DASCHLE AND DICK GEPHARDT? WHAT ARE YOU DOING UNDER THE TABLE?
SHHH!...
HOUSE OF JAVA
THE DEMOCRATS ARE KEEPING A LOW PROFILE.
CALL ME "LORETTA."
HOUSE OF JAVA .NET

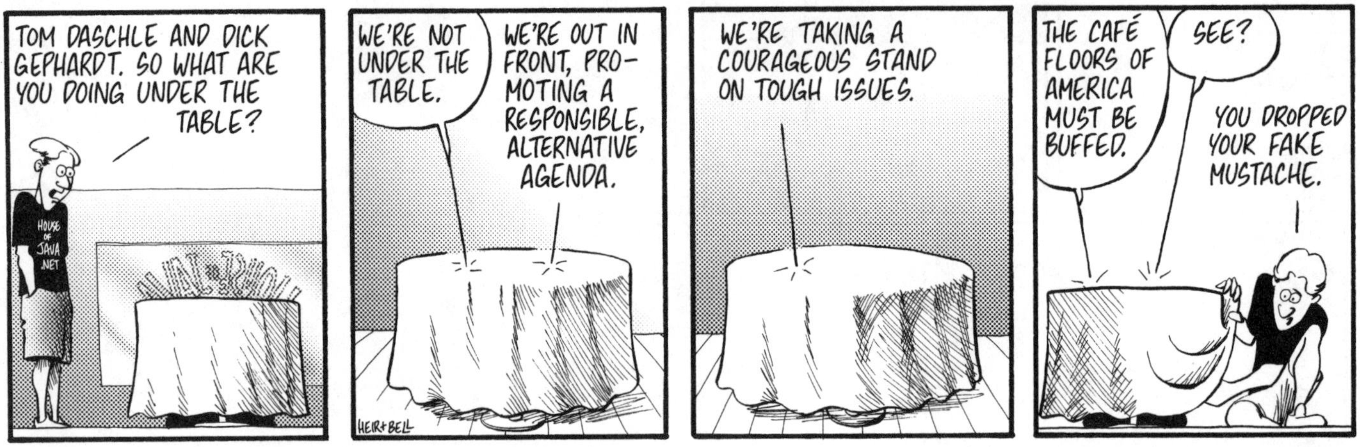
TOM DASCHLE AND DICK GEPHARDT. SO WHAT ARE YOU DOING UNDER THE TABLE?
HOUSE OF JAVA .NET
WE'RE NOT UNDER THE TABLE.
WE'RE OUT IN FRONT, PROMOTING A RESPONSIBLE, ALTERNATIVE AGENDA.
HEIR+BELL
WE'RE TAKING A COURAGEOUS STAND ON TOUGH ISSUES.
THE CAFÉ FLOORS OF AMERICA MUST BE BUFFED.
SEE?
YOU DROPPED YOUR FAKE MUSTACHE.

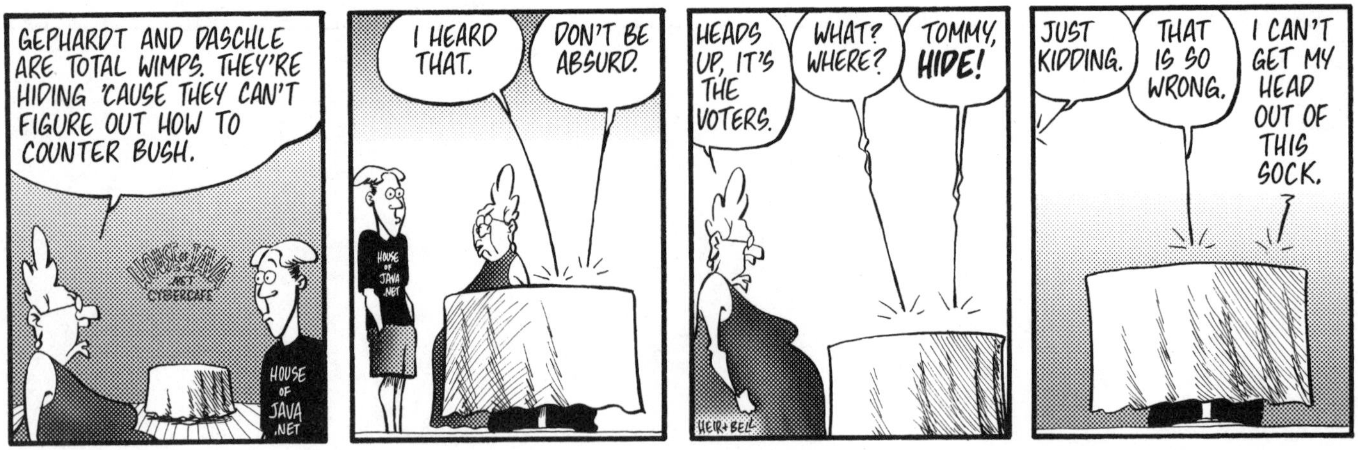
GEPHARDT AND DASCHLE ARE TOTAL WIMPS. THEY'RE HIDING 'CAUSE THEY CAN'T FIGURE OUT HOW TO COUNTER BUSH.
HOUSE OF JAVA .NET CYBERCAFE
HOUSE OF JAVA .NET
I HEARD THAT.
DON'T BE ABSURD.
HOUSE OF JAVA .NET
HEADS UP, IT'S THE VOTERS.
WHAT? WHERE?
TOMMY, **HIDE!**
HEIR+BELL
JUST KIDDING.
THAT IS SO WRONG.
I CAN'T GET MY HEAD OUT OF THIS SOCK.

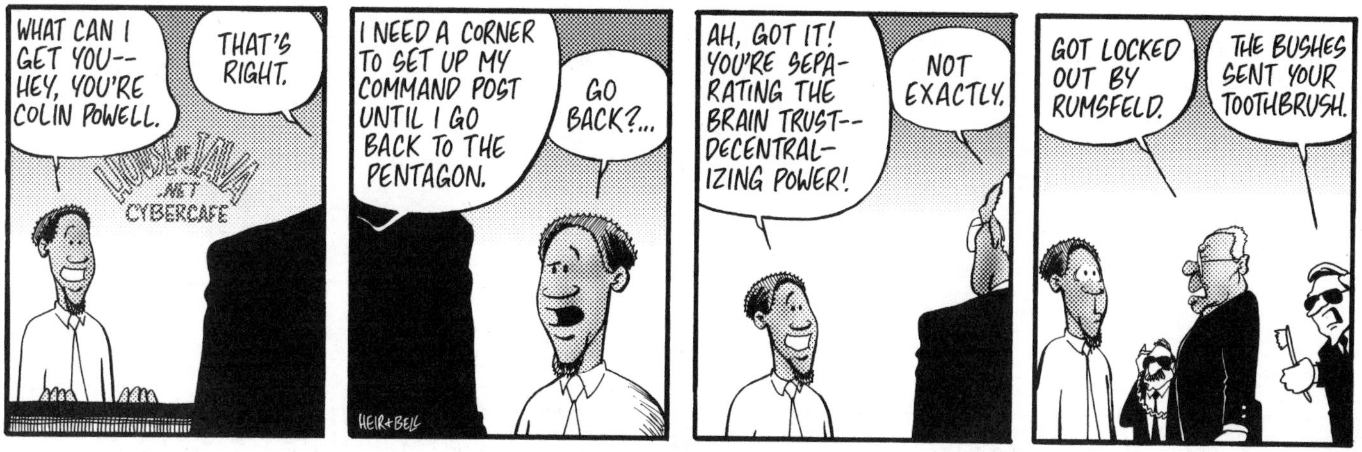
WHAT CAN I GET YOU-- HEY, YOU'RE COLIN POWELL.
THAT'S RIGHT.
HOUSE OF JAVA .NET CYBERCAFE
I NEED A CORNER TO SET UP MY COMMAND POST UNTIL I GO BACK TO THE PENTAGON.
GO BACK?...
HEIR+BELL
AH, GOT IT! YOU'RE SEPARATING THE BRAIN TRUST-- DECENTRALIZING POWER!
NOT EXACTLY.
GOT LOCKED OUT BY RUMSFELD.
THE BUSHES SENT YOUR TOOTHBRUSH.

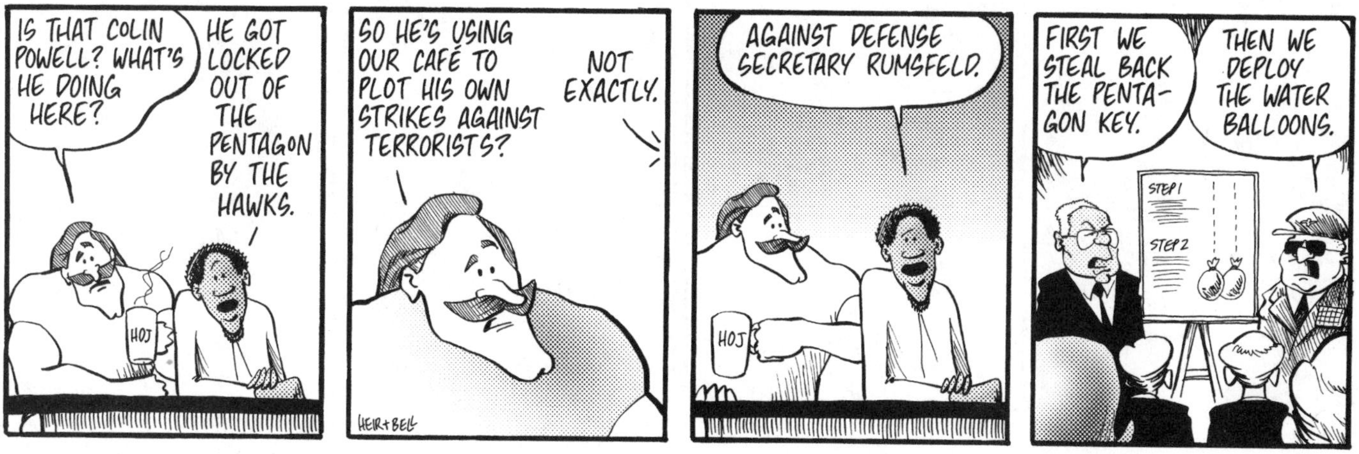
IS THAT COLIN POWELL? WHAT'S HE DOING HERE?
HE GOT LOCKED OUT OF THE PENTAGON BY THE HAWKS.
HOJ
SO HE'S USING OUR CAFÉ TO PLOT HIS OWN STRIKES AGAINST TERRORISTS?
NOT EXACTLY.
HEIR+BELL
AGAINST DEFENSE SECRETARY RUMSFELD.
HOJ
FIRST WE STEAL BACK THE PENTAGON KEY.
THEN WE DEPLOY THE WATER BALLOONS.
STEP 1
STEP 2

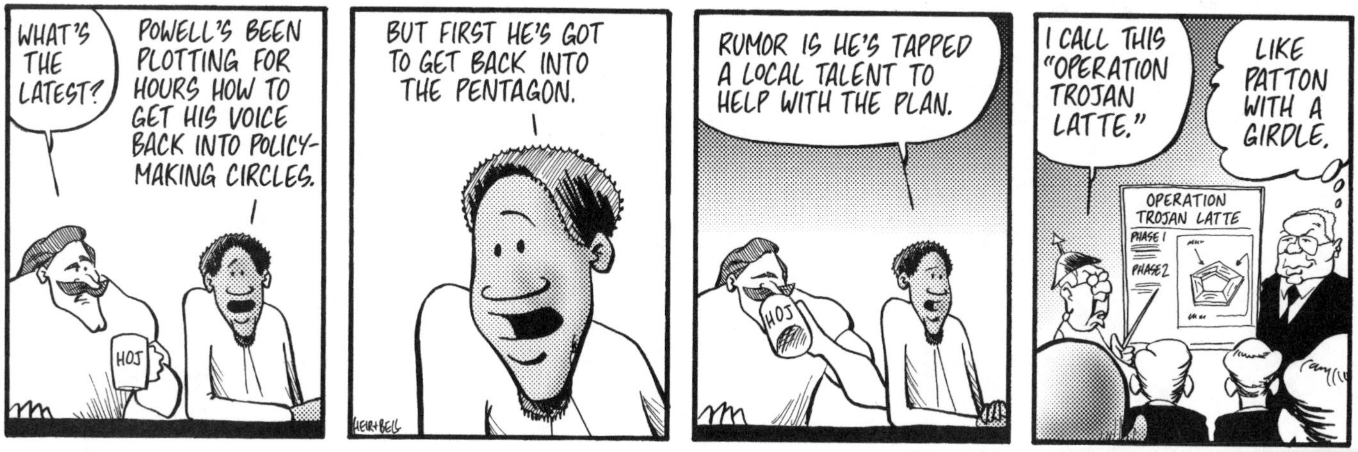
WHAT'S THE LATEST?
POWELL'S BEEN PLOTTING FOR HOURS HOW TO GET HIS VOICE BACK INTO POLICY-MAKING CIRCLES.
HOJ
BUT FIRST HE'S GOT TO GET BACK INTO THE PENTAGON.
HEIR+BELL
RUMOR IS HE'S TAPPED A LOCAL TALENT TO HELP WITH THE PLAN.
HOJ
I CALL THIS "OPERATION TROJAN LATTE."
LIKE PATTON WITH A GIRDLE.
OPERATION TROJAN LATTE
PHASE 1
PHASE 2

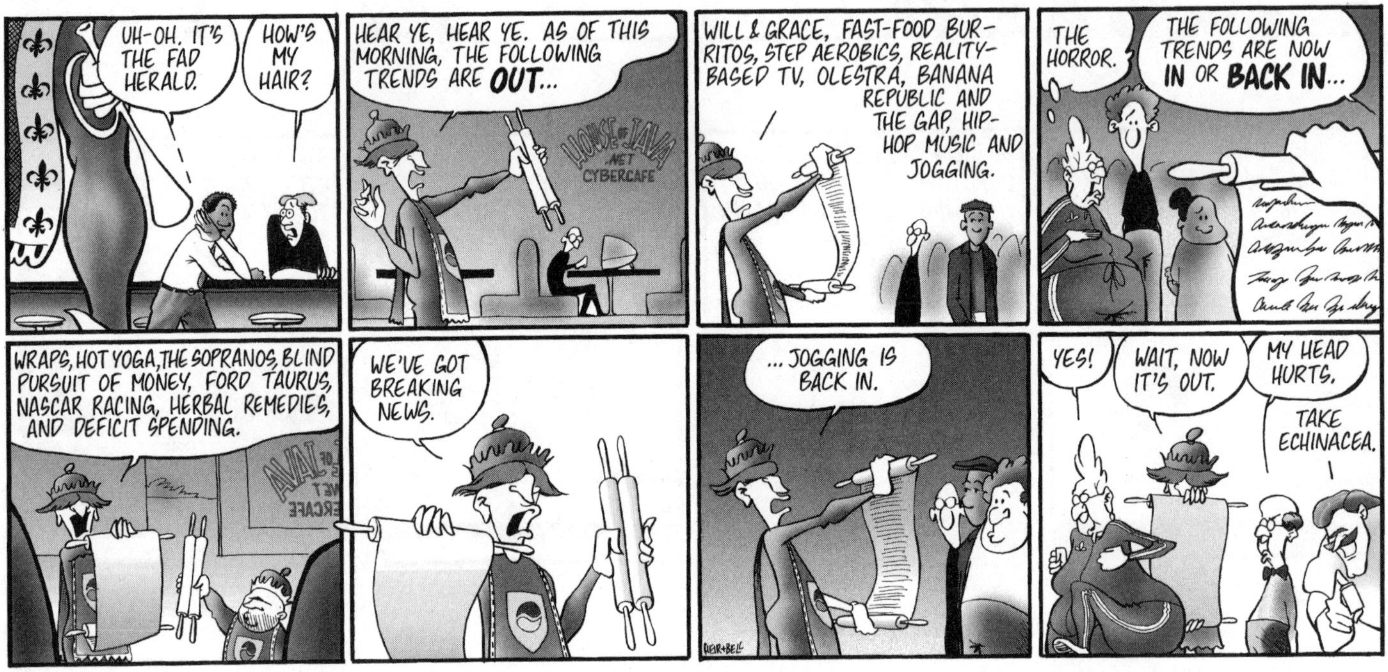
UH-OH. IT'S THE FAD HERALD.
HOW'S MY HAIR?
HEAR YE, HEAR YE. AS OF THIS MORNING, THE FOLLOWING TRENDS ARE **OUT**...
HOUSE OF JAVA .NET CYBERCAFE
WILL & GRACE, FAST-FOOD BURRITOS, STEP AEROBICS, REALITY-BASED TV, OLESTRA, BANANA REPUBLIC AND THE GAP, HIP-HOP MUSIC AND JOGGING.
THE HORROR.
THE FOLLOWING TRENDS ARE NOW **IN** OR **BACK IN**...
WRAPS, HOT YOGA, THE SOPRANOS, BLIND PURSUIT OF MONEY, FORD TAURUS, NASCAR RACING, HERBAL REMEDIES, AND DEFICIT SPENDING.
WE'VE GOT BREAKING NEWS.
...JOGGING IS BACK IN.
YES!
WAIT, NOW IT'S OUT.
MY HEAD HURTS.
TAKE ECHINACEA.

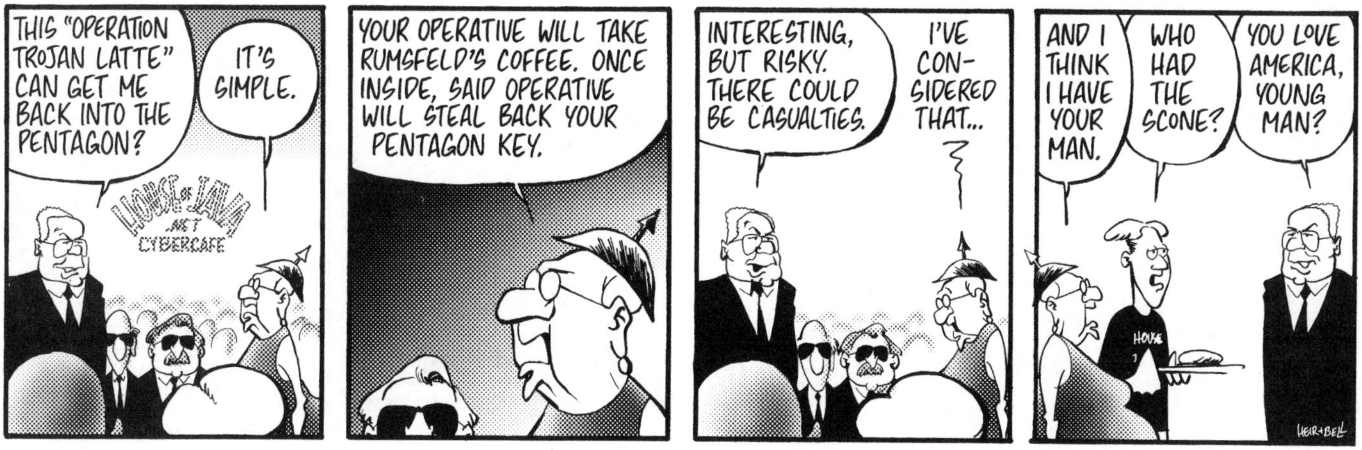
THIS "OPERATION TROJAN LATTE" CAN GET ME BACK INTO THE PENTAGON?
IT'S SIMPLE.
HOUSE of JAVA .NET CYBERCAFE
YOUR OPERATIVE WILL TAKE RUMSFELD'S COFFEE. ONCE INSIDE, SAID OPERATIVE WILL STEAL BACK YOUR PENTAGON KEY.
INTERESTING, BUT RISKY. THERE COULD BE CASUALTIES.
I'VE CONSIDERED THAT...
AND I THINK I HAVE YOUR MAN.
WHO HAD THE SCONE?
YOU LOVE AMERICA, YOUNG MAN?
HEIR+BELL

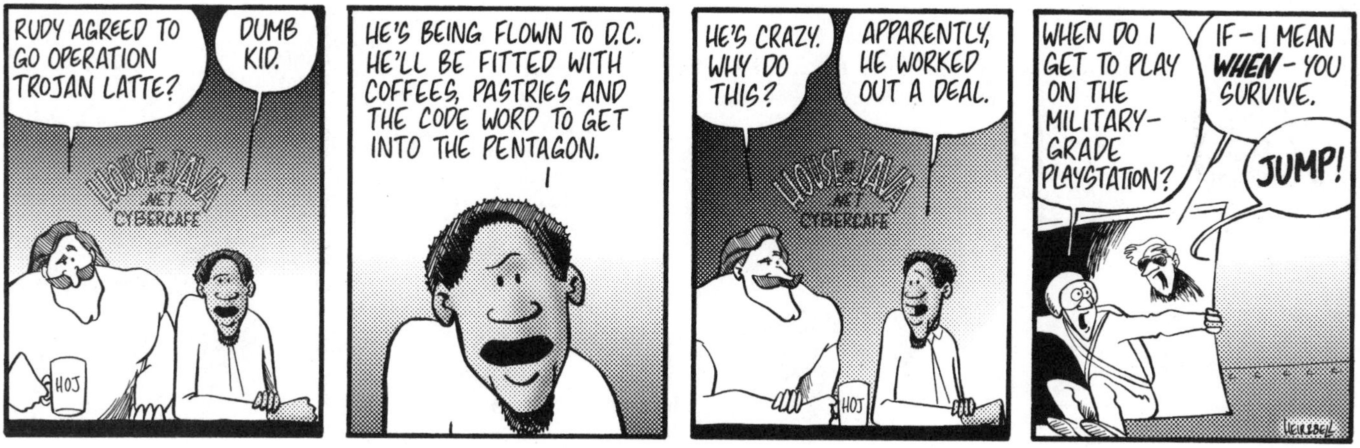
RUDY AGREED TO GO OPERATION TROJAN LATTE?
DUMB KID.
HOUSE of JAVA .NET CYBERCAFE
HOJ
HE'S BEING FLOWN TO D.C. HE'LL BE FITTED WITH COFFEES, PASTRIES AND THE CODE WORD TO GET INTO THE PENTAGON.
HE'S CRAZY. WHY DO THIS?
APPARENTLY, HE WORKED OUT A DEAL.
HOJ
WHEN DO I GET TO PLAY ON THE MILITARY-GRADE PLAYSTATION?
IF - I MEAN WHEN - YOU SURVIVE.
JUMP!
HEIR+BELL

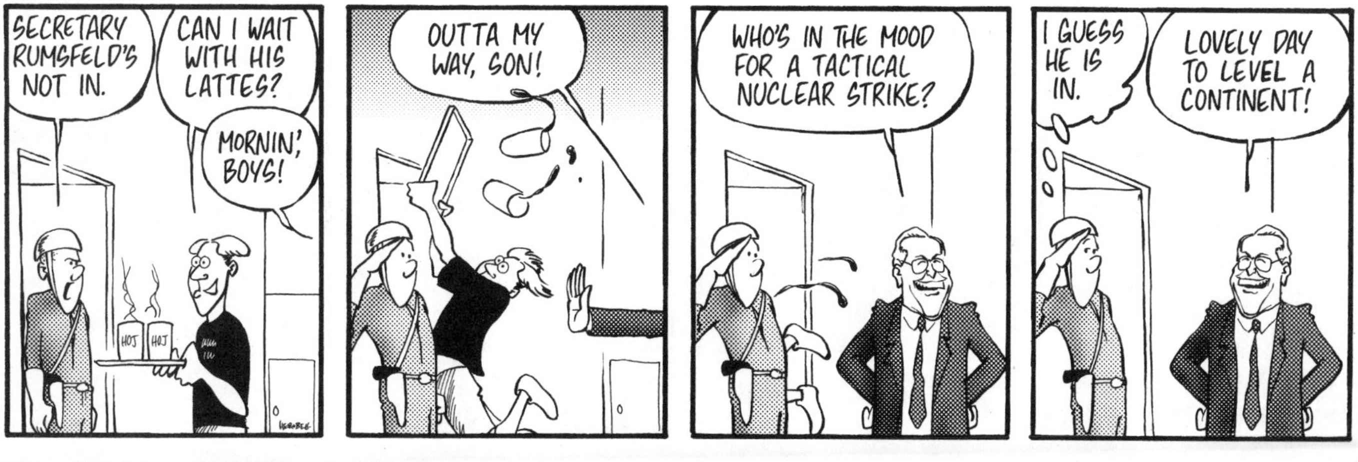
SECRETARY RUMSFELD'S NOT IN.
CAN I WAIT WITH HIS LATTES?
MORNIN', BOYS!
HOJ
HOJ
OUTTA MY WAY, SON!
WHO'S IN THE MOOD FOR A TACTICAL NUCLEAR STRIKE?
I GUESS HE IS IN.
LOVELY DAY TO LEVEL A CONTINENT!

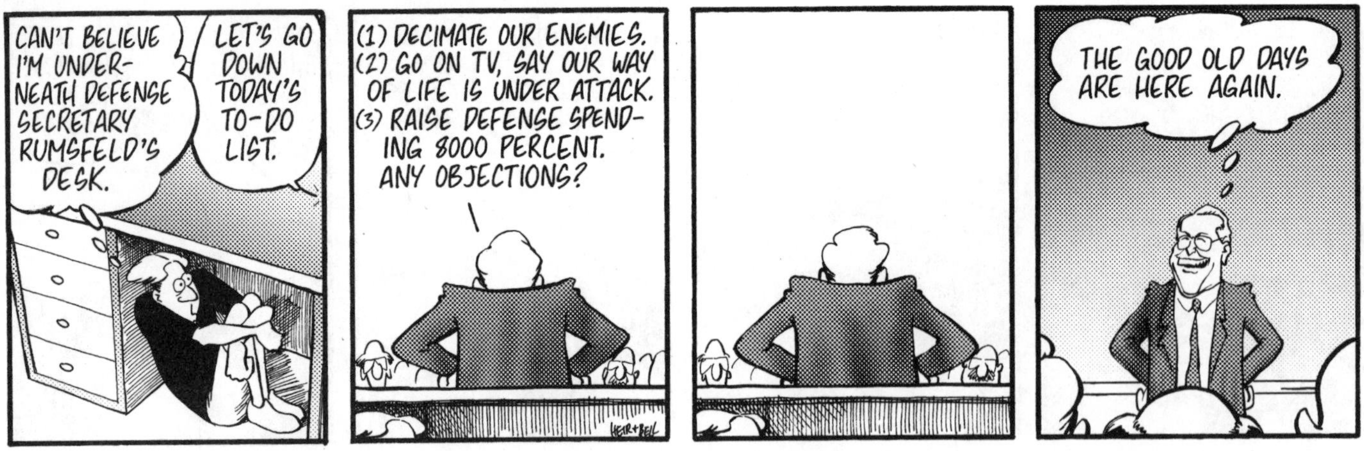
CAN'T BELIEVE I'M UNDER-NEATH DEFENSE SECRETARY RUMSFELD'S DESK.
LET'S GO DOWN TODAY'S TO-DO LIST.
(1) DECIMATE OUR ENEMIES. (2) GO ON TV, SAY OUR WAY OF LIFE IS UNDER ATTACK. (3) RAISE DEFENSE SPEND-ING 8000 PERCENT. ANY OBJECTIONS?
THE GOOD OLD DAYS ARE HERE AGAIN.

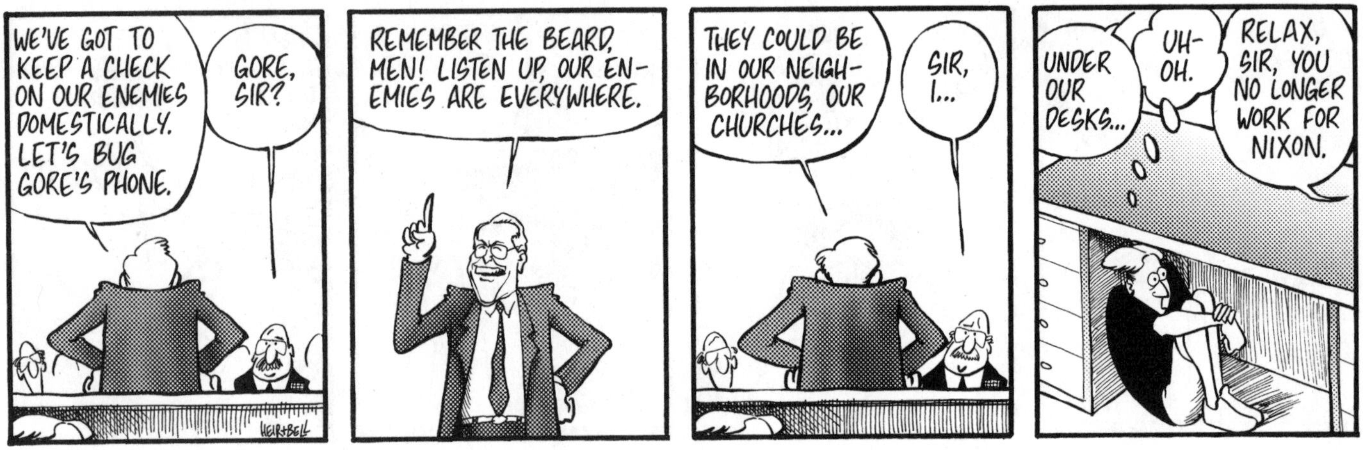
WE'VE GOT TO KEEP A CHECK ON OUR ENEMIES DOMESTICALLY. LET'S BUG GORE'S PHONE.
GORE, SIR?
REMEMBER THE BEARD, MEN! LISTEN UP, OUR EN-EMIES ARE EVERYWHERE.
THEY COULD BE IN OUR NEIGH-BORHOODS, OUR CHURCHES...
SIR, I...
UNDER OUR DESKS...
UH-OH.
RELAX, SIR, YOU NO LONGER WORK FOR NIXON.

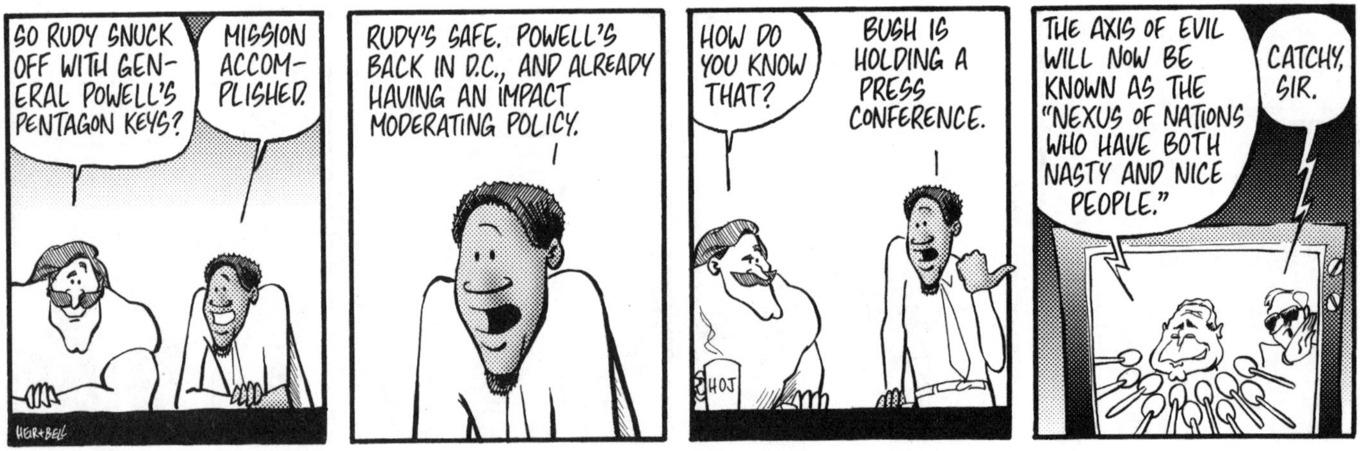
SO RUDY SNUCK OFF WITH GEN-ERAL POWELL'S PENTAGON KEYS?
MISSION ACCOM-PLISHED.
RUDY'S SAFE. POWELL'S BACK IN D.C., AND ALREADY HAVING AN IMPACT MODERATING POLICY.
HOW DO YOU KNOW THAT?
BUSH IS HOLDING A PRESS CONFERENCE.
THE AXIS OF EVIL WILL NOW BE KNOWN AS THE "NEXUS OF NATIONS WHO HAVE BOTH NASTY AND NICE PEOPLE."
CATCHY, SIR.

SEVENTH-INNING STRETCH, TIME FOR THE NEW VERSION OF "TAKE ME OUT TO THE BALLGAME."
NEW VERSION?
♪ TAKE ME OUT TO THE BALL GAME, TAKE ME TO PEPSI™ PARK... ♪
♪ BUY ME SOME FRITO LAY CRACKER JACKS™... METAMUCIL™ SURE HELPS YOU RELAX... ♪
♪ FOR IT'S ROOT, ROOT, ROOT, ROOT ROOT, ROOT BEER... ♫
♪ MILLER™ AND COORS™ AREN'T THE SAAAAME... ♪
♪ YES, IT'S ONE, TWO, THREE LUCKY STRIKES AT THE DUR-A-FLAME!™ ♪
*AMERICA'S PASTIME: SPONSORSHIP.
GO McYANKEES!
#1
*America is a wholly-owned subsidiary of Taco Bell™

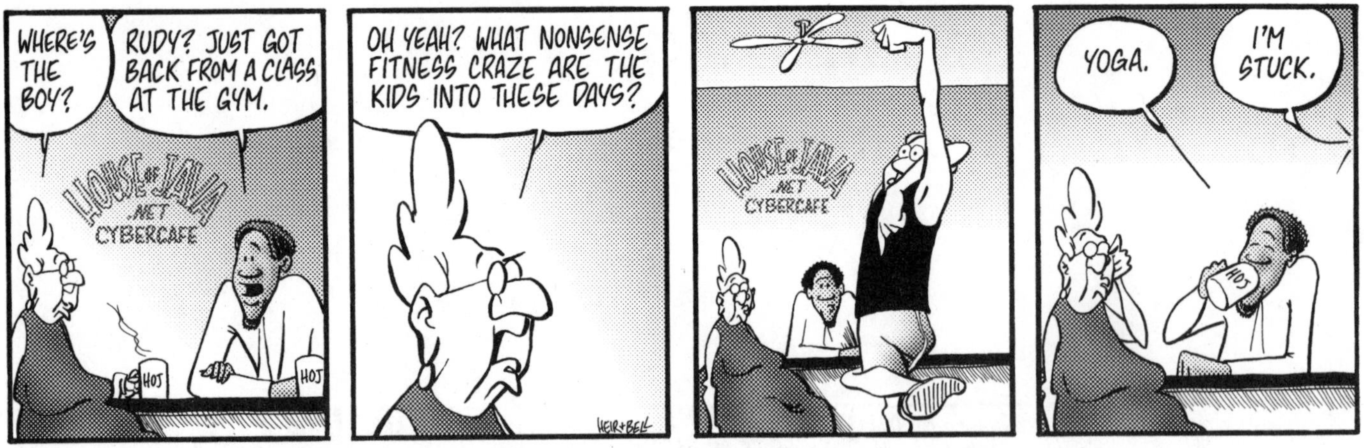
WHERE'S THE BOY?
RUDY? JUST GOT BACK FROM A CLASS AT THE GYM.
HOUSE OF JAVA .NET CYBERCAFE
HOJ
HOJ
OH YEAH? WHAT NONSENSE FITNESS CRAZE ARE THE KIDS INTO THESE DAYS?
HEIR+BELL
HOUSE OF JAVA .NET CYBERCAFE
YOGA.
I'M STUCK.
HOJ

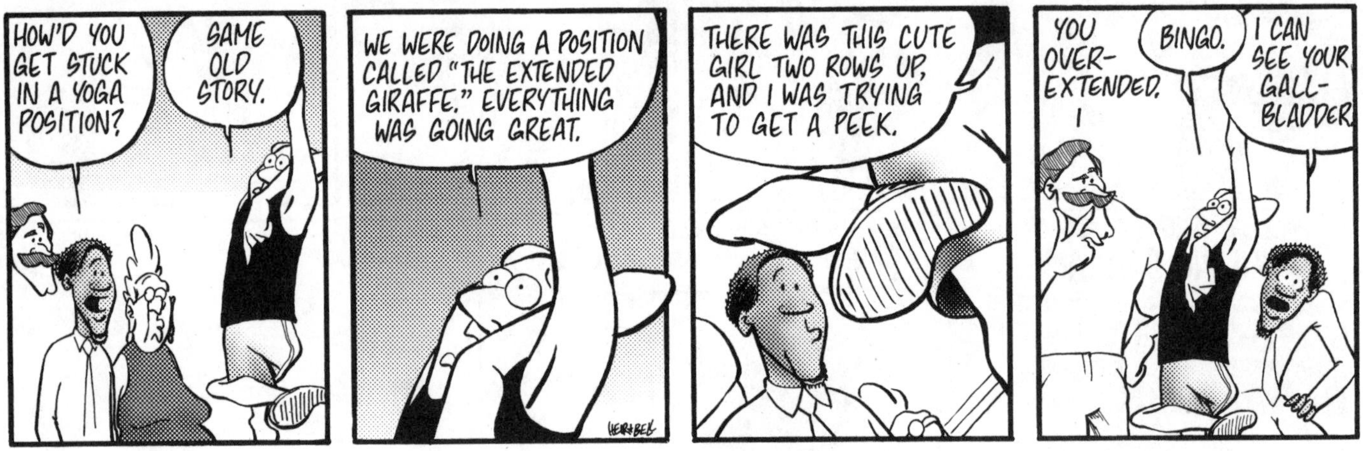
HOW'D YOU GET STUCK IN A YOGA POSITION?
SAME OLD STORY.
WE WERE DOING A POSITION CALLED "THE EXTENDED GIRAFFE." EVERYTHING WAS GOING GREAT.
HEIR+BELL
THERE WAS THIS CUTE GIRL TWO ROWS UP, AND I WAS TRYING TO GET A PEEK.
YOU OVER-EXTENDED.
BINGO.
I CAN SEE YOUR GALL-BLADDER

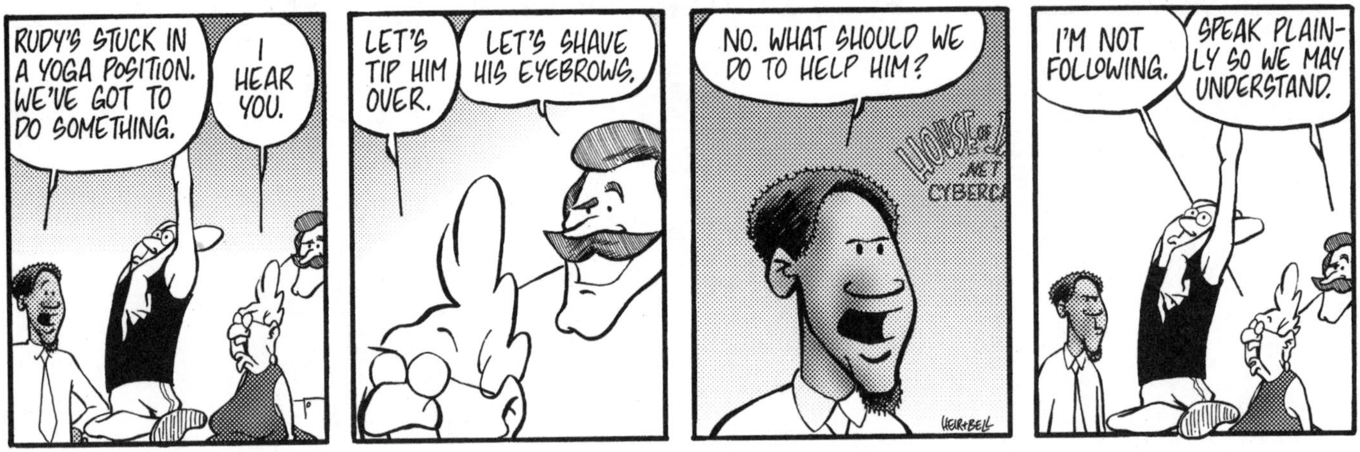
RUDY'S STUCK IN A YOGA POSITION. WE'VE GOT TO DO SOMETHING.
I HEAR YOU.
LET'S TIP HIM OVER.
LET'S SHAVE HIS EYEBROWS.
NO. WHAT SHOULD WE DO TO HELP HIM?
HEIR+BELL
I'M NOT FOLLOWING.
SPEAK PLAIN-LY SO WE MAY UNDERSTAND.

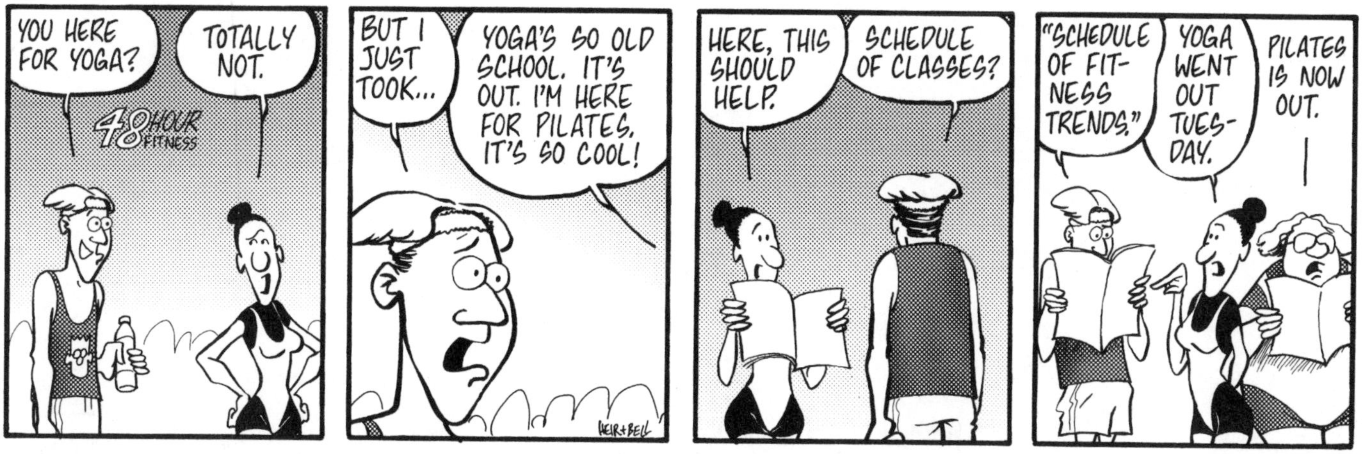
YOU HERE FOR YOGA?
TOTALLY NOT.
48 HOUR FITNESS
BUT I JUST TOOK...
YOGA'S SO OLD SCHOOL. IT'S OUT. I'M HERE FOR PILATES. IT'S SO COOL!
HEIR+BELL
HERE, THIS SHOULD HELP.
SCHEDULE OF CLASSES?
"SCHEDULE OF FIT-NESS TRENDS."
YOGA WENT OUT TUES-DAY.
PILATES IS NOW OUT.

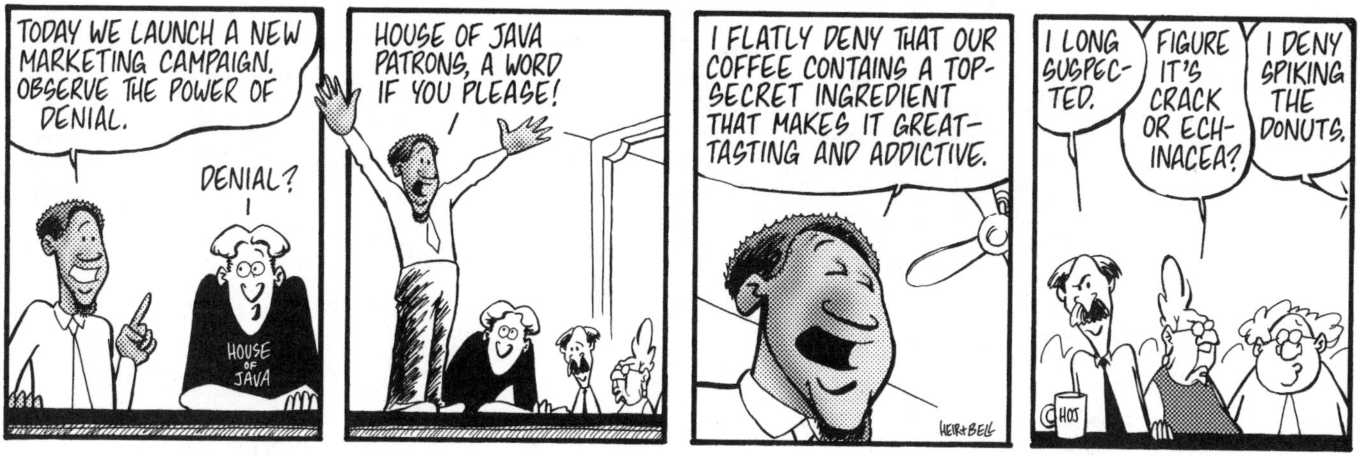
TODAY WE LAUNCH A NEW MARKETING CAMPAIGN. OBSERVE THE POWER OF DENIAL.
DENIAL?
HOUSE OF JAVA
HOUSE OF JAVA PATRONS, A WORD IF YOU PLEASE!
I FLATLY DENY THAT OUR COFFEE CONTAINS A TOP-SECRET INGREDIENT THAT MAKES IT GREAT-TASTING AND ADDICTIVE.
HEIR+BELL
I LONG SUSPEC-TED.
FIGURE IT'S CRACK OR ECH-INACEA?
I DENY SPIKING THE DONUTS.
HOJ

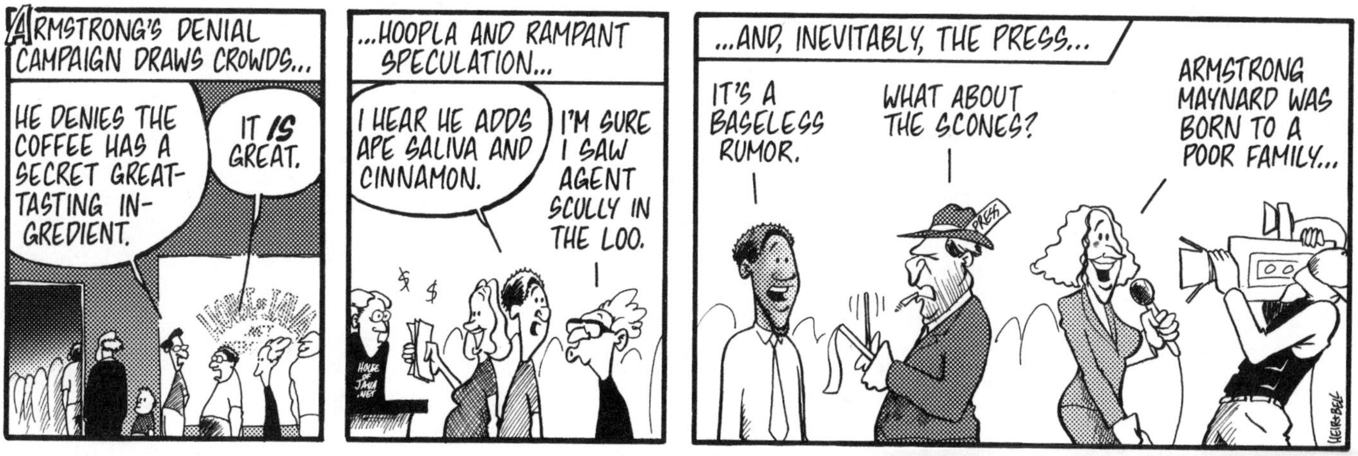
ARMSTRONG'S DENIAL CAMPAIGN DRAWS CROWDS...
HE DENIES THE COFFEE HAS A SECRET GREAT-TASTING IN-GREDIENT.
IT *IS* GREAT.
...HOOPLA AND RAMPANT SPECULATION...
I HEAR HE ADDS APE SALIVA AND CINNAMON.
I'M SURE I SAW AGENT SCULLY IN THE LOO.
...AND, INEVITABLY, THE PRESS...
IT'S A BASELESS RUMOR.
WHAT ABOUT THE SCONES?
PRESS
ARMSTRONG MAYNARD WAS BORN TO A POOR FAMILY...
HEIR+BELL

A STRUGGLING ECONOMY... RUEFUL SHAREHOLDERS... CALLS FOR EFFICIENCY, COST-CUTS, AND FEWER ADORABLE CATS... AND A SMOKE-FILLED ROOM OF CARTOON EXECUTIVES WITH A BLOCKBUSTER SOLUTION...

COMIC STRIP REVENUE IS DOWN, NEWS SPACE IS SHRINKING. LET'S QUIT BEATING EACH OTHER UP.

OF COURSE!

YOU'RE NOT SUGGESTING...

YES! A MERGER! A UNION OF EQUALS.

THREE COMIC STRIPS AS ONE. WE'LL CUT WRITERS AND ILLUSTRATORS, TRIM SALES STAFFS, AND FIRE REDUNDANT CARTOON CHARACTERS!

UNCLE MORT IS GONE!

AND SO, A MEGA-MERGER WAS SET ON TRACK: RUDY PARK,™ HAGAR THE HORRIBLE,® AND GARFIELD.® YET, AMIDST THE EUPHORIA, ONE QUESTION REMAINED: WHAT WILL CONSUMERS THINK?

THIS IS *SO* CONSUMER-FRIENDLY... I'VE WORKED UP A PROTOTYPE. I GIVE YOU: *RUDY, THE HORRIBLE CAT.*

RUDY THE **HORRIBLE CAT** by UNIVERSALLY UNITED KING MEDIA FEATURES, INC.

LATTE, YOU STINKY FUR-BALL.

HOUSE OF JAVA .NET CYBERCAFE

I HATE MONDAYS.

HOUSE OF JAVA .NET

NEXT WEEK: PART II- EFFICIENCIES, LAYOFFS, RUDY GETS FLEAS.

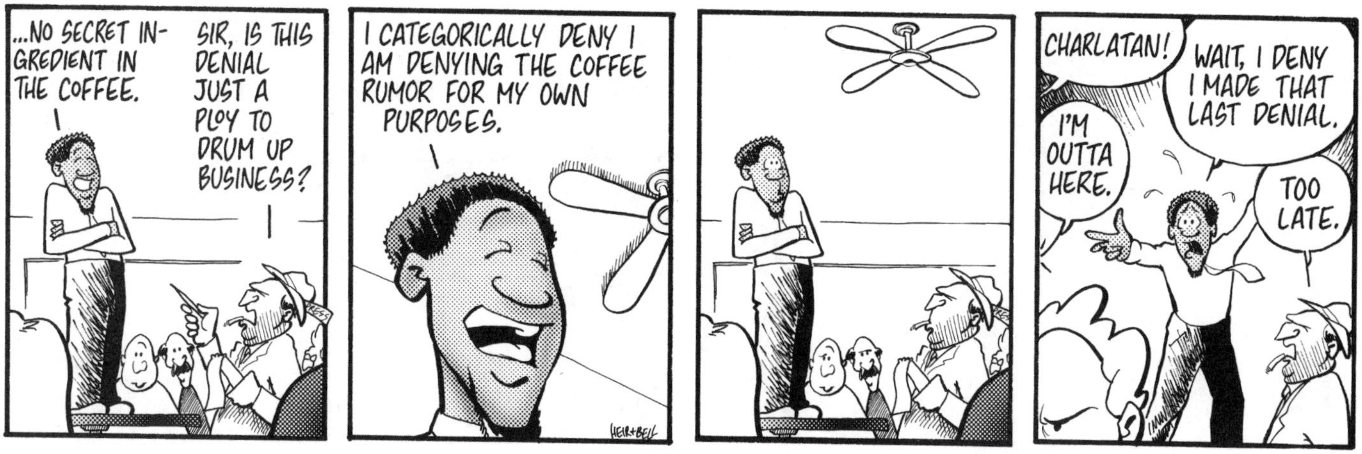
...NO SECRET INGREDIENT IN THE COFFEE.
SIR, IS THIS DENIAL JUST A PLOY TO DRUM UP BUSINESS?
I CATEGORICALLY DENY I AM DENYING THE COFFEE RUMOR FOR MY OWN PURPOSES.
HEIR+BELL
CHARLATAN!
WAIT, I DENY I MADE THAT LAST DENIAL.
I'M OUTTA HERE.
TOO LATE.

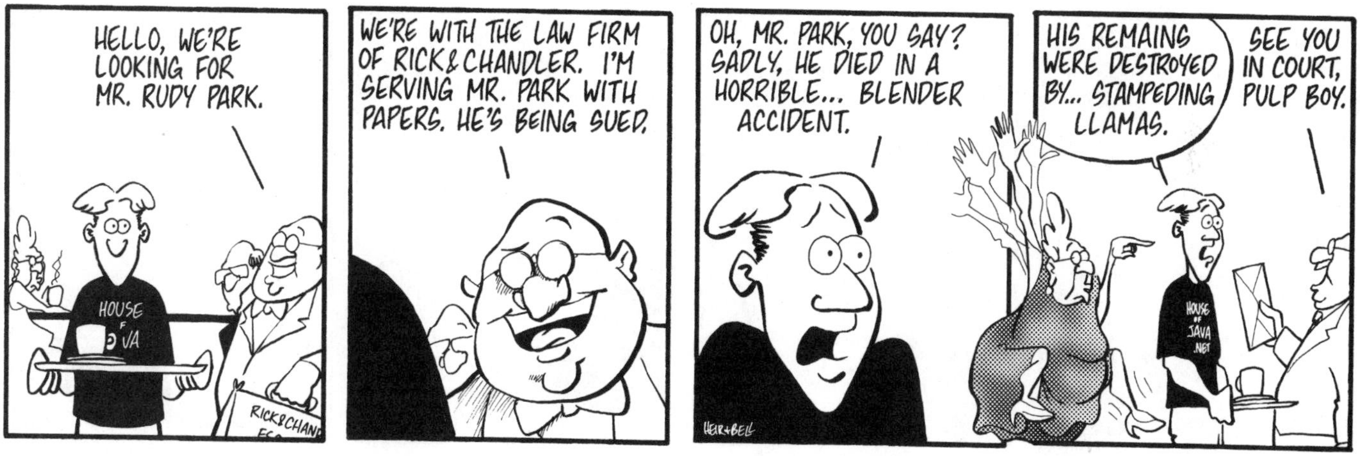
HELLO, WE'RE LOOKING FOR MR. RUDY PARK.
HOUSE OF JAVA
RICK&CHAND
WE'RE WITH THE LAW FIRM OF RICK&CHANDLER. I'M SERVING MR. PARK WITH PAPERS. HE'S BEING SUED.
OH, MR. PARK, YOU SAY? SADLY, HE DIED IN A HORRIBLE... BLENDER ACCIDENT.
HEIR+BELL
HIS REMAINS WERE DESTROYED BY... STAMPEDING LLAMAS.
SEE YOU IN COURT, PULP BOY.
HOUSE OF JAVA .NET

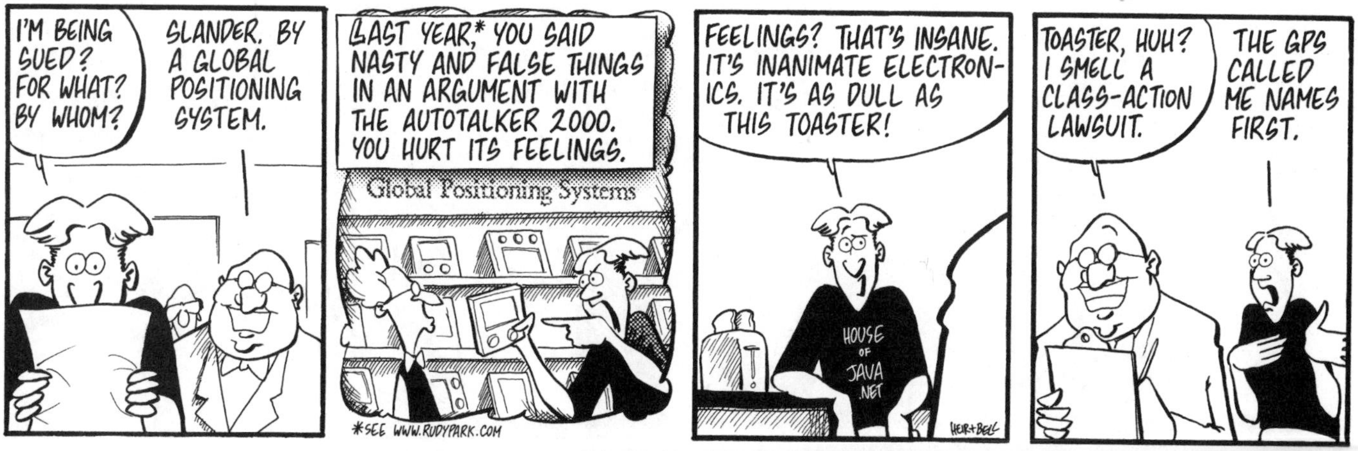
I'M BEING SUED? FOR WHAT? BY WHOM?
SLANDER. BY A GLOBAL POSITIONING SYSTEM.
LAST YEAR,* YOU SAID NASTY AND FALSE THINGS IN AN ARGUMENT WITH THE AUTOTALKER 2000. YOU HURT ITS FEELINGS.
Global Positioning Systems
*SEE WWW.RUDYPARK.COM
FEELINGS? THAT'S INSANE. IT'S INANIMATE ELECTRONICS. IT'S AS DULL AS THIS TOASTER!
HOUSE OF JAVA .NET
HEIR+BELL
TOASTER, HUH? I SMELL A CLASS-ACTION LAWSUIT.
THE GPS CALLED ME NAMES FIRST.

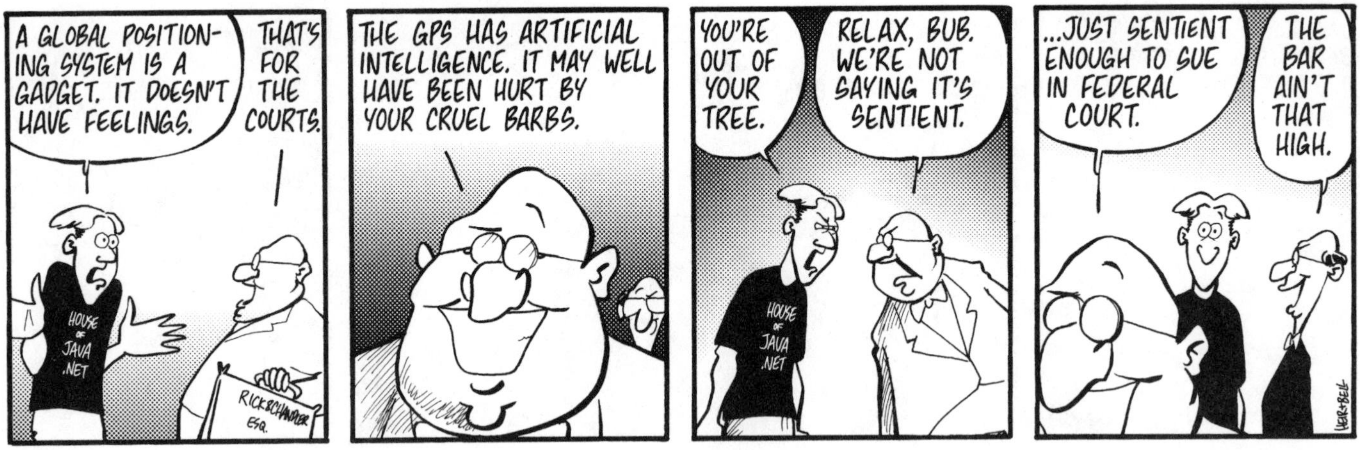
A GLOBAL POSITIONING SYSTEM IS A GADGET. IT DOESN'T HAVE FEELINGS.
THAT'S FOR THE COURTS.
HOUSE OF JAVA .NET
THE GPS HAS ARTIFICIAL INTELLIGENCE. IT MAY WELL HAVE BEEN HURT BY YOUR CRUEL BARBS.
YOU'RE OUT OF YOUR TREE.
RELAX, BUB. WE'RE NOT SAYING IT'S SENTIENT.
HOUSE OF JAVA .NET
...JUST SENTIENT ENOUGH TO SUE IN FEDERAL COURT.
THE BAR AIN'T THAT HIGH.
HEIR+BELL

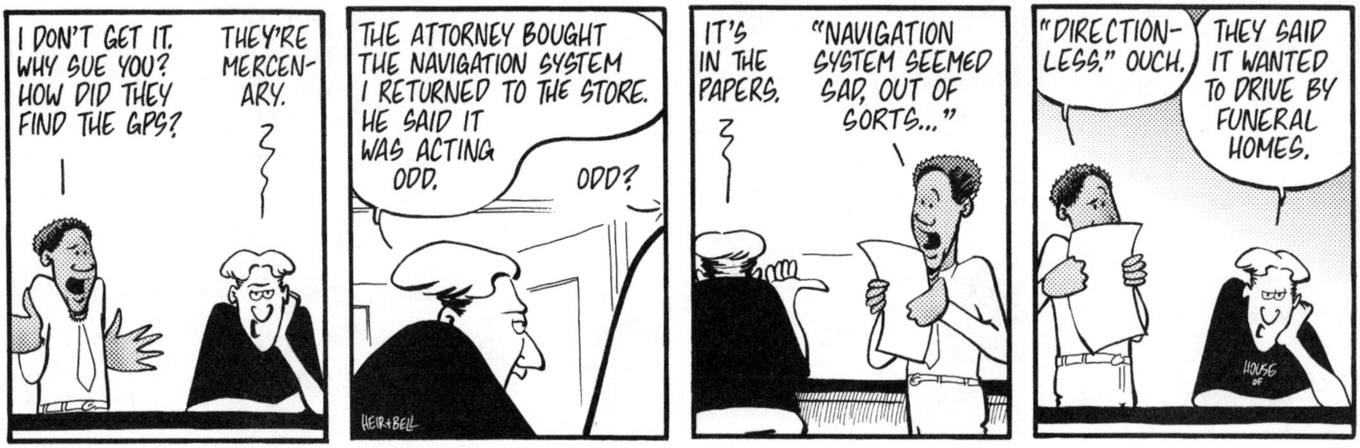
I DON'T GET IT. WHY SUE YOU? HOW DID THEY FIND THE GPS?
THEY'RE MERCENARY.
THE ATTORNEY BOUGHT THE NAVIGATION SYSTEM I RETURNED TO THE STORE. HE SAID IT WAS ACTING ODD.
ODD?
HEIR+BELL
IT'S IN THE PAPERS.
"NAVIGATION SYSTEM SEEMED SAD, OUT OF SORTS..."
"DIRECTIONLESS." OUCH.
THEY SAID IT WANTED TO DRIVE BY FUNERAL HOMES.
HOUSE OF

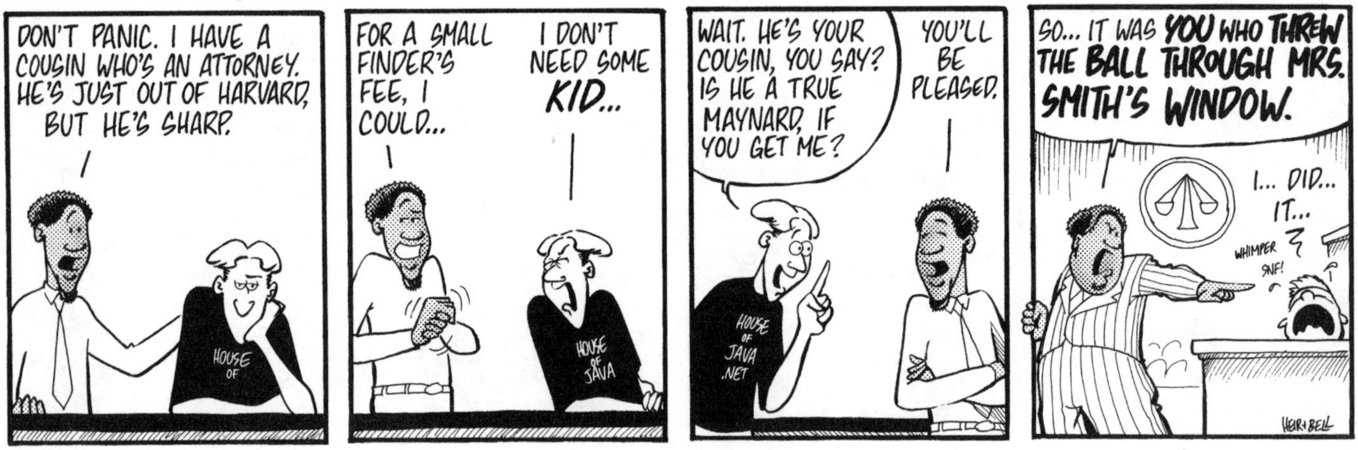
DON'T PANIC. I HAVE A COUSIN WHO'S AN ATTORNEY. HE'S JUST OUT OF HARVARD, BUT HE'S SHARP.
HOUSE OF
FOR A SMALL FINDER'S FEE, I COULD...
I DON'T NEED SOME KID...
HOUSE OF JAVA
WAIT. HE'S YOUR COUSIN, YOU SAY? IS HE A TRUE MAYNARD, IF YOU GET ME?
YOU'LL BE PLEASED.
HOUSE OF JAVA .NET
SO... IT WAS YOU WHO THREW THE BALL THROUGH MRS. SMITH'S WINDOW.
I... DID... IT...
WHIMPER
SNF!
HEIR+BELL

THE CAPTAINS OF INDUSTRY PROPOSED A MEGA-MERGER: RUDY PARK™, HAGAR THE HORRIBLE,® AND GARFIELD® WOULD BECOME "RUDY THE HORRIBLE CAT."™ BUT HURDLES MEANT TO PROTECT CONSUMERS AND EMPLOYEES LOOMED...

FROM REGULATORS...

UNITED STATES of AMERICA ANTI-TRUST DEPARTMENT

NEXT!

APPROVED

MERGER   MERGER

...FROM SHAREHOLDERS...

WE DOWNSIZE THE STAFF AND WATER DOWN THE LATTES, YOUR DIVIDEND RISES 4 CENTS.

GIDDY! GIDDY!

ANNUAL MEETING

...FROM THE UNION...

MAKE IT EASY ON YOURSELVES. DON'T MAKE US OUT-SOURCE...

YOU DON'T MEAN...

...LOW-COST IMMIGRANT LABOR.

I HATE MONDAYS.

...HAVING DEFTLY NAVIGATED THE OBSTACLES, THE CAPTAINS TURNED THEIR ATTENTION TO ONE LAST POTENTIAL STICKING POINT: THE CONSUMERS.

RUDY THE HORRIBLE CAT

HEIR&BELL

IT'LL MAKE YOU SMARTER! FASTER! A BETTER CHEF! LOVER! LAWN-MOWER CUTTER!

I LIKE THE GAP.® TACO BELL® GOOD... RUDY THE HORRIBLE CAT™ ROCKS...

NEXT WEEK: PART III—CONSUMER REVOLT, RUDY "FIXED."

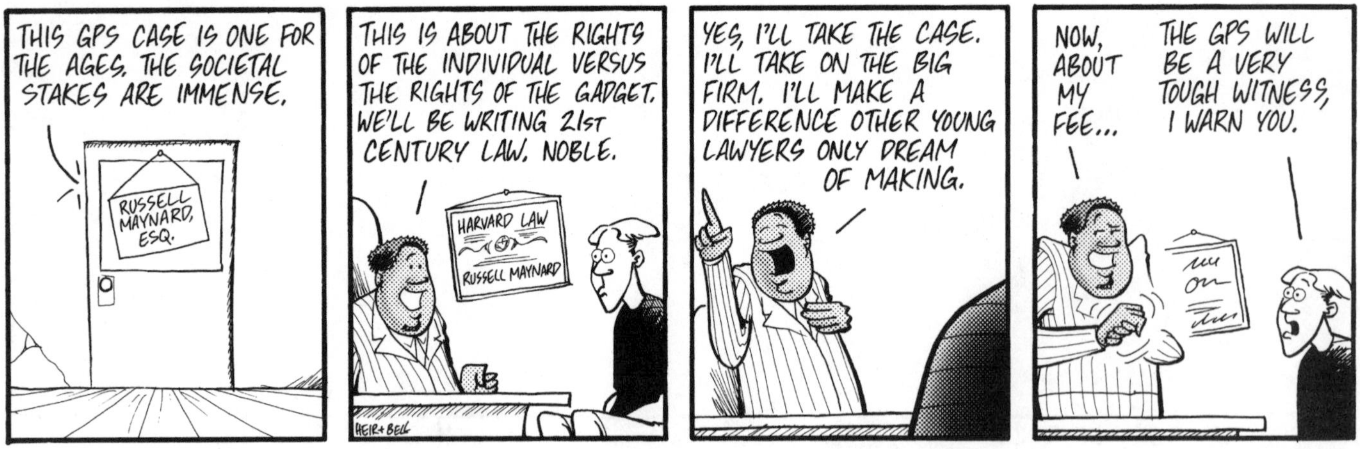
THIS GPS CASE IS ONE FOR THE AGES. THE SOCIETAL STAKES ARE IMMENSE.
RUSSELL MAYNARD, ESQ.
THIS IS ABOUT THE RIGHTS OF THE INDIVIDUAL VERSUS THE RIGHTS OF THE GADGET. WE'LL BE WRITING 21ST CENTURY LAW. NOBLE.
HARVARD LAW
RUSSELL MAYNARD
HEIR+BELL
YES, I'LL TAKE THE CASE. I'LL TAKE ON THE BIG FIRM. I'LL MAKE A DIFFERENCE OTHER YOUNG LAWYERS ONLY DREAM OF MAKING.
NOW, ABOUT MY FEE...
THE GPS WILL BE A VERY TOUGH WITNESS, I WARN YOU.

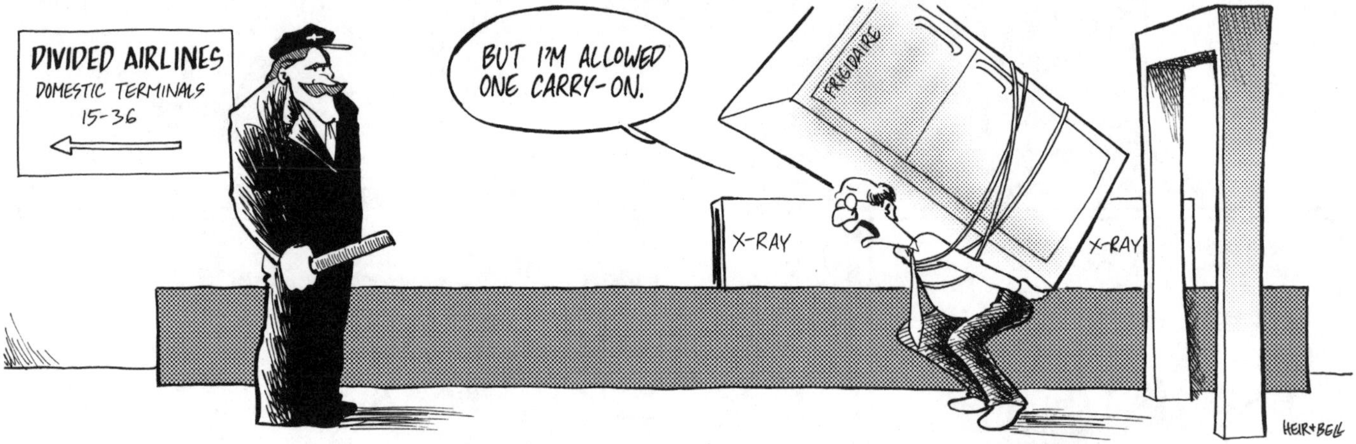
DIVIDED AIRLINES
DOMESTIC TERMINALS
15-36
BUT I'M ALLOWED ONE CARRY-ON.
FRIGIDAIRE
X-RAY
X-RAY
HEIR+BELL

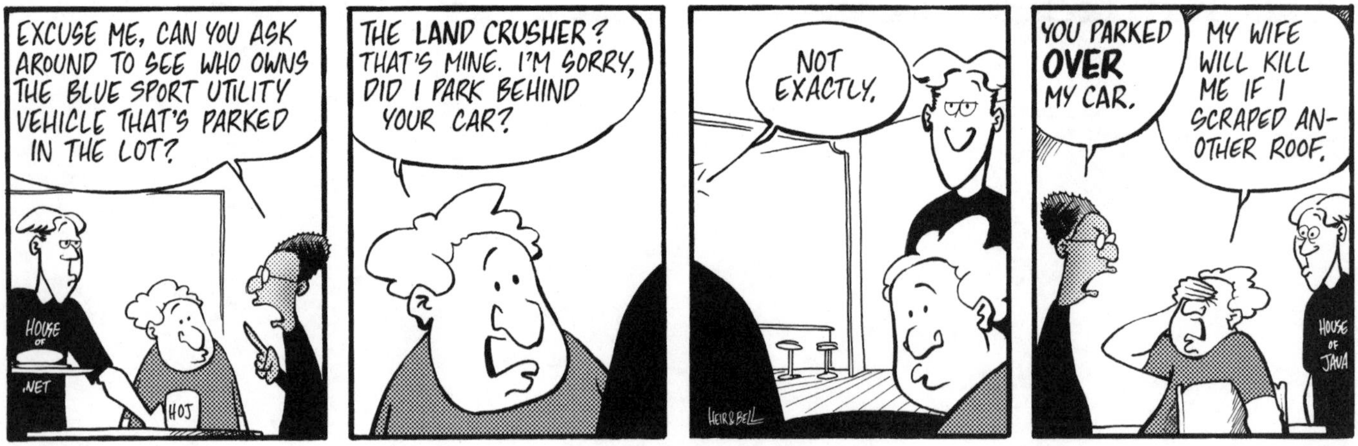
EXCUSE ME, CAN YOU ASK AROUND TO SEE WHO OWNS THE BLUE SPORT UTILITY VEHICLE THAT'S PARKED IN THE LOT?
HOUSE OF .NET
HOJ
THE LAND CRUSHER? THAT'S MINE. I'M SORRY, DID I PARK BEHIND YOUR CAR?
NOT EXACTLY.
HEIR&BELL
YOU PARKED OVER MY CAR.
MY WIFE WILL KILL ME IF I SCRAPED ANOTHER ROOF.
HOUSE OF JAVA

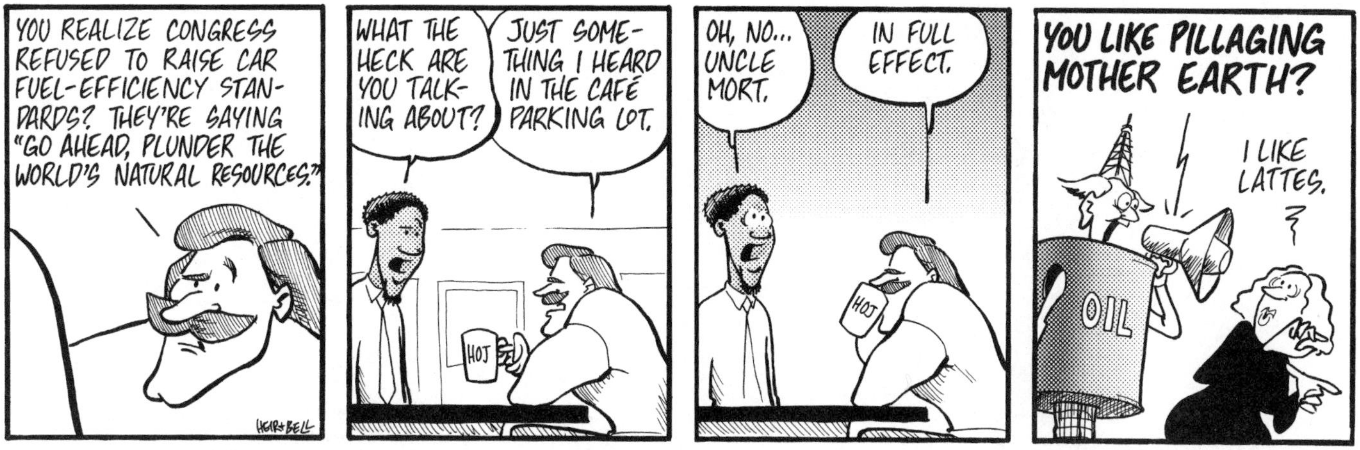
YOU REALIZE CONGRESS REFUSED TO RAISE CAR FUEL-EFFICIENCY STANDARDS? THEY'RE SAYING "GO AHEAD, PLUNDER THE WORLD'S NATURAL RESOURCES."
HEIR+BELL
WHAT THE HECK ARE YOU TALKING ABOUT?
JUST SOMETHING I HEARD IN THE CAFÉ PARKING LOT.
HOJ
OH, NO... UNCLE MORT.
IN FULL EFFECT.
HOJ
YOU LIKE PILLAGING MOTHER EARTH?
I LIKE LATTES.
OIL

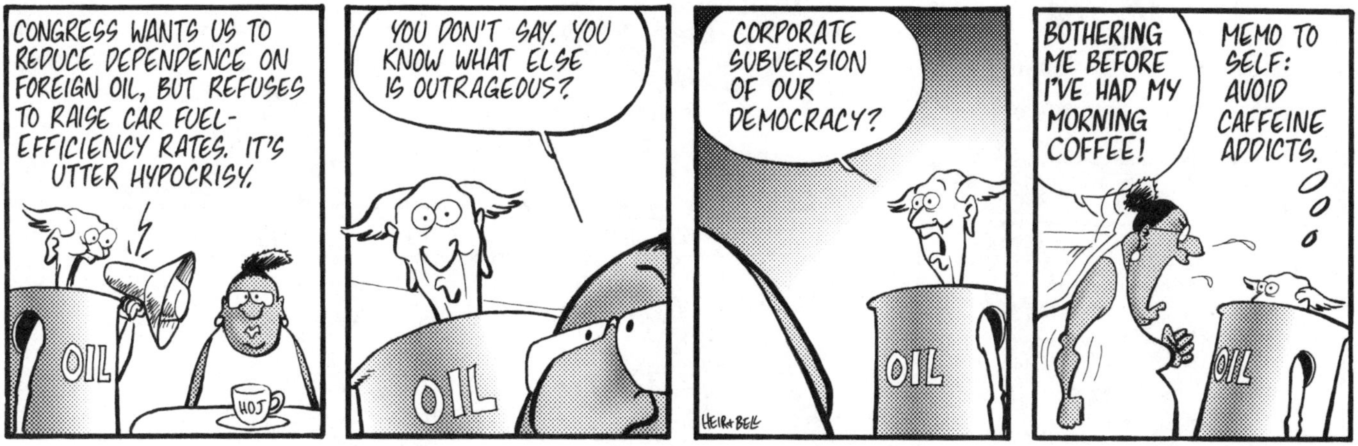
CONGRESS WANTS US TO REDUCE DEPENDENCE ON FOREIGN OIL, BUT REFUSES TO RAISE CAR FUEL-EFFICIENCY RATES. IT'S UTTER HYPOCRISY.
OIL
HOJ
YOU DON'T SAY. YOU KNOW WHAT ELSE IS OUTRAGEOUS?
OIL
CORPORATE SUBVERSION OF OUR DEMOCRACY?
OIL
HEIR+BELL
BOTHERING ME BEFORE I'VE HAD MY MORNING COFFEE!
MEMO TO SELF: AVOID CAFFEINE ADDICTS.
OIL

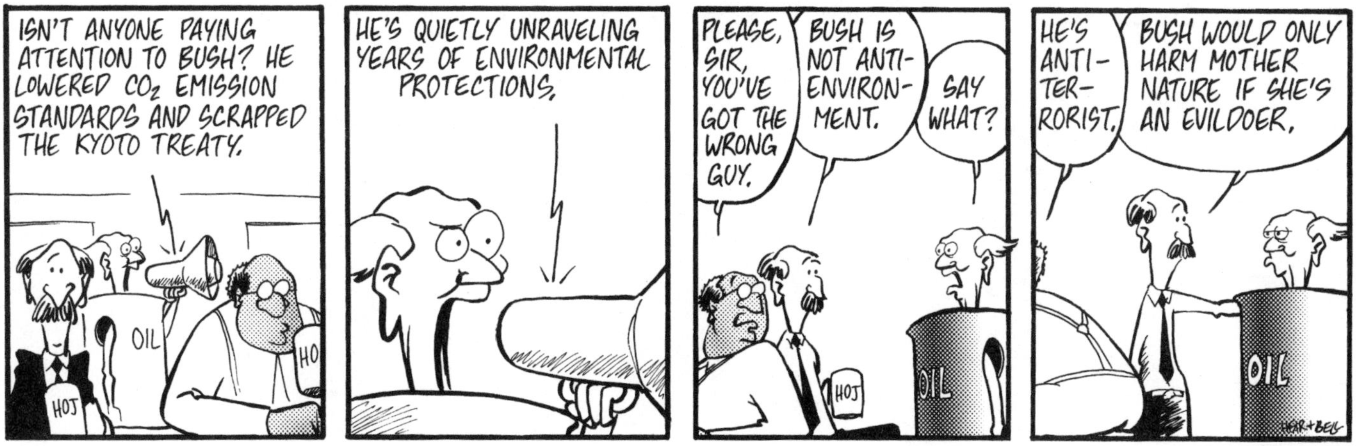
ISN'T ANYONE PAYING ATTENTION TO BUSH? HE LOWERED CO_2 EMISSION STANDARDS AND SCRAPPED THE KYOTO TREATY.
OIL
HOJ
HE'S QUIETLY UNRAVELING YEARS OF ENVIRONMENTAL PROTECTIONS.
PLEASE, SIR, YOU'VE GOT THE WRONG GUY.
BUSH IS NOT ANTI-ENVIRONMENT.
SAY WHAT?
HOJ
OIL
HE'S ANTI-TERRORIST.
BUSH WOULD ONLY HARM MOTHER NATURE IF SHE'S AN EVILDOER.
OIL
HEIR+BELL

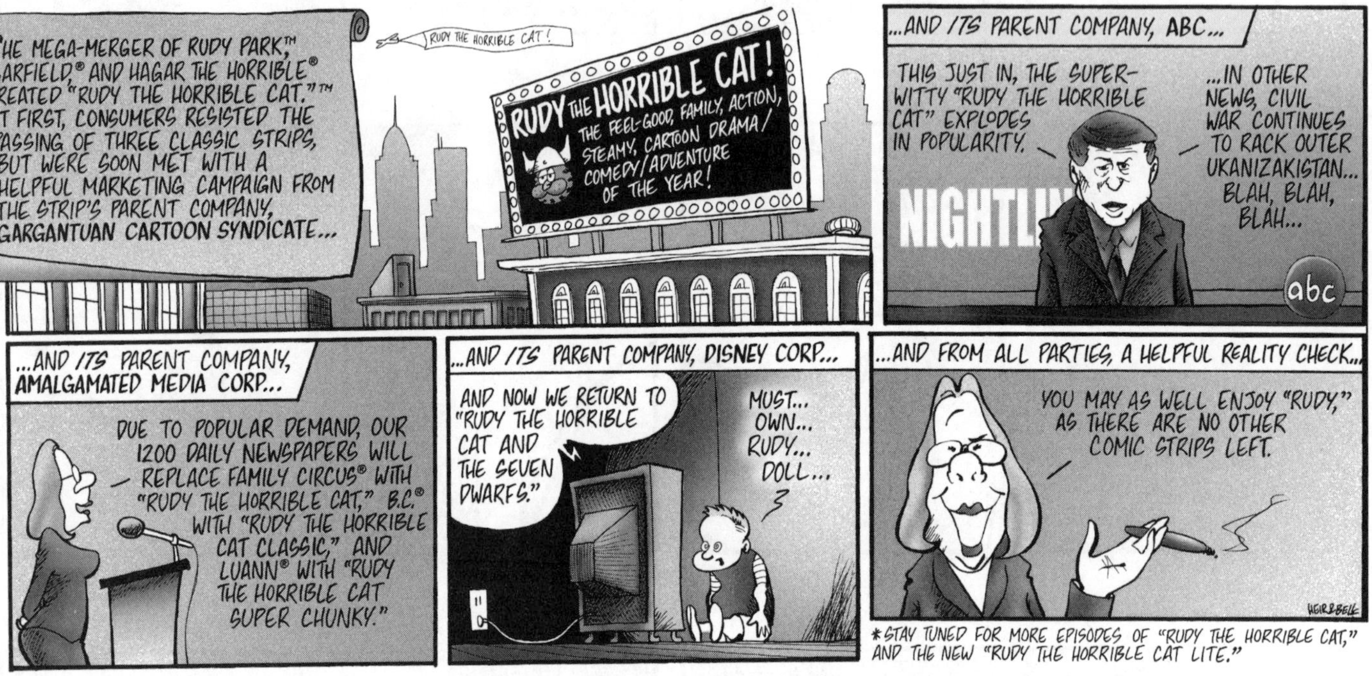
THE MEGA-MERGER OF RUDY PARK,™ GARFIELD,® AND HAGAR THE HORRIBLE® CREATED "RUDY THE HORRIBLE CAT."™ AT FIRST, CONSUMERS RESISTED THE PASSING OF THREE CLASSIC STRIPS, BUT WERE SOON MET WITH A HELPFUL MARKETING CAMPAIGN FROM THE STRIP'S PARENT COMPANY, GARGANTUAN CARTOON SYNDICATE...
RUDY THE HORRIBLE CAT!
RUDY THE HORRIBLE CAT! THE FEEL-GOOD, FAMILY, ACTION, STEAMY, CARTOON DRAMA/COMEDY/ADVENTURE OF THE YEAR!
...AND ITS PARENT COMPANY, ABC...
THIS JUST IN, THE SUPER-WITTY "RUDY THE HORRIBLE CAT" EXPLODES IN POPULARITY.
...IN OTHER NEWS, CIVIL WAR CONTINUES TO RACK OUTER UKANIZAKISTAN... BLAH, BLAH, BLAH...
NIGHTLI
abc
...AND ITS PARENT COMPANY, AMALGAMATED MEDIA CORP...
DUE TO POPULAR DEMAND, OUR 1200 DAILY NEWSPAPERS WILL REPLACE FAMILY CIRCUS® WITH "RUDY THE HORRIBLE CAT," B.C.® WITH "RUDY THE HORRIBLE CAT CLASSIC," AND LUANN® WITH "RUDY THE HORRIBLE CAT SUPER CHUNKY."
...AND ITS PARENT COMPANY, DISNEY CORP...
AND NOW WE RETURN TO "RUDY THE HORRIBLE CAT AND THE SEVEN DWARFS."
MUST... OWN... RUDY... DOLL...
...AND FROM ALL PARTIES, A HELPFUL REALITY CHECK...
YOU MAY AS WELL ENJOY "RUDY," AS THERE ARE NO OTHER COMIC STRIPS LEFT.
HEIRBBELT
*STAY TUNED FOR MORE EPISODES OF "RUDY THE HORRIBLE CAT," AND THE NEW "RUDY THE HORRIBLE CAT LITE."

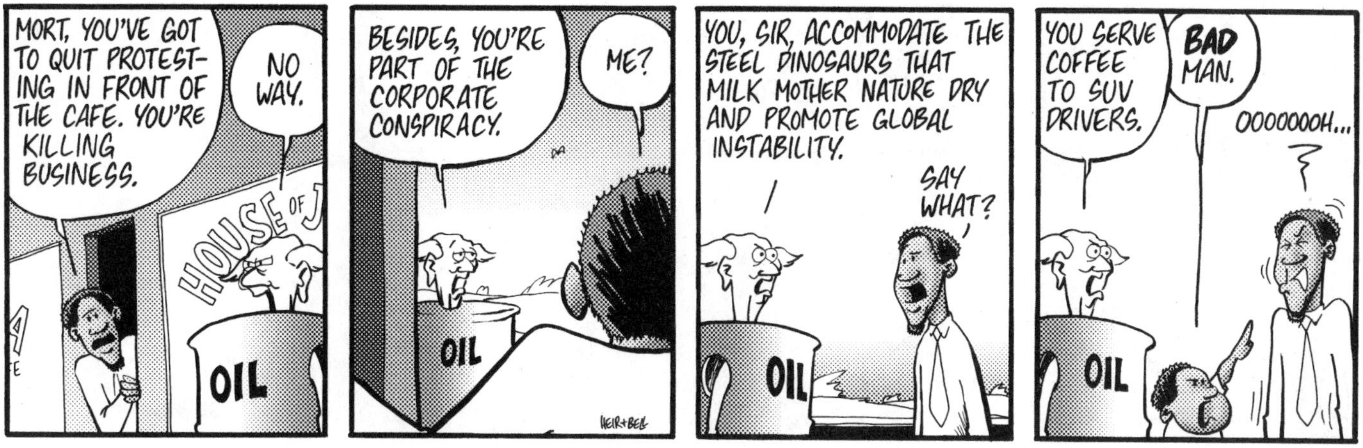
MORT, YOU'VE GOT TO QUIT PROTESTING IN FRONT OF THE CAFE. YOU'RE KILLING BUSINESS.
NO WAY.
HOUSE OF J
OIL
BESIDES, YOU'RE PART OF THE CORPORATE CONSPIRACY.
ME?
OIL
HEIR+BELL
YOU, SIR, ACCOMMODATE THE STEEL DINOSAURS THAT MILK MOTHER NATURE DRY AND PROMOTE GLOBAL INSTABILITY.
SAY WHAT?
OIL
YOU SERVE COFFEE TO SUV DRIVERS.
BAD MAN.
OOOOOOOH...
OIL

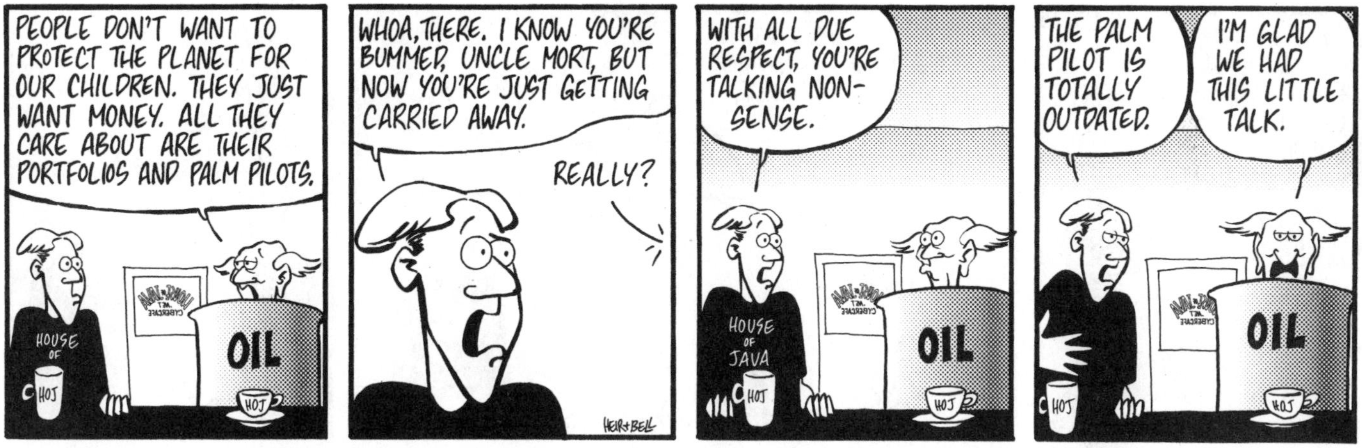
PEOPLE DON'T WANT TO PROTECT THE PLANET FOR OUR CHILDREN. THEY JUST WANT MONEY. ALL THEY CARE ABOUT ARE THEIR PORTFOLIOS AND PALM PILOTS.
HOUSE OF
OIL
HOJ
WHOA, THERE. I KNOW YOU'RE BUMMED, UNCLE MORT, BUT NOW YOU'RE JUST GETTING CARRIED AWAY.
REALLY?
HEIR+BELL
WITH ALL DUE RESPECT, YOU'RE TALKING NONSENSE.
HOUSE OF JAVA
OIL
HOJ
THE PALM PILOT IS TOTALLY OUTDATED.
I'M GLAD WE HAD THIS LITTLE TALK.
OIL
HOJ

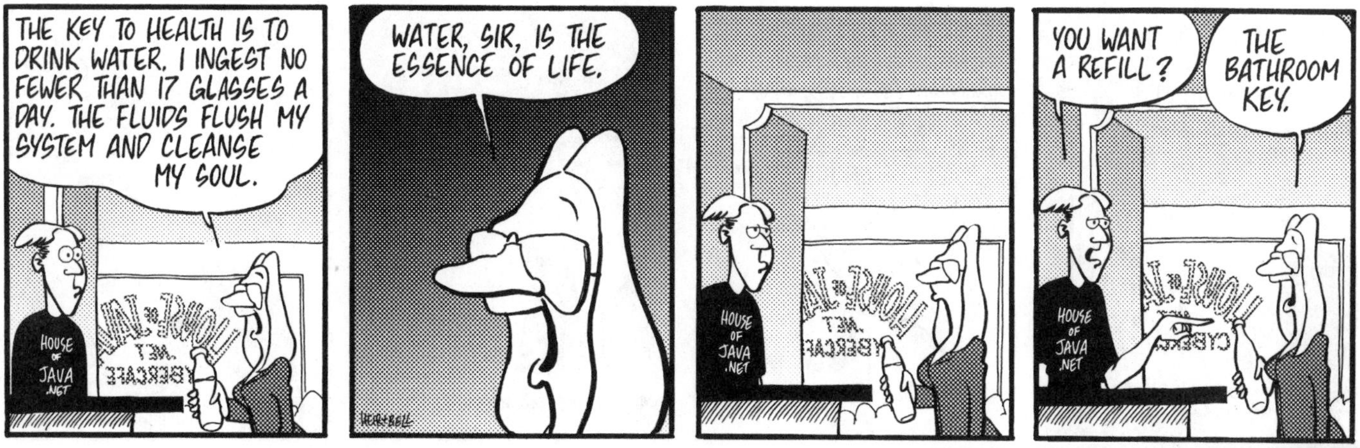
THE KEY TO HEALTH IS TO DRINK WATER. I INGEST NO FEWER THAN 17 GLASSES A DAY. THE FLUIDS FLUSH MY SYSTEM AND CLEANSE MY SOUL.
HOUSE OF JAVA .NET
WATER, SIR, IS THE ESSENCE OF LIFE.
HEIR+BELL
HOUSE OF JAVA .NET
YOU WANT A REFILL?
THE BATHROOM KEY.
HOUSE OF JAVA .NET

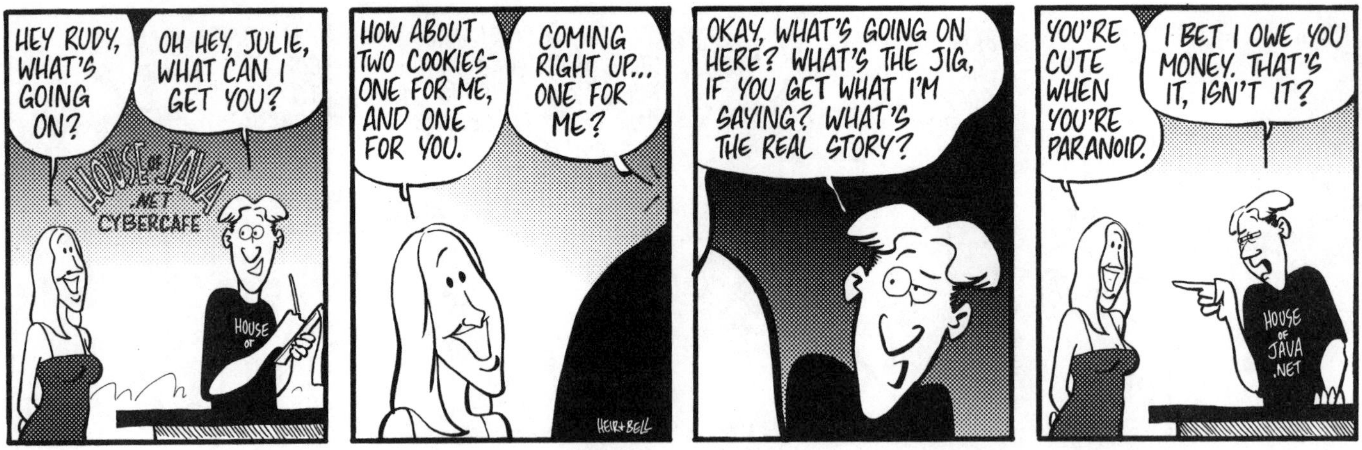
HEY RUDY, WHAT'S GOING ON?
OH HEY, JULIE, WHAT CAN I GET YOU?
HOUSE OF JAVA .NET CYBERCAFE
HOUSE OF
HOW ABOUT TWO COOKIES- ONE FOR ME, AND ONE FOR YOU.
COMING RIGHT UP... ONE FOR ME?
HEIR+BELL
OKAY, WHAT'S GOING ON HERE? WHAT'S THE JIG, IF YOU GET WHAT I'M SAYING? WHAT'S THE REAL STORY?
YOU'RE CUTE WHEN YOU'RE PARANOID.
I BET I OWE YOU MONEY. THAT'S IT, ISN'T IT?
HOUSE OF JAVA .NET

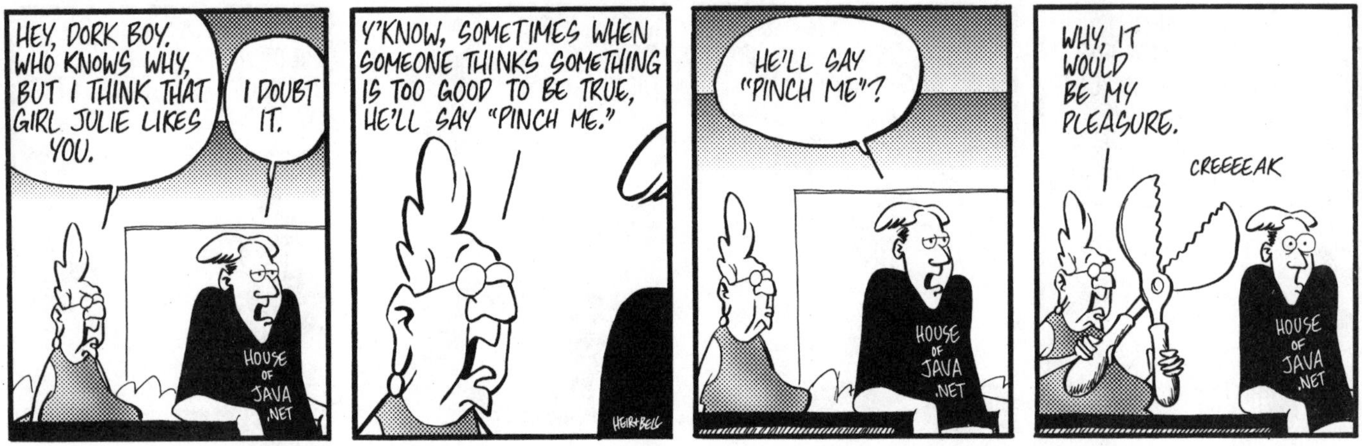
HEY, DORK BOY. WHO KNOWS WHY, BUT I THINK THAT GIRL JULIE LIKES YOU.
I DOUBT IT.
HOUSE OF JAVA .NET
Y'KNOW, SOMETIMES WHEN SOMEONE THINKS SOMETHING IS TOO GOOD TO BE TRUE, HE'LL SAY "PINCH ME."
HEIR+BELL
HE'LL SAY "PINCH ME"?
HOUSE OF JAVA .NET
WHY, IT WOULD BE MY PLEASURE.
CREEEEAK
HOUSE OF JAVA .NET

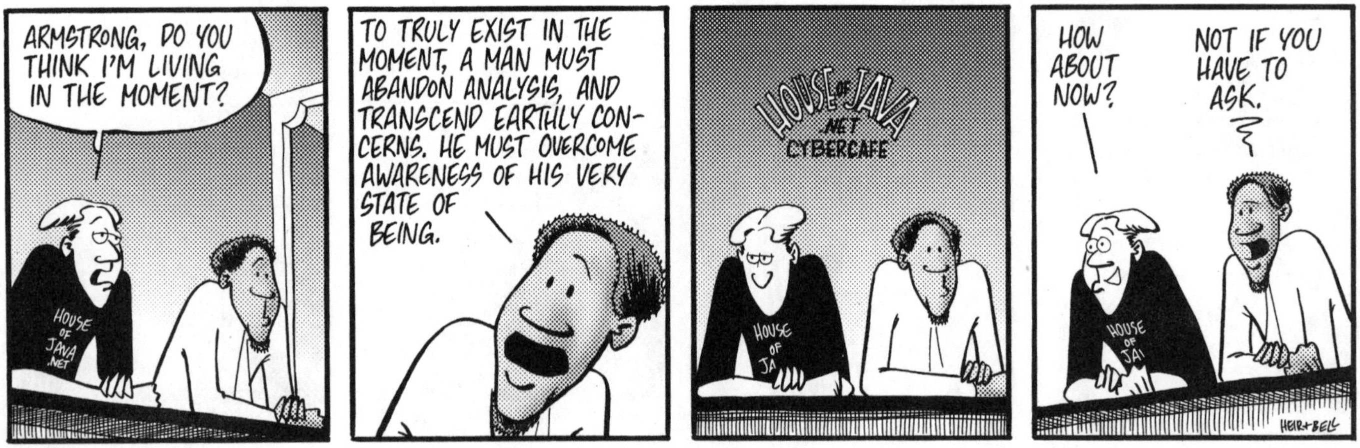
ARMSTRONG, DO YOU THINK I'M LIVING IN THE MOMENT?
HOUSE OF JAVA .NET
TO TRULY EXIST IN THE MOMENT, A MAN MUST ABANDON ANALYSIS, AND TRANSCEND EARTHLY CONCERNS. HE MUST OVERCOME AWARENESS OF HIS VERY STATE OF BEING.
HOUSE OF JAVA .NET CYBERCAFE
HOW ABOUT NOW?
NOT IF YOU HAVE TO ASK.
HEIR+BELL

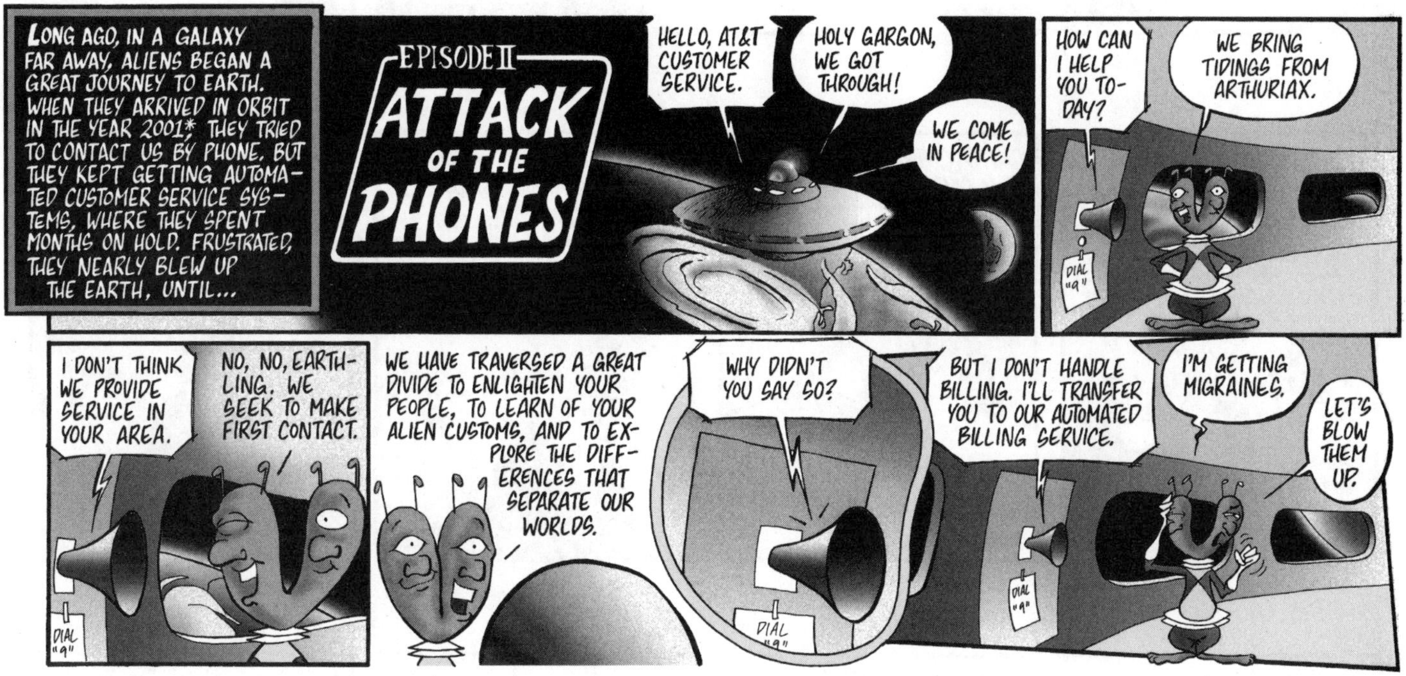
LONG AGO, IN A GALAXY FAR AWAY, ALIENS BEGAN A GREAT JOURNEY TO EARTH. WHEN THEY ARRIVED IN ORBIT IN THE YEAR 2001* THEY TRIED TO CONTACT US BY PHONE, BUT THEY KEPT GETTING AUTOMATED CUSTOMER SERVICE SYSTEMS, WHERE THEY SPENT MONTHS ON HOLD. FRUSTRATED, THEY NEARLY BLEW UP THE EARTH, UNTIL...
EPISODE II
ATTACK OF THE PHONES
HELLO, AT&T CUSTOMER SERVICE.
HOLY GARGON, WE GOT THROUGH!
WE COME IN PEACE!
HOW CAN I HELP YOU TODAY?
WE BRING TIDINGS FROM ARTHURIAX.
DIAL "9"
I DON'T THINK WE PROVIDE SERVICE IN YOUR AREA.
NO, NO, EARTHLING. WE SEEK TO MAKE FIRST CONTACT.
DIAL "9"
WE HAVE TRAVERSED A GREAT DIVIDE TO ENLIGHTEN YOUR PEOPLE, TO LEARN OF YOUR ALIEN CUSTOMS, AND TO EXPLORE THE DIFFERENCES THAT SEPARATE OUR WORLDS.
WHY DIDN'T YOU SAY SO?
DIAL "9"
BUT I DON'T HANDLE BILLING. I'LL TRANSFER YOU TO OUR AUTOMATED BILLING SERVICE.
I'M GETTING MIGRAINES.
LET'S BLOW THEM UP.
DIAL "9"

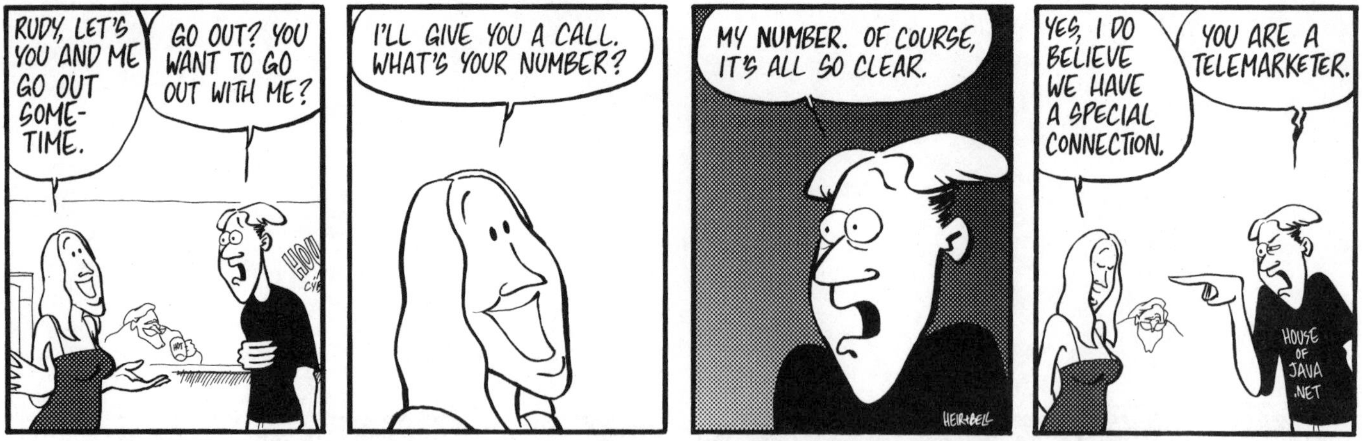
RUDY, LET'S YOU AND ME GO OUT SOME-TIME.
GO OUT? YOU WANT TO GO OUT WITH ME?
I'LL GIVE YOU A CALL. WHAT'S YOUR NUMBER?
MY NUMBER. OF COURSE, IT'S ALL SO CLEAR.
HEIR+BELL
YES, I DO BELIEVE WE HAVE A SPECIAL CONNECTION.
YOU ARE A TELEMARKETER.
HOUSE OF JAVA .NET

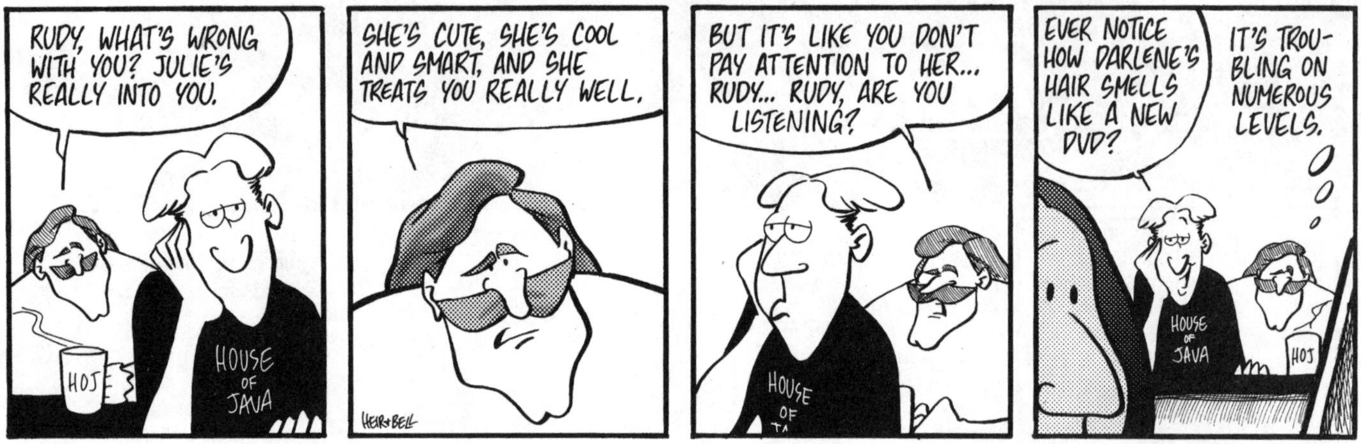
RUDY, WHAT'S WRONG WITH YOU? JULIE'S REALLY INTO YOU.
HOJ
HOUSE OF JAVA
SHE'S CUTE, SHE'S COOL AND SMART, AND SHE TREATS YOU REALLY WELL.
HEIR+BELL
BUT IT'S LIKE YOU DON'T PAY ATTENTION TO HER... RUDY... RUDY, ARE YOU LISTENING?
EVER NOTICE HOW DARLENE'S HAIR SMELLS LIKE A NEW DVD?
IT'S TROU-BLING ON NUMEROUS LEVELS.
HOUSE OF JAVA
HOJ

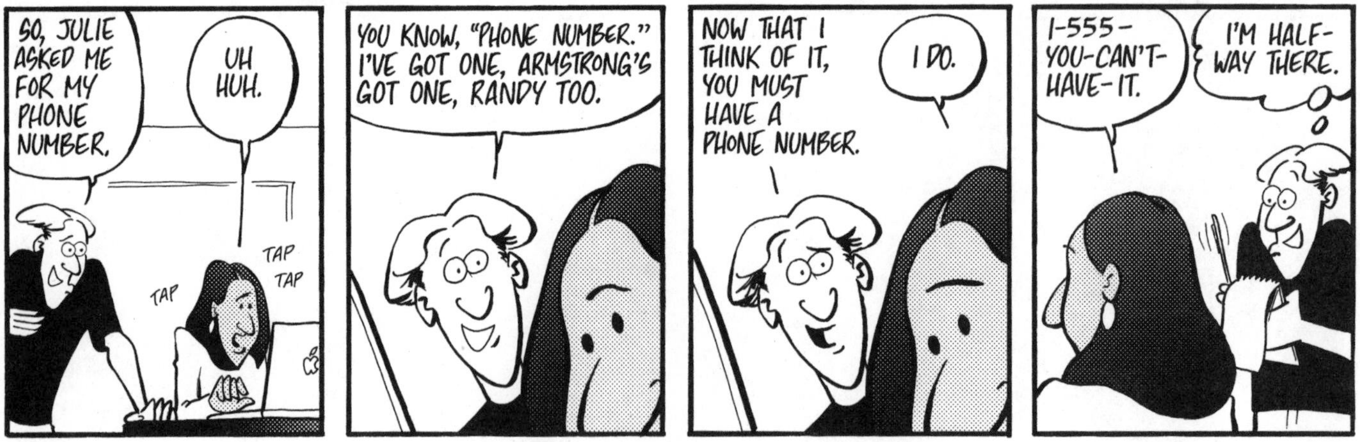
SO, JULIE ASKED ME FOR MY PHONE NUMBER.
UH HUH.
TAP
TAP TAP
YOU KNOW, "PHONE NUMBER." I'VE GOT ONE, ARMSTRONG'S GOT ONE, RANDY TOO.
NOW THAT I THINK OF IT, YOU MUST HAVE A PHONE NUMBER.
I DO.
1-555-YOU-CAN'T-HAVE-IT.
I'M HALF-WAY THERE.

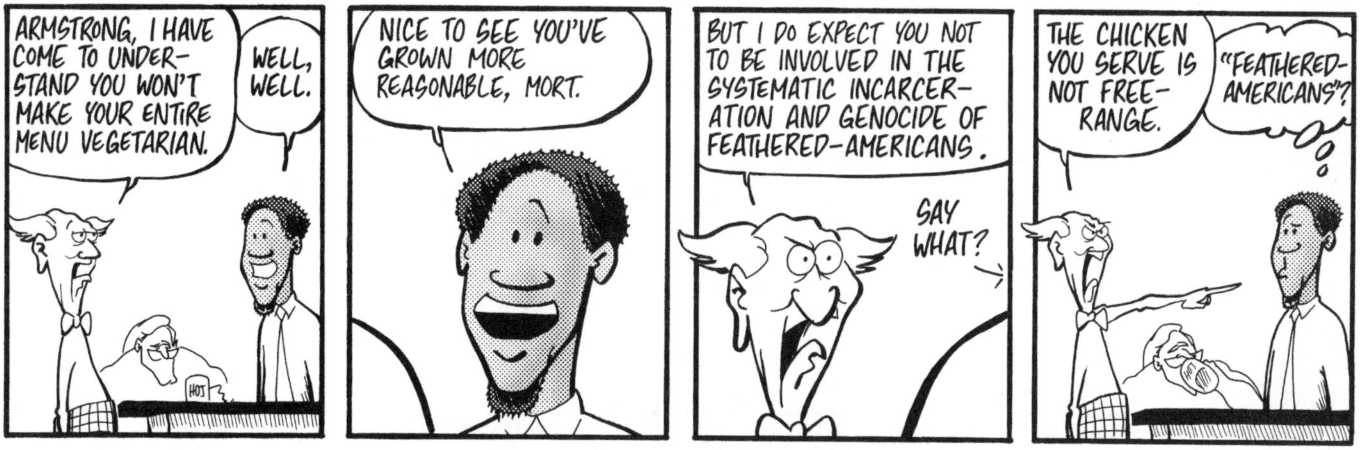
ARMSTRONG, I HAVE COME TO UNDERSTAND YOU WON'T MAKE YOUR ENTIRE MENU VEGETARIAN.
WELL, WELL.
NICE TO SEE YOU'VE GROWN MORE REASONABLE, MORT.
BUT I DO EXPECT YOU NOT TO BE INVOLVED IN THE SYSTEMATIC INCARCERATION AND GENOCIDE OF FEATHERED-AMERICANS.
SAY WHAT?
THE CHICKEN YOU SERVE IS NOT FREE-RANGE.
"FEATHERED-AMERICANS"?
HOJ

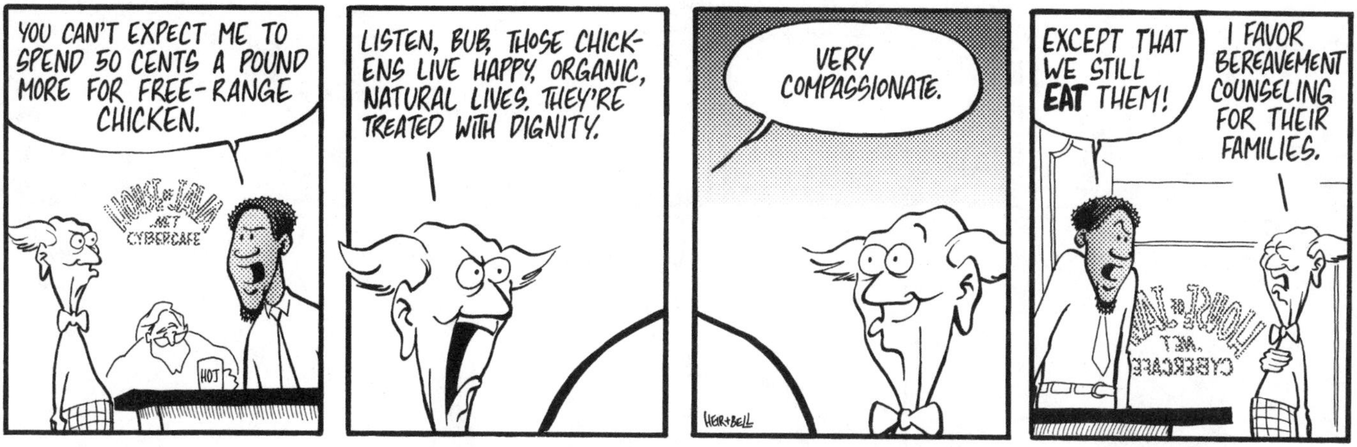
YOU CAN'T EXPECT ME TO SPEND 50 CENTS A POUND MORE FOR FREE-RANGE CHICKEN.
HOUSE OF JAVA .NET CYBERCAFE
HOJ
LISTEN, BUB, THOSE CHICKENS LIVE HAPPY, ORGANIC, NATURAL LIVES. THEY'RE TREATED WITH DIGNITY.
VERY COMPASSIONATE.
HEIR+BELL
EXCEPT THAT WE STILL **EAT** THEM!
I FAVOR BEREAVEMENT COUNSELING FOR THEIR FAMILIES.

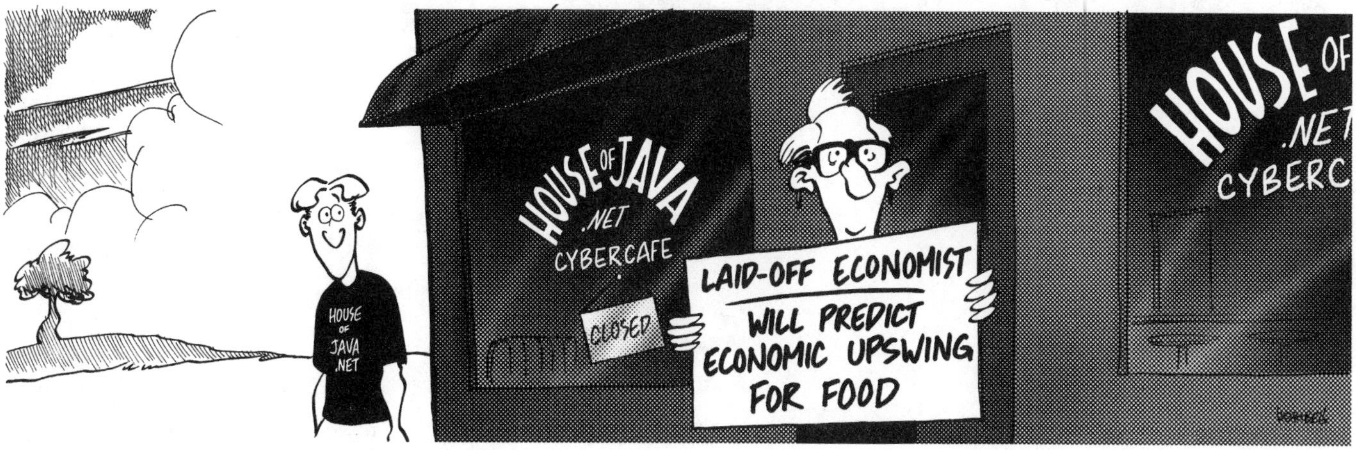
HOUSE OF JAVA .NET CYBERCAFE
HOUSE OF JAVA .NET
CLOSED
LAID-OFF ECONOMIST WILL PREDICT ECONOMIC UPSWING FOR FOOD
HOUSE OF .NET CYBERC

RUDY, RE-MEMBER VENTURE CAPITALISTS?
THE DOT-COM DARLINGS WHO'VE DISAPPEARED FROM THE FACE OF THE EARTH?
HOUSE OF JAVA .NET CYBERCAFE
HOJ
I THINK I FOUND 'EM.
A COFFEE AND WARM CUP OF MILK, PLEASE.
IT'S THE PARTNERS FROM MEREDITH & JONES. THEY MADE BILLIONS ON DOT-COMS, THEN LOST IT ALL. NOW THEY'RE TERRIFIED TO INVEST, OR EVEN TO SHOW THEIR FACES.
WE ARE NOT!
WE'RE WAITING FOR THE RIGHT TIME.
OH REALLY... SAY, WHAT'S THAT?
WHAT?
HEIR+BELL
IT'S AN INVESTMENT OPPORTUNITY.
WH-WHERE?
IT'S GETTING CLOSER. A SUREFIRE CAN'T MISS!
AAAAAH.
HOLD ME.
JUST KIDDING-JUST A GIANT, POISONOUS SPIDER.
THANK GOODNESS.
I WAIT FOR THE COOL RELEASE THAT IS DEATH.

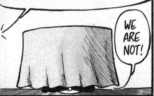

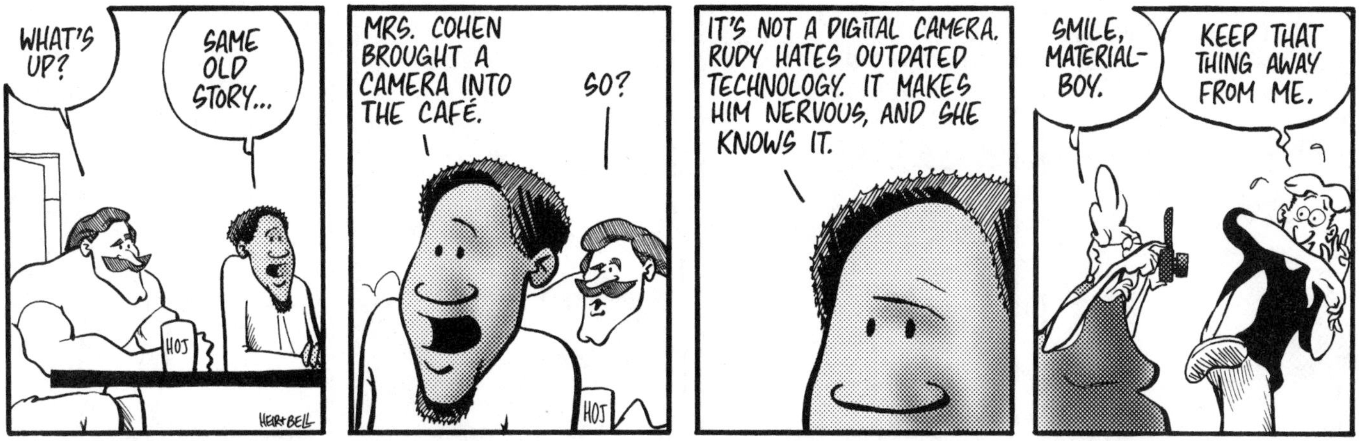
WHAT'S UP?
SAME OLD STORY...
MRS. COHEN BROUGHT A CAMERA INTO THE CAFÉ.
SO?
IT'S NOT A DIGITAL CAMERA. RUDY HATES OUTDATED TECHNOLOGY. IT MAKES HIM NERVOUS, AND SHE KNOWS IT.
SMILE, MATERIAL-BOY.
KEEP THAT THING AWAY FROM ME.

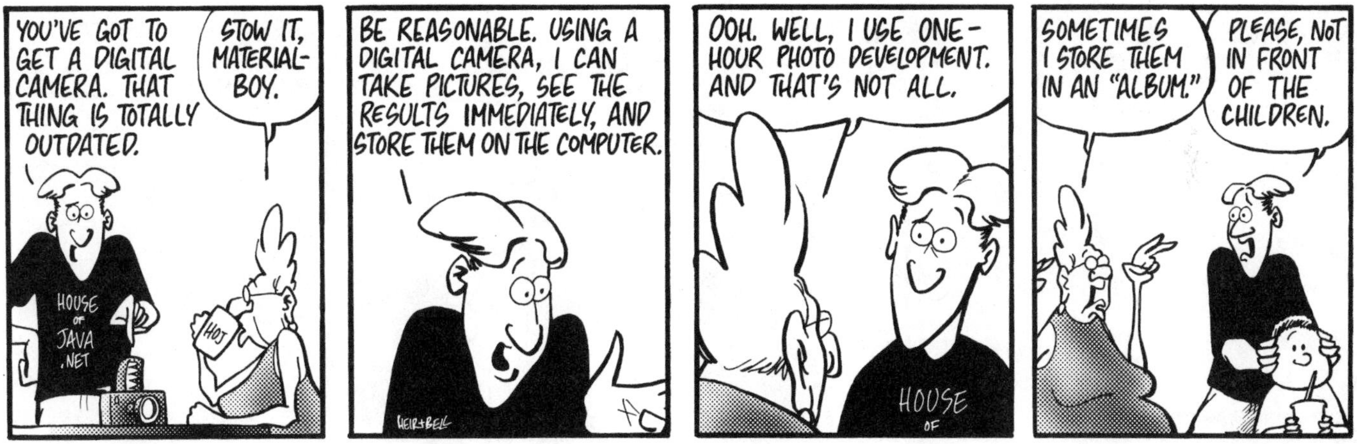
YOU'VE GOT TO GET A DIGITAL CAMERA. THAT THING IS TOTALLY OUTDATED.
STOW IT, MATERIAL-BOY.
BE REASONABLE. USING A DIGITAL CAMERA, I CAN TAKE PICTURES, SEE THE RESULTS IMMEDIATELY, AND STORE THEM ON THE COMPUTER.
OOH. WELL, I USE ONE-HOUR PHOTO DEVELOPMENT. AND THAT'S NOT ALL.
SOMETIMES I STORE THEM IN AN "ALBUM."
PLEASE, NOT IN FRONT OF THE CHILDREN.

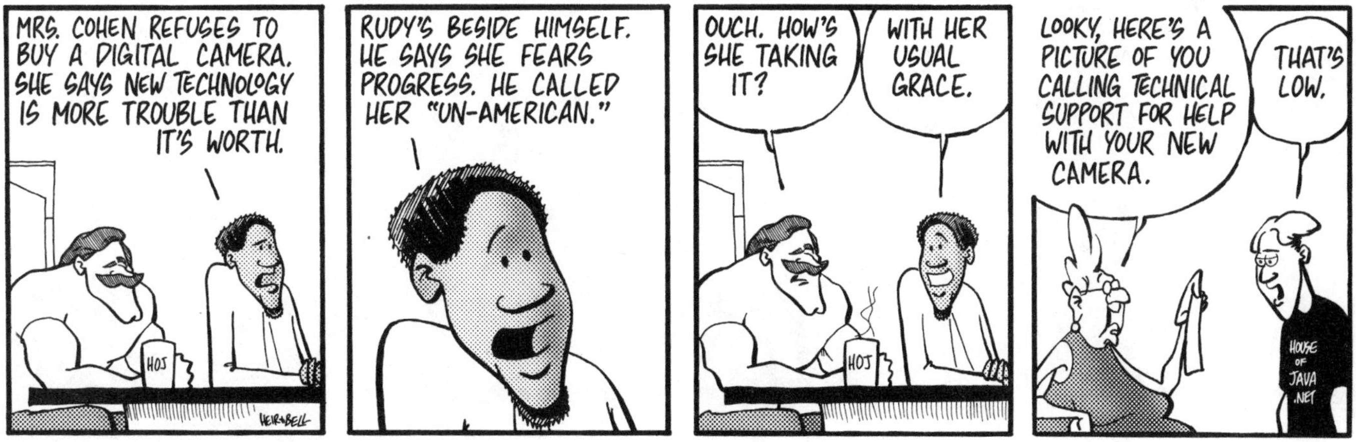
MRS. COHEN REFUSES TO BUY A DIGITAL CAMERA. SHE SAYS NEW TECHNOLOGY IS MORE TROUBLE THAN IT'S WORTH.
RUDY'S BESIDE HIMSELF. HE SAYS SHE FEARS PROGRESS. HE CALLED HER "UN-AMERICAN."
OUCH. HOW'S SHE TAKING IT?
WITH HER USUAL GRACE.
LOOKY, HERE'S A PICTURE OF YOU CALLING TECHNICAL SUPPORT FOR HELP WITH YOUR NEW CAMERA.
THAT'S LOW.

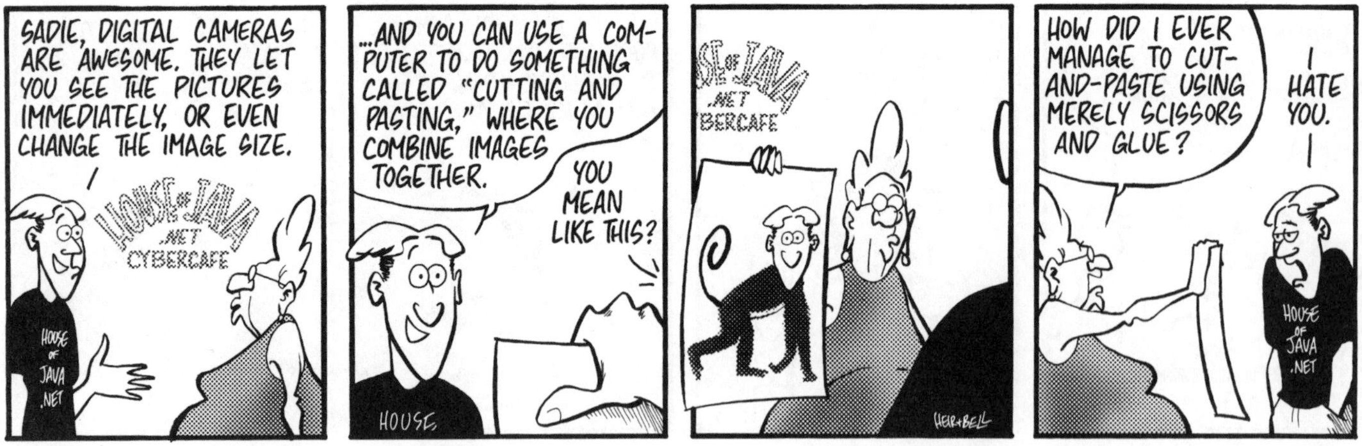
SADIE, DIGITAL CAMERAS ARE AWESOME. THEY LET YOU SEE THE PICTURES IMMEDIATELY, OR EVEN CHANGE THE IMAGE SIZE.
HOUSE OF JAVA .NET CYBERCAFE
...AND YOU CAN USE A COMPUTER TO DO SOMETHING CALLED "CUTTING AND PASTING," WHERE YOU COMBINE IMAGES TOGETHER.
YOU MEAN LIKE THIS?
HOW DID I EVER MANAGE TO CUT-AND-PASTE USING MERELY SCISSORS AND GLUE?
I HATE YOU.
HEIR+BELL

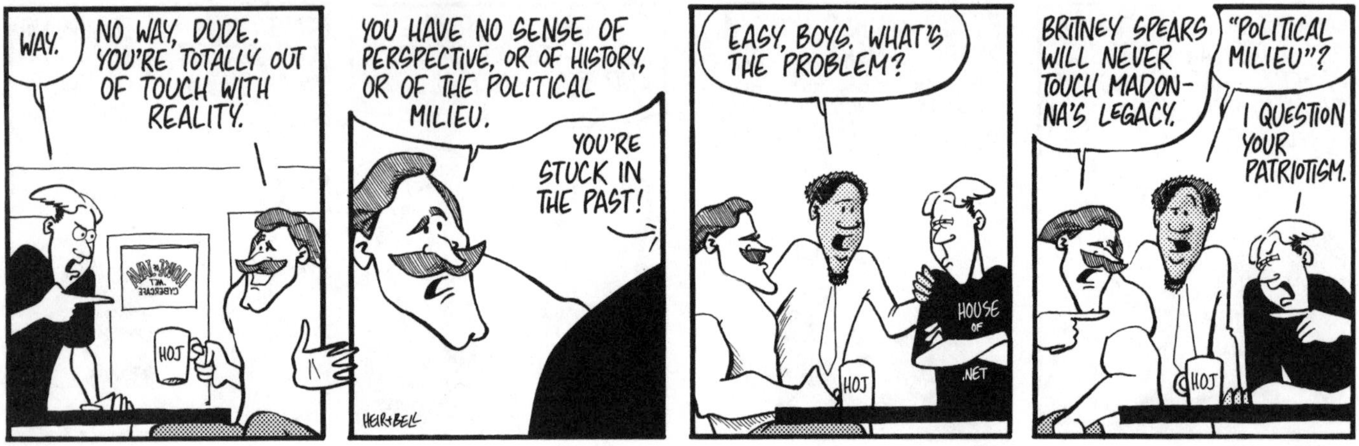
WAY.
NO WAY, DUDE. YOU'RE TOTALLY OUT OF TOUCH WITH REALITY.
YOU HAVE NO SENSE OF PERSPECTIVE, OR OF HISTORY, OR OF THE POLITICAL MILIEU.
YOU'RE STUCK IN THE PAST!
EASY, BOYS. WHAT'S THE PROBLEM?
BRITNEY SPEARS WILL NEVER TOUCH MADONNA'S LEGACY.
"POLITICAL MILIEU"?
I QUESTION YOUR PATRIOTISM.
HEIR+BELL

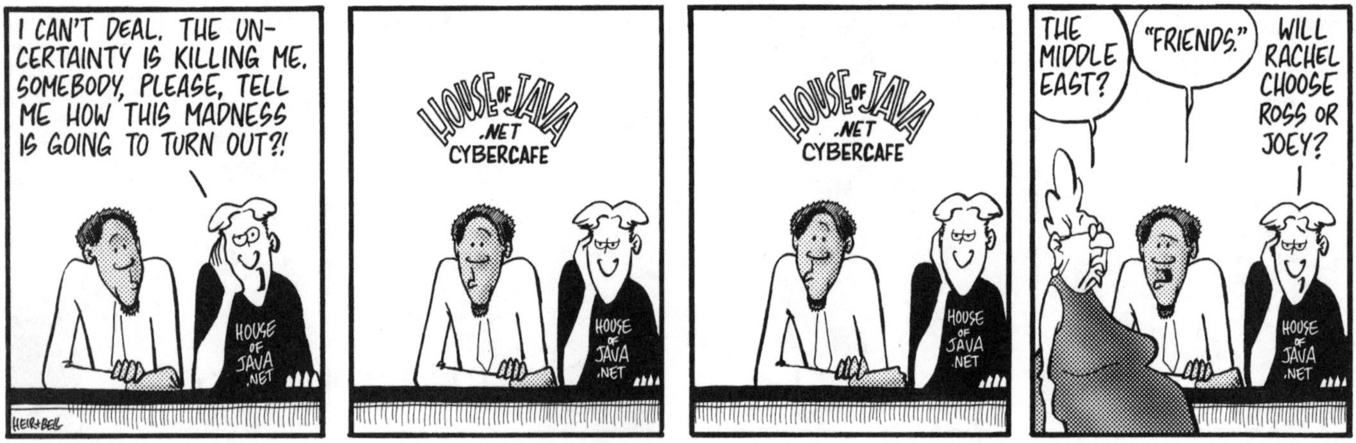
I CAN'T DEAL. THE UNCERTAINTY IS KILLING ME. SOMEBODY, PLEASE, TELL ME HOW THIS MADNESS IS GOING TO TURN OUT?!
HOUSE OF JAVA .NET CYBERCAFE
THE MIDDLE EAST?
"FRIENDS."
WILL RACHEL CHOOSE ROSS OR JOEY?
HEIR+BELL

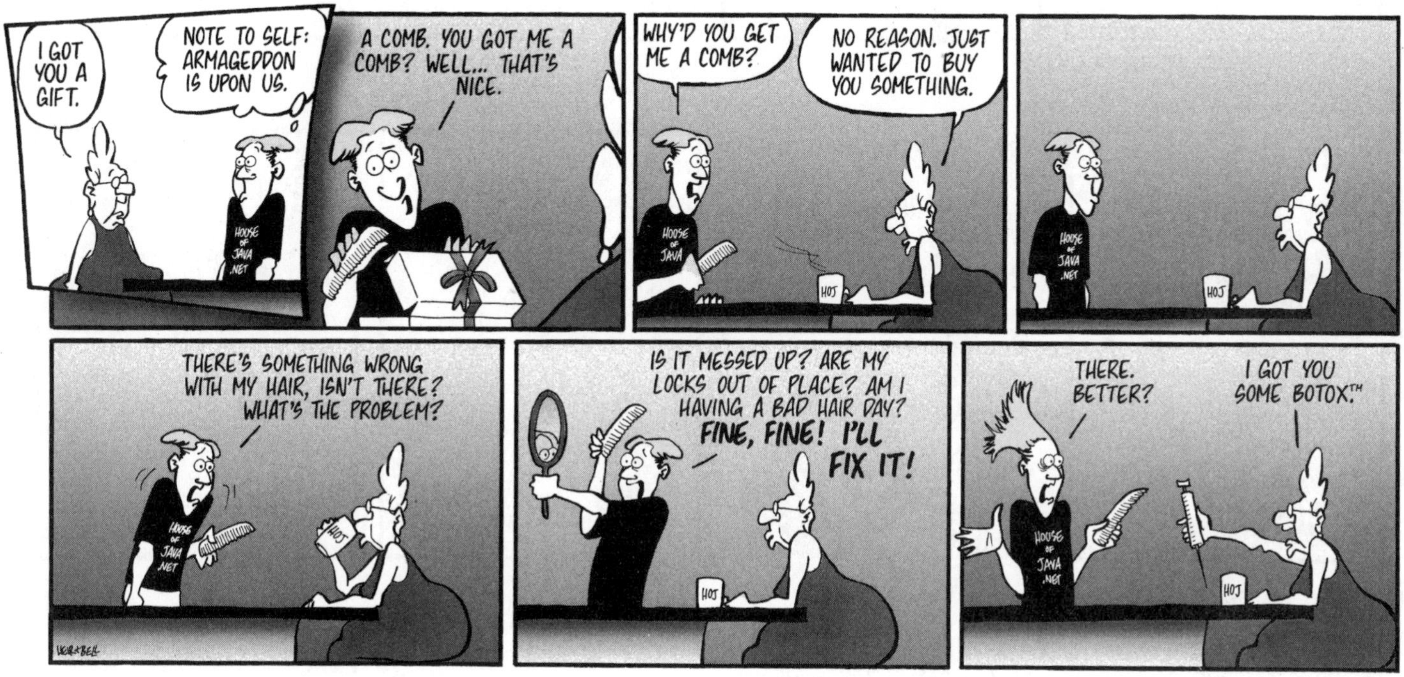
I GOT YOU A GIFT.
NOTE TO SELF: ARMAGEDDON IS UPON US.
A COMB. YOU GOT ME A COMB? WELL... THAT'S NICE.
WHY'D YOU GET ME A COMB?
NO REASON. JUST WANTED TO BUY YOU SOMETHING.
THERE'S SOMETHING WRONG WITH MY HAIR, ISN'T THERE? WHAT'S THE PROBLEM?
IS IT MESSED UP? ARE MY LOCKS OUT OF PLACE? AM I HAVING A BAD HAIR DAY? FINE, FINE! I'LL FIX IT!
THERE. BETTER?
I GOT YOU SOME BOTOX.™

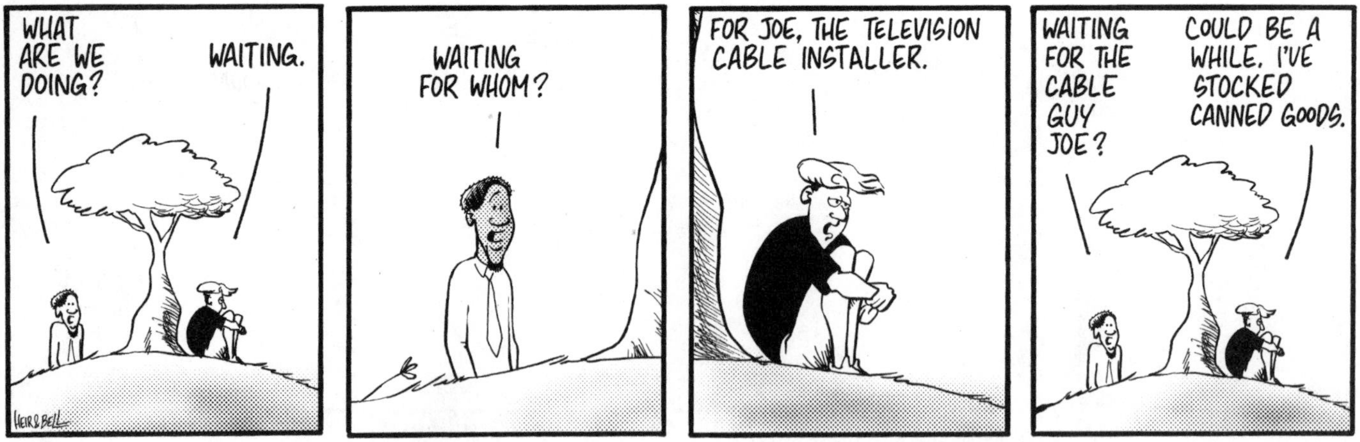
WHAT ARE WE DOING?
WAITING.
WAITING FOR WHOM?
FOR JOE, THE TELEVISION CABLE INSTALLER.
WAITING FOR THE CABLE GUY JOE?
COULD BE A WHILE. I'VE STOCKED CANNED GOODS.
HEIR&BELL

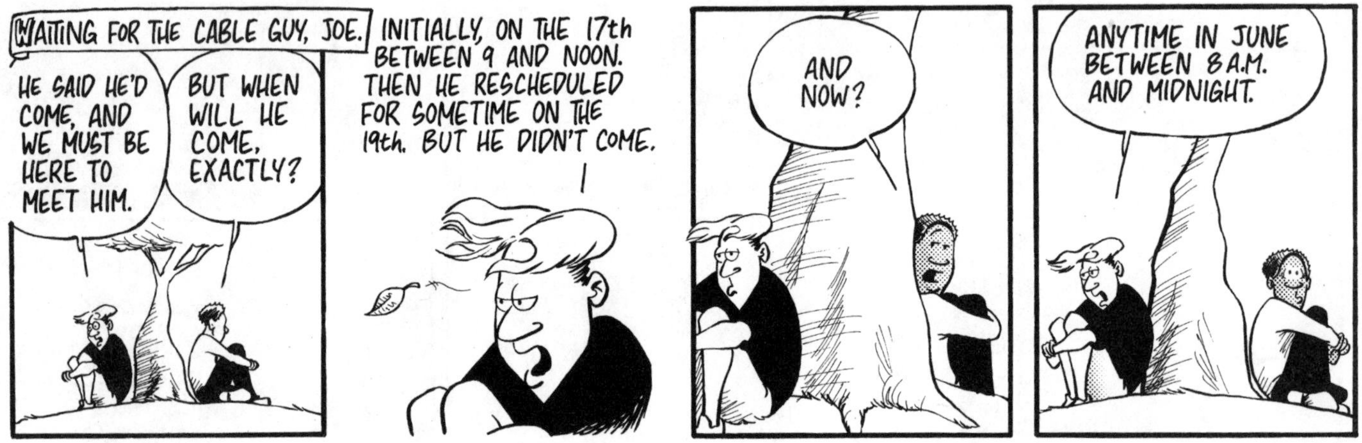
WAITING FOR THE CABLE GUY, JOE.
HE SAID HE'D COME, AND WE MUST BE HERE TO MEET HIM.
BUT WHEN WILL HE COME, EXACTLY?
INITIALLY, ON THE 17th BETWEEN 9 AND NOON. THEN HE RESCHEDULED FOR SOMETIME ON THE 19th. BUT HE DIDN'T COME.
AND NOW?
ANYTIME IN JUNE BETWEEN 8 A.M. AND MIDNIGHT.

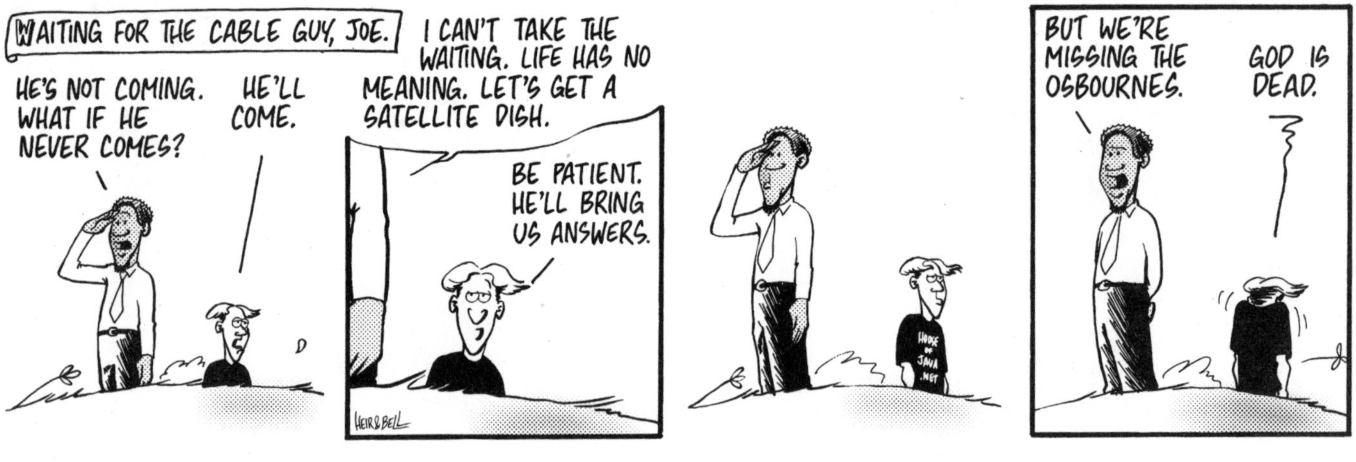
WAITING FOR THE CABLE GUY, JOE.
HE'S NOT COMING. WHAT IF HE NEVER COMES?
HE'LL COME.
I CAN'T TAKE THE WAITING. LIFE HAS NO MEANING. LET'S GET A SATELLITE DISH.
BE PATIENT. HE'LL BRING US ANSWERS.
HEIR&BELL
BUT WE'RE MISSING THE OSBOURNES.
GOD IS DEAD.

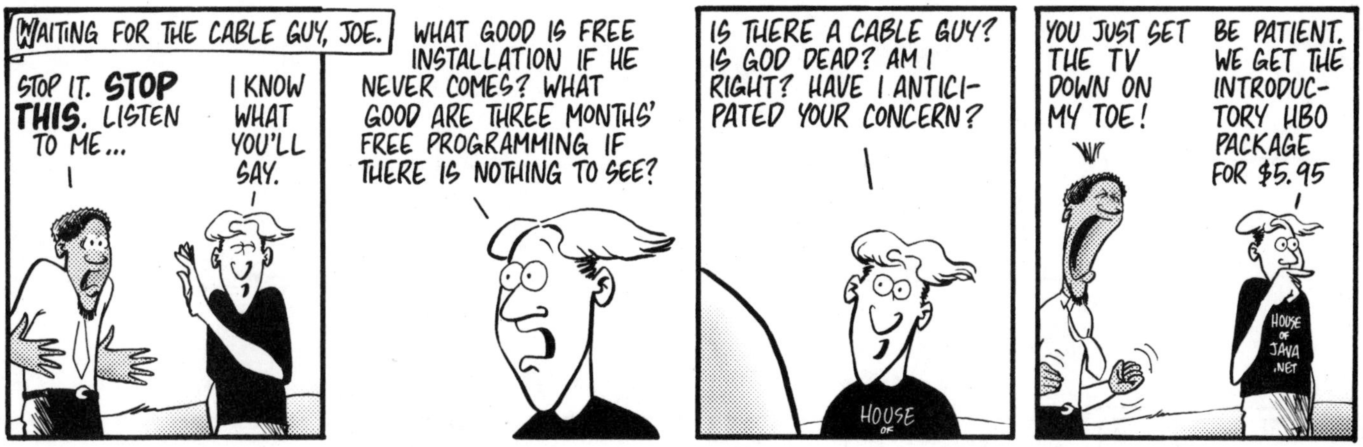
WAITING FOR THE CABLE GUY, JOE.
STOP IT. **STOP THIS.** LISTEN TO ME...
I KNOW WHAT YOU'LL SAY.
WHAT GOOD IS FREE INSTALLATION IF HE NEVER COMES? WHAT GOOD ARE THREE MONTHS' FREE PROGRAMMING IF THERE IS NOTHING TO SEE?
IS THERE A CABLE GUY? IS GOD DEAD? AM I RIGHT? HAVE I ANTICIPATED YOUR CONCERN?
HOUSE OF
YOU JUST SET THE TV DOWN ON MY TOE!
BE PATIENT. WE GET THE INTRODUCTORY HBO PACKAGE FOR $5.95
HOUSE OF JAVA .NET

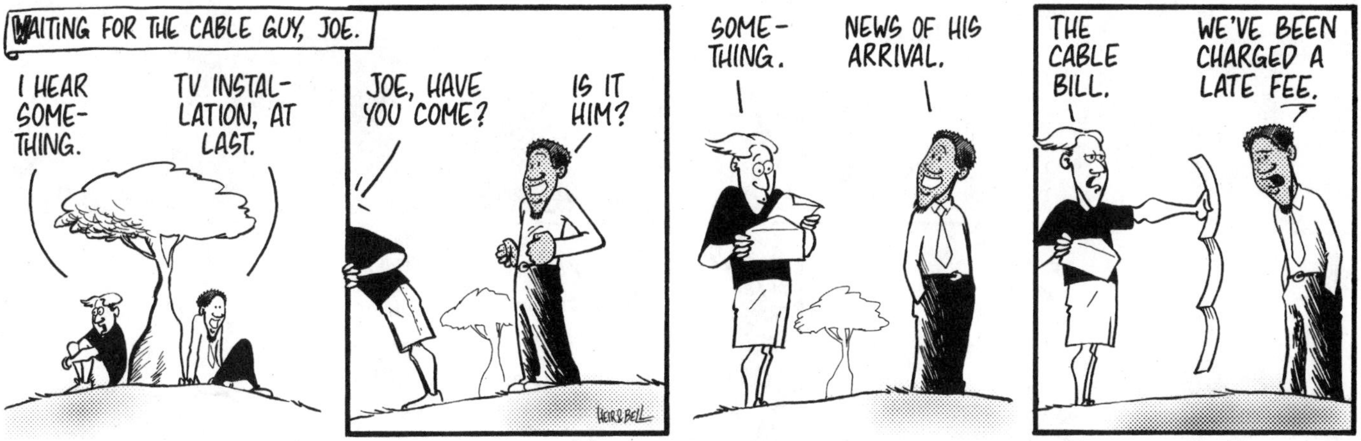
WAITING FOR THE CABLE GUY, JOE.
I HEAR SOMETHING.
TV INSTALLATION, AT LAST.
JOE, HAVE YOU COME?
IS IT HIM?
HEIR & BELL
SOMETHING.
NEWS OF HIS ARRIVAL.
THE CABLE BILL.
WE'VE BEEN CHARGED A LATE FEE.

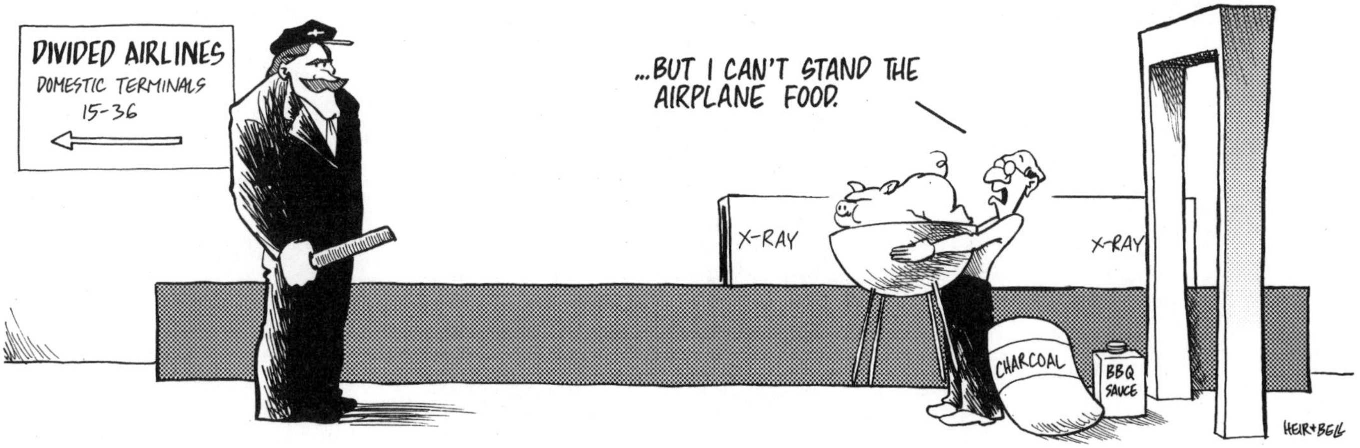
DIVIDED AIRLINES
DOMESTIC TERMINALS
15-36
...BUT I CAN'T STAND THE AIRPLANE FOOD.
X-RAY
X-RAY
CHARCOAL
BBQ SAUCE
HEIR+BELL

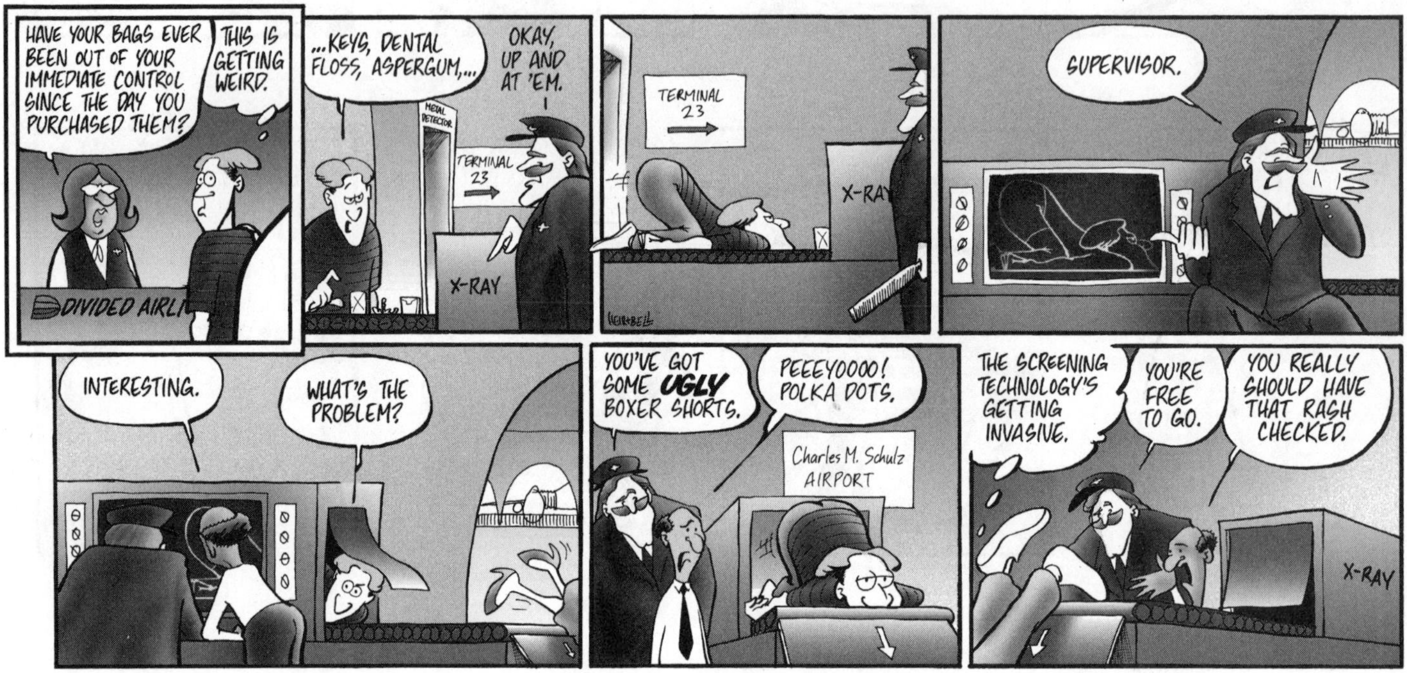
HAVE YOUR BAGS EVER BEEN OUT OF YOUR IMMEDIATE CONTROL SINCE THE DAY YOU PURCHASED THEM?
THIS IS GETTING WEIRD.
DIVIDED AIRLI
...KEYS, DENTAL FLOSS, ASPERGUM,...
OKAY, UP AND AT 'EM.
METAL DETECTOR
TERMINAL 23
X-RAY
TERMINAL 23
X-RAY
SUPERVISOR.
INTERESTING.
WHAT'S THE PROBLEM?
YOU'VE GOT SOME UGLY BOXER SHORTS.
PEEEYOOOO! POLKA DOTS.
Charles M. Schulz AIRPORT
THE SCREENING TECHNOLOGY'S GETTING INVASIVE.
YOU'RE FREE TO GO.
YOU REALLY SHOULD HAVE THAT RASH CHECKED.
X-RAY